BEHAVIOR
INTERVENTION
GUIDE

Kimberly J. Vannest, PhD

Cecil R. Reynolds, PhD

Randy W. Kamphaus, PhD

 PsychCorp

PsychCorp is an imprint of Pearson Clinical Assessment.

Pearson Executive Office 5601 Green Valley Drive Bloomington, MN 55437

PEARSON

For orders and inquiries:
800.627.7271
www.PearsonClinical.com

Dedication

To Frank, Karen, and Kevin for nearly a century's worth of combined experience working in schools and for your dedication to the development of children and youth, and to Jack—the reason for all that I do. KJV

To Henry J. L. Brathwaite V.
Thanks for adding another measure of inspiration. RWK

To Daphne D. Reynolds for her love, lessons in life, and model of service. CRR

About the Authors

Kimberly J. Vannest, PhD, is a Professor in the Educational Psychology Department at Texas A&M University. She is the author of more than 100 publications related to interventions for emotional and behavioral disorders, the reliable measurement of their effects, and valid analysis of treatment outcomes. She brings 20+ years of experience as an educator and scientist and remains actively involved in building school and community capacity for serving children and youth. She has received recognition for her research, teaching, and service, including a Yates Fellowship, a Regents Fellowship, and a Montague Teaching-Scholar award. She is an editorial board member or field reviewer for the leading journals in emotional and behavioral disorders, special education, school-psychology, assessment, positive behavior supports, and education policy.

Cecil R. Reynolds, PhD, is emeritus professor of educational psychology, professor of neuroscience, and Distinguished Research Scholar at Texas A&M University. Well known for his work in psychological testing and assessment and in neuropsychology, he is author or editor of more than 50 books, including *The Handbook of School Psychology*, the *Encyclopedia of Special Education*, and the two-volume *Handbook of Psychological and Educational Assessment of Children*. He also authored or coauthored more than 30 tests, including the BASC–3 Parenting Relationship Questionnaire (BASC–3 PRQ), BASC–3 Behavioral and Emotional Screening System (BASC–3 BESS), the Revised Children's Manifest Anxiety Scale, Second Edition (RCMAS-2), and the Reynolds Intellectual Assessment Scales–Second Edition (RIAS–2), and has published more than 300 scholarly works.

Dr. Reynolds has received a number of national awards for his work, including the Lightner Witmer Award from the American Psychological Association (APA) and Early Career Awards from two APA divisions (15, Educational Psychology; and 5, Measurement and Statistics). He is a recipient of the APA Division 16 Senior Scientist Award, the APA Division of Clinical Psychology Distinguished Assessment Psychologist Award, the APA Division 5 Messick Award for Lifetime Distinguished Contributions to Measurement Science, the National Academy of Neuropsychology's Distinguished Clinical Neuropsychologist Award, and several other national awards for his research on testing and assessment. Dr. Reynolds is the current editor-in-chief of two APA journals, *Psychological Assessment and Archives of Scientific Psychology*; former editor-in-chief of *Archives of Clinical Neuropsychology* and of *Applied Neuropsychology*; and has served as associate editor of the *Journal of School Psychology*. Active in professional affairs, he has served as president of the National Academy of Neuropsychology, a member of APA's Committee on Psychological Testing and Assessment, president of three APA divisions (5, 16, and 40), and on the executive committee of the National Association of School Psychologists. He is currently president of the American Academy of Pediatric Neuropsychology. Dr. Reynolds now practices forensic neuroscience in Austin, TX.

Randy W. Kamphaus, PhD, is professor and dean of the College of Education at the University of Oregon. He has received the Senior Scientist Award from the Division of School Psychology of the American Psychological Association (APA) and the Russell H. Yeany Jr. Research and Alumni Lifetime Achievement Awards from the College of Education at the University of Georgia, where he has twice received college-wide teaching awards. Dr. Kamphaus is best known for his research in classification methods, differential diagnosis, test development, and learning disability and attentiondeficit/hyperactivity disorder (ADHD) assessment. Dr. Kamphaus, coauthor of the BASC–3 Parenting Relationship Questionnaire, (BASC–3 PRQ) and BASC–3 Behavioral and Emotional Screening System (BASC–3 BESS), has served as principal investigator, co-investigator, and consultant on Institute of Education Sciences and other agency-funded research projects dealing with mental health screening, early intervention and prevention, child classification methods, prevalence of ADHD and conduct disorder in Latin America, and aggression reduction in schools. Dr. Kamphaus has authored or coauthored numerous books, psychological and educational tests, scientific journal articles, test reviews, and book chapters on these topics. As a licensed psychologist and a fellow of the APA, he has contributed extensively to his profession, having served as president of APA's Division of School Psychology and as a member of the APA Council of Representatives. He also participates in scholarship in the field through service as past-editor of *School Psychology Quarterly* and ad hoc reviewer for several other scientific journals.

Acknowledgments

There are many individuals who have contributed to the completion of this guide and to whom I am inspired by, or grateful to, or both.. Thank you to Rob Altmann for his exceptional work in both editions and Judy Harrison for her outstanding contributions to the original work, much of which remains an important part of this edition. Thanks also goes to the entire research and support team at Pearson for their excellent work including Alan Pierce, Ben Klaers, Laurie Anderson, Anne Trominski, Alanna Carmichael, and Susan Raiford.

Thanks to my co-authors, Cecil Reynolds and Randy Kamphaus, whose scholarship and encouragement are remarkable. Your influence on the field, and your dedication to children and the people who serve them humbles me beyond measure.

I would also like to acknowledge remarkable former students, now colleagues and dear friends whose shared experiences helped shape this work both past and present—Tara Hanway-Kalis and Denise A. Soares—thank you both.

I hope this guide helps create a world where all children get what they need for emotional and behavioral health.

Kimberly Vannest
Texas A&M University
April 2015

As always, but never enough, my appreciation and admiration to Julia, the best partner one could have in life, and a pretty terrific interventionist in her ongoing therapy practice. Her support and her lessons in loving and life continue to inspire me.

Cecil R. Reynolds
Texas A&M University
April 2015

I am grateful for the dedication and talent of my co-authors, Drs. Kimber Vannest and Cecil R. Reynolds, and Rob Altmann of Pearson. To my additional mentors, colleagues, and students who have contributed to this work in both direct and indirect ways—for these contributions, I am equally thankful.

Randy W. Kamphaus
University of Oregon
April 2015

Contents

Chapter 3. Interventions for Conduct Problems 45

Chapter 4. Interventions for Hyperactivity 69

Chapter 5. Interventions for Attention Problems .91

Chapter 6. Interventions for Academic Problems .113

Chapter 10. Interventions for Adaptability Problems 189

Chapter 11. Interventions for Functional Communication Problems 205

Chapter 12. Intervention for Social Skills Problems 221

References 227

List of Tables

List of Figures

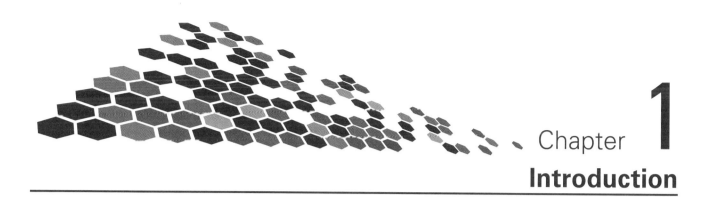

Chapter 1

Introduction

While scientific methods for diagnosing emotional and behavioral problems in children have made tremendous strides in recent years, intervention science has not kept pace. Many psychologists, teachers, and other professionals in the schools have access to tools that provide reliable and valid data for identifying the nature of a child's problems; however, they lack access to clear guidelines for taking the next step: designing and implementing research-supported interventions that effectively reduce a child's problem behavior and increase healthy or positive behavior.

As a component of the Behavior Assessment System for Children, Third Edition (BASC™–3; Reynolds & Kamphaus, 2015) product family, this BASC–3 Behavior Intervention Guide addresses the need for a comprehensive guide of effective interventions that are empirically matched to the specific problem(s) identified. This guide is grounded in intervention science and translates this science into everyday applications that are appropriate and effective for school applications and for consulting with parents (note: throughout this guide the term "parent" is used to refer to a parent or guardian caring for the child). As such, this guide fills a critical void in current professional resources by providing information about how to remediate emotional and behavioral problems.

Features

The BASC–3 Behavior Intervention Guide provides effective interventions for remediating emotional and behavioral problems experienced by children. The content includes interventions for some of the most common problem behaviors seen by teachers and parents and reported by children themselves. This guide is designed to bridge the gap between expert assessors and expert interventionists, and it is specifically well-suited for use with the BASC–3, a multimethod, multidimensional system used to evaluate the behavior and self-perceptions of children and young adults ages 2–25.

The comprehensive evaluation and summary of the best practices provided in this guide make it useful in a variety of contexts. This guide is informative for professionals involved in program development, post-screening decisions, intervention selection, assessment and diagnosis, special education qualification, Individualized Education Program (IEP) development, 504 plan development, teacher trainings, and Positive Behavioral Interventions and Supports (PBIS) planning. Many professionals have used the intervention guide that was based on the BASC–2 (i.e., the BASC–2 Intervention Guide; Vannest, Reynolds, & Kamphaus, 2008) and found it exceptionally beneficial, including school psychologists, clinical child and adolescent psychologists, pediatric psychologists, psychiatrists, family practitioners, school counselors, clinical social workers, behavioral specialists, behavior coaches, educational diagnosticians, directors of special education, and pediatricians, especially developmental pediatricians. The applicability of this guide extends beyond just those professionals who are trained and qualified to make an educational classification decision or diagnosis. This guide is relevant to teachers and teacher trainers. The BASC–2 Intervention Guide has been adopted by a number of university training programs in the U.S.

The interventions included in this guide were identified and selected through a rigorous process, with particular emphasis placed on demonstrated evidence of their effectiveness in the research literature and their practical applicability in a school setting. However, the interventions are also relevant to therapists working outside of school settings. Given the central role that school plays in a child's life, interventions that take place or are evaluated strictly outside of the school setting would be very limited in scope, and they probably would prove limited in their utility or benefits to the child and the family. The interventions provided in this guide appear in empirical research studies with evidence indicating the effective (or, at a minimum, considerably promising) treatment or management of behavioral and emotional disorders for children with a wide range of behavioral or emotional problems (e.g., aggression, hyperactivity, attentional difficulties, autism spectrum disorder, depression, severe emotional disturbances, social maladjustment, conduct disorder).

Interventions for certain problems (e.g., substance abuse, eating disorders, sexual disorders, gang affiliation) were intentionally omitted from this guide because their remediation requires considerable cooperation with and assistance from professionals outside of the school setting (e.g., medical or criminal justice personnel and agencies).

This guide offers a number of features for efficiently implementing effective behavioral and emotional interventions for children, including:

- comprehensive coverage of a wide range of emotional and behavioral problems, including aggression; conduct problems; hyperactivity; attention problems; academic problems; anxiety; depression; somatization; and problems with adaptability, functional communication, and social skills;

- descriptive overviews of each behavioral or emotional problem and the theoretical frameworks for understanding them;

- an easy-to-follow presentation of the critical components of each intervention to ease comprehension, decision making, and fidelity of implementation for greater sustainability;

- considerations for implementation of the interventions, including issues related to teaching, age or developmental level, and cultural or language differences;

- access on Q-global™ to summaries of empirical research studies that support the use of each intervention;

- a direct link between the interventions presented in the guide and the BASC–3 Teacher Rating Scales (TRS), Parent Rating Scales (PRS), and Self-Report of Personality (SRP), making the interventions easy for BASC–3 users to implement; and

- access on Q-global to suggestions for interventions based on the scores obtained on the BASC–3 TRS, PRS, and SRP forms.

A number of companion pieces for the guide enhance the ease with which interventions can be implemented and are available for separate purchase, including:

- the BASC–3 Behavior Intervention Guide Parent Tip Sheets, which facilitate effective parent participation in the remediation of their child's emotional and behavioral problems;

- the BASC–3 Behavior Intervention Guide Documentation Checklist, which helps the interventionist successfully document the steps taken during a child's intervention program and document the outcomes—facilitating discussions in meetings with parents, teachers, and school administrative personnel; and

- the Behavioral and Emotional Skill Building Guide, part of the BASC–3 family of products, a set of "Tier one" activities and "Tier two" small group lessons designed for general- and special-education teachers.

Chapter Structure

The number of interventions presented in each chapter varies depending on the prevalence of published effective interventions. Table 1.1 lists the interventions discussed in each chapter. As shown in the table, some interventions are unique to a specific problem, while others demonstrate effectiveness across a variety of problems.

Each intervention strategy is described in a narrative of essential concepts (THE BASICS). These help a professional quickly identify if the intervention described is appropriate for the context, resources, and skills; and if it is consistent with his or her approach to treatment. The PREP, IMPLEMENT, and EVALUATE (PIE) procedural steps provide a clear and concise set of instructions for the intervention.

Conceptually, the procedural steps draw from the collection of intervention strategies reported in the research literature, but their presentation is based largely on the authors' collective knowledge and experience implementing successful interventions with children with a broad range of emotional and behavioral problems. The procedural steps represent a "master list" of best practices for implementing these interventions.

Research supports the procedural steps and the use of each intervention for remediation of the corresponding behavioral or emotional problem. As the body of evidence supporting the use of these interventions is typically quite vast, a summary of the research is provided with this guide. Readers can access summaries of the research on Q-global™, Pearson's web-based scoring and reporting platform (at http://www.helloq.com) if they wish to review research detailing each intervention strategy's effectiveness. Guide users may request access to Q-global through the website.

Special considerations are discussed where appropriate. Consideration is given to the child's age and developmental level, the family's cultural and language background, and the context of the intervention (e.g., classroom-based approaches, group versus individual intervention). These considerations are provided to facilitate confident recommendations and to increase the likelihood of intervention success during selection and throughout planning, implementation, and evaluation.

Table 1.1 Intervention Types by Chapter

Chapter Title	Interventions
Interventions for Aggression	Bully Prevention
	Child-Centered Play Therapy (CCPT)
	Classroom Social Dynamics
	Cognitive Restructuring
	Counseling Groups
	Good Behavior Game (GBG)
	Incremental Theory Training
	Mindfulness Training
	Peer-Mediated Conflict Resolution and Negotiation
	Problem-Solving Training
	Replacement Behavior Training
	Social Skills Training
	Verbal Mediation
Interventions for Conduct Problems	Anger Management Skills Training
	Independent Group-Oriented Contingency Management
	Interdependent Group-Oriented Contingency Management
	Moral Motivation Training
	Multisystemic Therapy
	Parent Training
	Problem-Solving Training
	Social Skills Training
Interventions for Hyperactivity	Contingency Management
	Daily Behavior Report Cards (DBRC)
	Functional Behavioral Assessment
	Multimodal Interventions
	Parent Training
	Self-Management
	Task Modification
Interventions for Attention Problems	Classwide Peer Tutoring
	Computer-Assisted Instruction
	Contingency Management
	Daily Behavior Report Cards
	Modified Task-Presentation Strategies
	Multimodal Interventions
	Parent Training
	Self-Management

(continued)

Table 1.1 Intervention Types by Chapter *(continued)*

Chapter Title	Interventions
Interventions for Academic Problems	Advance Organizers
	Cognitive Organizers
	Instructional Strategies
	Mnemonics
	Peer Tutoring
	Classwide Peer Tutoring
	Self-Monitoring
	Self-Instruction
	Reprocessing Strategies
	Task-Selection Strategies
Interventions for Anxiety	Cognitive Behavior Therapy Integrated Approach
	Cognitive Restructuring
	Contingency Management
	Exposure-Based Techniques (Imaginal and In Vivo Desensitization, Emotive Imagery)
	Family Therapy
	Modeling (Live and Video)
	Psychoeducational Approach
	Relaxation Training
	Self-Monitoring and/or Self-Assessment
Interventions for Depression	Cognitive–Behavioral Therapy
	Psychoeducation
	Problem-Solving Skills Training
	Cognitive Restructuring
	Pleasant-Activity Training
	Relaxation Training
	Self-Management Training
	Family Involvement
	Interpersonal Psychotherapy
Interventions for Somatization	Behavioral Interventions
	Cognitive–Behavioral Therapy
Interventions for Problems with Adaptability	Behavioral Momentum
	Cognitive Behavior Management
	Functional Behavioral Assessment
	Precorrection
	Procedural Prompts
	Self-Management Training
Interventions for Functional Communication	Functional Communication Training
	Milieu Language Training
	Picture Exchange Communication System (PECS)
	Pivotal Response Training
	Video Modeling
Interventions for Social Skills Problems	Social Skills Training

Comprehensive Supports from Risk Reduction to Intervention

Several supplemental components—the BASC–3 Behavior Intervention Guide Parent Tip Sheets; the BASC–3 Behavior Intervention Guide Documentation Checklist; and the Behavioral and Emotional Skill Building Guide, part of the BASC–3 family of products—create a comprehensive and seamless approach to programming for risk reduction, problem prevention, and early and ongoing intervention. Access through Q-global to other supplemental materials that are helpful for preparation, implementation, and evaluation (e.g., handouts, posters, checklists, daily logs, and worksheets) is also available to guide users. These can streamline some of the more cumbersome aspects of preparing, thereby freeing up more time to focus on implementing the interventions.

BASC–3 BEHAVIOR INTERVENTION GUIDE PARENT TIP SHEETS

The BASC–3 Behavior Intervention Guide Parent Tip Sheets support professional practice by enhancing communication, knowledge, and skills. The tip sheets are designed for use by parents and they are most effective when used with guidance from a school psychologist or other professional responsible for implementing the interventions. The authors' collective clinical experience working with families suggests that parents appreciate the availability of these tip sheets and that their use enhances rapport between parents and therapists. As a result, parents may feel more valued and more included in the treatment process, which can ultimately improve an intervention's long-term success.

Each tip sheet corresponds to a particular chapter in this guide and provides a brief explanation of the nature and causes of the specified problem behavior, as well as some suggestions for how parents can best work with their child to help increase the chances of successful intervention. Each tip sheet also provides three or four intervention strategies for the relevant behavioral or emotional problem; while not as exhaustive as this guide, they correspond to the most appropriate subset of the strategies found herein. Additionally, each tip sheet includes a chart for tracking the use of the selected intervention and the child's progress in reducing the incidence of problem behavior(s) and increasing positive alternative behavior(s). Finally, each tip sheet lists several useful websites where parents with Internet access can find additional resources related to their child's specific behavior problems.

BASC–3 BEHAVIOR INTERVENTION GUIDE DOCUMENTATION CHECKLIST

When interventions are implemented fully and thoughtfully, effects are maximized. Partial, incomplete, or ill-advised implementation decreases the effect and defensibility of a particular intervention. The BASC–3 Behavior Intervention Guide Documentation Checklist serves as a tool for coaching fidelity, documenting implementation, and ensuring that treatment effects are not diminished by poor implementation.

BEHAVIORAL AND EMOTIONAL SKILL BUILDING GUIDE, PART OF THE BASC–3 FAMILY OF PRODUCTS

Children often express their emotional and behavioral problems in the classroom, and teachers are in a unique position to provide immediate help to correct problem behaviors. The Behavioral and Emotional Skill Building Guide, part of the BASC–3 family of products, is designed to include teachers and counselors or small group leaders in the intervention process and encourage their direct involvement in remediation of problem behaviors. While some teachers are very effective in managing classroom misbehavior and helping children deal with their emotional and behavioral problems, many teachers benefit from learning additional strategies. The skill building guide is designed to provide both general-education and special-education teachers with the tools they need to deal effectively with their students' emotional and behavioral problems, and it serves as an educational tool for teachers so they are better equipped to respond more independently in future cases.

The skill building guide provides three formats for tier one and tier two intervention. First is a nine-week curriculum of classroom discussion starters, activities, role-plays, and extension ideas (each taking 5–7 minutes and corresponding to a set of school-wide expectations); second is a set of comprehensive descriptions and basic steps for skill building across areas of common problems; and third is eight small group guides for targeted or tier two interventions. These can be used in any general- or special-education classroom setting, day treatment facility, or after-school program. As with the BASC–3 Behavior Intervention Guide Parent Tip Sheets, school psychologists or other professionals that are working with teachers can use the skill building guide as a tool for establishing a communication channel and engaging teachers to be a part of the solution for remediating a child's emotional and behavioral problems.

Relationship to Other BASC–3 Components

The BASC–3 Behavior Intervention Guide can be used independently, but it is also a part of a multimethod, multidimensional system used to evaluate the behavior and self-perceptions of children and young adults ages 2–25. Typically, emotional and behavioral difficulties have various facets. Consequently, these difficulties need to be assessed from a number of different viewpoints. Clinicians tend to obtain such views in a fairly ad hoc manner, using a variety of measures, observations, or other data that may prove difficult to integrate into a total picture. This is why the integrated assessment approach of the BASC–3 components is so desirable. Each component can be used individually or in various combinations that are best suited for the situation at hand. When used individually, the BASC–3 components are reliable and psychometrically sophisticated instruments that provide an array of beneficial data, providing the clinician with a coordinated set of tools for evaluation, diagnosis, and treatment planning. When used together, the BASC–3 components offer a comprehensive system for preventing, identifying, evaluating, monitoring, and remediating behavioral and emotional problems in children and adolescents.

The components of the BASC–3 system are presented in Table 1.2.

Table 1.2 Components of the BASC–3 System

Function	Component
Screening/Benchmarking	BASC–3 Behavioral and Emotional Screening System (BESS)
Comprehensive Assessment	BASC–3 Teacher Rating Scales (TRS)
	BASC–3 Parent Rating Scales (PRS)
	BASC–3 Self-Report of Personality (SRP)
	BASC–3 Parenting Relationship Questionnaire (PRQ™)
	BASC–3 Structured Developmental History (SDH)
	BASC–3 Student Observation System (SOS)
	BASC–3 Comprehensive Continuous Performance Test (CCPT)
Intervention	BASC–3 Behavior Intervention Guide
	BASC–3 Behavior Intervention Guide Parent Tip Sheets
	Behavioral and Emotional Skill Building Guide, Part of the BASC–3 Family of Products
	BASC–3 Behavior Intervention Guide Documentation Checklist
Monitoring Progress	BASC–3 Flex Monitor

BASC–3 BEHAVIORAL AND EMOTIONAL SCREENING SYSTEM (BESS)

The BASC–3 BESS is a brief screening tool designed to identify behavioral and emotional strengths and weaknesses in children and adolescents in preschool through high school. It includes Teacher, Parent, and Student Forms that are short (20, 29, and 28 items, respectively) and easy to complete, usually within 5 minutes or less for the Teacher and Parent Forms, and 5–15 minutes for the Student Form. Spanish forms are available for the Parent and Student Forms; both English and Spanish forms can be completed digitally or on paper. On each form, a Behavioral and Emotional Risk Index provides an overall indication for risk of having or developing a behavioral or emotional problem; additional scores are also provided that are used to identify specific risks for more specific problem areas.

BASC–3 TEACHER RATING SCALES (TRS)

The BASC–3 TRS is a comprehensive measure of both adaptive and problem behaviors in the school setting. It is designed for use by teachers or others who fill a similar role, such as teacher assistants or preschool caregivers. The TRS has three forms, with items targeted at three age levels: preschool (ages 2–5), child (ages 6–11), and adolescent (ages 12–21). The forms contain descriptors of behaviors that the respondent rates on a four-point scale of frequency, ranging from Never to Almost always. The TRS takes 10–15 minutes to complete for teachers with experience completing rating scales.

BASC–3 PARENT RATING SCALES (PRS)

The BASC–3 PRS, available in English or Spanish, is a comprehensive measure of a child's adaptive and problem behaviors in community and home settings. The PRS uses the same four-choice rating format as the TRS and takes 10–20 minutes to complete. Like the TRS, the PRS has three age-level forms: preschool, child, and adolescent.

BASC–3 SELF-REPORT OF PERSONALITY (SRP)

The BASC–3 SRP, available in English and Spanish, is an omnibus personality inventory consisting of statements that respondents answer in one of two ways. Some of the items (presented first on the record form) require a True or False response, while others use the four-point scale of frequency, ranging from Never to Almost always. The SRP takes about 20–30 minutes to complete. It has three age-level forms: child (ages 8–11), adolescent (ages 12–21), and young adults attending a postsecondary school (ages 18–25).

A fourth level of the SRP is the interview version (SRP–I), designed for children ages 6 through 7 years. The SRP–I contains a series of 14 questions asked by an interviewer, who then records the child's Yes or No responses, along with responses given to follow-up questions that are asked when a child provides an item response that indicates a possible behavioral or emotional problem.

BASC–3 PARENTING RELATIONSHIP QUESTIONNAIRE (PRQ)

The BASC–3 PRQ, available in English and Spanish, is designed to capture a parent's perspective of the parent–child relationship (or the perspective of a person serving a similar role). It assesses traditional parent–child dimensions, such as attachment and involvement, and it also provides information on parenting style, parenting confidence, stress, and satisfaction with the child's school. The BASC–3 PRQ is used in clinical, pediatric, counseling, school, and other settings where there is a need to understand the nature of the parent–child relationship. It is particularly important when implementing home-based intervention strategies and/or treatment monitoring. The BASC–3 PRQ can be completed in approximately 15 minutes. It should be administered to mothers and fathers (or caregivers) of children ages 2–18.

BASC–3 STRUCTURED DEVELOPMENTAL HISTORY (SDH)

The BASC–3 SDH, available in English and Spanish, provides a thorough review of social, psychological, developmental, educational, and medical information about a child that may influence diagnosis and treatment decisions. It is designed to be useful in numerous settings, including clinics, schools, and hospitals. The SDH is used either as a structured interview with a parent (or someone who fills a similar role) or as a questionnaire that can be filled out in a clinician's office, school, or at home. The SDH is available as an electronic/digital form and a paper form. When used in conjunction with the BASC–3 PRS, the digitally-administered version of the SDH can deliver supplemental items based on PRS scale scores that provide additional helpful information for making accurate classification or diagnostic decisions.

BASC–3 STUDENT OBSERVATION SYSTEM (SOS)

The BASC–3 SOS is 15-minute observation procedure designed to enable the professional to record and evaluate a student's behavior in a classroom environment. The SOS is available digitally using a smartphone, tablet, or laptop computer, and it is also available on paper.

BASC–3 COMPREHENSIVE CONTINUOUS PERFORMANCE TEST (CCPT)

The BASC–3 CCPT is a performance-based assessment of attentional control and executive functioning. It measures both visual and auditory performance in both traditional CPT and unique ways. It is used by psychologists when evaluating children and adults.

BEHAVIORAL AND EMOTIONAL SKILL BUILDING GUIDE, PART OF THE BASC–3 FAMILY OF PRODUCTS

The Behavioral and Emotional Skill Building Guide, part of the BASC–3 family of products, provides school-wide expectations, classroom management foundations, tier one interventions in the form of curricula (discussion starters, classroom activities, role-plays, and extension ideas), as well as conceptual descriptions and examples of common problems. Tier two interventions are a series of small group guides for more targeted intervention that promote and develop a number of core behavioral and emotional skills, such as communicating, problem solving, listening effectively, and relaxation strategies. The skill building guide is used by teachers, behavior coaches, counselors, social workers, or others who work in a school or similar setting. When used in conjunction with the BASC–3 BESS, the skill building guide can also be used by school administrators to enhance the skills of the student community and promote behaviors that lead to school-wide success.

BASC–3 FLEX MONITOR

The BASC–3 Flex Monitor is used to monitor and track the effect of a behavioral intervention implemented by a psychologist or other professional in a school or clinical environment. An Internet-based tool, the BASC–3 Flex Monitor provides a bank of behaviorally- or emotionally-based items that are selected to create a customized monitoring form that enables score comparisons to a nationally representative population sample. While creating forms, users can calculate reliability estimates based on a normative sample. In addition, existing forms can simply be selected and used to measure behavioral performance across a variety of common behavioral areas (e.g., hyperactivity, attention). Behavioral performance is measured and displayed over a period of time, thereby helping to establish the effectiveness of an intervention strategy.

Development

The interventions presented in this guide were selected based on published research demonstrating their effectiveness for use in remediating emotional and behavioral problems experienced by children. There is a large amount of variability in the methodologies used across these research studies, ranging from single-case studies to comprehensive meta-analyses. As a result, the criteria for evaluating the effectiveness of an intervention had to accommodate this variability. Standard criteria such as effect size, statistical significance, and clinical significance were considered. In addition, the authors also evaluated the merits of each study (e.g., quality of research design, apparent quality of treatment fidelity) based on their clinical and research experiences.

SELECTING BASC–3 SCALES TO INCLUDE

Before literature reviews were conducted, the BASC–3 TRS, PRS, and SRP scales were reviewed to determine which emotional and behavioral problems to include in this guide. Emphasis was placed on maximizing the coverage of BASC–3 scales and determining which emotional and behavioral problems had enough available evidence for intervention effectiveness. The decision to include many of the scales was fairly straightforward (e.g., Aggression, Hyperactivity, Anxiety). Some scales were combined because of their similarity to other scales within and across BASC–3 forms and their treatment in the research literature. For example, the Attitude to School, Attitude to Teachers, Learning Problems, and Study Skills scales were combined into a single Academic Problems chapter. This process resulted in only a few BASC–3 scales being omitted from this guide. For example, Atypicality is an important dimension to assess on the BASC–3, but it does not have a large research base demonstrating effective remediation strategies except in the case of specific disorders that may cause elevations on this scale (e.g., schizophrenia). More commonly, elevated Atypicality scores may be indicators of other problems that usually require additional follow-up. Table 1.3 shows the BASC–3 scales that are included in this guide.

SELECTING INTERVENTION STUDIES

For each problem area, a comprehensive literature review was conducted using electronic databases in psychology and education. Keywords for each subscale and for items within the scale (e.g., aggression, depression, lying) were used alone and in combination with keywords such as "treatment," "evidence-based practice," and "interventions." Abstracts were initially reviewed for the following criteria: evidence of treatment effect, age of study participants (2–21 years), and evidence of treatment fidelity; a few meta-analyses or critical studies include adult populations.

Table 1.3 List of BASC–3 TRS, PRS, and SRP Scales Included in Intervention Chapters

Scale	BASC–3 Form	Intervention Chapter(s)
Adaptability	TRS, PRS	Adaptability
Aggression	TRS, PRS	Aggression
Anxiety	TRS, PRS, SRP	Anxiety
Attention Problems	TRS, PRS, SRP	Attention Problems
Attitude to School	SRP	Academic Problems
Attitude to Teachers	SRP	Academic Problems

(continued)

Table 1.3 List of BASC–3 TRS, PRS, and SRP Scales Included in Intervention Chapters *(continued)*

Scale	BASC–3 Form	Intervention Chapter(s)
Conduct Problems	TRS, PRS	Conduct Problems
Depression	TRS, PRS, SRP	Depression
Functional Communication	TRS, PRS	Functional Communication
Hyperactivity	TRS, PRS, SRP	Hyperactivity
Interpersonal Relations	SRP	Social Skills
Learning Problems	TRS	Academic Problems
Social Skills	TRS, PRS	Social Skills
Somatization	TRS, PRS, SRP	Somatization
Study Skills	TRS	Academic Problems
Withdrawal	TRS, PRS	Anxiety

Note. TRS = Teacher Rating Scales, PRS = Parent Rating Scales, and SRP = Self-Report of Personality.

Studies that met at least some of these criteria were retained for further evaluation. For each retained research study or meta-analysis, reference lists were checked and additional research was included for review using the aforementioned criteria. A hand search was also conducted of the tables of contents of books and leading journals to cross-reference against all studies that had met our criteria for inclusion. This triangulation of three search methods provided a thorough view of the professional literature for each scale topic, including reviews of more than 1,000 studies.

Intervention methods provided in this guide were chosen because of the strength of the evidence for their effectiveness found in published research literature, based on standards established by professional organizations including the Council for Exceptional Children (CEC), the American Psychological Association (APA), the American Educational Research Association (AERA), and the National Association of School Psychologists (NASP). The annotated studies on Q-global are representative. For example, not all of the studies on aggression interventions are included, but all of them were used to create the step-by-step procedures and to determine the effects of intervention as presented in the Aggression chapter. The procedural steps for each intervention in this guide were determined by listing the procedures articulated in a given study (typically found in the research methodology procedure section) and comparing them across studies to identify common and uncommon steps, primary or critical components, and secondary or irrelevant components. This resulted in the creation of one master set of procedures that appeared to be relevant for use in the field rather than just as discrete research protocols. The procedural steps were reviewed by ad hoc consultation with school psychologists, counselors, and teachers where applicable. These procedural steps and the annotated research studies on Q-global provide general support for the use of the intervention methodologies as well as preliminary (albeit strong) evidence for the validity of the procedural steps as they are presented in this guide. It is anticipated that additional research will be conducted to further substantiate the strength of the interventions described in this guide and their effectiveness as they are used in field settings across ages and types of student problems.

It is helpful to note that several intervention methods (e.g., contingency management) appear as effective practice for more than one type of problem behavior. Each method is presented along with a review of the literature that supports its use for a specific issue and with the steps and examples for use in such a case. For example, the procedural steps for contingency management may differ slightly depending on which condition is being treated.

CREATING THE BASC–3 BEHAVIOR INTERVENTION GUIDE PARENT TIP SHEETS

Treatment is most effective when coordinated and applied across both home and school environments; therefore, parents are most often involved with child interventions to the extent possible and appropriate. The child should assent to parental involvement in treatment as appropriate.

The BASC–3 Behavior Intervention Guide Parent Tip Sheets were developed from the intervention strategies presented in this guide. Primary consideration was given to presenting information in a simple and engaging way. Readability of the text was paramount. Traditional readability metrics, such as the Flesch Reading Ease Score and the Flesch-Kincaid Reading Index, were used to evaluate the text written for the tip sheets. Whenever possible, sentences were rewritten to lower the reading difficulty level (as indicated by the readability metrics) while retaining the intended structure and tone of the text.

Some of the terminology describing the interventions was changed from how it was presented in the intervention guide to make it more meaningful to parents. For example, the phrase "contingency management" was replaced with "rewarding brave behavior" on the Anxiety tip sheet. Care also was taken to avoid simplifying the text so much that it may affect the utility of the document for any tip sheet user.

Using the Interventions

Effective development, adoption, and sustainability of an intervention is based in part on choosing an intervention that is appropriate given the child's strengths and weaknesses and the features of the setting in which the intervention is implemented. Understanding the child's background, his or her family, and the interventions that have been implemented or attempted previously facilitates this process. This guide is not a cookbook with a recipe for treating a particular problem behavior. Rather, it is a planning guide for the informed selection, implementation, and evaluation of efficient and effective treatment practices in schools, clinics, and homes. It provides step-by-step procedures for implementation of a selected intervention.

Children with emotional and behavioral disorders are frequently characterized by comorbidity of problems. As such, the simultaneous presentation of multiple symptoms necessitates prioritizing problems before addressing them. Some interventions may result in improvement to co-occurring behavior problems, but it is also fairly common to see one behavior improve while another gets worse or to see a new behavior emerge.

Given the comorbidity of many of the covered problems, prioritization can be complicated. Certainly, behaviors that indicate a threat to self or others or that result in property damage require some immediate resolution (e.g., aggression, conduct problems). Next to be addressed would be those problems that interfere with daily life or pose a threat to long-term adjustment and wellness (e.g., attention, academic problems, hyperactivity, depression, functional communication problems). Finally, consideration should be given to problems that may lead to stigmatization or struggles at school and in the community and that may create obstacles to becoming a more fully functioning individual (e.g., somatization, anxiety, social skills). These are not rules for triage but examples of how some conditions might be addressed in the context of the bigger picture.

Consider the relationship between the problems, both those that have been diagnosed and those for which the child is "at risk." For example, consider if the child's depression is caused by his or her learning problems or if the learning problems are caused by depression. Addressing one may eradicate the other. The severity of the problems should also be taken into consideration, and the most severe problems should be addressed first. For example, if a conduct problem is only a potential risk while social skills problems are so significant that they require immediate treatment, social skills interventions may require the most immediate attention.

USING THE BASC–3 Q-GLOBAL REPORTS

The BASC–3 Q-global Interpretive Summary Report with Intervention Recommendations generates an intervention guide narrative for Teacher Rating Scales, Parent Rating Scales, and Self-Report of Personality reports. This narrative includes information about the specific emotional and behavioral problems a child may be experiencing based on the ratings of items on the TRS, PRS, or SRP forms. It also includes a summary of up to two interventions for each identified problem area and a classification of BASC–3 subscale scores into primary (i.e., clinically significant) and secondary (i.e., at risk) intervention areas. For each intervention, a brief summary of the goal and the essentials of the intervention are provided. Procedural steps and considerations for implementing the intervention also are included.

Due to space considerations in the reports, the narratives generated are restricted to a maximum of three BASC–3 intervention areas. Interventions for problem areas beyond the top three will not be presented. Details of each intervention technique and their research basis, as well as additional intervention techniques not included in the narrative, can be found in this guide.

The interventions listed in the BASC–3 Q-global Interpretive Summary Report with Intervention Recommendations are based on the child's T scores. In the event of a tie between scales, scales are prioritized with respect to the impact of problems on the child, others, or academic performance. Scales associated with the Aggression, Conduct Problems, Depression, Hyperactivity, Attention Problems, Anxiety, and Academic Problems intervention areas are given priority over scales associated with other intervention areas. For example, consider a child who has a total of four TRS scales with a

T score of 75: Aggression, Conduct Problems, Depression, and Somatization. Given the limit of reporting no more than three significant scale elevations and the specified scale hierarchy, the software would generate interventions for Aggression, Conduct Problems, and Depression but would not list Somatization interventions (because Somatization has a lower priority ranking than the other scales). However, the software report would still identify Somatization as a problem area and would refer the user to this guide for information on specific intervention methods.

USING THE BASC–3 BEHAVIOR INTERVENTION GUIDE PARENT TIP SHEETS

The BASC–3 Behavior Intervention Guide Parent Tip Sheets are designed to be easily understood by parents, but it is still important to teach parents how to use them. First, each tip sheet contains three or four suggested intervention approaches. In many cases, it would be appropriate to indicate which intervention the parent should try first. This can be done by putting a star or a number next to the desired or prioritized intervention. Each tip sheet also includes a progress monitoring form for tracking progress and for documenting how often the parent works with the child. Some parents are unfamiliar with progress monitoring and they may need some initial guidance so they are not intimidated by the process. Also, it can be helpful to identify when the tip sheets' progress monitoring form should be returned to the therapist and when the sheets will be reviewed with the parents. Steps like these can help maximize parental involvement in the intervention process.

MONITORING PROGRESS

A key component to successful implementation of an intervention is determining its impact on a child's behavioral and emotional functioning. Interventions that improve a child's functioning are generally continued or systematically faded, while interventions that do not improve a child's functioning are modified or perhaps discontinued.

There are a number of ways to assess the impact of an intervention, all of which depend on the content of the intervention and the method of inquiry. Commonly used informal methods of monitoring progress in school and clinical settings, such as unstructured interviews or scheduled discussions, leave the degree of communication and the sensitivity of the measurement almost to chance. This informal approach is inadequate. For example, some questions, such as "How is it going?" or "Have things improved?" provide little information for data-driven decision making and they are unreliable methods of documenting results. The purposes for gathering the information (e.g., pre-referral data collection, clinical diagnosis, determining response to intervention, litigation documentation, monitoring progress on goals and objectives) and the behavior or condition being monitored may determine the number and types of monitoring procedures. For example, improving specific behaviors (e.g., staying seated in class, making eye contact) often requires frequent evaluation of the behaviors' effects.

This guide includes tools to help monitor progress. The BASC–3 Behavior Intervention Guide Parent Tip Sheets provide a form for progress monitoring at home. The BASC–3 Behavior Intervention Guide Documentation Checklist provides a method for articulating the level of intervention that occurred and the degree to which it was successful. Informal methods, such as a home–school note, a school–home note, or a daily behavior report card (DBRC), provide useful feedback to parents and professionals for assessing the effects of an intervention. Such approaches require relatively little effort, can be repeated frequently, and are well suited for answering questions for a specific period of time (e.g., math class performance, daily changes in aggression), but they should be treated as supplemental by the therapist. These approaches are not as helpful for evaluating behavioral and emotional functioning at a broader level or for determining if a child's functioning is still at an elevated or clinical level with respect to a normative population.

Another approach to evaluating the effectiveness of an intervention program is to use direct observation techniques (e.g., the BASC–3 Student Observation System [SOS]). In general, these techniques require a person to observe a child's behavior in a classroom or other setting for a specified time period (e.g., 15 minutes). At their most basic level, direct observation techniques utilize ratings that are categorized into a dichotomy (e.g., on-task and off-task behaviors), while more robust techniques capture ratings across a variety of behaviors and facilitate reporting on metrics such as the total number of positive and negative behaviors in frequency counts and percentages. These observational approaches require more time and effort than do informal checklists, and therefore, may not be used as frequently. However, they often provide a broader view of a child's behavioral and emotional functioning, which can be important for gaining a more complete perspective of the effects of an intervention program.

Another approach to evaluating the effectiveness of an intervention program is to use a standardized behavior rating tool like the BASC–3 Flex Monitor Report. Behavior rating forms are commonplace in school and clinical settings and they are very efficient for capturing information about a child's level of behavioral and emotional functioning. Although they are probably not appropriate for use on a daily basis, these reports can be used every few weeks and they provide an indication of both the degree of individual change (via changes in scale scores) and the current level of functioning (via comparisons to normative populations).

Over longer periods of time, a BASC–3 TRS, PRS, or SRP might prove useful if the child develops other problems while one problem is being addressed. A comprehensive rating scale like the TRS, PRS, and SRP can help monitor these trends in behavior and provide an early indication of newly forming problems. The BASC–3 Q-global reports also contain features that allow the user to monitor changes in a child's behavior over time. These changes can be evaluated graphically when using the BASC–3 Flex Monitor Report and the BASC–3 Q-global Interpretive Summary Report with Intervention Recommendations.

When choosing the method and frequency of evaluation, one must always carefully consider the link between the intervention method and the rating approach. Does the content of the intervention program align with the behaviors or emotions that are evaluated by the rating method? For example, an intervention method aimed at improving a child's attention level will probably focus on behaviors associated with staying on task and listening in class; if the child's attention problems manifest in a different form, that intervention method might be insufficient. Similarly, rating frequency should be specific to the case, reflecting a realistic time frame for the intervention to have a noticeable effect on the relevant behaviors and emotions. For example, reducing a child's depression or anxiety level to a normal range will likely require weeks or months, not days. Failing to consider this link may lead to inaccurate conclusions about the effectiveness of an intervention program.

Summary

The following chapters present evidence-based interventions to be considered when developing a treatment plan for children who have or are elevated levels of risk for developing specific emotional and behavioral problems. The interventions presented differ in their application of one or more behavioral, cognitive–behavioral, or social-learning theories, but they are all shaped by the fundamental goals of treatment (i.e., prevention, management, and remediation of problem behaviors).

The factors to consider for each individual child are as varied as the causes and consequences of the disorder. Professionals are encouraged to pay close attention to each intervention's considerations to select an intervention that will be most effective for achieving expected treatment outcomes. Additionally, an effective intervention strategy should consider the trajectory of a particular disorder's development, and the methods and strategies selected should specifically address a child's location in that trajectory. Last, it is essential to incorporate the interventions determined to be most effective for prevention and remediation of the problem behavior into the treatment plan.

Overall, treatment typically involves the remediation of more than one behavioral or emotional problem. Multiple problems (e.g., learning failure, attention deficits) interrelate in both direct and indirect ways. A treatment strategy can be seen as a system of intervention processes that is dependent on multiple variables working in concert. The goal of effective treatment should be the orchestration of these concurrent processes to maximize treatment success and to provide the greatest benefit to the child.

Chapter 2

Interventions for Aggression

Characteristics and Conditions of Aggression

WHAT IS AGGRESSION?

Aggression is characterized by hostile or destructive behaviors. These types of behavior include property damage, verbal aggression, self-oriented aggression, physical aggression, and sexual aggression (Crocker et al., 2006).

The social science literature commonly refers to two categories of aggression that differ in their goals: object-oriented aggression and person-oriented aggression. The goal of object-oriented aggression (sometimes called instrumental aggression) is to obtain an object that is desired or to escape an aversive situation. For example, a child may hit another child to get a toy that he or she wants or shove away a parent to avoid being given a bath. This type of aggression is found mainly in young children or individuals who lack verbal communication skills. Older children, however, tend to exhibit person-oriented aggression. The goal of person-oriented aggression is to obtain control, gain access to people or things, or escape from individuals; and behavioral motivation may include dominance and revenge. This category of aggression includes forms of direct and indirect aggression (i.e., victim present or not, respectively) and relational aggression (i.e., the use of peer relationships) to inflict harm on others (Reynolds & Fletcher-Janzen, 2007). For example, a child may hit another child as retribution for being embarrassed earlier in the day (direct physical aggression), spread rumors about another child (indirect aggression), or restrict friendships among peers to isolate others (relational aggression).

According to functional analysis literature, aggression can serve to escape or avoid people, task demands, social situations, or physiologic states (e.g., frustration, discomfort); or to gain access to people, objects, or social situations, events, or stimulation. Aggressive acts may also serve a self-stimulatory function or control function.

Children who exhibit aggressive behaviors may have inadequacies in problem solving, and specifically, they may have deficiencies identifying alternatives, considering consequences, and determining causalities. They may also engage in means–ends thinking and have difficulty understanding other perspectives. In other words, they do not understand the problem, think about or know of other options for behavior, or think about what will happen next. This trifecta of mismatch between their abilities and habits and societal expectations creates significant problems for these children and our communities.

HOW COMMON IS AGGRESSION?

Aggressive behaviors are reported as problematic in up to 20% of the total youth population, with differences by age and gender and also within disability type. Although most of the aggression seen in typical 2- to 3-year-old children will be replaced by appropriate behavior through maturation and development, one study found that 22.6% of adolescents (ages 12–17) had participated in a "serious fight" at school or work, and 16% had participated in a group-on-group fight (Marcus, 2007). In another study, nearly 8% reported attacking others with intent to seriously hurt someone (Office of Applied Studies, Substance Abuse and Mental Health Services Administration, 2010). According to Marcus (2007), adolescents engage in aggressive and violent behaviors (e.g., self-report of engaging in a physical fight) at rates of 42% for boys and 28% for girls. Studies have reported that aggression rates may be even higher in certain clinical populations (Kanne & Mazurek, 2011).

The BASC–3 Aggression scale measures both verbal and physical aggression. Verbal aggression includes behaviors such as arguing, name-calling, or vocalizing threats; relevant items from the Teacher Rating Scales (TRS) and Parent Rating Scales (PRS) include "Threatens to hurt others" and "Argues when denied own way." Physical aggression involves damage to property, self, or others; relevant items from the TRS and PRS include "Hits other children/adolescents" and "Breaks other children's things" or "Throws or breaks things when angry." More general behaviors indicating aggression are captured on the TRS and PRS with items such as "Bullies others" and "Loses temper too easily."

Theoretical Framework for Approaching Aggressive Behaviors

Although there are many theories on the causes of aggression, most approaches fit within one or more of five models: psychodynamic, drive theory, etiological/biological, social learning theory, and cognitive–behavioral perspectives. However, not all of these theories provide the support necessary to form the foundations for effective intervention strategies and the remediation of aggressive behaviors. The psychodynamic and drive theory models have limited utility and weak or unsupportable hypotheses. The biological attributions of aggression, although supportable, are insufficient as a sole basis from which to intervene in schools because extraneous factors may interfere with the intervention's selection, delivery, and sustainability. In contrast, the social learning and cognitive–behavioral theories provide strong evidence for the origins of aggression as a learned behavior and also offer a starting place for intervention utility in clinical and educational settings in particular. Therefore, the interventions presented in this chapter fit primarily within a social learning or cognitive–behavioral realm.

Interventions

This chapter presents 13 intervention strategies for remediating aggression (see Table 2.1). Most of the interventions are ready for adoption, but some require additional training or specialized materials. Table 2.1 provides a summary of where each strategy fits within a service implementation framework.

For some of the interventions in this chapter, supplemental materials (e.g., handouts, posters, checklists, daily logs, and worksheets) that are helpful for preparing, implementing, and evaluating the interventions can be found on Q-global.

Table 2.1 Interventions for Aggression

Intervention	Prevention[1]	Early Intervention[2]	Intensive Intervention[3]
Bully Prevention*	X	X	
Child-Centered Play Therapy (CCPT)*		X	X
Classroom Social Dynamics	X	X	
Cognitive Restructuring		X	X
Counseling Groups		X	X
Good Behavior Game (GBG)	X	X	
Incremental Theory Training*	X	X	X
Mindfulness Training*	X	X	X
Peer-Mediated Conflict Resolution and Negotiation*		X	X
Problem-Solving Training	X	X	X
Replacement Behavior Training		X	X
Social Skills Training	X	X	X
Verbal Mediation			X

[1] Prevention refers to skills that can be taught to all children or used universally; they promote better awareness and lessen the risk of problems.

[2] Early intervention includes techniques and strategies that address early warning signs or clinical signs of the risk of future problems. Early intervention may be specifically applied to one or more problems or generically applied as a skill set to prevent the development of a chronic problem. Early interventions can be delivered to groups or individuals.

[3] Intensive intervention focuses on individuals and individual problems, which are usually chronic, intensive, and require services due to the level of interference in daily functioning.

*May require additional training

 **BULLY PREVENTION**

DESCRIPTION

Group-based bully programs are intended to improve the school culture by changing faculty and student behaviors. Programs are school-wide and long-term, typically lasting several months to a year. Programs also modify how teachers perceive and interact with students on campus in relationship to bullying or bully-like behaviors (Espelage, Polanin, & Low, 2014).

Bully prevention programs involve staff-wide buy-in and professional development. The curricula, instruction, activities, and related materials can either be created or purchased. The key components of these programs involve developing awareness and skills because research indicates that most teachers typically do not intervene and most are unaware that this form of aggression is problematic. Instead, many misunderstand it to be part of socialization processes.

EXAMPLE

At a high school where violence and aggression are a part of the school culture, the administration and parents seek to change the culture by implementing training to make teachers and students aware of the problems associated with these behaviors; to help them develop a sensitivity to victims; and to teach them how to prevent, intervene, and recover after incidents. A program of ongoing staff development and student in-services is used to cover these topics through a created or purchased curriculum.

GOAL

Increase awareness and establish norms that communicate an intolerance for bullying.

THE BASICS

1. Lead teacher group workshops to increase awareness of bullying and its associated problems.

2. Help groups brainstorm interventions or choose from lists of options.

3. Help groups problem-solve methods for intervening and helping victims.

4. Codify prevention methods.

5. Teach relaxation and coping skills to be used with students.

HOW TO IMPLEMENT BULLY PREVENTION

 PREP

- Identify faculty-development days or workshops during which teachers and staff can participate in the program. Teachers and other staff and administrators compose groups to plan the program.

- Identify programs for purchase or self-develop one. Self-development involves creating 4–8 units of instruction and activities. Curriculum should be finished prior to the start of the program, ideally in a summer or pre-semester start. Curriculum content includes the following topics:

  ▲ awareness;

  ▲ intervening and helping victims;

  ▲ preventing and reporting; and

  ▲ planning for evaluating, modifying, and maintaining programs.

- Establish a calendar of awareness and training events to correspond with faculty and staff professional development and student assemblies.

IMPLEMENT

- Define bullying and why it is problematic in schools, communities, and even in the workplace. Relay costs (e.g., illness, jobs, feelings, damage, suicides, culture).

- Reach a consensus that school climate is important and that bullying is not conducive to a climate of respect and tolerance.

- Problem-solve methods for intervening and helping victims.

- Teach the procedures for what students and faculty are to do if they are bullied, and what to do if they become aware of or see bullying occurring.

- Codify prevention methods.

- Create a paper or electronic method for anonymous reporting.

- Identify any areas or times when bullying is problematic and address specifically (e.g., Are more faculty needed in a lunch room? Are more parents needed at a bus drop off? Should coaches be more active in supervising a locker room? Could older students serve as peer leaders to prevent problems from occurring where faculty are not inclined to supervise or monitor?).

- Train students, faculty, and staff in one or more coping, relaxation, or re-integration techniques for victims (e.g., how to stand up to a bully, where to get help, what to do if someone lets you down, how to build resiliency).

 EVALUATE

- Monitor office discipline referrals and parent reports to the office to determine program effectiveness.

EVIDENCE

A brief overview of research and annotated references supporting this intervention can be found on Q-global.

CONSIDERATIONS

It is possible that awareness of bullying may promote an initial rise in incident reporting. However, it is important to recognize that the rise may be due to increased social acceptance of reports and not to assume that the incidence of bullying is rising due to the program. Programs should not be partially implemented or their effectiveness may be blunted (Whitted & Dupper, 2005). Immediate improvement might not happen. According to one report from the National Association of School Psychologists, benefits of a program might not be realized for 3 years (Lazarus & Pfohl, 2010). Implementing a comprehensive program takes organization skills, creativity, time, support from educators, and resources to purchase curriculum materials (in some instances).

Consistent features of successful bullying prevention programs indicate schools can develop their own programs or participate in pre-packaged curriculums. Bullying prevention programs should attempt to (1) improve the school's culture (one long-time misconception about bullying is that it is a natural part of growing up), and (2) engage all adults and students in the school (Whitted & Dupper, 2005).

When teachers believe they can create or maintain a positive classroom environment, aggressive behavior of students in those classrooms appears to go down. Therefore, making teachers an integral part of intervention work is important because classroom teachers can impact student outcomes. Some adults will be resistant to the idea that bullying is a problem. To garner support, use a fact-based approach rather than one that appeals to sympathy. Discuss the incidence and outcomes of bullying rather than individual stories of something negative happening to other people.

Much of the work in this area continues to develop, and the experimental control for studies is improving and evolving. As such, these strategies hold promise, and they are based on principles that have demonstrated effectiveness in other areas.

CHILD-CENTERED PLAY THERAPY (CCPT)

DESCRIPTION

Child-Centered Play Therapy (CCPT) is based on the premise that children learn and communicate through play. Play therapy has a long history (Axline, 1947; Moustakas, 1959) and is rooted in a developmental approach. Play therapy is a developmentally responsive treatment for children who may be cognitively or verbally unable to describe abstract thought (Bratton, Ray, Rhine, & Jones, 2005).

CCPT can be administered only by professionals who have been trained and licensed or certified to conduct the therapy. Many training programs exist throughout the U.S. Registered play therapists must meet specific criteria and register with the Association for Play Therapy (see the University of North Texas' Center for Play Therapy website for more information). In addition, therapists must acquire toys to use during therapy. Examples of toys include clay, dolls, puppets, cars, phones, and toys that allow children to express aggression, such as a foam sword for playing soldier (see the University of North Texas' Center for Play Therapy website for a complete list). In addition, a room or space dedicated for treatment might be needed.

Play therapy involves establishing a therapeutic relationship and conducting therapy sessions. A therapeutic relationship is characterized by "nonjudgmental acceptance, empathy, and genuineness" (Bratton et al., 2013, p. 37). Therapeutic sessions generally are held weekly and last 30–50 minutes. The average number of treatments is 20 sessions, but this number can vary according to the Association for Play Therapy (n.d.).

EXAMPLE

Jon is a 3-year-old boy with aggressive and disruptive behaviors in a Head Start classroom. He is identified by his teacher as needing additional support and begins seeing a school counselor twice a week for 30 minutes of play therapy for 10 weeks.

GOAL

Teach children new strategies to express emotions and improve self-control through play.

THE BASICS

1. Allow children to play to learn new strategies to express a range of emotions, including anger and frustration, and to increase self-control.

2. Engage in nonjudgmental, empathetic, and genuine interactions.

HOW TO IMPLEMENT CHILD-CENTERED PLAY THERAPY

 PREP

- Participate in clinical training and licensure.
- Establish a location with appropriate materials (toys) to encourage emotional expression.
- Gather information about the child's behavior and situation through interviews with caregivers.

IMPLEMENT

- Build rapport with the child.
- Establish a therapeutic relationship.
- Engage in therapeutic sessions.

EVALUATE

- Employ clinical evaluation techniques to assess effectiveness, and consider having treatment outcome surveys completed by parents.

EVIDENCE

A brief overview of research and annotated references supporting this intervention can be found on Q-global.

CONSIDERATIONS

CCPT should be conducted only by trained professionals who have been properly supervised and professionally licensed and/or certified. See Landreth (2012) for an in-depth review of CCPT issues.

CLASSROOM SOCIAL DYNAMICS

DESCRIPTION

The classroom social dynamics intervention uses a class-wide approach to establish anti-aggression norms and to increase caring. It focuses on culture change at the classroom level using structured activities to increase empathy and responsiveness. Theoretically, the intervention is grounded in a cognitive and affective orientation. The classroom social dynamics intervention involves the teacher taking an active approach to managing classroom social patterns and peer relationships and to promote a more positive sense of a supportive peer community (Gest, Madill, Zadzora, Miller, & Rodkin, 2014). Teachers who involve themselves directly in discussions with children about peer relationships and who use strategies such as providing immediate consequences for aggression, assessing the social environment and behavior, creating positive social roles and opportunities, and involving themselves directly in resolving problems between children successfully reduce aggressive behavior (Gest et al., 2014).

EXAMPLE

Mr. Garcia's senior physics class uses the first week of school to discuss things that should be changed about a classroom in order to make school a better place and to brainstorm how to go about that change. The children in Ms. Dimmit's 1st grade classroom work though a similar process using age-appropriate language and examples about the social climate. Conflict, shaming, victimizing, criticizing, and rejection are themes that come up in both rooms, in different ways. Based on these discussions or activities, classroom rules are established.

GOAL

Change the culture of the classroom through direct involvement in discussions about peer relationships and by using assessment and structured activities to increase the focus on empathy and responsiveness.

THE BASICS

1. Establish classroom dynamics through direct teacher involvement in discussion about peer relationships and through quality interactions between the teacher and children.

2. Evaluate and identify areas for improvement.

HOW TO IMPLEMENT CLASSROOM SOCIAL DYNAMICS

 PREP

- Identify potential areas to improve by completing a classroom inventory and self-assessment on the quality of interactions along with the overall dynamics. This can be done informally through self-reflection and goal setting.
- Select one improvement target to work on during the following 6-week period.

 IMPLEMENT

- Based on assessment and discussion, implement a small change in teacher–student interactions one time per week for the first few weeks of the 6-week period (depending on your school calendar). A few small changes that have been shown to improve social dynamics include greeting children upon entrance and exit from the classroom, seeking structured and frequent opportunities for positive interactions, and creating opportunities for self-checking work.
- Increase to daily use gradually during the remaining weeks.

 EVALUATE

- Reflect on classroom practices or student interactions and social dynamics.
- Assess progress toward the goal of improving in one targeted area over the 6-week period.
- Determine what made the effort successful and if any barriers were responsible for a failure to stick to the target.
- Count and record aggressive acts by children at risk for aggressive behaviors and those who have demonstrated aggression. Monitor for decreased incidence of these behaviors.

EVIDENCE
A brief overview of research and annotated references supporting this intervention can be found on Q-global.

 # COGNITIVE RESTRUCTURING

DESCRIPTION
Cognitive restructuring (also referred to in the research literature as Rational Emotive Therapy [Ellis, 1962], social-judgment training, and attribution training [Harris, Wong, & Keogh, 1985; Meichenbaum, 1977]) is a strategy in which individuals learn to identify irrational or inaccurate beliefs and the events that lead to these beliefs. Irrational or inaccurate beliefs (i.e., cognitive distortions) often result in destructive emotions and subsequent maladaptive behaviors (e.g., aggression). For example, a child may irrationally identify a neutral look or comment from another person as aggressive or negative and respond aggressively. Or, a child may associate a teacher's request to come to the front of the classroom with being in trouble and, therefore, behave aggressively to avoid the negatively perceived encounter.

Because cognitive restructuring addresses the causal perceptions of success and failure—locus of control, stability, and controllability (Weiner, 1985)—the key to its use is modifying the beliefs that cause or lead up to the aggressive behavior. This modification of beliefs results in newly formed attributions. Through cognitive restructuring, children replace cognitive distortions that are disruptive and self-defeating by identifying irrational beliefs; understanding self-condemnation, frustration, intolerance, blame, and criticism of others; and learning to develop a system for disputing these beliefs (Ellis, 1986; Walen, DiGiuseppe, & Wessler, 1980; Wessler & Wessler, 1980; Young, 1977). As such, existing beliefs are replaced with more constructive ones that lead to more positive emotions and appropriate behaviors. Therefore, the beliefs are the target of the intervention, and generating solutions that can be applied and generalized during subsequent opportunities is the focus.

When using this intervention strategy with children, it can be helpful to use invented practice examples from stories, worksheets, or videos to develop skills for identifying irrational or mistaken attributions. With time and practice, the child can generate his or her own examples from past occurrences, and eventually, relate examples from current experiences. After achieving competence with the strategy it can be used as an "on the fly" intervention, with an adult quickly prompting a child to identify the "irrational" belief(s) that are supporting a current behavior.

It is important to understand that the child is the change agent in this intervention, while the person working with the child functions as a facilitator by assisting with the recognition, verbalization, and replacement of irrational beliefs. When modeling the procedures for the child, it is important to help the child develop more rational attributions so that he or she can gain more autonomy in using this technique. Either individual or group delivery of this technique is acceptable when implementing this intervention. Just-in-time services can be provided for children who have learned how to recognize signals and identify underlying beliefs. This assistance is gradually faded as children learn to progress independently through all steps and report back on their experiences.

EXAMPLE

Anthony is an 8-year-old boy who just started a new school. His 2nd-grade teacher passes back assignments by turning them face down on the desk so that children wait until all children have their papers before flipping them over to look at the score. Anthony has difficulty waiting and frequently puts his head on the desk to look under the paper. The teacher asks him to wait, but Anthony continues to peer under the paper until finally flipping it over angrily in frustration. The classroom routine includes the use of an interactive whiteboard following assignment review, but Anthony is usually in trouble by then and does not get a turn with the whiteboard, which creates more disturbance and sometimes leads him to have angry outbursts or push materials off the desk. Anthony believes the teacher is teasing him, just like the children at his former school. The school psychologist works with Anthony one-on-one to recognize the physical signs of frustration, to identify a rational explanation for turning grades over on the desk, and to verbalize and recognize that teachers do not tease children. Anthony and the school psychologist work through how to recognize teasing by facial features, tone of voice, and actions that are done to just one person, and not an entire classroom.

GOAL

Help the child to recognize emotional and behavioral signals that precede a problematic irrational behavior, identify irrational and inaccurate beliefs about others' behaviors, generate alternative explanations for behavior, and replace these irrational beliefs with more rational ones.

THE BASICS

1. Help the child recognize emotional or behavioral signals that precede a problematic irrational behavior.
2. Help the child identify beliefs responsible for the association between the emotional or behavioral signal and the irrational behavior.
3. Dispute the irrational or inaccurate belief.
4. Promote generalization of a more rational belief.
5. Develop a plan to internalize the rational belief.

HOW TO IMPLEMENT COGNITIVE RESTRUCTURING

 PREP

- Schedule time for individual, small group, or full-classroom meetings.

- Prepare three examples of misunderstanding or events from school that illustrate misattribution. Examples: (1) A student believes he gets in trouble because a teacher does not like him, when actually he just received a graded paper. (2) A child believes others are talking behind her back, but they are not talking about her at all. (3) A child feels his efforts in class do not make a difference.

 IMPLEMENT

Use the acronym "RIDGE" to easily recall the implementation steps.

- **Recognize emotional or behavioral signals that suggest a problem:** Discuss signals that might trigger a problematic irrational behavior. For example, a child might experience an emotional signal when reading teacher comments made on a homework assignment, such as a "funny" feeling in his or her stomach, an increased heartrate, or a general feeling of discomfort. Discuss awareness of these signals.

- **Identify beliefs that are responsible for the association between the emotional or behavioral signal and the irrational behavior:** Define the concept of irrational or inaccurate beliefs in daily life at school or with family. These beliefs, which are mistaken assumptions about a situation or person, can give rise to unnecessary conflict or feelings of self-condemnation, frustration, blame, and criticism of others.

- **Dispute the irrational or inaccurate belief:** Teach the child to look for facts that dispute the belief. "I'm dumb at math" can be disputed by any successes in math. "I'm disliked by everyone" is disproved by finding one friendly person or event. Provide the prepared examples and ask for children to point out possible inaccuracies in the belief being held.
  Ask children to write or share personal examples with you privately or with the group. Go through these personal illustrations and identify irrational thinking. The following are a few examples:

  ▲ "When I turn in homework it is always wrong because I'm dumb at math," could be corrected to, "I need some help to make sure I understand the homework, even when I think I do."

  ▲ "No one sits with me at lunch because they think I'm weird;" "I bring my lunch and most others buy theirs;" "My mom packs food from our native country and it smells/looks odd to others so nobody sits with me;" could be corrected to, "No one is really concerned with what I eat, they are focused on their own food;" or "No one is ignoring me, I just need to find someone who I can reach out to and become friends."

  ▲ "I must have been called to the office because I am in trouble," could be corrected to, "I got called to the office because someone needs me for something."

- **Generate a more rational belief:** Provide a generic thinking pattern to address problems discussed. For example, a child invites another child to play a game or go to a party and the invited child declines. The child who made the invitation thinks that the decline on the invitation means he is disliked. Instead, a new thinking pattern would involve thinking about the other side of the story and generating all possible, plausible other explanations (e.g., family responsibility, feels sick, agreed to work for someone, already had other plans, doesn't like the same activities.)
  "Three Truths and a Lie," where the child learns to create three reasonable other explanations and one that is ridiculous is another strategy that can be taught to the child. Three reasonable explanations for not accepting an invitation to a movie include "already seen the movie, can't sit still long enough to watch a movie, already has other plans," and one ridiculous explanation is "afraid of alien abduction." The child then compares and/or ranks the irrational belief being held to the more rational beliefs that were generated. In the movie example, the reasonable explanations are more likely to be true than the irrational belief of the child being disliked by peers.

- **Exemplify (create an example) to internalize the rational belief:** Replacing irrational thinking with more functional and more likely thoughts takes practice. Provide steps for doing so, such as repeating a corrective or replacement message, pairing this internal recitation with deep breathing, and visualizing examples that are counter to the irrational or problematic thinking.

 EVALUATE

- Meet as a follow-up with the individual, small group, or classroom; revisit the topic; and check for understanding of the concept and where it applies.

- Assess how many children can remember the RIDGE acronym and recall the techniques used in cognitive restructuring.

- Consider using an evaluation journal to identify when and where they use the replacement thoughts or beliefs in different environments. An evaluation journal can further enhance the potential effectiveness of this technique.

- Ask children to write a reflection, a response, or an example of using cognitive restructuring.

- Generalize and reinforce the use of rational thoughts by discussing their use in different situations.

- Judge mastery by responses, and follow-up with additional individual or group sessions as appropriate.

EVIDENCE
A brief overview of research and annotated references supporting this intervention can be found on Q-global.

CONSIDERATIONS

FOR TEACHING
Cognitive restructuring requires the willing participation of the child in addition to cognitive and verbal abilities. The adult teaching cognitive restructuring should be skilled in identifying distortions in a child's thinking. The cognitions of children and youth—their perspectives on what is real and what is a significant problem—are largely determined by their experience and age. Restructuring is intended to, for example, assist a child in understanding that if his or her friend doesn't sit by him or her at lunch, some external factor (e.g., the lunch line moving faster on one side of the cafeteria) may be involved as opposed to an imagined reason (e.g., the friend disliking the child).

FOR AGE AND DEVELOPMENTAL LEVEL
Children sometimes identify patterns of typical playground behavior expected from their friends differently than adults. Adult vernacular, examples, phrasing, and interactions are decidedly different than those of children and may be less socially valid. Consider the point of view of the child and the nuances of the environment or cultural expectations when considering appropriate behaviors and priorities.

The linguistic and emotional development of the child should be considered when identifying areas to change. For instance, at some ages or stages children may truly believe that they are not responsible for their problems. At others, they may assume all of the responsibility when doing so is not appropriate. Another example is related to prediction: Young children, perhaps up to age 8, have tremendous difficulty with prediction and may be unable to anticipate what might happen next or where a scenario is headed.

FOR CULTURAL AND LANGUAGE DIFFERENCES

There is considerable potential for familial, cultural, or economic values to influence a child's belief system about what is reality and what is a cognitive distortion. A mismatch often exists between a dominant culture and a minority one, or the culture of the school conflicts with that of the family.

Sensitivity to norms and assumptions should be a part of the cognitive restructuring approach. Parental perceptions of world events and cultural habits have a tremendous impact on youth perspectives. For example, an immigrant from a country in which police come in the middle of the night and remove people from their homes may transmit those beliefs and expectations to their children. Likewise, a family who has experienced parental incarceration for drug use or illegal activity may transmit values that are different from those expected by a teacher.

 # COUNSELING GROUPS

DESCRIPTION

Counseling groups assist in understanding aggression as a behavior. Sessions promote and practice identification of triggers and self-control. A therapeutic alliance between a trained counselor and a group or individuals is central to the development of group norms. Counseling groups are only semi-structured around the topic of decreasing aggression. Grouping aggressive individuals is not recommended as best practice. Aggression is best treated in groups where other models and other problems are discussed in addition to aggression.

Guidance curricula typically involve structured developmental lessons. Literature suggests these are more effective with older students (middle school or junior high) than with those in elementary school. Programs, such as Student Success Skills, have been systematically evaluated (Brigman, & Campbell, 2003; Lemberger, Brigman, Webb, & Moore 2011/2012; Villares, Lemberger, Brigman, & Webb, 2011). Counseling can follow protocols (O'Rourke & Worzbyt, 1996), but it may also include problem solving, self-instruction, modeling, role play, alternative thinking, social skills, and training.

EXAMPLE

Dr. Mortan runs a small counseling group of five boys identified as at-risk. One of these boys has problems with aggression; the other four boys are working on different support programs. Two of the boys have parents deployed in the military, one is struggling with anxiety related to a girlfriend and college applications, and the other lost a parent in an automobile accident. The group meets once a week during lunch. The children each have a "front of the line" pass to save time in the very short 35-minute lunch block (i.e., they are allowed to get trays or drinks and go to a classroom with their food). The large cafeteria is so busy that few people, if any, notice the group takes place.

Dr. Mortan runs three different groups per week, limits access to each group, and dismisses children from the group in as few sessions as possible, or after six sessions at most, to maximize access to children. Children are allowed to rejoin after awaiting the next opening.

GOAL

Help children to understand aggressive behavior, identify triggers, and practice self-control.

THE BASICS

1. Facilitate introductions and establish ground rules.

2. Establish goals.

3. Introduce the topic of aggression.

4. Examine responses to and consequences of aggression. Create assignments for practice.

5. Review practice sessions or homework from previous session, discuss personal strengths, and review goals.

6. Review progress.

HOW TO IMPLEMENT COUNSELING GROUPS

 PREP

- Locate a room for the meeting space.

- Identify lunch times or other group times that children can meet without fear of being ostracized.

- Arrange for front of line cafeteria access or bus transportation for early or late attendance at school as needed.

- Identify children for groups, get consent from parents, and get commitment from children to attend three sessions before opting out. Consider rotations, where six weeks is the maximum, children can rotate back in after others have an opportunity.

 IMPLEMENT

- Meet with children at the designated time.

- Lay out ground rules for respect and confidentiality.

- Explain when or how children can participate in a group.

- Using flash cards to write on, have children identify personal goals (e.g., decrease aggression). Alternatively, children could be handed a card with up to three goals or topics to choose from.

- Introduce what aggression is, what it looks like, where it comes from, and how often it occurs.

- Have children share when consequences of aggression have affected them personally and discuss as a group.

- Identify a practice assignment as homework for the next session (presumably a week away). When the group returns, review homework first in the session after re-establishing ground rules for respect and cooperation.

 EVALUATE

- Review individually reported progress on personal goals when the group meets, and ask children to share what they learned or remember from the prior week.

- Encourage or prompt children as needed when the group meets. Never skip a child who does not have anything to say. Allow them to pass so they have time to think, but warn them that you will come back in two minutes—or provide an option to share the next time or to participate later.

- Use professional judgment to monitor if children should be dismissed after 6 weeks or retained.

- Consider shorter or longer group sessions as necessary and as logistics allow.

EVIDENCE

A brief overview of research and annotated references supporting this intervention can be found on Q-global.

CONSIDERATIONS

Teachers can support counseling groups by providing feedback to the group leader about how new skills are being implemented or by providing data on diminishing or increasing aggression problems. Communication about the topic schedule assists teachers in this endeavor and allows teachers to reinforce topics or skills in the classroom setting to complement group participants' learning.

Parents may also benefit from knowing the schedule of topics, being informed of goals or plans, and participating in parent groups that correspond to what children are learning.

Groups of individuals experiencing trouble with conduct or similar problems generally should not be working together; they may simply learn additional maladaptive behaviors and form new networks. Aggression is best treated in groups where other models and other problems are discussed in addition to aggression.

 GOOD BEHAVIOR GAME (GBG)

DESCRIPTION

The Good Behavior Game (GBG) originated in the late 1960s during a prolific research era at the University of Kansas where the science of human behavior studies were focused on school-related problems. Originally a master's project by Barrish, Saunders, and Wolf, the first evaluation study was published in 1969 and many meta-analyses have since followed (see contemporary work by Bowman-Perrott, Burke, Zaini, Zhang, & Vannest, in press).

The GBG combines contingent reinforcement, token economies (or secondary reinforcers), and natural or social reinforcers in a classroom setting. The GBG starts out structured and predictable, but moves gradually to longer game times with less obvious start and stop times, and eventually, it becomes a part of the management of the group. The game is introduced to classrooms with two competitive teams vying for points. Set "play" times and teams are established by the teacher.

EXAMPLE

Mr. Jennings, a 6th-grade social studies teacher, finds the general behavior of his children to be noisy, disruptive, inattentive, and sometimes aggressive. He also notices high rates of pushing in class and physical fighting and other violence in the halls, which eventually leads to police involvement in the district. To correct the behavior issues, he divides each of his seven classes into two GBG teams by drawing an imaginary line down the middle of the classroom; the Left Team and Right Team are named by location. He announces that they will play a game on Monday, Wednesday, and Friday in his room. The team with the most points earns the last three minutes of class as quiet free time for phone use while the other team will write vocabulary words. The game time is 10 minutes during lecture and is designated by Mr. Jennings's personal trophy being placed on the front of his desk to identify that they are in game mode. The rules are to remain seated; raise hands to ask questions (teams must ask a minimum of three questions); and show respectful behaviors only (e.g., no acts of verbal or physical aggression, arguing, or protesting loss of points). Each team starts with 10 points and loses a point for any rule violations. Each time a rule is violated, Mr. Jennings says, "Minus one Left Team" or "Minus one Right Team" and continues his lecture.

GOAL

Improve children's social and academic performance and reduce aggressive behavior by using peers to provide corrective feedback and to promote adherence to classroom rules.

THE BASICS

1. Establish clear expectations of desired behavior.

2. Engage in repeated weekly play of the GBG.

3. Provide immediate reinforcement to teams.

4. Move from fixed, predictable game times to unpredictable and deferred reinforcements.

HOW TO IMPLEMENT GOOD BEHAVIOR GAME

 PREP

- Establish game times 3 times a week for 10 minutes each time.
- Locate/identify rewards or privileges to use in the game.
- Decide how to divide into two teams (e.g., class location front/back or left side/right side).
- Prepare a list of potential reinforcers.
- Create a chart of the teams' point totals and display the chart in an area visible to the entire class.

 IMPLEMENT

- Introduce the concept of the GBG to the class.
- Divide the class into two teams by location or another method.
- Explain that reinforcers are earned by the winning team and emphasize that reinforcers are awarded immediately.
- Explain the "Rules to Follow to Win" based on classroom expectations, such as: stay in seat unless given permission to leave for the restroom after raising your hand and being called on, or staying in your seat (e.g., not on the desk).
- Share the list of potential reinforcers with the children, ask them to generate a list of additional reinforcers, and then ask them to vote on a final reinforcer.
- Increase the play time 10 minutes per game every 3 weeks, up to a maximum of 3 hours per week.
- Transition from clear to uncertain start and stop times. Gradually begin to use game periods without start/stop time announcements with the goal of generalizing the skills to longer periods of time and fading the structured prompting.
- Begin to gradually delay any rewards to later in the school day (e.g., instead of immediately after the game ends, reward at the end of class, then at the end of the day, and then at the end of the week).
- Start to gradually use the game in different activities and at different times and schedules.
- Change reinforcers periodically to maintain children's interest.

 EVALUATE

- Check for understanding by asking children if they understand the game rules.
- Review problems targeted by the game to check whether incidences are fewer.
- Gather data periodically to assess continued effectiveness.

EVIDENCE

A brief overview of research and annotated references supporting this intervention can be found on Q-global.

CONSIDERATIONS

As described, the GBG is a preventative intervention for the general population of children. For this reason, children on Individualized Education Programs may need different levels of reinforcers, or they may need different penalties for rule violations in order to maintain inclusivity in the classroom and team membership. If a child is unable to maintain some of the behaviors expected of the whole class (e.g., raise your hand before speaking, remain attentive to class activities), those behaviors should be ignored so that the team is not degraded for their efforts and the individual with the disability is not viewed as detrimental to the team. Rather than address problems during GBG play times, ignore problem behavior in individuals with disabilities to the extent possible and address them later or establish separate individual expectations with different systems of reinforcement and privileges that are appropriate.

 # INCREMENTAL CHANGE THEORY TRAINING

DESCRIPTION

Incremental theory is grounded in personality change theory (Dweck, 2000) and is believed to be particularly well-suited for adolescent populations and violence reduction (Yeager & Dweck, 2012). Incremental theory training is designed to help children better understand their potential to change their own behavior and/or personality. This belief shift helps to contest personally-held beliefs that one is a certain type of person who is unable to change or must play a certain role, such as aggressor or victim. Hopefulness about change is hypothesized to lead to more change rather than helplessness about the personal choices or setbacks in making progress. Incremental change is rooted in change theory (Lindblom, 1959).

Incremental theory training requires some familiarity with personality change theory and enough understanding of the brain's anatomy to create materials and teach basic concepts to children. Unlimited graphics, descriptions, and concepts are available on the Internet.

EXAMPLES

Dr. Frank conducts weekly one-on-one sessions with Peter, a 10-year-old in a residential facility. Peter believes he has no control over his own behavior, that he is "bad" like his parents have described, and that he is destined to lead a life of poor choices and negative consequences. Dr. Frank works with Peter to teach fundamental concepts about the brain and the body at a level that Peter can understand. Across sessions, Peter learns about the ability to change and the degree of control we have over ourselves leading to less helplessness and greater recognition of positive choices and outcomes.

Ms. Koolmeyer is a high school science teacher who observes some of her students give up and believe they "just aren't good at science" and other students believe they are victims of their own behavior and "just can't help it" or are "always bad." She asks them if they believe they can change or if they know people who have changed. She teaches incremental theory to her students once a week for six weeks. In the first two sessions she teaches brain anatomy and how the brain chemically and physically changes with learning and describes and provides examples of how personality is part of the brain. In the next two sessions she presents examples of famous people who faced social difficulties but who gained acceptance, and scientific evidence supporting incremental theory. She assigns writing tasks in which children use incremental theory to deal with aggression and other conflict. In the last two sessions she talks about actions as distinct from feelings, and how both can be learned and changed, and she reinforces lessons from previous sessions by having the children perform skits in which they use ideas from incremental theory. In each of the six sessions there are group and individual activities, such as worksheets, practice activities, skits, discussions, and a small final writing assignment.

GOAL

Help children learn that personality is shaped by the brain and is subject to change through learning and feeling.

THE BASICS

1. Teach the science behind incremental theory.

2. Provide opportunities to practice in contexts that contribute to aggression (real or imagined).

HOW TO IMPLEMENT INCREMENTAL CHANGE THEORY TRAINING

 PREP

- Survey children prior to beginning the intervention to solicit examples of how people can change.

- Develop age-appropriate instructional materials and activities to cover two sessions each of three topics: neuroanatomy of the brain, personality as changeable, and the feelings and actions as distinct. Materials are also available through existing resources (see Yeager, Trzesniewski, and Dweck, 2013).

- Create a list of examples of famous people who overcame social adversity and changed how they were perceived. Popular films or books can provide additional examples.

- Implement the training with all children, or implement it one-on-one to reduce the likelihood of deviancy training (i.e., where children learn new ways to be inappropriate or use maladaptive behavior from other children with a larger repertoire).

 IMPLEMENT

- During sessions 1 and 2, discuss incremental theory's view of the brain as a malleable organ and personality as it relates to the brain. Expand on this idea to discuss how human qualities can also change.

- During sessions 3 and 4, present examples of famous people who faced social difficulties but who gained acceptance. Present scientific evidence supporting incremental theory. Assign writing tasks in which children use incremental theory to deal with aggression and other conflict.

- During sessions 5 and 6, discuss how actions are distinct from feelings and can be learned and changed. Reinforce lessons from previous sessions by having children perform skits in which they use ideas from incremental theory to resolve problems.

 EVALUATE

- Keep a record of session notes to evaluate and modify materials in future iterations.

- Ask children to record examples of personal growth or examples of change in themselves or others.

- Use a tracking sheet for each child to determine whether the number of aggressive behaviors has increased, remained stable, or decreased.

- Review individual progress and universal culture change in the class and on campus.

- Monitor the impact on office discipline referrals.

EVIDENCE

A brief overview of research and annotated references supporting this intervention can be found on Q-global.

CONSIDERATIONS

Teacher and/or staff training may be helpful in creating shared vocabulary and communicating theoretical approaches to working with children and youth who demonstrate aggression. Teachers may deliver certain topics of the program in class, or a school may identify this as a program of value for the entire population.

For Age and Developmental Level

The age and developmental level of the children should be considered during the development of materials. High school students can engage in deeper learning of content than can elementary students, but even young children are able to participate in explaining the concept of change and giving examples of when something has changed. Tangible demonstrations, such as watching an ice cube melt, may facilitate understanding of the concept. It was ice that became water; a solid that became a liquid. This illustration may help children grasp the abstract concept of personality change or incremental change theory—small steps, small change, leading to large or radical change over time.

For Cultural and Language Differences

The cultural and language differences of the participating children should be considered. Visual aids may help reduce language barriers. Asking children about their beliefs prior to engagement may be worthwhile because some cultures may attribute personality to a deity or consider it unchangeable.

 # MINDFULNESS TRAINING

DESCRIPTION

Mindfulness training procedures teach awareness of aggression and coping strategies related to aggression. Awareness is focused on emotions and other events that occur before aggressive behaviors (Parker, Kupersmidt, Mathis, Scull, & Sims, 2014). Coping strategies focus on training the mind to disengage from the feelings in order to control emotions and behavior (Milani, Nikmanesh, & Farnam, 2013; Peters et al., 2015). Strategies such as stress reduction and learning to observe feelings and thoughts without judgment are also taught (Milani et al., 2013).

EXAMPLE

Ms. Karen works in a group home with children, many of whom are fighting in the home or being aggressive at work. Some are at risk of losing community access. She employs weekly sessions of mindfulness training for residents and supervisors. When incidences occur, supervisors prompt residents and residents prompt one another to use these mindfulness strategies.

GOAL

Help children learn to disengage from feelings in order to control their emotions and behavior.

THE BASICS

1. Train the child in mindfulness strategies.
2. Help the child practice disconnecting from physiological reactions.
3. Help the child learn they are in control of their own responses.

HOW TO IMPLEMENT MINDFULNESS TRAINING

 PREP

- Create or use an existing 12-week training protocol (see Singh et al., 2013; steps are discussed in the IMPLEMENT section).
- Identify a time and location for 15- to 30-minute training and practice sessions.
- Teach parents the procedure.

IMPLEMENT

■ Objectives for the training sessions include:

▲ Week 1: Introduce the mindfulness program.

▲ Week 2: Teach the child to focus attention (e.g., meditation, observing breath).

▲ Week 3: Teach the child to focus attention on arousal states (e.g., observing breath, arousal states that follow anger, awareness of arousal states, breathing with awareness of arousal states).

▲ Week 4: Teach the child mediation on the soles of the feet (e.g., what is soles of the feet [SOF], SOF as shifting of attention, basic practice with SOF with joy- and anger-producing situations).

▲ Week 5: Engage in practice for arousal states and with triggers for anger and aggression.

▲ Weeks 6–8: Engage in SOF practice. Then, engage in SOF practice with triggers for anger and aggression.

▲ Weeks 9–11: Continue SOF practice, engage in SOF practice with support staff or a confederate.

▲ Week 12: Wrap up and discuss follow-up requirements.

■ During each training session, practice a meditation technique (e.g., the SOF technique). Parents may be included and may practice alongside the child. For example, to use the SOF technique:

▲ Use a soft voice.

▲ Ensure the child is seated comfortably in a soft chair with feet flat on the floor and hands resting on his or her thighs.

▲ Instruct the child to close his or her eyes to increase concentration and to narrow attentional focus to the present moment.

▲ Instruct the child to focus on the soles of his or her feet until a state of calmness is reached.

 EVALUATE

■ Review training materials for any necessary modifications.

■ Assess identified child outcomes. Children may self-report, or adults may observe and record changes in child behavior or uses of the strategy. Implementers may modify the protocol to involve fewer sessions.

■ Monitor outcomes after any modifications to ensure that desired results are still obtained.

EVIDENCE

A brief overview of research and annotated references supporting this intervention can be found on Q-global.

CONSIDERATIONS

FOR TEACHING

If time allows, mindfulness training may be delivered in a classroom or school-wide program. Current emphasis on standardized testing and curricula may render this impractical unless mentoring time, small-group time, or "homerooms" are a part of the school day. Mindfulness training may be more likely to occur via pull-out time with individuals or small groups of children. Be aware that "focus" training, such as this one, can be misconstrued as spiritual, prayerful, or meditative. To avoid misunderstandings with parents and school boards, be sure to articulate the purpose of the activities (i.e., decrease aggression) and the related steps or procedures.

Receptive language development and age may impact a child's ability to participate in this intervention. Be patient with teaching and learning sustained attention and focus as these are challenging skills that require practice.

PEER-MEDIATED CONFLICT RESOLUTION AND NEGOTIATION

DESCRIPTION
Peer-mediated conflict resolution and negotiation is a program that uses students as arbitrators who negotiate and resolve conflict among peers. A small group of students represents a cross-section of the student population and completes training to serve as peer mediators. Students or adults may refer cases for peer-mediated conflict resolution and negotiation, and participation in the program is voluntary.

Peer mediation, conflict resolution, and negotiation empower students to handle conflicts and misunderstandings. When peers mediate, school contexts and youth perspectives are naturally incorporated into negotiations. Peers may have unique vantage points from which to address the issues that arise in a school environment.

A peer-mediated program can have a powerful impact on a school campus when adequate time and care are involved in its initiation; therefore, these programs require a significant time investment during the organizational planning stages. Peer mediation is only as good as the training, support, and supervision provided by the adult coach. This intervention should be integrated into the school climate to be effective.

EXAMPLE
Two girls, Leah and Miranda, have a disagreement over who was invited to a party. This disagreement escalates into more aggressive fighting, unfortunately involving other groups of girls. A teacher completes a referral and sends Leah and Miranda to peer-mediated conflict resolution and negotiation. Trained peer mediators meet with the girls, help them resolve the conflict, and make follow-up contact.

GOAL
Foster student problem-solving leadership and allow peers (rather than adults) to address student-level problems.

THE BASICS
1. Train an advisor.
2. Establish a core team of student leaders.
3. Teach procedures for the peer-conflict resolution process on campus, including a referral system.
4. Monitor continuously and evaluate each semester.

HOW TO IMPLEMENT PEER-MEDIATED CONFLICT RESOLUTION AND NEGOTIATION

 PREP

- Obtain administrative support and commitment to the program.
- Create a committee (e.g., faculty, administration, and parents) that will make decisions about curriculum delivery and the selection of peer mediators.
- Identify adults who will maintain responsibility for program.

- Select a small group of students who can commit to serving as peer mediators. The group should represent a cross-section of the student population with respect to gender, age, grade, race/ethnicity, socioeconomic level, language, and other relevant characteristics.

- Train all program members in mediation processes. Mediation processes include active listening, communication, problem solving, negotiation, conflict resolution, and social skills. Training can range from a 2-day intensive workshop to 20 hours of training delivered in 30-minute sessions (see Johnson & Johnson, 2005). Role play may be one helpful method to use when teaching mediation and negotiation.

- Define the types of conflicts that are suitable for the mediation group to resolve.

- Define incidents that will not be mediated. For example, situations involving drugs, weapons, other illegal behaviors, abuse, harassment, and bullying are not appropriate for mediation (Block & Blazej, 2005).

- Establish logistic procedures for the program including the referral process, availability of and access to peer mediators, and any other necessary requirements at the school.

- Create forms to document the nature of conflicts and outcomes (i.e., conflict resolution status).

- Identify a system to track data about the program (e.g., number of cases referred to the program, types of conflicts, number of conflicts with a positive resolution).

- Articulate the specific procedures for lack of resolution (e.g., advisors or counselors attempt to settle the dispute).

IMPLEMENT

- Announce the program school-wide and explain the process for referrals and handling conflict. This can be done in an assembly or as a general announcement.

- Promote the program using flyers, posters, emails, and posts on the school district's or school's website.

- Explain to students and faculty how to initiate a conflict resolution, as well as how to refer students to the program.

- Elaborate on the types of conflicts that are suitable and unsuitable for the mediation group to consider.

- Maintain ongoing training and program support.

EVALUATE

- Follow up frequently with those involved in the process to determine the program's effectiveness and any further training needs.

- Track data about the program to determine if the incidence of aggressive behavior is reduced following implementation.

EVIDENCE
A brief overview of research and annotated references supporting this intervention can be found on Q-global.

CONSIDERATIONS
The establishment of a peer-mediated group requires advanced preparation and time and effort to obtain administrative approval, form a committee with different stakeholders, select peer mediators, train mediators, and maintain the mediation program. Furthermore, establishing a mediation program is costly if formal training and certification is involved.

FOR TEACHING

Teachers are most supportive when they are involved and informed of the process of peer mediation. This intervention is largely dependent on the support of building-level administration and faculty. Teams of individuals who sponsor and advise the process and peer mediators assist in the successful maintenance of the program. Some children and youth may be resistant to participating due to affiliation with groups who are in opposition to peaceful resolution of conflicts.

FOR AGE AND DEVELOPMENTAL LEVEL

Peer mediation has been typically used at the middle- and high-school levels; however, it may be appropriate for upper-elementary students in some cases. Children who are very young and not developmentally ready to understand conflict from another person's point of view may not benefit from this intervention.

FOR CULTURAL AND LANGUAGE DIFFERENCES

Social acceptability may be limited for some children based on their need for social independence. Recognize that cultural differences influence how groups identify, perceive, and manage conflict. Identifying cultural expectations for conflict resolution is beneficial and easily managed in this peer format.

 # PROBLEM-SOLVING TRAINING

DESCRIPTION

Problem-solving training teaches children a sequential and deliberate process for handling potentially negative situations that arise during the course of social interactions (Polsgrove & Smith, 2004). Problem solving is taught in group sessions through modeling, direct instruction, and guided practice. Problem-solving approaches rely on the development of skills that can be internalized and generalized to a variety of problems using the ICE method (i.e., Identify the problem, Create alternatives, and Evaluate options). The process is facilitated best if problem solving is taught at a universal level prior to establishment of reoccurring or individualized problems. Designing and practicing the technique also is important if problem solving is taught in response to a specific problem.

EXAMPLE

Nathan, a middle school student, frequently seeks help from his classmates during independent work time. He responds with verbally aggressive outbursts when his teacher asks him to stay on task and work quietly. He is referred to problem-solving training and learns to choose a more appropriate way to interact with his classmates and teacher. He identifies different ways to acknowledge the teacher while requesting help from classmates. He learns to express his academic concerns in a manner that is productive, rather than becoming verbally aggressive and disrupting the class.

GOAL

Teach the child a new skill set and to engage in different thinking and new behaviors to reduce aggression and other problem behaviors.

THE BASICS

1. Help the child recognize that a problem exists.

2. Define the problem accurately (e.g., whose problem is it and why).

3. Generate possible solutions.

4. Evaluate each solution for its pros and cons.

5. Design, implement, and evaluate the use of the solution.

HOW TO IMPLEMENT PROBLEM-SOLVING TRAINING

 PREP

- Identify one or two examples of triggers that lead to aggression.

- Review one or two examples of school-related aggression on record to initiate discussion. Use these examples if children have difficulty understanding any of the implementation steps below.

 IMPLEMENT

- Ask each child to identify one school-related aggression problem. Each child can also record an aggression problem on an index card to be collected. Review each child's card, and choose one of the cards to present to the group. Write the selected problem on the whiteboard (ensuring that the child's identity is not disclosed). If the children hesitate, provide prepared examples. Phase out prepared examples in subsequent sessions.

- Ask the children to define the problem thoroughly. Lead the children through identifying different perspectives and reinforcers of the problematic behavior.

- Ask the children to generate at least three alternative acceptable solutions. Encourage all legitimate attempts at solutions, regardless of how unrealistic they might be. These can be written on a board for the group to discuss in an open forum.

- Evaluate each potential solution. Elicit evaluative discussion of these solutions and if each meets the needs of all parties involved. Cross out solutions that the children decide are ineffective. List the costs and benefits of each solution. Ask the children to choose the best solution.

- Practice the plan. Ask the children to generate ideas for doing this. These could include role-play of the situation or simply talking about ways a child could practice.

- Incorporate the plan into an actual situation. Discuss situations in which the newly learned skill can be practiced, and encourage preparation to discuss its effectiveness at the next meeting.

- Teach the children to generalize these steps to other problems by using the acronym ICE (i.e., Identify the problem, Create alternatives, and Evaluate options).

- Create an evaluation plan for any problem behaviors and determine appropriate reinforcers. Choose a reinforcer that is desirable and use a 1:1 ratio for any new appropriate behavior (i.e., reinforce each instance of the target behavior).

 EVALUATE

- Check for comprehension by asking the children to demonstrate the process independently.

- Ask the children to report back on their ICE results after a plan has been implemented.

- Ask the children to identify particular places or times where they might want to use ICE for problem solving.

- Ask the children to rate the program.

- Monitor incidences of aggression to evaluate the effects of problem solving.

EVIDENCE
A brief overview of research and annotated references supporting this intervention can be found on Q-global.

CONSIDERATIONS

FOR TEACHING

When teaching problem-solving skills, allow time for modeling and guided practice. These steps are frequently skipped when teaching time gets compressed. Modeling and guided practice are critical for teaching problem-solving skills as they are not learned from worksheets or discussions and must be practiced. Children learn problem solving most effectively by experiencing it firsthand, primarily through role-play and practice situations. Teacher behavior may affect child outcomes (Frey, Hirschstein, & Guzzo, 2000). Therefore, supportive practices are critical, and teachers who involve children in identifying problems and constructing solutions will see better results.

FOR AGE AND DEVELOPMENTAL LEVEL

Children who are younger, developmentally delayed, or lack communicative skills have more difficulty than other children when using language to explain the actions of others. In these instances, symbols or puppets might be an alternative for instructional or communication needs. Offering fixed choices (e.g., asking "Which is the problem: x or y?") may help to bridge this functional gap. Examples or stories for younger children are most effective when well-matched to their age and developmental level.

FOR CULTURAL AND LANGUAGE DIFFERENCES

Choose language carefully during role-play. Be sensitive in encouraging and affirming student responses when working with children whose primary language and culture vary. Identifying the feelings or problems of others or taking their perspectives may be new task demands for some children. Language that identifies feelings varies for different cultures with respect to translation and in terminology that is available. Some languages do not have a vocabulary for emotions or feelings. These differences may result in the need for additional teaching.

FOR SAFETY

Role-play should be used with caution when working with children with histories of physical aggression. Adults should know the personal and social histories of each child with whom they are working. For example, if two adolescents have a history of aggression against one another, they may not be well-matched as independent role-play partners reenacting a problem-solving scenario about avoiding a fight. Children should not be coerced into participation. Successful intervention for aggression using problem-solving techniques requires a degree of willing participation.

 # REPLACEMENT BEHAVIOR TRAINING

DESCRIPTION

Replacement behavior training focuses on teaching new appropriate behaviors that can be used to replace undesirable behaviors (Naoi, 2011). Replacement behaviors are taught and reinforced to promote their adoption, maintenance, and generalization. The aggressive behavior (e.g., hitting or name calling) is replaced with an alternative behavior that fulfills the same need for the individual (Fischer, Iwata, & Mazalesk, 1997; Friman, Barnard, Altman, & Wolf, 1986; Hegel & Ferguson, 2000; Lerman, Kelley, Vorndran, Kuhn, & Larue, 2002). The replacement behavior is thought to be functionally equivalent to the initial behavior because it serves a similar purpose and allows the individual access to the same or greater contingencies of reinforcement (Naoi, 2011).

Reinforcement is central to teaching replacement behaviors. Initially, replacement behaviors are reinforced at a 1:1 ratio of reinforcement for each occurrence of the new behavior. This reinforcement schedule should be faded slowly over time (e.g., to a 1:2 and then a 1:4 ratio) while watching for natural contingencies of reinforcement (e.g., teacher praise, new friends, better grades). If natural contingencies do not occur, artificial reinforcers should be maintained.

Another key component in replacement behavior techniques is the identification of antecedents to the problem behavior. Similar to the process in other intervention techniques like frustration management training, relaxation training, and assertiveness training (Colter & Guerra, 1976; Wilkinson & Canter, 1982; Wolpe & Lazurus, 1966), identifying antecedents can help children recognize when a situation is prime for engaging in an undesirable behavior. This recognition can serve as a prompt or stimulus for the child to use the newly learned behavior that is more appropriate for the situation.

To some degree, replacement behavior training has its roots in basic applied behavior analysis. As such, it is successful largely based on the ability to identify contingencies in the environment that trigger and support the aggressive behavior. Identifying the setting events (i.e., variables that exert an influence on the interaction between antecedents and the child's response) and the antecedents to the behavior informs the function of the behavior (e.g., escaping a person or task versus access to a tangible or social reinforcer). Likewise, identifying the consequences (e.g., class laughter and attention for talking back to the teacher, lack of consequences for failure to do homework) that maintain the behavior is typically helpful in managing the aggression.

Teacher behavior and task demands are frequently found to be antecedents for certain types of maladaptive behaviors. However, eliminating task demands is not the preferred choice to manage aggression. Instead, finding ways to minimize the frustration of the task demand is the critical change needed (e.g., providing choices or quick access to help). Finally, matching the effort coefficient in the replacement behavior is paramount. For example, a student who aggresses by throwing a pencil to get immediate teacher attention or to avoid an aversive task may not find filling out a problem-solving worksheet to be a functionally equivalent behavioral replacement. Clearly, this task requires significantly more effort. Likewise, raising a hand and waiting 10 minutes for help is less efficient for the student than throwing the pencil and receiving immediate assistance.

EXAMPLES
Jackson is an elementary school student who frequently hits other students to gain attention from peers. His teacher uses replacement behavior training to teach him new verbal skills to use as replacements for the aggressive behavior. Use of these new verbal skills enables Jackson to receive attention from the teacher and classmates without hitting his classmates.

Katie is a high school student who verbally assaults teachers and peers when frustrated, resulting in an escape from the task or situation that is causing the frustration. During replacement behavior training she is taught an appropriate method of escaping the situation (e.g., asking to be excused, verbalizing her frustration) along with a replacement strategy for tolerating the frustration. Reinforcement would take the form of allowing the escape when appropriately sought.

GOAL
Reduce aggressive behavior by teaching and reinforcing (immediately with gradual fading) an alternate behavior that serves the same function as the aggressive behavior.

THE BASICS
1. Administer a functional behavioral assessment (FBA; see Chapters 4 and 10) to create an operational definition of the aggressive behavior and to identify the setting events, antecedents, and consequences contributing to or resulting from the aggressive behavior. Identify the function of the behavior (e.g., to escape or avoid, tangible reward, stimulation).

2. Identify and teach the child to engage in a socially acceptable replacement behavior that is as easy for the child as the problem behavior and that will result in the same outcome (e.g., to escape or avoid, tangible reward, stimulation).

3. Identify potential functionally equivalent reinforcers, prompt for and reinforce the replacement behavior, and ignore inappropriate behaviors.

4. Evaluate and revise as needed.

HOW TO IMPLEMENT REPLACEMENT BEHAVIOR TRAINING

 PREP

- Determine if the child will be an active participant in the intervention based upon the child's cognitive and developmental readiness and the specifics of the Intervention.
- Identify the target behavior and operationally define it.
- Identify who will be responsible for data collection for the FBA.
- Administer an FBA to identify the setting events, antecedents, and consequences contributing to or resulting from the aggressive behavior.
- Offer a hypothesis in the FBA about the function of the behavior (e.g., to escape or avoid, tangible reward, stimulation).
- Introduce the antecedent to test the hypothesis.
- Select a replacement behavior that serves the same function as the aggressive behavior.
- Identify potential reinforcers to increase the use of the replacement behavior.
- Identify who will teach and monitor replacement behavior use and reinforcement.

 IMPLEMENT

- Introduce the concept of replacement behavior training to the child.
- Teach the appropriate behavior that will be used to replace the problem behavior if the desired approach is to be more directive and use a direct-instruction model.
- If needed, remind the child to use the replacement behavior when the situation arises by using prompts or an agreed upon signal the child can use to communicate a need.
- Reinforce the use of the replacement behavior. Thank the child and honor the signal when used appropriately so that he or she learns that this behavior leads to his or her needs being met. If the child uses an inappropriate behavior, ignore the behavior and prompt him or her to use the signal, then move on quickly. This type of response ensures that the class is not drawn off task. If the teaching and training is in a small group, practice sessions may include an action plan to use when a child forgets.
- Fade the use of prompts and reinforcement gradually as the replacement behavior supplants the inappropriate behavior.

 EVALUATE

- Monitor the use of the replacement behavior.
- Monitor natural reinforcers or the use of periodic or unscheduled reinforcement.
- Consider tracking or having the child or another involved adult track the decrease in the inappropriate behavior and/or the increase in the replacement behavior. If charted or recorded, discuss in subsequent check-in meetings.
- Consider booster training sessions or additional reinforcement if the new appropriate behavior is not maintained.

EVIDENCE
A brief overview of research and annotated references supporting this intervention can be found on Q-global.

CONSIDERATIONS

FOR TEACHING

It is important to validate that the child is able to perform the new behavior and that he or she understands when it should be used. In addition, it is important to let all adults that work with the child know what the appropriate replacement behaviors are, thereby helping to generalize the new behaviors across settings (e.g., home, extracurricular activities, cafeteria, library, community). Using prompts can help to trigger use of the replacement behaviors; however, it is important to gradually fade out the prompts over time. Reinforcement of the new behaviors is important to their success. New behaviors should be reinforced according to a 1:1 ratio initially and then gradually faded.

It is important to consider the function of the maladaptive behavior, effort that will be required to learn and use a new behavior, and the capacity of the new behavior to provide the same benefit as the maladaptive behavior. The adult also must recognize that not all rewards are equally appealing: What seems like a good thing to one child may not be to another. By definition, reinforcement results in the maintenance or increase in a target behavior. Positive reinforcement involves the presentation of a pleasant stimulus and negative reinforcement involves the removal of an unpleasant stimulus, but both result in an increase in the target behavior. These are commonly misunderstood concepts. Positive and negative are misunderstood to be desirable and undesirable consequences (e.g., candy vs. yelling). This is inaccurate. When reinforcement occurs, the result is the maintenance or increase in a targeted behavior, regardless of the nature of the reinforcer. For example, if a teacher wants her students to remain quiet in class (target behavior) she could use reinforcement to increase that behavior. If either candy or attention in the form of yelling is provided, and the target behavior increases, this is positive reinforcement. In contrast, if a homework assignment is removed, and the target behavior (e.g., quiet students) increases, this is negative reinforcement.

Another important concept in reinforcement is "saturation." Reinforcers are generally strongest in a state of deprivation (e.g., a thirsty person is highly motivated for water, a hungry person for food, a lonely person for attention). Preferences and relative strength of reinforcers are child-specific and potentially time-specific. Peer attention is only effective when a child desires or needs attention.

FOR AGE AND DEVELOPMENTAL LEVEL

Inadequate functional language and communication abilities are often precursors to aggressive behaviors. Language abilities should be assessed and, when determined to be a contributing factor in the aggressive behavior, communication skills (verbal or pictorial) should be a primary focus. Teaching older children the concepts involved in replacement behavior training allows them to learn a valuable skill set that will generalize beyond the current problem. Replacement behavior training is a valuable tool that offers options to children whose current inappropriate behavior is meeting their needs with unfortunate consequences.

 # SOCIAL SKILLS TRAINING

DESCRIPTION

Social skills generally refer to skills that enable effective functioning when interacting with others. Social skills have been defined by Gresham (1986) as having dimensions of peer acceptance, behavioral skills, and social validity. Social skills training or similar intervention programs generally present a child with a series of lessons each targeting a specific social skill so that the child can apply newly learned skills when opportunities arise.

Oftentimes, aggressive behaviors in children are linked to the absence of particular social skills. This lack of social skills indicates a deficiency in the child's social competency. While social skills and social competency may seem synonymous, they are not. Social competency is a construct that includes social skills as well as other important factors, such as positive relationships with others, accurate and age-appropriate social cognition, absence of maladaptive behaviors, and effective social behaviors (Vaughn & Hogan, 1990). Social competency, therefore, is necessary for successful treatment and remediation of aggressive behaviors.

Social competency is made up of discrete skills that must be taught in isolation and then integrated seamlessly into the individual's life and actions. Typically, when a child lacks social competency, the behavioral deficiency is addressed through a program of training based on a series of related skills. For example, it is insufficient to teach a child to "be nice," "behave," or "play fair" because the skill sets that make up "nice" and "fair," such as taking turns and sharing, have to be taught individually and then incorporated into the child's general behavior. Children must have enough exemplars to be adaptable to a variety of appropriate situations. Therefore, particular attention must be paid to context. For example, the skills associated with handshaking as part of a greeting could generalize to formal situations such as job interviews or meeting adults in social settings. However, such skills are not as relevant to 4th graders greeting each other on a playground. Similarly, teaching a child how to request a turn to speak to an adult respectfully, without interrupting, is an appropriate and expected skill for settings such as a restaurant or classroom but would not transfer to a pickup basketball game in a park.

Social skills training is grounded in a behaviorist framework. It places a strong emphasis on behavior replacement training and differential reinforcement to distinguish inappropriate behavior from behaviors that exhibit strong social validity. These training programs often require a child to generate multiple strategies for engaging in appropriate social behavior. These strategies may include expressing empathy, becoming aware of the consequences of one's own and others' behavior, and identifying appropriate paths to reach desired goals.

Many social skills improvement programs have been developed (Alberg et al., 1994; Johnson, Bullis, Mann, Benz, & Hollenbeck, 1999; McGinnis, 2012; McGinnis, Sprafkin, Gershaw, & Klein, 2012; Rutherford, Chipman, DiGangi, & Anderson, 1992; Walker et al., 1983). However, the basic procedural steps can be implemented without the use of such formalized programs.

EXAMPLES

A 1st-grade student may grab objects from playmates rather than making requests or waiting his or her turn, a behavior that may be perceived as aggressive. Such behavior may be remediated through social skills training that focuses on developing skills associated with making requests and sharing.

A freshman in high school who frequently interrupts the conversations of others may experience social rejection and isolation that may result in aggressive or retaliatory responses toward those responsible for his dejected feelings. This student would benefit from learning specific conversation skills, such as joining a conversation, taking turns in conversations, and/or active listening.

In both scenarios, the skills learned in the lessons should be practiced and then applied or transferred to the next occurrence of an appropriate situation.

GOAL

Prevent and remediate components of aggression through instruction in the use of prosocial skills as an alternative.

THE BASICS

1. Determine any social skill deficits.
2. Demonstrate appropriate social skills via explanations and explicit modeling.
3. Apply learned social skills in contrived scenarios.
4. Provide feedback and reinforcement for appropriate responses.
5. Apply learned social skills in an actual situation.

HOW TO IMPLEMENT SOCIAL SKILLS TRAINING

 PREP

- Organize the schedule of meetings.

- Form small groups of children who have similar aggression problems.

- Establish performance goals.

- Set boundaries, consequences, and rules for participation.

- Determine common social skills or social competency deficits (e.g., turn-taking, assertiveness, patience, response to negative feedback) that may be responsible for triggering the children's aggressive actions and prioritize them for intervention. These determinations are made from assessments, recommendations from teachers and parents, and child self-disclosures or self-assessment.

 IMPLEMENT

- Introduce only one specific social skill for each session (e.g., "Today we will talk about listening effectively and seven steps that will help us do that.")

- Use visual representations of each step associated with the social skill being taught. Write the steps on note cards or paper. Ask the children to recite the steps. Model the correct behavior associated with each step.

- Establish performance goals, such as, "I want to spend more time talking to my mom, and less time yelling," or "I want to stop throwing my books when I'm feeling mad in class."

- Engage the children in a discussion (e.g., brainstorming) centered on recent events that required use of the new skill. For example, "When was a time you wished you could talk instead of yelling?"

- Introduce and model the new skill. For example, make eye contact, take a deep breath, and say, "I understand what you are saying," rather than yelling.

- Encourage the children to role-play the skill while others coach them. For example, set up a scenario where you role-play the mother and try to get the child to start yelling. The child uses the new social skill of "make eye contact, breathe deeply, and verbalize calmly." Practice just the one skill taught during each session.

- Facilitate the retention of learned behaviors at the next meeting by reviewing skills that were taught during previous intervention sessions. Ask the children about opportunities to use the skill, review progress, or make modifications when things did not go as planned. For example, the child says, "I looked at my mom, took deep breaths, and said, 'I understand what you are saying,' but she kept yelling and thought I was making fun of her, so I started yelling back!"

- Maintain skill acquisition by holding periodic refresher sessions.

- Encourage children to use journals to record or keep track of skills used and the subsequent outcome. Journals can be optional or assigned as homework to record daily personal experiences with the newly learned social skills. As available and if appropriate, encourage them to read journal entries aloud for the group depending on child and counselor preference.

- Distribute copies of the skill steps to teachers and parents and ask them to monitor and record use of the skill. Monitor these records if available.

- Schedule routine observations such as weekly classroom walk-throughs or monthly classroom observations to monitor social skills as time permits.

EVIDENCE

A brief overview of research and annotated references supporting this intervention can be found on Q-global.

CONSIDERATIONS

For Teaching

Instructors should allow time for modeling and guided practice when planning to implement social skills training. Children need to learn by doing, primarily through role-play and frequent practice situations. Teacher behavior may affect child outcomes (Frey et al., 2000), so social skills modeling throughout a school day will serve to strengthen children's skills. Supportive, nurturing practices are also critical for successful outcomes of social skills training, as are teachers who present opportunities for children to use social skills. Generalized application of social skills training to groups of children prevents individual children from being stigmatized and reduces violence and aggression across the population. Individual targeting and lengthening of treatment will improve results for children.

For Age and Developmental Level

Many children's social skills are limited by lack of experience or age-appropriate training. For children with autism spectrum disorder or other developmental disabilities, social skills are affected more profoundly. While reinforcers that trigger aggression often become evident during typical interventions, they may not apply to individualized treatments for aggression. A child with disabilities or social skills that differ significantly from those of his or her peers may not experience the benefits of treatment (e.g., increased friendships, greater social understanding). Therefore, although social skills training is necessary in its own right, it may not be the most effective intervention for aggression in every case.

 VERBAL MEDIATION

DESCRIPTION

Verbal mediation refers to the use of language to promote a positive influence on a person's cognitions and behavior. More specifically, verbal mediation refers to the use of private self-talk (i.e., not heard by others) for the purpose of self-regulation of behavior. While language traditionally is considered to be a tool used to communicate with others, it can also be used to communicate with oneself and as a way to self-regulate behavior (Berk, 1992; Skinner, 1953; Vygotsky 1930/1978; Vygotsky, 1934/1987).

Verbal mediation has been referred to as a core component in cognitive modeling (Bandura, 1986) and self-instruction training (Hinshaw & Erhardt, 1991; Kaplan & Carter, 1995; Meichenbaum, 1985) and has led to self-monitoring and self-regulation strategies. Short-term memory also utilizes verbal mediation during rehearsal of phonological information in the phonological loop of working memory (Baddeley & Hitch, 1974).

Teaching verbal mediation involves identifying the current self-talk that occurs prior to incidents of aggression and replacing maladaptive self-speech with a new script. Alternatively, if no self-talk occurs prior to incidents of aggression, then a new script is created to self-regulate aggression. Depending on the age and developmental level of the child, the script may be as simple as, "I will not hit on the playground," or as complex as several sentences describing the antecedent or setting of the event, the plan for action, and the desired outcome. For example, a teenager who regularly gets provoked during lunch by another child might create and internalize a script such as: "When I see Jose, he will try to bait me into fighting with him. When I see Jose, I will walk in the other direction and smile. I will win by smiling and having a good day."

EXAMPLES

A kindergartner might softly repeat the directions his mother gave him to refrain from biting his little brother, saying, "I will not bite Tommy, I will not bite Tommy."

An 8th grader might move his lips silently while repeating a phrase in his head, encouraging himself not to get frustrated or angry in the face of adversity.

A high school senior may silently repeat a mantra not to get angry when cut off in traffic by another driver.
In each case, self-talk is used to mediate the aggressive behavior.

GOAL

Help children achieve self-regulation by internalizing verbal directions, procedures, or rules that assist them in controlling aggressive behavior.

THE BASICS

1. Demonstrate cognitive modeling (i.e., teacher says, teacher does).

2. Implement overt external guidance (i.e., teacher says, child does).

3. Teach overt self-guidance (i.e., child says, child does).

4. Implement faded overt self-guidance (i.e., child whispers, child does).

5. Achieve covert self-instruction (i.e., child thinks, child does).

HOW TO IMPLEMENT VERBAL MEDIATION

 PREP

- Identify the child's targeted problem behavior through observation, assessment, referral, and parent/teacher or student report.

- Create self-talk scripts that specifically address identified target areas. For example, for a young child who is frequently touching and tripping other children, create and teach a script of self-talk about keeping "mustangs in the stables (hands in pockets) and hoofs clip-clopping on the trail (feet walking in line)." For a child who uses verbal aggression when anxious, create a self-soothing script, such as, "I'm cool, I'm cool, I'm cool like ice." The scripts can be about self-direction, self-instruction, or self-soothing.

 IMPLEMENT

- Introduce the concept of verbal mediation at a level that is age-appropriate. Emphasize that verbal mediation uses private self-talk to help manage behavior. Discuss the fact that private self-talk should not be heard by others.

- Model the scripts for the child while saying the steps (teacher says, teacher does). For example, a child becomes frustrated when he takes reading tests, and sometimes hits the desk with his fist. The teacher models the script: "When I become frustrated during tests, I will count to 10 in my head while slowly breathing in and out." The teacher quietly counts to 10 while slowly breathing in and out.

- Recite the script as the child role-plays (teacher says, child does). The teacher reads the script: "When I become frustrated during tests, I will count to 10 in my head while slowly breathing in and out." The student then quietly counts to 10 while slowly breathing in and out.

- Transfer the skill to the child by instructing him or her to follow the script verbally as he or she follows through with the actions (child says, child does). The child says: "When I become frustrated during tests, I will count to 10 in my head while slowly breathing in and out." The child then quietly counts to 10 while slowly breathing in and out.

- Begin fading the verbal prompts by having the child whisper the script (child whispers, child does). The child whispers the self-talk while slowly breathing in and out.

- Encourage the child to implement private self-talk where he or she simply "thinks" the script (child thinks, child does). The child will think the words in his or her head, while slowly breathing in and out.

 EVALUATE

- Ask the child to demonstrate independent use of the technique.

- Offer a hypothetical scenario and ask the child to practice verbal mediation. The child should say the script while slowly counting and breathing.

- Observe or interview the child to determine if generalization has occurred and consider planning an opportunity for the child to use this technique in a new scenario.

- Ask the child to keep a log or journal of when he or she used the self-talk script in different situations where aggressive behavior was likely to occur.

EVIDENCE

A brief overview of research and annotated references supporting this intervention can be found on Q-global.

CONSIDERATIONS

FOR TEACHING

Children will need opportunities to practice, and training and rehearsal would ideally be paired with a reinforcer, at least initially, until contingency reinforcers occur naturally. The skill sets associated with verbal mediation can be rehearsed with a variety of topics, not just aggression. The awareness and development of self-talk will improve a child's ability to create and use verbal scripting for aggression issues, especially those that are more difficult to address. Teacher modeling is very beneficial in this endeavor. Teachers can overtly engage in self-talk throughout the day to help children observe how it can be applied independently. Children can also engage in revising internal speech by having "sessions" where they engage in an activity, talking out loud to themselves about each action.

FOR AGE AND DEVELOPMENTAL LEVEL

When using verbal mediation as an intervention for aggression, it is important to consider the verbal and cognitive abilities of the child. If the child's language abilities are limited, this intervention will be less functionally useful. However, if language exists, children of all ages can benefit from this technique. The naturally occurring condition of self-talk makes it ideal as an intervention across the age spectrum because, although the complexity of the self-talk will differ across ages, the mediating factors of the self-talk should not.

Chapter 3

Interventions for Conduct Problems

Characteristics and Conditions of Conduct Problems

WHAT ARE CONDUCT PROBLEMS?

Conduct disorder, as defined by the *Diagnostic and Statistical Manual of Mental Disorders*, Fifth Edition, (*DSM–5*; American Psychiatric Association, 2013) is a childhood disorder in the category of disruptive, impulse control, and conduct disorders characterized by aggressive and destructive activities that interfere with successful life functioning. Children with conduct disorder usually exhibit a repetitive and persistent pattern of behaviors in which the basic rights of others or major age-appropriate societal norms or rules are violated.

The *DSM–5* assigns behaviors associated with conduct disorder to one of four categories: (1) aggression to people and animals, (2) destruction of property, (3) deceitfulness or theft, and (4) serious violations of rules. Aggression to people and animals includes overt antisocial behaviors such as fighting, assaulting or causing physical harm to others, bullying, using weapons, threatening or intimidating others, stealing while confronting a victim, sexual misconduct, and cruelty to people and/or animals. Destruction of property includes behaviors such as setting fires or using other means with the intent of destroying property. Deceitfulness or theft include behaviors such as lying to attain tangibles or intangibles; lying to avoid responsibility; stealing without victim confrontation; and breaking into another person's house, building, or car. Serious violations of rules include staying out late at night starting at a young age, truancy, and running away.

Dealing with children with conduct problems can be extremely challenging and frustrating for professionals and caregivers. There is enormous resistance to change, in part due to the intrinsically rewarding nature of these behaviors for the individuals (Frick, 2006; Tarolla, Wagner, Rabinowitz, & Tubman, 2002). These change-resistant and stable behaviors are symptoms of a chronic disability that often manifests problems into adulthood (Borduin & Schaeffer, 1998; Kazdin, Siegel, & Bass, 1992; Tarolla et al., 2002), and the behavioral trajectory of this population can lead to incarceration at a high cost to society (Hemphill, Toumbourou, Herrenkohl, McMorris, & Catalano, 2006; Mpofu & Crystal, 2001; Tarolla et al., 2002). Therefore, prevention for children at elevated levels of risk and treatment for those already identified as having conduct problems are critical in interrupting the progression of the disorder and thus preventing serious long-term consequences. Longitudinal research has established risk factors for children in the early stages of the behavioral trajectory of conduct problems, and strong evidence exists for a wide range of effective prevention and intervention programs (Brestan & Eyberg, 1998; Frick, 2006; Tarolla et al., 2002; Wilson, Gottfredson, & Najaka, 2001).

HOW COMMON ARE CONDUCT PROBLEMS?

The prevalence rates for Conduct Problems range from 2–10% with higher rates among males and rising rates from childhood to adolescence (APA, 2013).

The BASC–3 Conduct Problems scale includes a selection of items that measure aspects from each of the four categories: aggression to people or animals; destruction of property; deceitfulness or theft; and serious violations of rules. Items from the Teacher Rating Scales and Parent Rating Scales related to conduct problems include "Breaks the rules," "Sneaks around," and "Hurts others on purpose." While conduct problems or conduct disorders (sometimes referred to as delinquency) are related to aggression, researchers have recognized differences between the two conditions (van der Put et al., 2012) and they have studied them independently (de Haan, Prinzie, & Deković, 2010).

Theoretical Framework for Approaching Conduct Problems

Most theoretical approaches for remediating conduct problems involve behavioral, cognitive–behavioral, or social learning theories. For example, children with conduct problems often have deficits in social information processing; therefore, cognitive–behavioral theory is applicable (Frick, 2000; Lipsey & Wilson, 1998). It is also well established that children whose parents lack effective parenting skills are at a greater risk for developing conduct problems; therefore, some strategies originate in social learning theory (Patterson, Chamberlain, & Reid, 1982; Patterson, Reid, & Dishion, 1992; Woolgar & Scott, 2005). In addition, a large quantity of empirical evidence indicates support for the treatment of conduct problems using multimodal or multisystemic approaches that combine theoretical perspectives (Frick, 2000; Kazdin et al., 1992; Lochman & Wells, 2004; Woolgar & Scott, 2005). These approaches combine behavioral, cognitive–behavioral, and/or social learning (including family-based) perspectives, and do not exclude a biological orientation.

Effective intervention for conduct problems is as much about timing in the development of the disorder as it is about the use of specific theoretical approaches. The systematic development of conduct disorder is such that early intervention is the most critical component for children or adolescents identified with elevated levels of risk. Therefore, methods and strategies in this chapter have been specifically selected to address the development of conduct problems through early prevention and intervention.

Interventions

Interventions in this chapter include prevention as well as remediation efforts. When choosing interventions, practitioners are encouraged to pay close attention to the considerations for use of each intervention, to be cognizant of timing in the developmental trajectory of the disorder, and to recognize which interventions are most effective for prevention and which are most effective for remediation.

The intervention strategies for preventing and/or remediating conduct problems have been classified into nine categories. Note that the multimodal and multisystemic interventions are combinations of various intervention strategies (see Table 3.1).

For some of the interventions in this chapter, supplemental materials (e.g., handouts, posters, checklists, daily logs, and worksheets) that are helpful for preparing, implementing, and evaluating the interventions can be found on Q-global.

Table 3.1 Interventions for Conduct Problems

Intervention	Prevention[1]	Early Intervention[2]	Intensive Intervention[3]
Anger Management Skills Training	X	X	X
Independent Group-Oriented Contingency Management	X	X	X
Interdependent Group-Oriented Contingency Management	X	X	X
Moral Motivation Training	X	X	X
Multimodal Interventions			X
Multisystemic Therapy			X
Parent Training	X	X	X
Problem-Solving Training		X	X
Social Skills Training	X	X	X

[1] Prevention refers to skills that can be taught to all children or used universally; they promote better awareness and lessen the risk of problems.

[2] Early intervention includes techniques and strategies that address early warning signs or clinical signs of the risk of future problems. Early intervention may be specifically applied to one or more problems or generically applied as a skill set to prevent the development of a chronic problem. Early interventions can be delivered to groups or individuals.

[3] Intensive intervention focuses on individuals and individual problems, which are usually chronic, intensive, and require services due to the level of interference in daily functioning.

ANGER MANAGEMENT SKILLS TRAINING

DESCRIPTION

Children identified as having conduct problems frequently do not use appropriate anger management techniques. Anger ranges from mild irritation to rage (Pilania, Mehta, & Sagar, 2015). Although anger is a natural state, extreme or prolonged anger that interferes with life functioning is problematic. Anger management skills training focuses on behaviors and not feelings. The training takes a cognitive–behavioral, skill-building approach to reducing socially inappropriate responses to anger. Prosocial techniques for coping with feelings of anger are taught in time-specified sessions (e.g., 30 minutes or 1 hour) conducted weekly over a number of weeks.

EXAMPLES

Marcus, a 17-year-old, becomes physically and verbally aggressive whenever another boy speaks to his girlfriend. Small heterogenous groups work on school challenges every Wednesday after school. He is taught to identify the cause of his anger and his physiological reactions. He learns to walk away from the situation as an anger management technique.

William, a 6-year-old, scratches at teachers' faces and kicks when asked to leave the sandbox. The therapist teaches William in individual sessions about the schedule, taking turns, and how to recognize "feelings." A small trampoline is provided in a safe, cushioned area of the playground for William because he has stated he enjoys trampolines. William is taught to walk away from the sandbox toward the trampoline and play on it rather than scratching and kicking when he recognizes feelings of anger.

GOAL

Decrease the incidence of physical aggression, verbal aggression, and revenge-seeking behaviors by teaching children to recognize anger triggers and to use alternative coping techniques.

THE BASICS

1. Help the child recognize the events or triggers that cause anger, including thinking patterns or physiological reactions.

2. Select an anger management technique that the child is willing to try.

3. Evaluate the effectiveness and appropriate use of the technique.

4. Modify the technique as needed.

HOW TO IMPLEMENT ANGER MANAGEMENT SKILLS TRAINING

 PREP

- Locate or create materials to introduce the components, physiological reactions, and methods for managing anger.

- Find heterogeneous groups to avoid deviancy training (i.e., where children learn new ways to be inappropriate or use maladaptive behavior from other children with a larger repertoire), or identify times for individual work.

IMPLEMENT

■ Introduce the components of anger, such as anger triggers and physiological signs of anger arousal (cues).

■ Ask the child to name things that make him or her angry (triggers), and create a list on a whiteboard, overhead projector, or poster.

■ Discuss the physiological reactions (cues) to anger experienced by the child.

■ Model the triggers and ask the child to identify the cues to anger arousal.

■ Explain the reasons why physical and verbal aggression are ineffective methods of anger management. These reasons include social consequences (e.g., losing friendships), legal ramifications, and moral considerations.

■ Explain that prosocial anger management methods are those that do not result in verbal or physical aggression or negative consequences for actions.

■ Introduce prosocial anger management techniques such as relaxation (e.g., counting or deep breathing), assertiveness skills, anticipation (e.g., recognizing physical signs of anger), self-instruction (e.g., substituting appropriate self-talk for anger-arousing thoughts), self-evaluation, and problem solving.

■ Encourage the child to keep a journal of anger-provoking incidents experienced throughout the day (if he or she can write) and to record his or her prosocial responses.

■ Give the child visual cues, such as note cards with pictures or text, explaining the method to use, if necessary.

■ Allow the child to role-play the triggers and cues. Set up safe situations for the child to practice the anger management techniques and to learn how to transfer the new skill(s) to everyday situations.

 EVALUATE

■ Test the skill(s) in real-life situations by setting up an unexpected event for the child.

  ▲ Tell the child that another person (e.g., parent, teacher, or friend) will try to make him or her angry so that he or she can practice the newly learned skills. It is critical to provide a warning to the child that a practice event is forthcoming.

  ▲ After the event occurs, the child reports on these occurrences and explains what prosocial methods were used successfully and to what degree.

■ Instruct the child to keep a log of incidents throughout the day that make them feel angry.

■ Begin subsequent sessions by discussing these logs.

■ Reinforce participation and completion of the course in a social situation (e.g., an awards ceremony).

EVIDENCE

A brief overview of research and annotated references supporting this intervention can be found on Q-global.

CONSIDERATIONS

FOR TEACHING

Socially acceptable anger management techniques are rarely reinforced within the peer groups of children, and home and community environments sometimes are not conducive to their use. Therefore, multimodal or multisystemic therapy is often necessary to maintain the skills learned in anger management programs. Exercise caution when using anger management programs in groups of children with conduct problems. Such use can lead to deviancy training and can form new deviant peer groups. Anger management techniques often are better taught in heterogeneous groups or in individual sessions.

FOR CULTURAL AND LANGUAGE DIFFERENCES

Anger, aggression, and conduct problems may be modeled and reinforced at home as a part of gender roles that are influenced by cultural beliefs (e.g., a dominant and aggressive patriarch or matriarch). Unfortunately, behaviors that are used to manage other family members can generalize to the school setting (e.g., intimidating a teacher who referred a student for a behavioral problem, being unwilling to seek help or work with others who are trying to help). Intervention can be difficult in such situations, but is still advised and certainly warranted. Intervention should reinforce the idea that the school environment has a culture that maintains certain expectations of its students and its students' parents.

 # INDEPENDENT GROUP-ORIENTED CONTINGENCY MANAGEMENT

DESCRIPTION

Group-oriented contingency management interventions take one of several forms. One form is independent interventions. These might include, for example, a token economy where contingencies are in place for all but are assigned based on individual behavior (Bandura, 1969). The target behaviors or responses are the same for each individual in the group.

A token economy system is a behavioral technique that allows children to earn points or tokens that later can be exchanged for positive reinforcers. Token economy systems are based on operant learning theory (Skinner, 1931) and combine differential reinforcement with a response-cost technique, providing a concrete visual representation of teacher approval (Alberto & Troutman, 2003; Bushell, 1973). A child can earn tokens for demonstration of the desired behavior or set of behaviors and can also have tokens removed for inappropriate behavior. This removal is called "response cost." Response cost is considered punishment if it results in a subsequent reduction in the targeted problem behavior.

Token distribution and removal is done on a specific ratio, much like a banking system. A child earns tokens by engaging in certain behaviors, and tokens are spent by exchanging them for tangible or intangible reinforcers. The tokens take on the reinforcing quality of the item for which they can be exchanged, providing immediate or delayed self-reinforcement for the individual. Fees or fines occur when a child engages in inappropriate or undesirable behavior, resulting in removal of the token(s). The cost of these undesirable behaviors should be explained prior to engaging in the token economy.

EXAMPLE

In an elementary school classroom, expectations (or rules) are in place for all students and posted. The students have their names on a large magnetic poster with game-like pieces. Students engaging in certain behaviors earn or lose individual pieces. At the end of each day, the children count their pieces and exchange them for an activity. Students may choose to trade in the pieces for immediate access to different areas of the classroom, or they can save them for later by leaving them on their name.

GOAL

Increase appropriate behavior and reduce antisocial and disruptive behavior by immediately and systematically reinforcing appropriate behavior and punishing problem behavior, creating a direct link between behavior choices and consequences.

THE BASICS

1. Create a visual chart of behaviors that will earn tokens, with values assigned for each behavior.

2. Specify when reinforcers are earned and for what the tokens are exchanged.

3. Follow the schedule for assigning or distributing the tokens and reinforcers, and exchange tokens for reinforcers.

HOW TO IMPLEMENT INDEPENDENT GROUP-ORIENTED CONTINGENCY MANAGEMENT

 PREP

- Acquire or develop the physical tokens necessary (e.g., magnets on a board, a list of names and points on a whiteboard, paper currency, bingo chips, paper tickets, a point sheet).

- Identify behaviors of interest and replacement behaviors in concrete, observable terms.

- Create a visual aid or chart that represents the behaviors that result in earning reinforcers and those that result in loss.

- Identify the method for removing reinforcers, and list the procedure. Considerations might include whether students return items that were earned (and how they do so) or pay a fine for items that cannot be returned (e.g., food snacks).

- Establish the reinforcers that can be exchanged for tokens and the rate in tokens for each reinforcer. Display the exchange rates in a highly visible place.

 IMPLEMENT

- Review the prepared information and materials (physical tokens, methods for removing reinforcers, exchange system) with the participating children.

- Teach group members which behaviors earn points and which result in a loss of points.

- Provide a visual cue to the children for use in tracking points. A visual cue can be a tangible token or other visual aids (e.g., a daily point sheet, group points tallied on a whiteboard or a chart). Explain the system and point to the visual representation of the behavior and the amount of points to be earned or lost.

- Demonstrate procedures by modeling and role playing with the children. Have the children practice the targeted behavior followed by acceptable replacement behaviors.

- Award or remove points throughout the recording/scoring period.

- Allow the children to exchange the tokens or points for reinforcers at a predetermined time (e.g., once a day or twice a week).

 EVALUATE

- Keep track of specific behaviors and identify if they have improved with the use of this system.

- The reinforcer schedule may need to be frequent initially for children with conduct problems.

EVIDENCE

A brief overview of research and annotated references supporting this intervention can be found on Q-global.

CONSIDERATIONS

FOR TEACHING

Teachers should avoid using tokens as bribery, randomly offering tokens for jobs, or using threatening comments when utilizing a token economy system (Goldstein, 1995). The difference between bribery and appropriate use of reinforcement can be subtle and is often determined by the situation in which the reinforcer is offered. For example, consider a child who begins to whine and refuses to engage in work that is requested by the teacher. As the child begins to stamp his feet and becomes louder and louder, the teacher responds by telling the child to go back to his seat and sit down. The child responds to this latest request from the teacher by expressing his disdain for math even more loudly. In an effort to end the child's tantrum, the teacher responds by telling the child he can go to recess early if he stops. In this case, the token (i.e., recess) serves as a bribe rather than an appropriate reinforcement. Tokens should be clearly articulated in advance and used consistently to reinforce appropriate behavior, not as bribes to end inappropriate behavior while it is occurring. In the example, a more efficient response by the teacher might have been to calmly use a reminder about earning tokens at the beginning of the lesson to prevent the child from engaging in the tantrum. Then, if the child began to act up, the teacher could calmly redirect his attention while ignoring the initial behavioral response.

FOR AGE AND DEVELOPMENTAL LEVEL

A young child may engage in very inappropriate behavior when things are taken away, so consider carefully if the child's age or developmental level is appropriate for use of a token economy. Regardless of age, methods to earn back lost tokens should be clear to all children. The quality of reinforcers is another general consideration. Reinforcers must be sufficient to compete with naturally occurring reinforcement from problem behaviors, and access to other reinforcers should be limited as much as possible. Moreover, it is important that the reinforcement schedule be appropriately distributed so that enough tokens can be earned to outweigh the loss of tokens in order to avoid apathy. Satiation can occur with reinforcers, so modifications or routine changes can maintain interest. The reinforcers, as well as the program, should be frequently evaluated for effectiveness and modified as needed. Positive strategies are generally more effective and should be attempted before response-cost strategies.

FOR CULTURAL AND LANGUAGE DIFFERENCES

Although there has been recent interest in studies examining the role of culture in the success of individual- and group-level reinforcers, no definitive patterns of their use have emerged. In fact, most children successfully learn differences between school and home expectations and respond remarkably well to transitions. It is important to note that cultural and language factors may necessitate additional training (e.g., providing more examples and nonexamples) so that the token system is clearly understood. Families may also require additional information about earning or losing points to prevent miscommunication and inconsistent reinforcement schedules. In some families, the behavior of children may be influenced, in part, by cultural perspectives regarding family identity, pride, and respect, and these factors should be considered when presenting and explaining token systems.

 # INTERDEPENDENT GROUP-ORIENTED CONTINGENCY MANAGEMENT

DESCRIPTION

Another form of group-oriented contingency management interventions are interdependent approaches. As described in the previous section on independent interventions in this chapter, group-oriented contingency management can take several forms. Interdependent interventions may reinforce the cumulative behavior of a group as a whole and focus on group performance (Bandura, 1969). The target behaviors or responses are the same for each individual in the group and response contingencies (i.e., expected behaviors for reinforcement) remain in effect for each group member (Alberto & Troutman, 2003). A group collective goal contributes to improvement of the larger group's performance.

EXAMPLE

Several students in a 4th-grade classroom are ignoring directions, stealing from other students, and exhibiting aggressive behaviors. The teacher splits the class into two teams and institutes the management plan. The teams are given points for following directions and practicing defined prosocial behaviors, and points are deducted for engaging in inappropriate behaviors.

GOAL

Decrease classroom disruption and antisocial behavior and increase appropriate and on-task behavior by systematically reinforcing appropriate behavior at a group level.

THE BASICS

1. Create a visual chart of behaviors that will earn points and rule violations that will result in a loss of points.

2. Divide the children into teams and identify reinforcers.

3. Use a highly visible scoreboard to record points, and provide scheduled reinforcement.

HOW TO IMPLEMENT INTERDEPENDENT GROUP-ORIENTED CONTINGENCY MANAGEMENT

 PREP

- Determine the target behavior (based on assessment) that can best be addressed by means of a group intervention.

- Establish goals and objectives for the children and key stakeholders.

- Determine specific techniques to be used.

- Create a strategy for reinstating the contingency plan on an intermittent schedule to maintain behavioral progress.

- Divide the class or group into teams.

- Create the scoreboard.

- Identify the reinforcers. Reinforcers can include activity, social, edible, or tangible rewards.

- Identify the reinforcement schedule and post it in a highly visible place.

 IMPLEMENT

- Teach group members which behaviors earn points and which result in a loss of points.

- Check for understanding by asking the children to demonstrate inappropriate behaviors and prosocial behaviors.

- Visibly record points on the board. The game can be played in innings, quarters, or intervals throughout the school day.

- Follow the reinforcer schedule. Reinforcement should occur at least daily.

 EVALUATE

- Monitor reinforcement strength and level of participation, and reinforce the winning team daily.

- Modify reinforcers often to prevent boredom or satiation.

EVIDENCE

A brief overview of research and annotated references supporting this intervention can be found on Q-global.

CONSIDERATIONS

FOR TEACHING

Responsibility to meet a goal is shared by a group. Children with conduct problems may target the individual whose behavior results in a loss of points or failure to reach a goal if the teacher misapplies the system to individual behavior rather than "team" or group behavior. Contingencies should be applied to performance of the *group*. This requires teamwork, but may allow an individual to "hide" in the performance of others. If well-behaved children are not meeting goals due to the group, they are likely to perceive the experience as punishment. To counter this, rotate teams frequently and maintain social- and behavior-specific praise throughout the day.

Harris and Sherman (1973) found that interdependent group-oriented contingency management did not significantly impact academic progress. Consideration should be given to effective instructional techniques to be used in conjunction with the intervention. Johnson, Turner, and Konarski (1978) found that the positive effects of the intervention began to diminish after 2 months. Refresher sessions can be used intermittently after conclusion of the initial intervention to prevent loss of positive results.

FOR AGE AND DEVELOPMENTAL LEVEL

Younger children require steadier, more prolonged use of the intervention in order to generalize the skills to other contexts. Reinforcers and contingencies should be age-appropriate and based on the developmental level of the children. Reinforcer selection can be done in several different ways. Groups can vote on reinforcers from a reinforcer menu or spin a reinforcer wheel, or the teacher can use mystery motivators (Sheridan, 1995). Younger children are more likely to make selections from a list, whereas older children might respond better to creating a list as a group and then making individual decisions. Reinforcers are also unlikely to be equally strong across all members of a group, but randomization of reinforcers may be suitable.

FOR CULTURAL AND LANGUAGE DIFFERENCES

Peer pressure, peer competition, and peer recognition are factors to consider when using interdependent group-oriented contingency management (Embry & Straatemeier, 2001). While these factors can be motivating, they may not be as effective in cultures for which competition is less important or even discouraged. Rotating group membership is one way to negate some of this effect. By frequently changing membership in teams, the stigmatizing effect for less competitive individuals can be reduced or removed. An additional method for lessening this effect would be the distribution of points for appropriate team-oriented group behavior (e.g., cooperation, mutual respect).

 # MORAL MOTIVATION TRAINING

DESCRIPTION

Training in morality or "ethics" is a widely accepted goal of education (Gordijn, 2015). Several models exist for adults, but there are fewer models for children and youth. Moral motivation training is a group-oriented cognitive intervention designed to accelerate moral reasoning development (Arbuthnot & Gordon, 1986). Moral motivation training can decrease antisocial behavior by increasing the level of moral functioning of children with inadequate moral reasoning skills through role-play and group discussions of a variety of moral dilemmas. The ultimate intent of the role-play and group discussions is to reach a consensus among the members of the group, reflecting moral maturity (Palmer, 2005).

Moral motivation training is expected to help children progress to more advanced levels of moral development as defined by Kohlberg (1969) and originally described in the work of Piaget (1932). Kohlberg delineated three levels of moral development: (1) preconventional, (2) conventional, and (3) postconventional. At the preconventional level, an individual's moral judgment is concrete and self-centered. At the conventional level, moral judgments are based on relationships with others, and at the postconventional level, moral judgments are based on societal needs.

Moral motivation training uses the cognitive skills of listening and discussing to develop internalized rules for and conceptual understanding of ethics or to create an awareness of social justice, right and wrong, and relative right and wrong. Procedurally, this can be accomplished in small- to medium-size groups as long as there is room for discussion and participation by all members. One-on-one discussions may also be used but may generate less discussion. Discussion in a child/adult dyad may be less effective because the child may feel compelled to present the ideas that he or she believes the adult wants to hear.

EXAMPLE

With a group of children, the trainer reads a scenario in which a parent is ill and the family can't afford medicine. The children are asked to determine if it would be appropriate for a child to steal the needed medicine for the parent. Adding information to the scenario (e.g., the parent will die without the medicine, the owner of the pharmacy is on the verge of bankruptcy) increases the difficulty of the decision and creates opportunities for debate amongst the children. The focus of the exercise is less on resolving the dilemma and more on the reasoning processes used to achieve an answer.

GOAL

Improve poor conduct through both education in morals and development of reasoning and empathy.

THE BASICS

1. Determine the discussion group members and the moral developmental stage of each member.

2. Introduce active listening skills to the members.

3. Present and discuss with the group moral dilemmas that are often created by selfish behavior.

4. Identify possible solutions to the dilemmas.

5. Present probing questions to advance the moral developmental stage of the group members.

HOW TO IMPLEMENT MORAL MOTIVATION TRAINING

PREP

- Assess the children's current levels of moral reasoning by asking brief, informal questions that present common moral dilemmas.

IMPLEMENT

- Read a moral decision-making scenario to the group, and request a decision for the presented problem.

- Challenge the group's decision by encouraging group members at higher moral reasoning levels to debate the decision.

- Add more details to the scenario that make the decision more difficult.

- Continue to ask group members functioning at higher moral levels to challenge the moral reasoning of those at lower levels. Also have children challenge each other by articulating decisions considered further up in the hierarchy of moral levels.

EVALUATE

- Track improvements in conduct problems directly, and alter the moral scenarios to make them more relevant, as needed.

  ▲ Formal assessment of responses to moral reasoning scenarios (e.g., selecting the correct answer from multiple choices, developing in the hierarchy of moral levels) can help you to track a child's moral decision-making skills, but this is supplemental to the improvement of conduct problems.

EVIDENCE

A brief overview of research and annotated references supporting this intervention can be found on Q-global.

CONSIDERATIONS

FOR TEACHING

If conveyed in a classroom setting, moral motivation training may best be accomplished in civics, social studies, or liberal studies classes. Groups should ideally include only one or two individuals identified as having conduct problems or being at risk for developing conduct problems. In addition, group membership should include youths assessed at different levels of moral reasoning in order to challenge individuals to think and rethink scenarios.

FOR AGE AND DEVELOPMENTAL LEVEL

Young and very young children are unlikely candidates for moral motivation training due to the cognitive and language demands of the intervention. Preteens and teens, however, are ideal candidates for the discussion because their age groups are more experienced with moral dilemmas and more likely to be familiar with social rules and norms.

FOR CULTURAL AND LANGUAGE DIFFERENCES

The studies that provide the evidence for using this intervention method are somewhat dated and Eurocentric in nature. This does not invalidate the findings; however it does suggest that the user should consider how culture might influence the developmental stages of ethical or moral reasoning. In some cultures, definitions of the self or of relationships may or may not hold as much influence for determining behavioral and cultural norms. Expectations or belief in a greater good may also vary across cultures, with some adopting higher principles earlier.

 # MULTIMODAL INTERVENTIONS

DESCRIPTION

Multimodal interventions consist of a combination of two or more affective, social, behavioral, and cognitive components (Webster-Stratton & Hammond, 1997). Multimodal interventions (i.e., MMIs) are sometimes described as multisystemic therapy (i.e., MST). Although they are not identical, their similarities are worth noting. MST is typically implemented by highly trained professionals and is often used by community mental health and child protective agencies. MMIs involve multiple interventions more broadly. Implementing MST may be more difficult in some educational environments (Borduin et al., 1995; Henggeler, Melton, & Smith, 1992; Tarolla et al., 2002). MST is discussed in a subsequent section of this chapter.

In general, most MMIs for conduct problems combine child treatment with parent training to improve efficacy. However, efficacy also exists when combining different intervention approaches with the child only. For instance, Goldstein (1988) lists a great deal of empirical research pointing to the combined use of social skills training, problem-solving training, and moral motivation training.

EXAMPLE

Johnny, a 15-year-old with conduct problems, is failing all of his classes, is absent from school a majority of the time, and has been arrested for shoplifting. Johnny is caught stealing from a classmate and becomes aggressive with the teacher when confronted. When Johnny's mother arrives at school, the teacher notices that the mother uses harsh language and threatens to take away all of his privileges for a year. When Johnny raises his voice, his mother begins to withdraw the threats of punishment to avoid embarrassment in front of the teacher. Johnny is exhibiting behavior that suggests he has deficits in problem solving and social skills; therefore, both problem-solving and social skills training should be prescribed. Additionally, parent training should be provided to assist Johnny's mother in using more effective parenting skills.

GOAL

Decrease antisocial and delinquent behavior by implementing two or more types of intervention approaches to address the complex and highly reinforcing nature of the conduct problems.

THE BASICS

1. Provide multiple treatments with appropriate personnel simultaneously or in sequence.

2. Determine the responsible parties for implementing and monitoring treatments and communication methods.

HOW TO IMPLEMENT MULTIMODAL INTERVENTIONS

 PREP

- Identify the key stakeholders who can contribute to assessment of the conduct problems and can provide reliable information about treatments and progress.

- Select the exact interventions within the multimodal framework, based on assessment results that indicate the causal factors associated with the conduct problems.

- Determine the length of treatment based on the severity of the causal factors. Treatment may be provided for longer periods of time than with single interventions.

- Identify the specific members of the team who will provide services (e.g., psychologist, social worker, case worker) based on the prescribed intervention.

 IMPLEMENT

- Implement the interventions simultaneously, as described in the PREP, IMPLEMENT, and EVALUATE sections for each intervention.

- Seek to generalize treatment effects to natural environments.

 EVALUATE

- Track and monitor the conduct related problem behaviors throughout the program.
  - ▲ Note any improvements and communicate them to others on the team.
  - ▲ Check interventions for fidelity if there is a noted lack of responsiveness to make sure all aspects of the system are adhering to the plan.

EVIDENCE

A brief overview of research and annotated references supporting this intervention can be found on Q-global.

CONSIDERATIONS

FOR TEACHING

Multimodal interventions involve coordination across multiple professionals, in and out of the school environment. This coordination may or may not involve the classroom teacher. Collaborative relationships, a team approach, and shared goals are critical components for successful implementation, progress monitoring, and information sharing across treatment providers.

FOR FAMILIES

MMIs are prescribed for children with serious or early-onset conduct problems for whom family factors are contributors to the problem. Because of this, professionals must ensure that families understand the commitment required, and expectations between the therapist and the family must be stated explicitly. However, family participation is often difficult to achieve, so opportunities for encouragement should be maximized when possible.

FOR AGE AND DEVELOPMENTAL LEVEL

Developmental changes in children co-occur with sequential treatments; hence, trainings about childhood stages may need to be revisited if the family of a 5-year-old continues to receive treatment for several years. Techniques that were appropriate at age 5 may need modification as the child gets older.

FOR CULTURAL AND LANGUAGE DIFFERENCES

Parent buy-in and consent for a multimodal intervention might be confounded by unknown or less-than-understood differences about cultural perceptions of individual treatments and combinations of treatments.

 # MULTISYSTEMIC THERAPY

DESCRIPTION

Multisystemic therapy (MST) is a short-term, home-based, family-focused intervention used with children who have severe conduct problems (Henggeler, Schoenwald, Borduin, Rowland, & Cunningham, 1998). Implementing MST may be more difficult in some educational environments (Borduin et al., 1995); nevertheless, MST is discussed in this chapter due to its demonstrated effectiveness in remediating severe conduct problems in children (Frick, 2000; Henggeler, Cunningham, Pickrel, Schoenwald, & Brondino, 1996; Tarolla et al., 2002). MST is characterized as an action-oriented, intensive, in-home treatment provided by qualified mental health providers that addresses behavior across all areas of functioning, generally lasting for 3–4 months (Henggeler et al. 2006; Thomas, 2006). Parent training and coping skills training are used with the child, family, school, and peer group to simultaneously provide a combination of all effective treatments in multiple environments based on the family systems approach.

EXAMPLE

Albert, an 18-year-old, is currently taking medication for attention-deficit/hyperactivity disorder (ADHD). He has been arrested multiple times for felony activities, is at risk for out-of-home placement, and has earned only enough credits in high school to be considered a first-semester sophomore. He is a member of a gang and has been suspended from school 10 out of the last 20 days. He lives with his mother, who is unemployed and is diagnosed with bipolar disorder and is an alcoholic; his 16-year-old sister who has been diagnosed with anxiety and depression; and his sister's 2-year-old son. To address these factors, the MST team devises a treatment plan to address all issues within Albert's home, school, and social environments and includes team members from the school, community, mental health agency, and juvenile justice system.

GOAL

Reduce delinquent, criminal, antisocial, and aggressive behavior; and increase family cohesion while empowering families to solve future problems.

THE BASICS

1. Select highly trained professionals with small caseloads.

2. Coordinate services with multiple community and school agencies.

3. Implement problem-solving training.

4. Complete a strengths based assessment to determine the behavioral problems and reinforcers within all environments.

5. Engage in individual and comprehensive case conceptualization.

6. Create a treatment plan, integrating action-oriented interventions, family strengths and responsibilities, and services into all environments.

7. Establish accountability of all treatment teams.

8. Implement behavioral and cognitive–behavioral interventions.

9. Engage in case management.

HOW TO IMPLEMENT MULTISYSTEMIC THERAPY

 PREP

- Create MST teams with a supervisor who oversees the MST therapist and observes therapy in the child's home.

- Provide extensive training for MST therapists by a multisystemic therapy consultant before beginning the intervention and provide continuing education (e.g., once a month).

- Provide adolescents with the ability to contact their MST therapists around the clock, and prepare the therapists to provide services by making home visits.

 IMPLEMENT

- Write and implement a highly individualized treatment plan that addresses all domains of child functioning. Such plans may include:

  ▲ Teaching cognitive–behavioral skills (e.g., problem-solving or anger management) to the child.

  ▲ Teaching effective discipline skills (e.g., differential reinforcement, response-cost techniques, contracting skills) to the parents.

  ▲ Teaching observational skills (e.g., association with deviant peers and school truancy issues) for parents to use in monitoring peer group relations.

  ▲ Assisting families in parent–school relationships by participating in parent–teacher meetings and special-education meetings, assisting with homework completion, and handling school disciplinary referrals.

  ▲ Teaching family management strategies (e.g., scheduling, family member responsibilities such as chore lists).

- Hold weekly MST team meetings for peer and supervisory consultation.

- Consult and meet regularly with individuals from other agencies who are providing services to the child (e.g., teachers, school administrators, probation officers, child protective services case managers, and mental health case workers).

 EVALUATE

- Evaluate outcomes continuously and modify the treatment plan as needed, with assistance from peer and supervisory consultants.

- Ensure treatment generalization by assigning homework to be completed by the entire family based on the interventions being used, and provide feedback on completion and success at every session.

- Provide a referral for the less intensive treatment following the completion of MST.

EVIDENCE

A brief overview of research and annotated references supporting this intervention can be found on Q-global.

CONSIDERATIONS

FOR TEACHING

MST is unlikely to occur in the classroom, but it may involve a teacher for data collection or interviews to determine needs. Academic deficits should not be overlooked, however, because severe conduct disorders often interfere with school attendance and participation.

FOR FAMILIES

MST is appropriate for severe conduct disorders. It requires a great deal of in-home intervention, with sessions provided on a daily to weekly basis (Thomas, 2006). There may be a number of obstacles to overcome when implementing MST. For example, defensive family patterns can significantly interfere with problem-solving and communication skills training (Margolin, Burman, & John, 1989). To address this problem, the therapist must understand the function of the behavior and how it is maintained by the family system. It is important that the therapist not make value judgments about the behavior as moral or immoral. In addition, for MST to be optimized, alliances must be established between the therapist and the child, as well as between the therapist and the mother (Robbins et al., 2006).

 PARENT TRAINING

DESCRIPTION

Parent training is a parent-focused, psychoeducational (or social learning) intervention that facilitates appropriate interactions between children and parents, leading to an increase in positive interactions and a decrease in coercive interactions (Dean, Myors, & Evans, 2003; Dishion & Andrews, 1995). Parent training teaches specific parenting skills and effective child management techniques by focusing on the thought processes and behaviors of the parent. This type of instruction assists parents in avoiding the use of coercive disciplinary procedures to obtain behavioral compliance. Such disciplinary procedures often result in children mimicking coercive communication patterns and becoming resistant to learning functional social skills (Martinez & Forgatch, 2001). Bor and Sanders (2004) identified parental coercive behaviors as hitting, scolding, and shouting. Children's coercive behavior frequently reflects actions modeled by a parent and is often exhibited as hitting, yelling, and throwing objects while refusing to comply with a request.

The combination of parental coercive behavior and child coercive behavior results in a negative cycle that begins with a directive given by the parent. In one scenario, the child's negative behavior is negatively reinforced (e.g., after the child gives a coercive response such as whining, the parent does not persist with the directive and the child does not comply). In a second scenario, the parent's negative behavior is negatively reinforced (e.g., the child's coercive behavior stops when the parent uses continual and escalating coercive behaviors, such as shouting).

EXAMPLE

Katy, a 5-year-old who exhibits conduct problems, is often deceitful and violates the rights of others by bullying or destroying property. When Katy wants the toy another child is playing with, she aggressively demands that the child give her the toy. If this doesn't get the result she wants, she screams and becomes more violent. If an adult intervenes, Katy immediately acts innocent, blaming the other child for the confrontation. In parent training, Katy's parents are taught to recognize this coercive cycle and to reinforce Katy when she verbally asks for what she wants and/or states her feelings verbally. Her parents are also taught to discipline Katy for her inappropriate behaviors with natural consequences, such as not being allowed to play with a child whom she has bullied for a specific period of time or taking away the object Katy was trying to acquire.

GOAL

Decrease antisocial behavior and reduce the likelihood of conduct problems by increasing the use of effective parenting skills and positive disciplinary techniques.

THE BASICS

1. Teach or coach parents to understand coercive parent–child interactions and their cycle.

2. Teach appropriate skill sets through modeling, including:

    a. effective reinforcement strategies and different types of reinforcers (e.g., verbal praise, social reinforcers, tangible reinforcers, and activity reinforcers);

    b. observation skills;

    c. play skills;

    d. response-cost techniques;

    e. timeout procedures;

    f. punishment and extinction;

    g. relationship enhancement skills (e.g., partner support, communication, and problem solving);

    h. token economy and reward charts;

    i. contingency contracts;

    j. mood management;

    k. self-determination;

    l. relaxation techniques;

    m. stress reduction techniques;

    n. anger management techniques; and

    o. self-monitoring and self-reward.

HOW TO IMPLEMENT PARENT TRAINING

PREP

- Determine if group or individual parent training will work for the trainer and the setting.

- Conduct an intake assessment with the family. Include an evaluation of the family climate to determine the needs of the family and any barriers to success, a broad overview of the goals of the intervention, the relevance of the information to be presented, and the responsibilities of the parents in the process.

- Identify skill deficits and formulate the goals and objectives that can be achieved by implementing family and parent management techniques.

- Determine the logistics of the intervention's implementation, including format, location, and the time of the intervention.

- Find a mutually satisfactory time for meeting, and determine the appropriate number of training sessions that might be needed. Consider creating a partnership contract to agree on the number of times to meet and the techniques to learn.

IMPLEMENT

- Teach a specific parenting technique, using descriptions and examples to demonstrate relevance to the individual.

- Verbally describe the technique.

- Discuss parental concerns about using the technique, and provide evidence of its effectiveness so that families know what to expect.

- Model the technique. Ask the parents for an example of a time when the technique could have been effective, and role-play the technique using the given example. If conducting training in after-school or parent groups, role-play examples with several parents so everyone who attends is involved and contributes.

- Bring the child into the session and briefly explain the technique to him or her for individual family sessions in the home. Have the parents role-play the technique with the child. Provide feedback after the performance, highlighting positive statements regarding the parents' implementation.

- Encourage independent implementation by requesting the use of the technique a specific number of times by the next session.

- Request that the parents document the effects, including any problems encountered, and note any questions they have.

- Begin each session by reviewing the effective parenting technique discussed in the previous session, reviewing the homework assignment, and answering specific parental questions.

 EVALUATE

- Monitor both parent training and the parent's application of the training to determine the effects of the training topics.

- Continue parent training at the rate and duration needed to sustain effectiveness.

EVIDENCE
A brief overview of research and annotated references supporting this intervention can be found on Q-global.

CONSIDERATIONS

FOR FAMILIES
Behavioral parent training is effective as a preventative measure and as an intervention (Taylor, Eddy, & Biglan, 1999). Certain factors should be considered when implementing them for either purpose. It may be best to limit training groups to no more than 16 participants or eight families. Parents benefit most by spending approximately 45 hours in training (Patterson & Narrett, 1990). It is critical to establish maintenance procedures after the intervention has ended because behavioral difficulties often resurface. There may be certain barriers to achieving success with behavioral parent training, including family stressors, lack of parent compliance with therapeutic expectations, the need for treatment flexibility due to heterogeneous family characteristics, and therapist feelings of hopelessness and ineffectiveness.

FOR AGE AND DEVELOPMENTAL LEVEL
Behavioral parent training is most effective for children ages 5–10 (Patterson & Narrett, 1990). Parent training is certainly appropriate for children at the pre-K level, but conduct problems are unlikely to appear at very early ages. Additionally, there is less learned behavior to address and parent–child relationship history to consider for younger children.

FOR CULTURAL AND LANGUAGE DIFFERENCES
Some research suggests therapists may be insensitive to cultural differences in parenting attitudes and parental expectations of child behavior and the intervention process (Forehand & Kotchick, 2002). Parents might bring preconceived notions about therapy that are not cognitive–behavioral in nature. Moreover, many parents have strong beliefs about child-rearing practices, and overcoming resistance for successful implementation may prove difficult (Kazdin, 2005). Because of these and other barriers, additional techniques to encourage parent participation are often necessary. Parents also may need specific assistance with implementing interventions in the home. At times parental issues may emerge that require alternate treatment methods or referrals to different agencies. While some of these issues are not specific to culture or language, they are certainly influenced by differences.

PROBLEM-SOLVING TRAINING

DESCRIPTION

Problem solving is the application of a set of skills to address situations that may be resolved in different ways. Problem-solving training teaches children a sequential and deliberate process for handling potentially negative situations that arise in social interactions (Polsgrove & Smith, 2004). Problem solving is taught through modeling, direct instruction, and guided practice. Problem solving approaches rely on the development of skills that can be internalized and transferred to a variety of problems and settings.

Evaluation of a child's current problem-solving skill level prior to developing a problem-solving strategy facilitates development of an effective intervention. Children differ widely in their ability to understand and implement problem-solving strategies. For example, a child may be able to recognize when a problem exists but have trouble defining it. In such cases, the initial problem-solving approach should focus on defining the problem and setting goals.

The best strategy for assessing the child's current level of problem-solving functioning is to provide a scenario and ask the child to retell the problem in the scenario as he or she sees it. This skill assessment method can help to identify possible issues with problem-solving skills. For instance, inaccurately identifying the problem or articulating nonsensical or unrelated reasons for the actual problem behavior may indicate weaknesses in problem identification. Other answers might properly identify the problem but demonstrate an inability to generate alternative responses. Reviewing the steps of problem assessment in this manner with one or more examples should provide a thorough screening of a child's current level of functioning.

Teaching problem-solving skills to children with conduct problems may be best achieved using real or imaginary examples from school, provided they are relevant. Skits or role-play involving a teacher with one or more children can be used for demonstration, although written examples or videos may also be appropriate. Such examples should provide background information about the situation, model the behaviors to be learned, and guide children through a problem scenario they are asked to solve. Upon completion of the examples, children can be asked to answer questions about the scenarios or to review the main points of each example. Children can provide answers in a variety of ways, including on a chalk or whiteboard, a worksheet, large index cards, or a flip chart. When children provide answers, it is important they are recognized for their contributions. Initially all efforts should be encouraged (correct answers can be emphasized later). This support for participation will provide clarity about where children are in their problem-solving skills.

The best example scenarios are ones that the child has seen or experienced and ones that can be carried through each step of problem solving. Although the child may not initially be able to work through all of the steps, he or she will become more proficient with each step as more examples are given. After learning the problem-solving elements through pre-generated examples, the approach can be reinforced by asking the child to generate his or her own problem scenarios.

EXAMPLE

As part of a language arts lesson in a public high school, Ms. Miller asks Owen to decorate and write his own thank you cards to his classmates to develop social skills. Owen begins to whine and eventually draws inappropriate images and writes profanity in the card, showing it to friends and eliciting laughter. Ms. Miller refers Owen to the office and has him wait while she meets with the counselor to inform her about the classroom behavior. In his subsequent meeting with the counselor, Owen explains that he can't draw and doesn't know what goes in a thank you card or what to say. He knows that inappropriate cartoon drawings are funny, whereas poor quality artwork may receive condemnation from peers. The counselor and Owen review options for self-advocacy to get assignments modified. Owen suggests he leave the classroom and the counselor asks about consequences of that choice. They discuss the consequences and then Owen suggests that he could request another assignment (knowing that is a school-expected answer). They engage in continued discussion about the consequences of that option. They discuss the physical signs of discomfort from the assignment that created a sense of urgency to escape. Owen is eventually guided to minimum compliance. He recognizes he could have drawn symbols or shapes and simply written "thank you" inside the card and avoided the classroom disruption. Later, he could tell the teacher that he knows his assignment wasn't the best but that he didn't know how to draw or what to write. Owen learned and practiced the steps of problem recognition, generating alternatives, and making selections. The counselor may follow up with Owen in the future and suggest the use of this strategy with other problems.

GOAL
Engage the child in thinking about alternatives based on consequences and help add a skill set to the child's repertoire that can be used to prevent or reduce a variety of problems, including profanity, underage drinking, need for attention, and the desire to fight.

THE BASICS

1. Help the child recognize that a problem exists.

2. Identify the problem and its consequences with the child.

3. Generate possible solutions with the child.

4. Evaluate the consequences of various solutions with the child.

5. Help the child select and implement the best solution.

HOW TO IMPLEMENT PROBLEM-SOLVING TRAINING

 PREP

- Determine the method of problem solving training to be used (i.e., response to problem solving behavior, a priori as a prevention strategy, group lesson).

- Prepare one or two examples of problems that lead to conduct problems as examples for opening discussions for preventative interventions or group lessons. The examples of problems should address each of the steps to initiate discussion.

 IMPLEMENT

- Use an example to identify and discuss a behavioral incident. The example may include a direct observation, reading a written scenario that describes an incident, or viewing a video demonstration. Ask questions that lead the child to identify cues as if making predictions in a story, such as overt feelings, facial representations, and potential feelings. If using a video, pausing and rewinding with cues like, "Did you see…?" can be helpful. As a replacement for verbal cuing, provide questions ahead of time for the child to respond to during a role-play or video.

- Generate alternative solutions to the social problem presented in the example, listing them on a whiteboard, overhead projector, or poster.

- Brainstorm the likely positive and negative consequences of each solution and verbally or visually represent them. To allow anonymity in group settings, children can write these on paper and the responses can be collected and shared on the classroom board by the group facilitator. If anonymity is unimportant, then the facilitator can ask children to provide descriptions in their own words and can use simple indicators (e.g., red checkmark, green star) using markers on a whiteboard to reflect the positive and negative consequences.

- Determine the best solution through discussion and feedback.

- Have children struggling with individual problems identify their own targeted behavior or provide the suggestion saying, "I notice you sometimes hit other children," or "You shared with me earlier that you need to work on not yelling at your friends or teachers." For children who have difficulty providing a response, discuss ways the child in the example can respond appropriately and get what he or she needs. Ask the children if they believe the plan is reasonable, being sure to consider the needs of each person in the situation.

- Practice the plan and ask the child to generate ideas to do so. These could include role playing the situation in the group or simply talking about ways a child could practice.

- Implement the plan. When discussing a real situation, ask the child to identify situations prior to the next meeting to practice the new skill.

- Create an evaluation plan and determine appropriate reinforcers. Choose reinforcers that are desirable to the child, and use a 1:1 ratio (e.g., reinforce each instance of the target behavior) for any new behavior.

- Inform the child that he or she will be asked to report back at the next meeting if the plan is used in a real situation.

- Teach the child the steps to problem solving by using the acronym ICE (i.e., Identify the problem, Create alternatives, Evaluate options) to ensure retention of the methodology and increase the child's potential to use the methodology to generalize to other problems.

 EVALUATE

- Assign homework that asks the child to practice the behaviors in real situations and to record key aspects in a notebook (e.g., type of incident, solutions tried, outcome).

- Review the notebook with the child at the next session and evaluate the implementation.

- Continue to monitor conduct problems.

EVIDENCE
A brief overview of research and annotated references supporting this intervention can be found on Q-global.

CONSIDERATIONS

FOR TEACHING
Problem-solving training can be incorporated readily into a variety of academic lessons. At the most basic level, the ability to recognize choices or options for reaching a solution is parallel to seeing a variety of viewpoints or multiple solutions to a problem. The more frequently problem solving is practiced across different scenarios, the more likely it will generalize and transfer to other settings. Ideally, both generalization and transfer are programmed into the scheduling and curriculum for frequent opportunities to improve skill fluency.

FOR CULTURAL AND LANGUAGE DIFFERENCES
Problem solving can be different across cultures because of how problems are identified. Some cultures do not assign ownership for problems. Events are seen as random occurrences and not as the results of human actions. For example, a description used to indicate a broken glass might be "the glass broke" rather than "he broke the glass." Another example would be the relationship of future events to the spiritual or divine. Some culturally-related religious beliefs may reflect a perceived lack of control or self-determination that deems the need for certain safety precautions, medicines, or other preventative measures unnecessary because problems that occur are viewed as manifestations of supernatural or divine control.

SOCIAL SKILLS TRAINING

DESCRIPTION

Students with childhood-onset conduct problems exhibit a lack of competency in specific social skills. This lack of competency directly relates to antisocial behaviors and results in an increased risk of continuing on the conduct problems trajectory. This situation can be remediated with direct social skills instruction. Social skills are taught through a process that involves visually representing and modeling the skill, doing role-play and practicing the skill, and then transferring and maintaining the skill in the natural social environment of the child.

Social skills training is a cognitive–behavioral approach that involves teaching children the necessary prosocial skills to facilitate successful functioning in their typical environments. Social skills training is necessary for children with deficits in social competency, which are commonly found among those with conduct problems. Social skills and social competency are not synonymous. Social competency is made up of discrete skills that must be taught in isolation and then integrated seamlessly into the individual's life and actions. Typically, when a child lacks social competency the behavioral deficiency is addressed through a program of training based on a series of related skills. For example, it is insufficient to teach a child to "be nice," "behave," or "play fair" because the skill sets that make up "nice" and "fair," such as taking turns and sharing, have to be taught individually and then incorporated into the child's general behavior. Children must have enough exemplars to be adaptable to a variety of appropriate situations. Therefore, particular attention must be paid to context. For example, the skills associated with handshaking as part of a greeting could generalize to formal situations such as job interviews or meeting adults in social settings. However, such skills are not as relevant to 4th graders greeting each other on a playground. Similarly, teaching a child how to request a turn to speak to an adult respectfully, without interrupting, is an appropriate and expected skill for settings such as a restaurant or classroom but would not transfer to a pickup basketball game in a park.

Social skills training is grounded in a behaviorist framework, placing a strong emphasis on behavior replacement training and differential reinforcement to distinguish inappropriate behavior from behaviors that exhibit strong social validity. These training programs often require a child to generate multiple strategies for engaging in appropriate social behavior. These strategies may include expressing empathy, becoming aware of the consequences of one's own and others' behavior, and identifying appropriate paths to reach desired goals.

Many social skills improvement programs have been developed (Alberg et al., 1994; Johnson et al., 1999; McGinnis, 2012; McGinnis et al., 2012; Rutherford et al., 1992; Walker et al., 1983). However, the basic procedural steps can be implemented without the use of such formalized programs.

EXAMPLE

Johnny, an 8-year-old with conduct problems, is redirected by his teacher for talking in class. He turns and hits Suzy. He was talking to Suzy and blames her for getting him in trouble. Johnny should be taught the social skill of dealing with an accusation.

GOAL

Prevent and remediate components of conduct problems through instruction in the use of prosocial skills as an alternative.

THE BASICS

1. Determine any social skills deficits.

2. Demonstrate appropriate social skills via explanations and explicit modeling.

3. Apply learned social skills in contrived scenarios.

4. Provide feedback and reinforcement for appropriate responses.

5. Apply learned social skills in an actual situation.

HOW TO IMPLEMENT SOCIAL SKILLS TRAINING

 PREP

- Organize the schedule of meetings.

- Form small groups of children who have similar problems.

- Establish performance goals.

- Set boundaries, consequences, and rules for participation.

- Determine common social skills or social competency deficits that may be responsible for triggering the child's conduct problems and prioritize them for intervention. These determinations are made from assessments; recommendations from teachers, parents, and caregivers; and child self-disclosures or self-assessment.

 IMPLEMENT

- Introduce only one specific social skill for each session (e.g., "Today we will talk about listening effectively and seven steps that will help us do that.")

- Use visual representations of each step associated with the social skill being taught. Write the steps on note cards or paper. Ask the children to recite the steps. Model the correct behavior associated with each step.

- Establish performance goals, such as, "I want to spend more time talking to my mom, and less time arguing about what I've done wrong," or "I want to stop disobeying my teachers."

- Engage the children in a discussion (e.g., brainstorming) centered on recent events that required use of the new skill. For example, "When was a time you wished you could talk to your mom instead of arguing?"

- Introduce and model the new skill. For example, make eye contact, take a deep breath, and say, "I understand what you are saying," rather than arguing.

- Encourage the children to role-play the skill while others coach them. For example, set up a scenario where you role-play the mother and try to get the child to start arguing. The child uses the new social skill of "make eye contact, breathe deeply, and verbalize calmly." Practice just the one skill taught during each session.

- Facilitate the retention of learned behaviors at the next meeting by reviewing skills that were taught during previous intervention sessions. Ask the children about opportunities to use the skill, review progress, or make modifications when things did not go as planned. For example, the child says, "I looked at my mom, took deep breaths, and said, 'I understand what you are saying,' but she kept arguing and thought I was making fun of her, so I started arguing back!"

- Maintain skill acquisition by holding periodic refresher sessions.

- Encourage children to use journals to record or keep track of skills used and the subsequent outcome. Journals can be optional or assigned as homework to record daily personal experiences with the newly learned social skills. As available and if appropriate, encourage them to read journal entries aloud for the group depending on child and counselor preference.

 EVALUATE

- Distribute copies of the skill steps to teachers and parents and ask them to monitor and record use of the skill. Monitor these records if available.

- Schedule routine observations such as weekly classroom walk-throughs or monthly classroom observations to monitor social skills as time permits.

EVIDENCE

A brief overview of research and annotated references supporting this intervention can be found on Q-global.

CONSIDERATIONS

For Teaching

Deficits can occur in a variety of social skills commonly used in the classroom. Many social skills can be targeted for development during daily instruction (e.g., preparing for a stressful conversation, expressing a complaint to others, dealing with group pressure, responding to others' feelings, avoiding fights with peers, dealing with an accusation from adults or peers, expressing affection, helping others, dealing with failure). Many social skills lessons can be incorporated into regular curriculum through readings for literature or social studies, assigned topics for language arts or story writing, or even problems for mathematics where a narrative or paragraph is used.

For Cultural and Language Differences

Social skills training, although effective in small groups, might be more effective in one-on-one settings with children from cultures where public discussion of individual challenges, emotions, and choice-making is perceived as inappropriate, or where social skills expectations differ based on gender or age group. Some children may not be expected to be assertive, to discuss feelings, or to respond to stress or anger. Even helpfulness may be interpreted as subservience, weakness, or a lack of such culturally esteemed qualities as independence or strength.

Chapter 4

Interventions for Hyperactivity

Characteristics and Conditions of Hyperactivity

WHAT IS HYPERACTIVITY?

Hyperactivity is one of the symptoms used to identify the heterogeneous condition attention-deficit/hyperactivity disorder or ADHD (APA, 2013). The hyperactive/impulsive subtype of ADHD is relatively infrequent (Fair et al., 2010). Behavior deficits in this area are associated with regional brain abnormalities and changes in functional and structural connectivity (Cao, Shu, Cao, Wang, & He, 2014). Individuals with the hyperactivity/impulsivity subtype of ADHD show brain connections that are different than those found in individuals with other subtypes (Cao et al., 2014).

Hyperactivity is present when for at least six months or more symptoms are evident in children under the age of 16, and five months or more when individuals are over age 17. The *DSM–5* lists symptoms such as fidgeting and squirming, leaving a seat unexpectedly, running or climbing inappropriately, failing to stay quiet, having difficulty waiting for a turn, or frequently interrupting and intruding socially. Hyperactivity problems can occur alone or can co-occur with attention problems. According to the *DSM–5*, they are usually exhibited by children in both home and school settings and can worsen in situations that require sustained mental effort or when situations lack intrinsic appeal (APA, 2013). Hyperactivity/impulsivity is less indicative of some long-term negative outcomes than other ADHD subtypes (Loya, 2011) and is differentially related to specific quality of life domains (Gjervan, Torgersen, Rasmussen, & Nordahl, 2014). It functions specifically as a predictor of social functioning and mental health.

HOW COMMON IS HYPERACTIVITY?

ADHD is reported to occur in 5% of children and about 2.5% of adults. However, some studies estimate a much higher rate, and rates vary across time (Centers for Disease Control and Prevention, 2014). Diagnosis increased 3% a year in the last two decades and 5% between 2003 and 2011. Males are more likely than females to be identified, with a ratio of approximately 2:1 in children and 1.6:1 in adults. ADHD symptoms remain into adulthood for up to 60% of children diagnosed with ADHD (Weiss & Murray, 2003).

As a subtype, not much data is available specific to hyperactivity and impulsivity. Deficient inhibition processes appear to be linked to smaller prefrontal and basal ganglia volumes (Halperin & Healey, 2011) and to problems with brain structures and neural networks (Chang, Hung, Huang, Hatfield, & Hung, 2014).

The BASC–3 Hyperactivity scale focuses on the hyperactivity and impulsivity aspects of attention-deficit/hyperactivity disorder (ADHD). The Teacher Rating Scales, the Parent Rating Scales, and the Self-Report of Personality measure hyperactivity with items such as "Acts out of control," "Has trouble staying seated," "Is overly active," and "People tell me to be still." Items from the three forms that help identify impulsivity include "Acts without thinking," "Cannot wait to take turn," and "I talk while other people are talking." Even though the clinical assessment field makes a conceptual distinction between impulsive responding and hyperactivity, impulsivity is included here because the research literature indicates that, from a psychometric perspective, it is nearly impossible to distinguish impulsive responding from hyperactivity.

Theoretical Framework for Approaching Hyperactivity

First described in 1845 in a children's book with a character dubbed "Fidgety Philip" (Hoffman, 1845), hyperactivity is not a new or under-researched condition, although many misconceptions remain regarding causation, such as poor parenting, excess sugar consumption, or lack of discipline (Reynolds, Vannest, & Harrison, 2012). Research suggests a neurological component to hyperactivity and impulsivity. Socioeconomic status (i.e., parental education and household income), family functioning (i.e., quality and quantity of stimulation and support for the child in the home environment, symptoms of depression in the mother), prenatal toxins (i.e., illicit drugs and smoking), being male, and age of the mother have been associated with the severity of hyperactivity symptoms and may play causal roles in ADHD (Sagiv, Epstein, Bellinger, & Korrick, 2013). Conversely, a host of studies on sugar and food additives indicate no clear evidence to support their role in hyperactivity or impulsivity (Flora & Polenick, 2013). Although approximately 5% of children see improvement with controlled diets, treatment approaches such as those that restrict sugar intake are not effective interventions for most (Searight, Robertson, Smith, Perkins, & Searight, 2012).

Behavioral, cognitive, psychoeducational, cognitive–behavioral, pharmacological, and neuropsychological treatments appear to have the greatest efficacy and the greatest breadth of evidence. A comprehensive review of pharmacological treatments are beyond the scope of this text; however, the U.S. Food and Drug Administration (FDA) has approved some medications for the treatment of ADHD and provides a list of short-term, long-term, and rare but serious side effects on their webpage (FDA, 2011). The website also provides information about signing up for consumer updates by email and an RSS Feed for current reporting on related issues.

Interventions

A variety of interventions demonstrate effectiveness for reducing or eliminating hyperactive and impulsive behavior. Some interventions can work to prevent the demonstration of these behaviors. Hyperactivity and impulsivity are rarely measured or studied in isolation. Therefore, this chapter includes interventions for associated problems that typically occur in the school setting (e.g., academic failure, off-task behavior, impulsive behaviors such as interrupting or being out of one's seat) as well as those problems that directly reflect hyperactivity or impulsivity. Descriptions of interventions that are considered efficacious as evidenced by their publication in the peer-reviewed research are provided. Evidence-based interventions for improving hyperactivity are listed in Table 4.1. For some of the interventions in this chapter, supplemental materials (e.g., handouts, posters, checklists, daily logs, and worksheets) that are helpful for preparing, implementing, and evaluating the interventions can be found on Q-global.

Table 4.1 Interventions for Hyperactivity

Intervention	Prevention[1]	Early Intervention[2]	Intensive Intervention[3]
Contingency Management	X	X	X
Daily Behavior Report Cards (DBRC)		X	X
Functional Behavioral Assessment			X
Multimodal Interventions		X	X
Parent Training		X	X
Self-Management	X	X	X
Task Modification		X	X

[1] Prevention refers to skills that can be taught to all children or used universally; they promote better awareness and lessen the risk of problems.

[2] Early intervention includes techniques and strategies that address early warning signs or clinical signs of the risk of future problems. Early intervention may be specifically applied to one or more problems or generically applied as a skill set to prevent the development of a chronic problem. Early interventions can be delivered to groups or individuals.

[3] Intensive intervention focuses on individuals and individual problems, which are usually chronic, intensive, and require services due to the level of interference in daily functioning.

 CONTINGENCY MANAGEMENT

DESCRIPTION

Contingency management is used to modify the consequent events that maintain hyperactive and impulsive behavior (DuPaul & Weyandt, 2006; Pfiffner & Haack, 2014). Contingency management involves shaping the child's existing behavior and providing opportunities for the new, desired behavior to become internalized. The target behavior can be behavioral and/or academic. Specific behavioral objectives for children with hyperactivity may include increasing the duration of productive learning time, decreasing episodes of hyperactivity, decreasing the frequency of verbal reprimands to correct behavior, or decreasing the number of disruptive, off-task activities.

Contingency management programs for hyperactivity include the individual or combined use of behavioral intervention strategies such as token economies; point systems; verbal praise; response cost; timeout from peers, reinforcers, attention, or privileges; varying amounts and frequency of teacher attention; verbal reprimands; and removal of praise (Chronis, Jones, & Raggi, 2006; Harlacher, Roberts, & Merrell, 2006; Pelham & Gnagy, 1999).

Social reinforcement can be incorporated into a contingency management plan through increasing verbal praise and posting records of achievement (Blackman & Silberman, 1980). Response cost may be an effective part of a contingency management plan for children with ADHD (Pfiffner & O'Leary, 1987). The degree of intensity or complexity of a contingency management plan varies based on the individual needs of the child (Daly, Creed, Xanthopoulos, & Brown, 2007; Pelham & Gnagy, 1999). Studies indicate that a lack of emotion-recognition abilities in children with hyperactivity contributes to problem behavior (Chronaki et al., 2015). This finding underscores the importance of providing additional support to manage external environments because children may have difficulty responding to instruction when they are experiencing processing deficits.

EXAMPLES

Clint, a 16-year-old with hyperactivity, blurts out answers often and talks without permission during class. He taps his pencil on his desk, gets out of his seat, and roams around the room. He and his teacher, Mrs. Gustafson, write a contingency management plan that institutes a point system to address his disruptive behavior. If Clint sits in his seat quietly during a lesson, he earns points that Mrs. Gustafson records on his point sheet. On Friday, if he has enough points, he is allowed to run errands for the teacher. If he doesn't have enough points, Clint has to sweep the classroom.

Sam's nickname is "Motorboat," which represents well the 3-year-old's perpetual motion as he moves from one activity to the next, never attending to anything for very long. His parents and preschool teacher, Ms. Lila, remark that he seems almost "driven" to move, as though engine-powered. He fidgets when at the table or in settings where other children his age can sit for periods of time. Mom tried a sticker chart at the end of the day, but Ms. Lila pointed out that the end of a full day was too long for Sam to wait. Now, mom carries stickers, and when Sam sits still for a brief, set period of time he earns a sticker. Sam knows how to use the timer on his mom's smart phone to keep track of the time and prompt his mom for the sticker.

GOAL

Decrease the child's activity levels that negatively impact learning by reshaping the environment to reinforce or eliminate behaviors.

THE BASICS

1. Define the behavioral objectives clearly in operationally defined terms.

2. Identify pre-established and taught routines for earning and losing reinforcers.

3. Provide appropriate levels and types of reinforcers to shape behavior.

4. Deliver contingencies consistently at fixed or random intervals.

5. Implement response-cost contingencies as needed.

HOW TO IMPLEMENT CONTINGENCY MANAGEMENT

 PREP

- Select a behavior to target. There may be several that are problematic, but only choose one to start.

- Define the child's behavior in operational terms.

- Identify who will record baseline data on the frequency (i.e., how often) and/or severity (i.e., how much) of the hyperactivity. Use this information as a sample of functioning (e.g., length of time child remains seated, amount of time child waits before blurting out an answer) before the intervention to permit evaluation of the degree of post-intervention improvement.

- Consider the child's preference for reinforcers. For example, if the child enjoys computer games, computer time can be earned or lost. Reinforcement surveys can help to determine reinforcers that are appropriate and meaningful to the child.

 IMPLEMENT

- Use the baseline data to set behavioral goals. Common goals include increasing the amount of time spent on task or decreasing the amount of off-task behavior during a specific interval. Modest increases in the amount of time spent on task, such as 20%, are more appropriate than large increases, such as 100%. If age appropriate, review the goals with the child or have the child participate in goal setting.

- Review the rules for providing reinforcers and ensure that the child understands them by asking him or her to repeat them back or to demonstrate when contingencies will occur and for what.

- Use a 1:1 ratio of behavior to reinforcement (i.e., every time the child performs the appropriate behavior, he or she is reinforced for it) when teaching new skills. This strengthens the association between engaging in appropriate behavior and receiving the reinforcer. If the behavior is a performance problem and not a skill problem, then it may be sufficient to reinforce less frequently (e.g., one out of three times the child performs the appropriate behavior). Intermittent intervals may also work, such as providing a non-scheduled ratio of reinforcement to behavior.

  - ▲ Consider using tokens or points that can be cashed in for reinforcers at the end of a specified time period as a modification to the intervention if necessary. For example, if the child is on task, a token is earned, but if the child is off task, a token is lost. After the child has earned a certain amount of tokens (or at the end of the day or week), he or she chooses an appropriate reinforcer. Token systems are typically more effective once basic behavioral goals have been met, and the tokens can be used to maintain the behavior.

- Use an electronic or paper visual aid to track behavior. This will assist the child in understanding progress and which specific behaviors are being targeted.

- Provide the reinforcer to the child when he or she meets the goal. Do not provide the reinforcer if the goal is not met. Previously earned reinforcers, such as tokens, may be taken away when a goal is not met.

EVALUATE

- Collect and examine data during the use of contingency management. You should expect to see large changes in behavior in a few days. If you do not, reconsider the implementation. Ensure reinforcement opportunities are consistent and not missed. If it seems that reinforcement opportunities have been inconsistent or missed, revisit the implement phase.

- Remain aware of the potential for satiation or boredom with a reinforcer, such as filling up on candy or getting tired of listening to music.

  ▲ After consistent effects are established, thin and fade the schedule of reinforcement to become more unpredictable and more irregular over time to avoid creating dependency on rewards to obtain appropriate behavior.

EVIDENCE

A brief overview of research and annotated references supporting this intervention can be found on Q-global.

CONSIDERATIONS

For Teaching

Teachers are generally adept at procedures that involve classwide prompting or acknowledgement and may need only minimal coaching to be effective with students with hyperactivity. Some issues that typically frustrate teachers include having to modify systems and provide immediate reinforcement, having to consistently apply the system, and the process of setting goals to encourage and change behavior. Teachers must modify the structure of token economy systems when the child loses more points than he or she earns (Abramowitz & O'Leary, 1991), or children may lose interest or be unable to access the reinforcer. Reinforcement must be immediate for children with hyperactivity; contingencies that are hours, days, or weeks away are unlikely to be effective. Behavioral interventions for hyperactivity require long-term consistency (Pelham & Gnagy, 1999). Once a child engages in appropriate behaviors, fading may occur, but monitoring should continue and the intervention reapplied when necessary. Goal setting or criteria setting for access to reinforcers is as critical as immediate access. If a child is engaging in hyperactive behaviors 90% of the time, a goal of 0% is unrealistic. Goals need to be gradual, and intermediate steps toward reaching a long-term solution are important for reducing hyperactivity. Goals should also be specific when possible, targeting the relevant behaviors that are characteristic of hyperactivity. For example, fidgeting and running around a classroom may have a differential impact on the setting and these behaviors might need to be addressed separately, even if both actions are part of hyperactivity.

For Age and Developmental Level

Special consideration should be given to the amount of reinforcement provided when using contingency management with children who experience hyperactivity. Hyperactivity is often associated with a low level of frustration tolerance. As a result, the use of continuous reinforcement can be particularly effective. While reliance on continuous reinforcement can sometimes be faded successfully, reinforcement should be reintroduced immediately if behavior levels fall below expectations. Continuous external reinforcement of appropriate behavior serves as a functional replacement for self-regulation skills, which may or may not be developed.

When asking children to generate a list of desired reinforcers, it is important to remind them to list things that are both realistic and age appropriate. Consider asking a parent to list some examples of attainable reinforcers and then giving the child the option to choose from that list. When generating a list of reinforcers, consult with teachers or other adults who may be able to provide information about the child's preferences and high-interest activities. Young children may be more comfortable with a small number of choices (e.g., a fruit snack, rocking in a chair, choosing a song for circle time). Older children may prefer access to music, social time with peers, one-on-one time with a teacher, or alone time. Consider the effects of satiation; if the child has unlimited or extensive access to the reinforcer, the reinforcer weakens over time. To maintain effectiveness and avoid habituation, periodically change or rotate the reinforcer.

DAILY BEHAVIOR REPORT CARDS (DBRC)

DESCRIPTION

Daily behavior report cards (DBRCs; also referred to as home notes, home-based reinforcement, daily report cards, and school–home notes) are used to record a child's behavior each day (Chafouleas, Riley-Tillman, & McDougal, 2002; Riley-Tillman, Chafouleas, & Briesch, 2007). Here, DBRCs are discussed as a specific intervention strategy for children with hyperactivity. School–home communication is typically recommended but not required.

A DBRC is implemented to change behavior by providing systematic feedback on performance and progress to children and parents, followed by appropriate reinforcement. The result is decreased hyperactive or impulsive behaviors during specific tasks and conditions.

There are many variations of DBRCs that make this approach easy to customize for a particular child or situation. A DBRC can include a short list of three to five appropriate behaviors with a scale to rate each behavior. Scales can be alphabetical, numerical, symbolic, or topographical. DBRCs are completed at the end of specified time periods by one or more teachers and then reviewed with the child. DBRCs can be used with more than one teacher. These records can be managed and shared in various ways using either electronic transmission or a simple log or notebook kept for parent signatures (Burke & Vannest, 2008). DBRCs provide a reliable way to track behavioral goals and objectives that are included in an individualized education program (IEP; Vannest, Davis, Davis, Mason, & Burke, 2010), and to monitor progress in response to intervention (RTI) models.

EXAMPLES

Lonnie is a 1st-grade student who has difficulty attending to tasks. Each morning, Lonnie's teacher reads a short book to the class. While she reads, Lonnie often sprawls out on the floor, picks at the carpet, and fidgets with his shirt. Lonnie does not answer questions about the story, indicating he was most likely not attending. Using a DBRC, his teacher identifies the target behaviors of sitting, listening, and attending to the morning's story. She circles one of several icons next to each behavior to assign a value; a yellow sunshine for a good morning, a white windy cloud icon for a so-so morning, and a black rainy storm cloud for a not-so-good morning. The chart is sent home daily for his parents to sign. After reading time, Lonnie's teacher allows him to look at a graph of his rate of attending to the story, and she praises each daily increase. When Lonnie gets picked up, his mother rewards him with 10 minutes of game time on the phone during the ride home for each day that he receives a "sunshine."

Stephanie is an 8th grader who argues, interrupts classmates, impulsively slaps her friends on the arm, and has difficulty sitting still in class. A DBRC is established for her with the target behaviors of "waiting to speak," "friendly hands with friends," and "seat in the chair." These behaviors are scored as A, B, C, and D letter grades and the report card is sent electronically in the teacher's communication system that connects parents to student grades.

GOAL

Decrease the child's hyperactive and impulsive behavior during specific tasks and conditions through monitoring, feedback, and communication with children and parents at home.

THE BASICS

1. Define the target behaviors.

2. Monitor and record behaviors daily.

3. Provide reinforcement when the child exhibits the target behaviors.

4. Communicate results to children and parents.

HOW TO IMPLEMENT DAILY BEHAVIOR REPORT CARDS

PREP

- Identify the target behaviors for improving behavior.

- Identify the rater of the target behavior.

- Identify if the DBRC will be used for communication, monitoring, or performance feedback, and if it will involve contingencies. Contingencies may be delivered at school during feedback sessions and at home for performance at school.

- Create and explain the rating system to raters. For example, assign a letter grade to the child's performance for each day. Each target behavior is rated daily. Letter grades (instead of frequency of behavior, for example) are preferable because they are usually more meaningful to children and parents.

- Explain the behavioral anchors (i.e., typical behavior for earning each grade) to avoid variance among raters or differences in personal tolerance levels. For example, appropriate behavior during 10 out of 20 minutes of class time may earn a 'C,' 15 minutes may earn a 'B,' and 17 minutes or more might earn an 'A.'

IMPLEMENT

- Ask the rater to begin ratings on a specific day and during a specific time period.

- Show ratings to the child in feedback sessions and provide brief, encouraging feedback. For example, "You earned a 'B' because you were out of your seat twice. If you are only out of your seat one time or less, you will earn an 'A.' Good job, keep it up!"

- Consider graphing or charting progress, depending on the age, developmental level, and interest of the child.

- Consider using the ratings as part of a checking in and checking out system. The child may check in at the beginning of the day to get a pep talk and receive reminders of goals or targets, and then check out at the end of the day to review performance and discuss goals or targets for the next day.

- Reward the child either at home or school for meeting performance goals. This step may or may not be needed for some children.

EVALUATE

- Compare the ratings from before the intervention with the ratings during the intervention to determine if the change occurring is large enough to be useful for the school setting.

- Changes in behavior should be moderate to large when the intervention is used throughout the day.

- Ensure reinforcement has been used consistently if the change is not moderate to large. Reassess reinforcer quality and feedback quality. Consider graphing or charting performance goals if those visual aids are not currently in place.

EVIDENCE

A brief overview of research and annotated references supporting this intervention can be found on Q-global.

CONSIDERATIONS

This intervention works better when the reinforcement communicated is positive instead of negative. DBRCs are not meant as a channel for communicating punishment or for reporting daily bad behavior. Ideally, they are used to provide objective and frequent feedback to the child and to communicate progress to the parents.

It is important to be accurate with the estimate of current performance and to avoid overrating when creating the initial behavior rating. For example, classifying a child's current level of on-task behaviors as a "B" grade might indicate that his or her current performance level is above average, calling into question why the report card is needed in the first place. In addition, this grade may not allow the child enough room for improvement, leading to increased frustration. Instead, "C" or "D" grades should be anchored as a child's present level of performance. Identify areas for improvement in a way that is not damaging to a child's feelings or self-concept. If a child is upset by these initial ratings, explain why the current level of performance is hindering his or her success in school and how he or she can improve. Set appropriately high expectations and provide encouragement.

Using letter grades to rate behavioral performance, unlike more typical measures of behavior (e.g., frequency counts, duration measures), may appear subjective or unfair to the child and parents. However, the ease of understanding letter grades outweighs the possible benefits of using behavior measures that seem more scientific yet are not accessible to the child and parents. Discuss the behavioral anchors (i.e., typical behavior for earning each grade) with the child and parents before implementing DBRCs, and explain how the grades will be used to minimize differences among multiple raters, lessening any impact on the child's behavior grades.

When setting performance goals, be sure to set a level that is challenging but attainable. Goals should become more difficult with time to encourage shaping of the behavior to the desired level (Chronis et al., 2006). Setting unattainable goals only leads to frustration.

FOR AGE AND DEVELOPMENTAL LEVEL
Younger children often respond quickly and positively to teacher attention and feedback. An older child may be embarrassed to receive daily grades on behavior for fear it may suggest to peers that he or she has a problem.

FOR CULTURAL AND LANGUAGE DIFFERENCES
Communication with parents is a critical component of DBRCs. Effective communication with parents may necessitate use of the home language. It is important to give careful consideration to facilitating accurate explanation of the DBRC's purpose and the process.

 # FUNCTIONAL BEHAVIORAL ASSESSMENT

DESCRIPTION
Functional behavioral assessment (FBA) is a method for identifying the purpose or communicative function of a behavior and the circumstances that maintain it (DuPaul & Eckert, 1997). Interventions based on data that are collected during the functional assessment are chosen to modify or eliminate the maintaining circumstances (Gresham, Watson, & Skinner, 2001).

FBA should not be confused with a functional analysis (FA), which refers to the use of experimental manipulation of environmental events to assess the functions these events have on behavior (Horner, 1994). An FBA does not manipulate or attempt to control the environment. The use of an FBA is not a single test or observation, but rather a multi-method strategy consisting of observations, interviews, and a review of records regarding the child's behavior and environmental conditions associated with presence or absence of problem behaviors (Gresham, Watson, & Skinner, 2001). An FBA for a child with hyperactivity allows therapists to determine the reason for the maladaptive behaviors (DuPaul & Ervin, 1996)—in other words, what the child hopes to achieve through the behavior (e.g., to gain sensory stimulation; to gain access to objects, events, or people; to escape certain events, situations, or people). Knowing the behavior's function helps the therapist address effectively the two primary goals of an intervention: (1) eliminating problem behaviors by modifying the antecedents and/or consequences of the behavior, and (2) teaching appropriate replacement behaviors. Through an FBA, therapists assess the effect of antecedents and consequences on the observed behavior. Antecedents to behaviors associated with hyperactivity (e.g., overactivity, inappropriate verbalizations, disruptive behavior) may be identified as being asked to complete a potentially difficult task. The function of the subsequent aberrant behavior may be stimulation, such as self-soothing, or may be to achieve an escape from a difficult task. The results of an FBA can be used to select interventions aimed at increasing acceptable behaviors that are functionally equivalent (i.e., accomplish the same purpose) to the problem behaviors.

EXAMPLE

Jacob is an 8-year-old with hyperactivity. Jacob's math teacher, Mrs. Barry, gives the class independent practice time each day. The independent practice is usually a math worksheet with over 30 multiplication problems. Every day, Jacob works on his worksheet for about 5 minutes and then starts meowing like a cat or drumming with his pencils on his desk. His peers laugh and Mrs. Barry sends Jacob out into the hall to finish his work, which he does not complete. An interdisciplinary team completes an FBA and determines that the function of the behavior is either to escape from difficult tasks, garner peer attention, or sometimes both. Testing this hypothesis, the team assists the teacher in keeping Jacob in the room (e.g., removing the escape) and find that he continues to engage in the behaviors. The team then asks the laughing peers to please stay quiet the next time this occurs and they will earn extra free time. In doing so, the team determines that Jacob's disruptive behavior is being maintained by the peer attention rather than the escape. To remediate Jacob's disruptive behavior, the interdisciplinary team identifies additional ways to modify the existing reinforcers of peer attention.

GOAL

Determine the function of a specific hyperactive behavior and identify one or more replacements or environmental modifications to effectively enable the child to decrease the hyperactive behavior while still accomplishing the desired effect or eliciting the same environmental response.

THE BASICS

1. Conduct an FBA (including interviews and direct observation).

2. Operationalize the target behavior.

3. Observe and record the antecedents.

4. Observe and record the consequences.

5. Develop hypotheses for why the behavior occurs.

6. Evaluate or test the hypotheses.

7. Select a functionally equivalent replacement or intervention.

HOW TO IMPLEMENT FUNCTIONAL BEHAVIORAL ASSESSMENT

 PREP

- Gather collateral information (e.g., interview with parents and teachers, review of records) and observe the child in the environment in which the hyperactive behaviors are occurring.

 IMPLEMENT

- Identify and operationally define the target behavior. Interview parent(s) and teacher(s) to gather information about the specific situations in which the child tends to exhibit hyperactive behaviors.

- Identify observers to collect data before and after the targeted behavior. Observers may include the therapist or other adults involved with the child's day-to-day activities.

- Observe (or have other adults observe) the child during typical times when the hyperactive behavior is exhibited.

- Determine the antecedent(s) of the hyperactive behavior.

- Generate a testable hypothesis about the function of the behavior and test it when possible.

- Observe the child again to test the hypothesis, targeting the identified problem situations.

- Using the results of the FBA, choose an appropriate intervention to help the child develop the skills to accomplish the same function through socially acceptable behaviors.

 EVALUATE

- Assess the use of the intervention or the functional equivalence of any replacement behavior to determine if the hyperactive behavior identified in the FBA has decreased.

- Use parent, child, and teacher reports to provide information about the level of hyperactivity. Use direct observations—and frequency, duration, latency, or rating scales—to monitor effects and/or progress.

EVIDENCE

A brief overview of research and annotated references supporting this intervention can be found on Q-global.

CONSIDERATIONS

FBA is a technically sound approach to intervention planning; however, an assessment is only as reliable as the data that are collected. In some situations, the function of a child's behavior may be nearly self-evident and minimal effort may be required to collect high-quality data that are both valid and reliable. However, some other behaviors may be more difficult to operationally define and the antecedents more difficult to determine. In these situations, collecting good data and finding clear patterns in the child's behavior may be much more challenging. In instances where the behavior is topographically complicated or not readily observed (e.g., occurs with high intensity but low frequency or occurs at times or in locations not accessible to school personnel), a team of professionals should remain involved until sufficient data are gathered to produce a solid hypothesis about the behavior's function.

Therapists who already have extensive professional experience working with a certain child may be tempted to draw conclusions about the function of a particular behavior without formal data collection procedures. This practice is inadvisable. It is crucial to view preliminary ideas about the behavior's possible function as a hypothesis only and to enter the observation/hypothesis-testing step with an open mind. Data tend to become a self-fulfilling prophecy when the observer feels strongly invested in an a priori hypothesis. This is not to suggest that professional knowledge of and history with the child should not influence what kind of data are collected and what data collection methods are used (e.g., identifying the conditions or behaviors of interest and choosing the time periods for observation). However, there is a marked difference between drawing on one's experience to conduct informed data collection and undertaking data collection to support a biased or predetermined attribution of cause.

For Teaching

Some teachers and/or administrators may be hesitant to participate in formal data collection due to the time-consuming nature of the process. This may be particularly true if the problem behavior interferes with classroom or campus life or if parents are demanding immediate, effective intervention. In some cases, a "best match" approach, in which the intervention is based on professional judgment and informal assessment of the conditions surrounding the problem behavior, is warranted. Teachers may need support in classroom settings; including training, help supervising students, or assistance in data collection responsibilities.

FOR AGE AND DEVELOPMENTAL LEVEL

Functional assessments are applicable to any age or developmental level, making this approach a strong intervention method for problem behaviors. However, use caution when describing a young child as hyperactive, given that young children are characteristically more active.

FOR CULTURAL AND LANGUAGE DIFFERENCES

This guide relies on a primarily cognitive–behavioral and biological perspective of the theoretical basis for understanding hyperactivity. Other cultures may not share this view and may instead believe hyperactivity has a spiritual origin, or may view hyperactivity as a maladaptive trait that should not be addressed.

 # MULTIMODAL INTERVENTIONS

DESCRIPTION

Multimodal interventions for hyperactivity are multiple solutions for previously learned maladaptive behaviors, current performance, and future learning, based on the view that multiple factors within the child and his/her environment impact these behaviors. Multimodal interventions typically involve both home and school environments. Multimodal interventions involve teaching new skills to reduce hyperactivity and prevent future problems while also remediating any deficits that exist academically, socially, or in self-regulation. These combination treatments are more complex to initiate and involve multiple participants. Sometimes it is difficult to ascertain which relative parts are responsible for improvements. The effect of the whole treatment is often more beneficial than the sum of its parts. The synergy from multiple interventions applied at the same time can help shape self-regulating individuals who need little or no intervention to exhibit more functional behavior, allowing them to achieve their goals without outside support.

Because consistent application of treatments is most effective, children improve most quickly when parents and schools work together to set expectations for behavior and implement consequences. One or both parents may report that their child is "just like I was" in school and that this apparent genetic link may contribute to a lack of compensatory skills. Parents may believe that the child's hyperactivity is simply something to be outgrown, so psychoeducation may be necessary to enlist parent involvement and support.

Multimodal interventions are more significantly effective than single treatments alone. According to some studies (Abikoff & Hechtman, 1994; MTA Cooperative Group, 2004), multimodal interventions are the most effective school-based interventions for hyperactivity, although the effects of multimodal interventions may diminish over time (Swanson et al., 2008a, 2008b). In addition, the strongest evidence of effectiveness for interventions to decrease hyperactivity supports the use of psychostimulant medication and/or multimodal interventions with stimulant medication and contingency management (Barkley, 2006; Brown & Sammons, 2002; Crenshaw, Kavale, Forness, & Reeve, 1999; MTA Cooperative Group, 1999; Pelham & Gnagy, 1999; Tamm & Carlson, 2007). The use of pharmacology for ADHD has been increasing, with 6.1% of children ages 4–17 taking medication for the disorder in 2011 (Centers for Disease Control and Prevention, 2014). Such use of medication is implemented under the control of the parents in careful consultation a physician and may be administered in school settings with parent consent. Feedback on drug effects and side effects may originate from school officials more often than parents, because task demands in these settings are different.

A complete discussion of psychostimulant medication interventions is beyond the scope of this guide. However, therapists frequently choose interventions for children who have been prescribed psychostimulant medication by a physician; therefore, evidence for the use of behavioral interventions in combination with psychostimulant medications is presented. It is recommended that behavioral interventions be attempted first to determine if they are sufficient alone.

EXAMPLE

Mya was diagnosed with ADHD by a child psychiatrist and takes methylphenidate with breakfast and lunch. However, the effects of her medication begin to wear off in the afternoon while she is still in school. When this happens, Mya begins to act out in class, move around the room, disrupt her classmates' work, and speak loudly. When she arrives home, her behavior is unmanageable for her parents, who become easily irritated and complain that it takes Mya 2 hours to complete what should be about 30 minutes of homework. To address Mya's declining behavior at school and uncontrollable behavior at home, the school psychologist designed a multimodal behavior management plan to assist her teacher and parents. The plan involved a combination of intervention methods to remediate her disruptive behaviors, including additional or different dosages of medication to extend the effects, task modification in the classroom to limit disruptions and improve her focus, and training to assist her parents in managing her behavior at home.

GOAL

Identify and provide a comprehensive approach to treatment by addressing the physiological, social, and behavioral aspects of hyperactivity and improving the child's self-regulation.

THE BASICS

1. Provide multiple treatments with appropriate personnel simultaneously or in sequence, including:

    a. Functional behavioral assessment,

    b. Contingency management,

    c. Parent training,

    d. Self-management, and/or

    e. Task modification.

2. Determine the responsible team members for implementing and monitoring treatments.

HOW TO IMPLEMENT MULTIMODAL INTERVENTIONS

 PREP

- Use individual assessments or team evaluation to determine the causal factors associated with the hyperactive behavior, and identify the exact interventions to be used from the multimodal framework based on assessment results.

- Decide on a length of treatment based on the severity of the causal factors. (With multimodal interventions, treatment may be provided for longer periods of time than with single interventions.)

- Identify the specific team members (e.g., psychologist, social worker, case worker, parents) to provide services based on the prescribed interventions.

 IMPLEMENT

- Implement the interventions simultaneously.

- Fade interventions in frequency or duration systematically to transfer new skills to the classroom or home environment, without as much structure or support.

- Use progress monitoring data or repeated measures of performance to determine success or growth on the targeted hyperactive behavior.

- Track any potential medication side effects, such as changes in mood, weight or appetite, sleep patterns, or other behaviors as suggested by the physician.

- Implement booster sessions as needed.

- Review the number of interventions used and their complexity and determine their overall acceptability by those involved (e.g., ask implementers their opinion informally, survey formally).

EVIDENCE

A brief overview of research and annotated references supporting this intervention can be found on Q-global.

CONSIDERATIONS

As with individual approaches, it is important to identify the best treatment options for everyone involved. Pharmacology has generally been shown to be an effective intervention. However, the most recent findings from a comprehensive, longitudinal study suggest that while pharmacological approaches have demonstrated effectiveness at 14 and 24 months, follow-up assessments at 36 months showed pharmacological approaches to have no greater effects than behavioral or combined treatment approaches (Swanson et al., 2008a, 2008b).

Medication effects appear to not stand out from behavioral treatments long term without consistent behavioral management (Hinshaw & Arnold, 2014). As stressed in other sections of this guide, the decision to use psychopharmacological interventions is a matter for careful consideration among parents, the child, and the physician who would manage such an intervention. Small negative effects have been seen in height and weight measures at one year, but these diminish and do not appear to impact long-term growth (Faraone, Biederman, Morley, & Spencer, 2008). Less intrusive interventions, such as strategy use and skill instruction, typically should be attempted before trying more complicated ones.

Parents, counselors, and teachers should not take a wait-and-see attitude or leave improvement to chance or future development. Instead, early action involves little risk, especially interventions that involve school–home communication, teaching skills, and modifying problem behavior. It is best to keep an open mind toward proactive approaches that benefit children (even those who may not warrant a diagnosis of attention-deficit/hyperactivity disorder).

 PARENT TRAINING

DESCRIPTION

Parent training as an intervention for hyperactivity consists of educating parents about hyperactivity and teaching effective parenting techniques to be used in the home (Daly et al., 2007; Pelham & Gnagy, 1999). Parent training is difficult to implement successfully due to the many barriers (Wymbs et al., 2015). Most programs involve multiple sessions in a set program of study. For example, parents are taught problem-solving skills; how to give effective directions; how to properly reinforce desired behaviors by establishing clear expectations; how to modify antecedents and consequents of the child's behavior; how to monitor behavior; and how to use positive attention, tangible rewards, response cost, and timeout from positive reinforcers appropriately (Chronis, Chacko, Fabiano, Wymbs, & Pelham, 2004; Chronis et al., 2001; DeNisco, Tiago, & Kravitz, 2005). Studies indicate most parents prefer individual training to group training, and most are interested in active skill building and problem solving (Wymbs et al., 2015).

Parenting interventions are based on a gene-environment explanation of the developmental course of hyperactivity in ADHD and potential negative parenting, such as coercive, intrusive, and restrictive practices (Doyle, 2004). Children who are more difficult to parent are more susceptible to negative parenting techniques and more affected by harsh parenting (Sheese, Voelker, Rothbart, & Posner, 2007; Swanson et al., 2008a, 2008b). The focus is on early intervention and training for the child and parents, particularly where barriers exist in the home or community to receiving services.

EXAMPLE

Kevin's hyperactivity keeps him moving at full speed. He has relationship problems with friends and family and engages in high-risk behaviors that keep both his parents stressed and depressed as they try to engage Kevin and help him to be more successful. Parent training may help Kevin's parents understand factors that contribute to hyperactivity and to structure a workable family plan designed to reduce Kevin's hyperactive behavior.

GOAL

Help parents develop skills for handling hyperactive behaviors and develop greater understanding of factors that contribute to hyperactivity.

THE BASICS

1. Discuss goals and expected outcomes in an introduction session.

2. Teach or coach parents to help them understand the biological, behavioral, and cognitive aspects of hyperactivity.

3. Teach and review parenting skills through modeling strategies and rehearsing, and by using videos and other prepared materials in a number of scheduled weekly sessions. Cases, shared examples, or brainstorming sessions can be used to identify parenting errors and provide effective solutions.

4. Assign homework and review in each session.

HOW TO IMPLEMENT PARENT TRAINING

 PREP

- Conduct an intake assessment with the family. This assessment includes an evaluation of the family climate to determine the needs of the family and any barriers to success, including cultural–parental expectations (Kotchick & Forehand, 2002).

- Identify skill deficits and then formulate the goals and objectives that can be achieved by implementing family and parent management techniques. The targets of the intervention are the child's hyperactive behaviors as well as the actions of the parents that appear to reinforce these behaviors.

- Determine if group or individual parent training will work for the implementer and the setting.

- Identify the instructor and location for trainings.

- Create or purchase materials for training (see the parent tip sheets that may be purchased to accompany this guide for prepared strategies and information).

- Determine the duration (e.g., two hours) and the number of sessions (e.g., 3, 5, or 10).

- Consider the following sample topics:

    ▲ Effective reinforcement strategies and different types of reinforcers (e.g., verbal praise, social activities, toys)

    ▲ Observation skills

- ▲ Play skills
- ▲ Response-cost techniques
- ▲ Timeout procedures
- ▲ Self-regulation/monitoring skills
- ▲ Token economy
- ▲ Reward charts
- ▲ Contingency contracts
- ▲ Self-reward
- ■ Arrange for transportation, meals, and childcare, as needed, to promote participation.
- ■ Invite or assign parents or caregivers to training sessions.
- ■ Provide a broad overview of the goals of the intervention, the relevance of the information to be presented, and the responsibilities of the parents in the process (e.g., follow-through, attendance).

IMPLEMENT

- ■ Begin the intervention by teaching parents to use effective discipline techniques, such as differential reinforcement and timeout procedures.
- ■ Use the parent training materials that were created or purchased during the prep phase to introduce new topics.
- ■ Explain the relevance and importance of the topics to hyperactivity.
- ■ Model or view examples of parenting errors and effective parenting skills that can serve as solutions.
- ■ Role-play and answer questions.
- ■ Problem-solve challenges to the skill.
- ■ Provide corrective feedback.
- ■ Assign simple homework.
- ■ Encourage independent implementation by requesting the use of the technique a specific number of times before the next session. Additionally, request that the parents document the effects, problems encountered, and any questions that arise.
- ■ Assist parents throughout the process in choosing effective and preferred parenting and child management techniques.
- ■ After training sessions are completed, refresher sessions or periodic individual sessions may be needed to review and maintain the skills learned. In many cases, parents will receive training in three or four topics over several sessions.

EVALUATE

- ■ Conduct surveys at the end of each session to assess satisfaction and utility of the information.
- ■ Directly observe changes in parenting skills during the parent training sessions and instruct or redirect accordingly.
- ■ Have a parent or outside observer (e.g., family member, teacher) complete a progress monitoring form regarding the child's hyperactive behaviors.

EVIDENCE

A brief overview of research and annotated references supporting this intervention can be found on Q-global.

CONSIDERATIONS

As Anastopoulos, DuPaul, and Barkley (1991) explain, a critical element for successfully implementing parent training is establishing trusting, collaborative relationships between the instructor and the parents/caregivers. To this end, instructors are advised to convey genuine understanding and support, avoid professional jargon, incorporate humor, and keep the discussion grounded in realistic examples and scenarios. Some parents may prefer to receive parent training in a multifamily group context while others may prefer an individual-family basis; this decision is based largely on parent preference, the clinical judgment of the therapist, and logistical considerations. Ideally, both parents will attend the training sessions. If this is not feasible, consider asking the parents or caregivers to alternate attendance to the training sessions or share the information via audio recording (Anastopoulos et al., 1991).

FOR AGE AND DEVELOPMENTAL LEVEL

Early intervention is often shown to be effective and is particularly relevant for parent training. Providing training to parents of young children as early as possible can have a positive effect on a child's typical behavior patterns and routines as well as on parenting styles.

FOR CULTURAL AND LANGUAGE DIFFERENCES

Communication is critical for parent training; thus, using the primary language of the family and understanding the values of the family are essential to building an effective partnership. If beliefs about the condition or the treatment are radically different than those of the school, all key stakeholders would benefit from a discussion about expectations for success in the school setting while maintaining an attitude of tolerance and understanding for the culture of the home.

 **SELF-MANAGEMENT**

DESCRIPTION

Self-management strategies for hyperactivity are techniques that children can use to monitor their own activity level, record the results, and compare this level to a predetermined acceptable level of activity (Reid, Trout, & Schartz, 2005). Self-management in this context involves a combination of three behavioral techniques: self-monitoring, self-monitoring plus reinforcement, and self-reinforcement (Mace, Belfiore, & Hutchinson, 2001; Reid et al., 2005). Self-monitoring is the process of observing and recording one's own activity level. A teacher or other professional can add reinforcement to self-monitoring by rewarding the child for exhibiting appropriate activity levels. In self-reinforcement, the child defines his or her own goal for the level of activity and provides a self-reward when the goal is achieved (Christie, Hiss, & Lozanoff, 1984; Reid et al., 2005). A child's ability to produce this automatic response through internalized controls can decrease his or her situation-specific, inappropriate hyperactivity.

EXAMPLES

Ying, a 17-year-old with ADHD, moves and sings when driving with the radio on. On two occasions, Ying has run the same stop sign, almost causing an accident each time. After these two incidents, her mother refused to let her drive to school. As an alternative to removing all of her driving privileges, self-monitoring could be implemented to reduce or eliminate the effect of Ying's hyperactive, off-task behavior while driving. Ying can be taught to self-monitor her activity level internally or using a cuing device such as a watch or electronic reminder while driving, and to reinforce her own appropriate behavior.

Todd is challenged by hyperactivity. He fidgets frequently, tapping his pencil on the desk and his feet on the floor. When he hears classmates talking, he jumps into the conversation regardless of the task he is engaged in. Todd is taught to monitor his fidgeting and impulsive talking by using a low cost app on his phone. Todd records his behaviors electronically and syncs to his mother's phone when he gets home. When he meets his goal, Todd is allowed to purchase a dessert for himself.

GOAL

Increase the child's awareness of his or her own level of activity in order to produce an automatic response without relying on external reinforcement or prompting.

THE BASICS

1. Teach the child to monitor his or her own activity level.

2. Teach the child to record his or her own activity level.

3. Teach the child to check against self-determined goals.

4. Teach the child to reinforce him- or herself.

HOW TO IMPLEMENT SELF-MANAGEMENT

 PREP

- Determine the specific area for self-management of hyperactivity (e.g., impulsivity control, hyperactive behavior).

- Determine the cuing method for the self-management (e.g., audio cue tape, wrist counter, teacher signal).

- Identify the paper self-recording form.

- Identify a goal.

- Determine a reinforcer.

- Gain commitment for participation from the child.

- Determine if an adult will provide simultaneous monitoring and recording for accuracy checks later. (If so, be sure to demonstrate to both the child and adult during the IMPLEMENT step.)

 IMPLEMENT

- Teach self-monitoring procedures to the child including any new replacement behaviors (e.g., relaxation, deep breathing).

- Model the replacement behavior and indicate the level (i.e., the frequency and/or intensity) at which it should occur. Consider role-playing the expected level and behavior with the child as a check for understanding.

- Explain what cuing is and how it will work. Discuss and determine how often the cue will be heard or seen (e.g., every 30 seconds for 10 minutes, or every 1 minute for 20 minutes during a certain class or instructional time).

- Demonstrate how the child will record his or her attention to task when the cue is heard. The cues or prompts can be audio recorded or generated by a watch with intermittent beeps; intervals from 15 seconds up to 2 minutes can be used, depending on the child. At the sound of each prompt, the child records his or her activity level by placing a checkmark on the self-monitoring sheet.

- Ask the child to demonstrate the techniques and check for his or her understanding.

- Start the cuing and prompt if necessary to remind the child to record.

- Monitor activity levels and the replacement behavior. Provide a basic level of reinforcement for participation even if goals are not met, and provide a higher level of reinforcement when goals are met.

- If an adult was monitoring the child at the same time, ask the child and adult to compare their recording forms.

  ▲ Place scores on a single graph to facilitate the comparison.

  ▲ Discuss if the scores are dramatically different—allowing for some degree of error is acceptable and expected.

  ▲ Highly praise and encourage perfectly matched scores as a goal depending on the number of intervals.

- Encourage the child to self-reinforce the behavior both for displaying appropriate activity levels and consistently and accurately recording the replacement behavior. Reinforcement is phased out as naturally occurring reinforcement takes place (e.g., better grades, better skills, less discipline in classrooms).

EVIDENCE

A brief overview of research and annotated references supporting this intervention can be found on Q-global.

CONSIDERATIONS

FOR TEACHING

When teaching children to self-manage, it is important to thoughtfully consider the goal of the intervention. If the objective is to reduce fidgety behaviors, the intervention and outcome will be different than improving a class of behaviors, such as listening or assignment completion. For example, targeting fidgety behaviors may result in solely monitoring and recording the tapping of a foot or pencil, which may not produce the same results that monitoring on-task behavior or task completion might. However, reducing fidgety behaviors may be the primary goal in other situations. For example, if a child's behavior interrupts the other children's class work or creates a negative relationship with the teacher, it may be best to focus on reducing those behaviors, even if the child's overall academic performance is not targeted.

Self-management techniques can be effective even when a child is inaccurate in his or her recording. Accuracy, and thus attention to detail, can be encouraged by matching the child and teacher ratings. If teacher ratings aren't available or viable, the child can submit self-recorded information to another adult (for a contingent reward). The most efficient rewards using this approach are self-rewards (i.e., those given by the child to himself or herself), not rewards from the adult with whom the child has contact.

 # TASK MODIFICATION

DESCRIPTION

Task modification as an intervention for hyperactivity involves modifying aspects of specific instructional tasks or assignments or behavioral expectations. Task modifications are nearly limitless. Tasks are altered using antecedent instructional modifications based on information obtained through a functional behavioral assessment (FBA; Ervin, DuPaul, Kern, & Friman, 1998; Kern & Clemens, 2007; Raggi & Chronis, 2006). A number of recommended modification strategies are discussed in this section (and see also Carbone, 2001; Kern & Clemens, 2007; Montague & Warger, 1997; and Salend, Elhoweris, & van Garderen, 2003), and most professionals will be able to identify a host of ideas not identified in this brief review of the literature.

Modify Intratask Stimulation

One way to modify a task is to change the intratask stimulation (i.e., stimulation that occurs within the task; Zentall, 1989; Zentall & Leib, 1985). Examples of intratask stimulation include adding color to written assignments, decreasing task-overlapping noise, requiring structured response patterns, and adding motor activity to rote tasks (Drechsler, Rizzo, & Steinhausen, 2010; Zentall & Dwyer, 1989; Zentall & Leib, 1985; Zentall & Meyer, 1987; Zentall & Shaw, 1980).

Offer a Choice of Instructional Activities

Teachers can modify tasks by giving the child a choice of activities or assignments (Dyer, Dunlap, & Winterling, 1990; Koegel, Dyer, & Bell, 1987). Encouraging children to engage in active decision making and to exercise control over making choices can help increase their level of attention. Using this approach, children choose activities, materials, or a task sequence within a set of instructional materials outlined by the teacher (Dunlap et al., 1994; Kern, Bambara, & Fogt, 2002; Powell & Nelson, 1997).

For example, a child might choose the order of the completion of assignments, decide which group of children he or she will work with, or select among types of responses (e.g., oral, written). However, this approach is successful only when the choices offered to the child are relevant to the curriculum or learning objectives. Consideration should be given to ensure that learning goals are not compromised. For example, choosing between two equally unattractive options will be unpopular with the child, and doing only half of the assignment versus doing all of the assignment will be unacceptable to the teacher. Agreeing on the conditions for each choice is critical and is best done prior to any possible conflicts between child and teacher interests.

Use High-Interest Activities and Hands-on Demonstrations

Activities and tasks that are novel and interesting to children can increase work productivity (Carbone, 2001; Clarke, et al., 1995). Providing moderate levels of auditory stimuli (e.g., music) during familiar tasks with structured responses, and in turn, reducing classroom noise while children are engaged in learning new concepts, can provide cues to the different types of attention each task requires (Scott, 1970; Zentall, 1983). Teachers can begin lessons with high-interest activities that require participation and facilitate attention. Examples include demonstrating practical applications (especially in subjects such as math or science), playing music or film clips, engaging in role-plays, or using examples related to current events (either community or world events, or events related to child activities).

Provide Increased Opportunities to Respond

In this strategy, children are given increased opportunities to respond to academic material using varied response methods, such as written responses, the class answering in unison, and individual answer cards (Montague & Warger, 1997; Sutherland, Alder, & Gunter, 2003). When children have more opportunities to respond, they tend to be more engaged and attentive and, as a secondary benefit, academic performance tends to improve. Counting the number of responses per child per hour is one way to monitor the amount of interaction between the children and the teacher (and consequently how difficult it may be for children to exhibit appropriate classroom behavior). For example, if a class has 20 children, and the teacher asks 20 questions during a 20-minute presentation, each child should actively participate approximately one time. However, a teacher could instead use individual answer cards and ask each child to write a response on his or her card and then show the teacher his or her response by holding up the card. In this case, every child participates 20 times in 20 minutes and appropriate behavior is maintained due to the pace and immediacy of the task.

Vary the Pace of Instruction

Briskly paced instruction increases levels of on-task behavior because rapid pacing is thought to require more effort (Kern & Clemens, 2007; Skinner, Johnson, Larkin, Lessley, & Glowacki, 1995). Teachers can increase the pacing of their instruction either by increasing their rate of presenting material or by decreasing the length of instructional pauses (Kern & Clemens, 2007).

EXAMPLE

Ian, a 12-year-old with ADHD, becomes highly frustrated when he is unable to complete all five essay questions on a written assignment in history class. His teacher insists that he write the answers to all five questions before moving on to the next lesson. Using task modifications, the teacher may ask Ian to answer three of the five questions before moving on or can allow Ian to type his answers on a computer.

GOAL

Modify task presentation in order to increase the child's engagement and manage hyperactivity by exercising control over his or her environment or experience of novelty.

THE BASICS

1. Assess the instructional preferences and abilities of the person presenting the information to identify feasible modifications.

2. Conduct an FBA to determine the function of the hyperactive behavior.

3. Assess the needs and abilities of the child to identify the best candidates for an effective modification from the list of feasible modifications.

4. Select from among the best candidates one or more strategies that best fit the content of the lesson and meet the needs of the child in the situation as determined by the FBA.

5. Prepare necessary materials to facilitate the modification.

6. Present the task using the modified strategy.

7. Monitor effectiveness of the modification and adjust as necessary.

HOW TO IMPLEMENT TASK MODIFICATION

 PREP

- Use assessment or observation data to determine which strategies best fit the person delivering the content, the needs of the child, and the content of the lesson.

- Identify the differences in when, where, and how the typical group instruction or tasks vary from those for a targeted or individual group, or if the strategy will be a menu-like choice selection for all children.

- Prepare materials if necessary, and plan the modification if it involves changing presentation style or a modification to the environment (e.g., music).

 IMPLEMENT

- Present the task using the modified strategy.

 EVALUATE

- Engage in direct observation of the child's hyperactive behavior and class performance as a whole.

- Determine which modifications seem to have the greatest positive impact and which are ineffective using observational data. Continue use of those modifications that are effective, and discontinue those that are not.

EVIDENCE

A brief overview of research and annotated references supporting this intervention can be found on Q-global.

CONSIDERATIONS

FOR TEACHING

Teachers may perceive this approach as adding to their workload, cheating, or providing an advantage, especially in a time of high-stakes testing and competitive academic conditions. First, remind teachers that initial time investment does not require more time but rather different time, and may result in more instructional time and less time spent managing a child's behavioral problems in the long run. In many schools, there are often a few teachers who are very skilled in implementing task modifications. They can be invaluable resources for other teachers learning how to incorporate this strategy into their own teaching programs efficiently and effectively. Second, consider carefully the modifications included in individualized education programs for both classroom and annual assessment. Modifications in classroom and assessment conditions are sometimes expected to be parallel, regardless of test validity issues. Be cautious to distinguish between modifications and accommodations.

Chapter 5

Interventions for Attention Problems

Characteristics and Conditions of Attention Problems

WHAT ARE ATTENTION PROBLEMS?

Attention problems are defined as chronic and severe inconsistencies in the ability to maintain and regulate focus on tasks for more than short periods of time (Barkley, 1997). Attention problems are often characterized by distractibility, inability to concentrate or to maintain attention to tasks for long periods of time, disorganization, failure to complete tasks, and a lack of study skills (Atkins, Pelham, & Licht, 1985; Evans et al., 2006; Kerns, Eso, & Thomson, 1999; Mash & Barkley, 2003; Reynolds & Kamphaus, 2015). Children with attention problems exhibit an inability to control and direct attention to the demands of a task (Loge, Staton, & Beatty, 1990; Semrud-Clikeman et al., 1999) and are frequently distracted by internal distractions or by irrelevant stimuli, even in a relatively quiet classroom environment. Attention problems are related to academic development, even after controlling for other variables (Arnold, Kupersmidt, Voegler-Lee, & Marshall, 2012). Attention problems are often experienced by children diagnosed with attention-deficit/hyperactivity disorder (ADHD), as well as children with acquired brain injury (Sohlberg, McLaughlin, Pavese, Heidrich, & Posner, 2000), depression (APA, 2013), acute stress (Hancock & Warm, 2003), and anxiety (LaBerge, 2002). However, significant attention problems, herein defined as those that rise to the level of interfering with academic learning, can exist and require management in the absence of any other clinical or educational disorder.

Physiologically, studies of children with ADHD suggest attention problems are due to dysfunctions of pathways that communicate with the prefrontal and frontal cortex (Todd & Botteron, 2001). Dopamine genes and neurotransmitters are believed to play a primary role in the development of attention problems (Comings et al., 2000; Cook et al., 1995). Twin studies indicate that differences in attention are largely explained by genetics (Rietveld, Hudziak, Bartels, van Beijsterveld, & Boomsma, 2004).

HOW COMMON ARE ATTENTION PROBLEMS?

Attention problems frequently co-occur with other problems, but attention deficits are most typically reported within the diagnosis of ADHD. According to the National Survey of Children's Health conducted in 2011–2012, 11% of school-age children in the U.S. received a diagnosis of ADHD by a health care provider, with 1 in 5 high school boys receiving a diagnosis compared to 1 in 11 girls (Visser et al., 2014). Like many similar disorders, boys are more likely to be identified and more likely to have more serious problems (Offord, Boyle, Fleming, Blum, & Grant, 1989). The average age of diagnosis is 7 years (Visser et al., 2014).

The BASC–3 Attention Problems scale is useful for identifying problems associated with ADHD when considered alongside the Hyperactivity scale. Nevertheless, it is important to distinguish problems with attention from problems with hyperactivity because attention tends to have a stronger relationship with academic problems than hyperactivity does (Arnold et al., 2012; Hartley, 1998). Items that measure attention on the Teacher Rating Scales, Parent Rating Scales, and the Self-Report of Personality include "Listens to directions," "Has trouble concentrating," and "I have trouble paying attention to what I am doing."

Theoretical Framework for Approaching Attention Problems

Research suggests there is no single cause of attention problems. While a variety of causes have been cited (including brain injury, food additives, and genetics; National Institute of Mental Health, 2006), there is strong evidence supporting a neurobiological basis that stems from irregular and inefficient transmission of information (DuPaul & White, 2006; Solden,

1995). In such cases, children experience extreme difficulty filtering irrelevant information from the environment (Semrud-Clikeman et al., 1999). Riccio, Reynolds, and Lowe (2001) have provided a discussion of the neurobiological basis of attention in the context of performance-based measures of attention and the relation of attention problems to learning as well as to impulsive response styles.

While this chapter focuses on interventions that are primarily behavioral, psychopharmacology can also play a role in the treatment of attention problems. Psychostimulant medications and behavioral interventions are commonly used in combination when treating attention problems and have been shown to be effective in reducing attention problems (Chronis et al., 2006; DuPaul & Eckert, 1998; DuPaul & Weyandt, 2006). Medication interventions are beyond the scope of this guide. However, therapists frequently find themselves choosing interventions for children who are prescribed stimulant medication by a licensed physician. Evidence for the use of behavioral interventions in combination with psychostimulant medications is discussed in this chapter within the multimodal intervention section in the context of concurrent treatment per physician recommendation. In the authors' view, the best practice is to implement behavioral interventions first to determine if they are sufficient.

Interventions

The interventions included in this chapter are behavioral and cognitive–behavioral. They involve strategies that include programmatic instruction via technology, changing the environment to support structured learning, and learning new behaviors and thinking routines. Evidence-based interventions for improving attention are listed in Table 5.1. For some of the interventions in this chapter, supplemental materials (e.g., handouts, posters, checklists, daily logs, and worksheets) that are helpful for preparing, implementing, and evaluating the interventions can be found on Q-global.

Table 5.1. Interventions for Attention

Intervention	Prevention[1]	Early Invervention[2]	Intensive Invervention[3]
Classwide Peer Tutoring	X	X	
Computer-Assisted Instruction	X	X	X
Contingency Management	X	X	X
Daily Behavior Report Cards (DBRC)		X	X
Modified Task-Presentation Strategies		X	X
Multimodal Interventions		X	X
Parent Training		X	X
Self-Management	X	X	X

[1] Prevention refers to skills that can be taught to all children or used universally; they promote better awareness and lessen the risk of problems.

[2] Early intervention includes techniques and strategies that address early warning signs or clinical signs of the risk of future problems. Early intervention may be specifically applied to one or more problems or generically applied as a skill set to prevent the development of a chronic problem. Early interventions can be delivered to groups or individuals.

[3] Intensive intervention focuses on individuals and individual problems, which are usually chronic, intensive, and require services due to the level of interference in daily functioning.

 CLASSWIDE PEER TUTORING

DESCRIPTION

Classwide peer tutoring (CWPT) is a multicomponent and multistrategy treatment program (Greenwood, Delquadri, & Carta, 1997; Greenwood, Maheady, & Delquadri, 2002; Harlacher et al., 2006) that consists of peer tutoring and interdependent, group-oriented contingency management. CWPT is an instructional intervention characterized by trained and monitored peers supporting, instructing, and providing immediate corrective feedback to each other on academic assignments (Greenwood, Maheady, & Carta, 1991). CWPT is based on the principles of maximizing student-engaged time, providing frequent opportunities for practice, increasing rates of student responding and feedback loops, and minimizing errors in learning and off-task behavior. CWPT also incorporates an element of progress monitoring by recording performance over time. Interdependent group-oriented contingency management is a system of providing positive reinforcement to a group of children for the cumulative behavior of the entire group (Alberto & Troutman, 2003). The combination of progress monitoring and interdependent group-oriented contingency management creates a system to enhance attention and learning for children with attention problems.

EXAMPLE

Mr. Elia's philosophy class has weekly quizzes on names of theoreticians and their major works. Two self-named teams (the Piagets and the Montessoris) consist of rotating partners who spend the last 10 minutes of each class quizzing each other from a preprepared notebook containing questions, a recording sheet, and a key. Points are awarded to the individual pairings as well as the overall teams. The team scores are recorded on a board to monitor as a class who is approaching a preset winning level and who could earn a grand prize at the end of the semester.

GOAL

Reduce attention problems through more one-on-one engagement with and immediate feedback from a peer.

THE BASICS

1. Establish student or team pairs.

2. Explain procedures and allow practice.

3. Have tutor present problem to tutee.

4. Have tutee present solution to tutor.

5. Have tutor provide feedback (praise, encouragement, and corrections).

6. Monitor tutoring time.

7. Reinforce appropriate behavior.

HOW TO IMPLEMENT CLASSWIDE PEER TUTORING

 PREP

- Establish age-based (i.e., same- or different-age students) as well as ability-based (i.e., same- or differing-ability levels) pairs or groups.

- Maintain these pairs or groupings for a specific period of time that is long enough for the tutor and tutee to become comfortable with each other and for the instruction to complete a sequence.

- Teach, model, and practice the procedures for tutoring during the first part of the intervention, regardless of the arrangement method. Once the procedures are established, implement the peer-tutoring sessions.

- Define the tutoring context, such as when tutoring will occur, its duration, and the general rules that apply to the tutoring sessions.

- Define the objectives of the tutoring program for the students. Objectives can be written academic or social goals, and can be individually- or group-based, but should include both tutor and tutee learning.

- Choose the subject or content area to be taught during the tutoring program.

- Notify parents of the upcoming peer tutoring. The notice should include information about the purpose of peer tutoring, the role of the children involved, the date tutoring begins, the skills to be practiced or taught, and the contact information for further questions.

- Write a lesson plan for the tutors. The plan should be scripted for reading and following directions, including the examples and the correction procedures.

- Train the tutors. In the first tutoring session, the teacher models being the tutor by actually doing the tutoring during this lesson. While modeling, the teacher should monitor the tutors' understanding of the process.

 IMPLEMENT

- Have the tutor first provide an example of the problem or question during the peer-tutoring sessions. The tutee then attempts to solve the problem. Based on the response, the tutor praises the correct answer, records the point or points, and presents the next problem. If the tutee provided an incorrect response, the tutor says, "Try again." After the second response attempt, the tutor either praises a correct response or provides the correct answer and moves on to the next problem or question. Points for a correct answer on the first attempt are more than for a correct answer given on a second attempt.

 EVALUATE

- Monitor the tutoring process. During subsequent sessions, observe peer-tutoring sessions for child focus, understanding of the process, and child progress.

- Evaluate the program by determining if the initial objectives have been met. For example, has attention improved for the class and any targeted children?

- Provide feedback to children and other interested parties (e.g., parents, school administrators) about the program's success or lessons learned.

EVIDENCE
A brief overview of research and annotated references supporting this intervention can be found on Q-global.

CONSIDERATIONS
Time for material development and child training must be taken into consideration before implementing CWPT (Harlacher et al., 2006). It is important that teachers continually monitor tutor–tutee teams, especially in order to systematically assign points as reinforcers for appropriate behavior and good tutoring. Additionally, it may be wise to avoid pairing students with attention problems together initially, to allow the entire class to adapt smoothly to CWPT procedures.

 # COMPUTER-ASSISTED INSTRUCTION

DESCRIPTION
As an intervention for attention problems, computer-assisted instruction (CAI) presents academic content on a computer to supplement direct teacher instruction. CAI can be an effective way to heighten a child's attention and interest. Learning software provides an opportunity to control and maintain the frequency of feedback and the level of engagement. Computers do what teachers cannot—provide a constant source of activity and stimulation. For rote memorization tasks, complex research and synthesis, and creation of new knowledge, CAI is well suited as an intervention for students with attention problems (Xu, Reid, & Steckelberg, 2002).

EXAMPLES
Gwynne carries a laptop and uses it to take notes in all her classes. She finds the novelty and constant activity more engaging than pencil-and-paper tasks. It keeps her focused and less distracted by peers.

Jack enters his classroom daydreaming each morning when school starts. The teacher uses a computer center in her 2nd grade room. Jack knows to go to the computers first. This routine has immediate appeal for Jack, and he walks purposefully to the computer to start math fact games rather than the seatwork his friends begin.

Karen has difficulty paying attention to a science lecture in which her teacher lists types of rocks and describes their differences. As she tries to recall names, such as *sedimentary* and *igneous*, she misses the explanation of the assignment. While the rest of the class is engaged in the activity, Karen wanders the perimeter of the room to look at other children's work to see what to do. The teacher spends 10 extra minutes with Karen, teaching the lesson and demonstrating the assignment again just for her. To help children like Karen, the teacher chooses a program from the Internet that relates the content covered in the rock unit. During lecture time, Karen can use the computer to listen to descriptions of rock types and watch videos that show the rock formations.

GOAL

Increase attention by incorporating individual computer time to provide more interactive learning and variation in how information is conveyed (e.g., color, sound, movement, rapid pacing).

THE BASICS

1. Provide a desktop, laptop, or tablet.
2. Utilize software or an app that:
   a. defines instructional objectives,
   b. highlights essential materials (e.g., large print, color),
   c. provides multiple methods of presentation (e.g., visual, auditory, text/graphic),
   d. divides content into smaller bits of information efficiently, and
   e. provides immediate feedback.

HOW TO IMPLEMENT COMPUTER-ASSISTED INSTRUCTION

 PREP

- Coordinate with technology and administrative support to obtain local grants, or utilize existing computer labs or tablet devices.
- Search online for programs (i.e., supplemental or replacement) that support classroom instruction.
- Ensure the materials are aligned with the state's curriculum frameworks or that they support the content goals of the classroom.

 IMPLEMENT

- Utilize the resources on a regular or scheduled basis for individuals or classrooms.

 EVALUATE

- Compare the individual's or class's grades before and while using a CAI system.
- Compare the individual's or class's attendance and discipline records to see if CAI provides an environment that reduces disruptive or inattentive behavior.

EVIDENCE

A brief overview of research and annotated references supporting this intervention can be found on Q-global.

CONSIDERATIONS

Consider possible CAI logistic issues; certain details can derail an otherwise thoughtful program. Ensure there are sufficient electrical outlets to support a computer and printer, and that outlets are located near the equipment. Determine if firewalls in the district protect children while allowing them to use computers for research, or if they simply run software. Assess if the computer or device has adequate server and memory space to save work, send attachments with email, and receive large files.

Neglecting to address these issues can lead to larger ones. For example, one school district received a large grant to purchase computers, but it had no funds to hire technical support and no teacher with time or expertise to run a computer lab. Another district purchased computers for a lab, but its brand-new computer room didn't have adequate power or sufficient network strength to support the entire lab of computers running simultaneously.

FOR TEACHING

In order to be effective, interventions must be consistent and persistent (Evans et al., 2006). This is especially true for CAI to remediate attention problems. Sporadic implementation may frustrate children, as it often takes several sessions for them to become acquainted with the details of a program.

While a school-supported computer lab can be a wonderful resource, a program of this nature requires substantial investment and maintenance. An individual teacher can implement CAI without such resources, although initially it may require substantial time to find and manage good software. Children should not be placed in front of computers if the teacher has not had the time to find and teach an appropriate program. Despite the preparation required, finding good computer software or content that maintains the child's interest and generates positive learning outcomes is well worth the effort. School psychologists may offer to help by locating resources or volunteering to supervise during transition times.

 CONTINGENCY MANAGEMENT

DESCRIPTION

Contingency management as an intervention for attention problems uses positive and/or negative consequences for maintaining, or failing to maintain, attention to tasks (Wolery, Bailey, & Sugai, 1988). Contingency management may involve establishing behavioral objectives for children with attention problems, such as increasing the duration of attention, decreasing episodes of inattention, decreasing the latency between requests and attending to the task, or decreasing the number of prompts required to gain the child's attention. Consider a response-cost system whereby all reinforcements (i.e., points/tokens) are given at the beginning of the day, with the goal of ending the day with a minimum number to earn a reward (Gimpel & Holland, 2003). Inappropriate behavior results in the loss of a point/token. This approach integrates positive reinforcement and response cost (i.e., negative consequences) into individual behavior intervention plans with the goal of increasing desired behavior and decreasing problem behavior (Harlacher et al., 2006). Contingency management works best when it is used consistently in both home and school environments (DuPaul & White, 2006). A token economy system is an example of an effective contingency management system. Details for implementing a token economy are found in the Independent Group-Oriented Contingency Management intervention in Chapter 3.

EXAMPLE

During independent seatwork in a general education classroom, Clint often talks to the child sitting behind him before completing his assignment. His teacher can use positive reinforcement (e.g., earning additional free-time options) and negative consequences (e.g., forfeiting his turn to feed the classroom's pet turtle) as contingency management to motivate Clint to complete his seatwork. Clint can earn reinforcers for increasing the length of time he attends to tasks or for reducing the amount of time it takes him to get back on task.

GOAL

Shape existing behavior or provide an opportunity for new behavior to take root and become a part of a child's daily routine.

THE BASICS

1. Define the behavioral objectives clearly in operationally defined terms.

2. Provide appropriate levels and types of reinforcers to shape behavior.

3. Implement response-cost contingencies as needed.

HOW TO IMPLEMENT CONTINGENCY MANAGEMENT

 PREP

- Define the child's behavior in operational terms, and determine the baseline rating of typical attention span.

- Choose just one or two concerns to target. Never choose more than three; it will become too unwieldy and not practical to implement.

- Identify who will record baseline data on the frequency (i.e., how often) or severity (i.e., how much) of the attention problem. Use this information as a sample of functioning before the intervention to permit evaluation of the degree of post-intervention improvement.

- Consider the child's preference for reinforcers. For example, if the child enjoys computer games, computer time can be earned or lost. Reinforcement surveys can help to determine reinforcers that are appropriate and meaningful to the child.

 IMPLEMENT

- Use the baseline data to set behavioral goals. Common goals include increasing the amount of time spent on task or decreasing the amount of off-task behavior during a specific time interval. Modest increases in the amount of time spent on task, such as 20%, are more appropriate than large increases, such as 100%. If age appropriate, review the goals with the child or have the child participate in goal setting.

- Review the rules for providing reinforcers, and ensure that the child understands them by asking him or her to repeat them back or to demonstrate when contingencies will occur and for what.

- Use a 1:1 ratio of behavior to reinforcement (i.e., every time the child performs the appropriate behavior, they are reinforced for it) when teaching new skills. This strengthens the association between engaging in appropriate behavior and receiving the reinforcer.

  ▲ Consider using tokens or points that can be cashed in for reinforcers at the end of a specified time period as a modification to the intervention if necessary. For example, if the child is on task, a token is earned, but if the child is off task, a token is lost. After the child has earned a certain amount of tokens (or at the end of the day or week), he or she chooses an appropriate reinforcer. Token systems are typically more effective once basic behavioral goals have been met, and the tokens can be used to maintain the behavior.

- Use an electronic or paper visual aid to track behavior. This will assist the child in understanding progress and which attention levels are being targeted.

- Provide the reinforcer to the child when he or she meets the goal. Do not provide the reinforcer if the goal is not met. Previously earned reinforcers, such as tokens, may be taken away when a goal is not met.

- Collect and examine data during the use of contingency management. You should expect to see large changes in behavior in a few days. If you do not, reconsider the implementation. Ensure reinforcement opportunities are consistent and not missed. If reinforcement opportunities appear to be inconsistent or missed, revisit the implement phase.

- Remain aware of the potential for satiation or boredom with a reinforcer, such as filling up on candy or getting tired of listening to music.

- After consistent effects are established, thin and fade the schedule of reinforcement to become more unpredictable and more irregular over time to avoid creating dependency on rewards to obtain appropriate behavior.

EVIDENCE

A brief overview of research and annotated references supporting this intervention can be found on Q-global.

CONSIDERATIONS

FOR AGE AND DEVELOPMENTAL LEVEL

Special consideration should be given to the amount of reinforcement provided when using contingency management with children who experience attention problems. Attention problems often are associated with a low level of frustration tolerance. As a result, the use of continuous reinforcement can be particularly effective. While reliance on continuous reinforcement can sometimes be faded successfully, reinforcement should be reintroduced immediately if behavior levels fall below expectations. Continuous external reinforcement of attention serves as a functional replacement for self-regulation skills, which may or may not be developed.

When asking children to generate a list of desired reinforcers, it is important to remind them to list things that are both realistic and age appropriate. Consider asking a parent to list some examples of attainable reinforcers and then giving the child the option to choose from that list. When generating a list of reinforcers, consult with teachers or other adults who may be able to provide information about the child's preferences and high-interest activities. Young children may be more comfortable with a small number of choices (e.g., a fruit snack, rocking in a chair, choosing a song for circle time). Older children may prefer access to music, social time with peers, one-on-one time with a teacher, or alone time. Consider the effects of satiation; if the child has unlimited or extensive access to the reinforcer, the reinforcer weakens over time. To maintain effectiveness and avoid habituation, periodically change or rotate the reinforcer.

DAILY BEHAVIOR REPORT CARDS

DESCRIPTION

Daily behavior report cards (DBRCs; also referred to as home notes, home-based reinforcement, daily report cards, and school–home notes) are used to record a child's behavior each day (Chafouleas et al., 2002; Riley-Tillman et al., 2007). Here, DBRCs are discussed as a specific intervention strategy for students with attention problems. School–home communication is typically recommended but not required.

A DBRC is implemented to change behavior by providing systematic feedback on performance and progress to children and parents, followed by appropriate reinforcement. The result is increased attention (or decreased inattention) during specific tasks and conditions.

There are many variations of DBRCs that make this approach easy to customize for a particular child or situation. For example, a DBRC can include either a short list of appropriate behaviors, with each behavior receiving a grade, or a single behavior that the child is working on. DBRCs can also be used with more than one teacher. These records can be managed and shared in various ways using either electronic transmission or a simple log or notebook kept for parent signatures

(Burke & Vannest, 2008). DBRCs provide a reliable way to track behavioral goals and objectives that are included in an individualized education program (IEP; Vannest et al., 2010), and to monitor progress in response to intervention (RTI) models.

EXAMPLE

Mario is a 3rd grader who has difficulty attending to tasks. Each morning, Mario's teacher reads a short book to the class. While she reads, Mario often sprawls out on the floor, picks at the carpet, and fidgets with his shirt. Mario does not answer questions about the story, indicating he was most likely not attending. Using a DBRC, his teacher identifies the target behaviors of sitting, listening, and attending to the morning's story. She then assigns a letter grade to evaluate these target behaviors, which are used to operationally define attention in this situation. A grade higher than a "C" means that he engaged in the target behaviors. This grade is given to Mario, charted in a report, and sent home daily for his parents to sign. After reading time, Mario's teacher allows him to look at a graph of his attention and she praises each daily increase. At home, his mother rewards him with 30 minutes of computer game time for each day that he receives an "A" or "B" grade.

GOAL

Increase the child's attention to specific tasks and conditions through monitoring, feedback, and communication with children and parents at home.

THE BASICS

1. Define the target behaviors.

2. Monitor and record behaviors daily.

3. Provide reinforcement for exhibiting the target behaviors.

4. Communicate results to children and parents.

HOW TO IMPLEMENT DAILY BEHAVIOR REPORT CARDS

 PREP

- Identify the target behaviors for improving attention.

- Identify the rater of the target behavior.

- Identify if the DBRC will be used for communication, monitoring, or performance feedback, and if it will involve contingencies. Contingencies may be delivered at school during feedback sessions and at home for performance at school.

- Create and explain the rating system to raters. For example, assign a letter grade to the child's performance for each day. Each target behavior is rated daily. Letter grades (instead of frequency of behavior, for example) are preferable because they are usually more meaningful to children and parents.

- Explain the behavioral anchors (i.e., typical behavior for earning each grade) to avoid variance among raters or differences in personal tolerance levels. For example, attending during 10 out of 20 minutes of class time may earn a "C," 15 minutes may earn a "B," and 17 minutes or more might earn an "A."

IMPLEMENT

- Ask the rater to begin ratings on a specific day and during a specific time period.

- Show ratings to the child in feedback sessions and provide brief, encouraging feedback. For example, "You earned a 'B' because you sat and listened for 15 minutes. If you sit and listen for 17 or more minutes, you will earn an 'A.' Good job, keep it up!"

- Consider graphing or charting progress, depending on the age, developmental level, and interest of the child.

- Consider using the ratings as part of a checking in and checking out system. The child may check in at the beginning of the day to get a pep talk and receive reminders of goals or targets, and then check out at the end of the day to review performance and discuss goals or targets for the next day.

- Reward the child either at home or school for meeting performance goals. This step may or may not be needed for some children.

 EVALUATE

- Compare the ratings from before the intervention with the ratings during the intervention to determine if the change occurring is large enough to be useful for the school setting.

  ▲ Changes in behavior should be moderate to large when the intervention is used throughout the day.

- Ensure reinforcement has been used consistently if the change is not moderate to large. Reassess reinforcer quality and feedback quality. Consider graphing or charting performance goals if those visual aids are not currently in place.

EVIDENCE

A brief overview of research and annotated references supporting this intervention can be found on Q-global.

CONSIDERATIONS

This intervention works better when the reinforcement communicated is positive instead of negative. DBRCs are not meant as a channel for communicating punishment or for reporting daily bad behavior. Ideally, they are used to provide objective and frequent feedback to the child and to communicate progress to the parents.

It is important to be accurate with the estimate of current performance and to avoid overrating when creating the initial behavior rating. For example, classifying a child's current attention level as a "B" grade might indicate that his or her current performance level is above average, calling into question why the report card is needed in the first place. In addition, this grade may not allow the child enough room for improvement, leading to increased frustration. Instead, "C" or "D" grades should be anchored as a child's present level of performance. Identify areas for improvement in a way that is not damaging to a child's feelings or self-concept. If a child is upset by these initial ratings, explain why the current level of performance is hindering his or her success in school and how he or she can improve. Set appropriately high expectations and provide encouragement.

Using letter grades to rate behavioral performance, unlike more typical measures of behavior (e.g., frequency counts, duration measures), may appear subjective or unfair to parents and students. However, the ease of understanding letter grades outweighs the possible benefits of using behavior measures that seem more scientific yet are not accessible to the child and parents. Discuss the behavioral anchors (i.e., typical behavior for earning each grade) with the child and parents before implementing DBRCs, and explain how the grades will be used to minimize differences among multiple raters, lessening any impact on the child's behavior grades.

When setting performance goals, be sure to set a level that is challenging but attainable. Goals should become more difficult with time to encourage shaping of the behavior to the desired level (Chronis et al., 2006). Setting unattainable goals only leads to frustration.

FOR AGE AND DEVELOPMENTAL LEVEL

Younger children often respond quickly and positively to teacher attention and feedback. An older child may be embarrassed to receive daily grades on behavior for fear it may suggest to peers that he or she has a problem.

FOR CULTURAL AND LANGUAGE DIFFERENCES

Communication with parents is a critical component of DBRCs. Effective communication with parents may necessitate use of the home language. It is important to give careful consideration to facilitating accurate explanation of the DBRC's purpose and the process.

MODIFIED TASK-PRESENTATION STRATEGIES

DESCRIPTION

Modified task-presentation strategies refer to a collection of specific options that can be used to increase the interest level of an activity with the goal of increasing the amount of time a child is attentive and engaged. Tasks are altered using antecedent instructional modifications based on information obtained through a functional behavioral assessment (Ervin et al., 1998; Kern & Clemens, 2007; Raggi & Chronis, 2006). A number of recommended modification strategies are discussed in this section (and see also Carbone, 2001; Kern & Clemens, 2007; Montague & Warger, 1997; and Salend et al., 2003).

OFFER A CHOICE OF INSTRUCTIONAL ACTIVITIES

Encouraging children to engage in active decision making and to exercise control over making choices can help increase their level of attention. Using this approach, children choose activities, materials, or a task sequence within a set of instructional materials outlined by the teacher (Dunlap et al., 1994; Kern et al., 2002; Powell & Nelson, 1997).

For example, a child might choose the order of the completion of assignments, decide which group of children he or she will work with, or select among types of responses (e.g., oral, written). However, this approach is successful only when the choices offered to the child are relevant to the curriculum or learning objectives. Consideration should be given to ensure that learning goals are not compromised. For example, choosing between two equally unattractive options will be unpopular with the child, and doing only half of the assignment versus doing all of the assignment will be unacceptable to the teacher. Agreeing on the conditions for each choice is critical and is best done prior to any possible conflicts between child and teacher interests.

PROVIDE GUIDED NOTES AND INSTRUCTION IN ATTENDING TO RELEVANT INFORMATION

In this strategy, the teacher provides guided notes to help the child follow along during lectures and class presentations. Guided notes contain some information about the lecture or presentation, but spaces are left for children to fill in the most relevant and important ideas. Schematic maps that outline relationships between concepts and require children to fill in relevant details are another useful form of guided notes. For example, a teacher may outline his or her own lecture notes and create a second set for the children, with only the beginnings of key points or section headers, leaving space for children to complete the rest. Additionally, the teacher can provide direct instruction on note taking, help directly with note taking, or involve a peer who can help (Evans, Pelham, & Grudberg, 1995). These strategies help correctly focus attention and require an active written response, which increases attending behavior.

USE HIGH-INTEREST ACTIVITIES AND HANDS-ON DEMONSTRATIONS

Activities and tasks that are novel and interesting to children can increase work productivity (Carbone, 2001; Clarke, et al., 1995). Providing moderate levels of auditory stimuli (e.g., music) during familiar tasks with structured responses, and in turn, reducing classroom noise while children are engaged in learning new concepts, can provide cues to the different types of attention each task requires (Scott, 1970; Zentall, 1983). Teachers can begin lessons with high-interest activities that require participation and facilitate attention. Examples include demonstrating practical applications (especially in subjects such as math or science), playing music or film clips, engaging in role-plays, or using examples related to current events (either community or world events, or events related to child activities).

Modify In-Class Assignments and Responses

There are many ways assignments can be modified to accommodate children who struggle with attention problems. However, modifications are not a permanent solution for many children. In addition, modifications eventually should be phased out so that task demands in class resemble task demands in a living or post-school environment. While modifications and supports are in place, interventions to increase attention on a long-term basis must also be implemented. Examples of allowable modifications include using technology when completing written assignments (Council for Exceptional Children, 1992; Kern, Childs, Dunlap, Clarke, & Falk, 1994; Kern & Clemens, 2007), dividing longer assignments into multiple shorter tasks, reducing the number and types of items (Kern et al., 1994), allowing oral responses, giving written directions with expectations for completing the assignment (Ervin et al., 1998), and listening to music while doing work (Abikoff, Courtney, Szeibel, & Koplewicz, 1996).

Modify Homework

Homework requires good attention skills on many levels. The child must bring the work home, understand the directions for starting the assignment, remember to complete the assignment, and return the assignment to school. While these aspects of homework are taken for granted by many, they can be a source of stress for children with attention problems. Homework can be modified very successfully by decreasing the amount given, allowing extended time for its completion, using routine procedures (e.g., homework planners), providing assistance through one-on-one or group tutoring or via the telephone or Internet (Habboushe et al., 2001; Salend et al., 2003; Stormont-Spurgin, 1997), or allowing it to be completed at school instead of at home.

Highlight Relevant Material or Key Information with Colors, Symbols, or Font Changes

Providing cues in large or complex tasks and lessons can help children attend to the most relevant material and filter out unnecessary stimuli that prevent them from attending to the correct information. Possible cues include using highlighters or using larger or different fonts or graphics. These cues can be facilitated with computer word-processing programs or via child teams that identify these cues prior to presentation of the lesson. Adding novelty through color increases intra-task stimulation, and when used judiciously, stresses the importance of task features (Zentall, 1993). Teachers may also do this with the class as a group by leading children through exercises (e.g., main ideas are highlighted in one color, vocabulary words in another color).

Provide Increased Opportunities to Respond

In this strategy, children are given increased opportunities to respond to academic material using varied response methods, such as written responses, the class answering in unison, and individual answer cards (Montague & Warger, 1997; Sutherland et al., 2003). When children have more opportunities to respond, they tend to be more engaged and attentive and, as a secondary benefit, academic performance tends to improve. Counting the number of responses per child per hour is one way to monitor the amount of interaction between the children and the teacher (and consequently how difficult it may be for children to sustain attention). For example, if a class has 20 children, and the teacher asks 20 questions during a 20-minute presentation, each child should actively participate approximately one time. However, a teacher could instead use individual answer cards and ask each child to write a response on his or her card and then show the teacher his or her response by holding up the card. In this case, every child participates 20 times in 20 minutes and attention is maintained due to the pace and immediacy of the task.

Vary the Pace of Instruction

Briskly paced instruction increases levels of on-task behavior because rapid pacing is thought to require more attending effort (Kern & Clemens, 2007; Skinner et al., 1995). Teachers can increase the pacing of their instruction either by increasing their rate of presenting material or by decreasing the length of instructional pauses (Kern & Clemens, 2007).

GOAL

Modify task presentation in order to maximize the child's attention and engagement.

THE BASICS

1. Assess the instructional preferences and abilities of the person presenting the information to identify feasible modifications.

2. Conduct an FBA to determine the function of the attention problems.

3. Assess the needs and abilities of the child to identify the best candidates for an effective modification from the list of feasible modifications.

4. Select from among the best candidates one or more strategies that best fit the content of the lesson.

5. Prepare necessary materials to facilitate the modification.

6. Present the task using the modified strategy.

7. Monitor effectiveness of the modification and adjust as necessary.

HOW TO IMPLEMENT MODIFIED TASK-PRESENTATION STRATEGIES

 PREP

- Use assessment or observation data to determine which strategies best fit the person delivering the content, the needs of the child, and the content of the lesson.

- Identify the differences in when, where, and how the typical group instruction or tasks vary from those for a targeted or individual group, or if the strategy will be a menu-like choice selection for all children.

- Prepare materials if necessary, and plan the modification if it involves changing presentation style or a modification to the environment (e.g., music).

 IMPLEMENT

- Present the task using the modified strategy.

 EVALUATE

- Engage in direct observation of the child's attention problems and class performance as a whole.

- Determine which modifications seem to have the greatest positive impact and which are ineffective using observational data. Continue use of those modifications that are effective, and discontinue those that are not.

EVIDENCE

A brief overview of research and annotated references supporting this intervention can be found on Q-global.

CONSIDERATIONS

FOR TEACHING

Instructional interventions require compatibility between teacher disposition and skill. A teacher may be less willing to make changes because he or she is committed to a particular style or teaching method based on personal values and beliefs about education. A teacher may also view an attention problem as lack of effort rather than a valid learning problem. He or she may feel threatened or appear insensitive when instructional changes are suggested for children who are already demanding and who represent a fraction of the population the teacher must serve. A well-intentioned teacher, on the other hand, may simply not have enough time or resources to adapt his or her lesson plans. Always keep the complex relationship between teachers and children in mind. Teachers and children often have reciprocal behaviors, and the dynamics of this exchange may reinforce or punish the type of teaching used in the classroom. Rely on the experience of the classroom teacher and his or her appraisal of the situation, and anticipate the level of control and effort teachers may expect when recommending changes in instructional behaviors.

Because there are many different types of instructional modification interventions for attention problems, they have the largest likelihood of success when implemented after a functional behavioral assessment. Such an assessment can help to uncover the antecedents and consequences and reveal the environmental and setting-based conditions that set the stage for the attention problems. For example, a child who struggles to bring back completed homework will not find high-interest, novel, or engaging classroom activities helpful in learning the specific attention skill needed to improve his or her grades.

 # MULTIMODAL INTERVENTIONS

DESCRIPTION

Multimodal interventions for attention problems are multiple solutions for previously learned maladaptive behaviors, current performance, and future learning, based on the view that multiple factors within the child and his/her environment impacts these behaviors. Multimodal interventions typically involve both home and school environments. For this reason, and because consistent application of treatments is most effective, children improve most quickly when parents and schools work together to set expectations for behavior and implement consequences. The use of pharmacology for ADHD has been increasing, with 6.1% of children ages 4–17 taking medication for the disorder in 2011 (Centers for Disease Control and Prevention, 2014). Such use of medication is implemented under the control of the parents in careful consultation with a physician and may be administered in school settings with parent consent. Feedback on drug effects and side effects may originate from school officials more often than parents, because task demands in these settings are different. One or both parents may report that their child is "just like I was" in school and that this apparent genetic link may contribute to a lack of compensatory skills. Parents may believe that the child's inattention in school is simply something to be outgrown.

Multimodal interventions involve teaching new skills to improve attention and prevent future problems while also remediating any deficits that exist academically, socially, or in self-regulation. These combination treatments are more complex to initiate and involve multiple participants. Sometimes it is difficult to ascertain which relative parts are responsible for improvements. The effect of the whole treatment is often more beneficial than the sum of its parts. The synergy from multiple interventions applied at the same time can help shape self-regulating individuals who need little or no intervention to maintain attention in a way that is functional, allowing them to achieve their goals without outside support.

EXAMPLE

Randall is a bright, energetic 6-year-old who loves to disassemble objects. His daydreaming makes him difficult to teach in the classroom, and repeating instructions frustrates his teacher. His mom thinks Randall is a typical boy, much like her three brothers. She thinks Randall simply needs more time to mature and jokes that his future wife will need to organize things like she does for her brothers. Randall's dad, however, disagrees and believes Randall needs more discipline.

Randall's teacher, Mr. Johnson, is concerned that he is not an immature or indulged 6-year-old, but rather a child who struggles to pay attention. Randall's inattention may be at the root of his poor reading performance, which is significantly below his peers. During a parent–teacher conference, Mr. Johnson describes Randall's reading problems and new behavior of showing signs of frustration and aggression when he is frequently reprimanded for not paying attention or doing his work. After asking about a family history of attention problems, Mr. Johnson suggests assessment to rule out attention problems. The assessment confirms that Randall is suffering from attention problems and supports Mr. Johnson's theory about Randall's reading performance.

Several weeks later, Randall is evaluated for the effects of a psychostimulant medication and contingency management plan (both resulting from the assessment). As part of a contingency management plan, Randall receives cookies and milk as an after-school snack when he comes home with a good teacher report. His teacher and parents closely monitor

Randall's response to the medication, looking for any changes in sleep, appetite, weight, and motor activity. Both the school and his parents communicate weekly via email about Randall's progress. Randall seems happier in class and says that the medicine takes away the noise of the cars in the parking lot and the clicking heels in the hallway. Randall's improved ability to attend has lessened Mr. Johnson's frustration, and he now has more time to focus on positive classroom activities instead of Randall's discipline issues.

GOAL

Identify and provide a comprehensive approach to treatment that can help address current performance problems; remediate deficits in skills across social, behavioral, or academic domains; and build a strong foundation for learning the new skills necessary for success in school and beyond.

THE BASICS

1. Provide multiple treatments with appropriate personnel simultaneously or in sequence, including:

    a. Contingency management,

    b. Daily behavior report cards,

    c. Modified task-presentation strategies,

    d. Self-management of attention,

    e. Classwide peer tutoring, and/or

    f. Computer-assisted instruction.

2. Determine the responsible team members for implementing and monitoring treatments.

HOW TO IMPLEMENT MULTIMODAL INTERVENTIONS

 PREP

- Use individual assessments or team evaluation to determine the causal factors associated with the attention problems, and identify the exact interventions to be used from the multimodal framework based on assessment results.

- Decide on a length of treatment based on the severity of the causal factors. (With multimodal interventions, treatment may be provided for longer periods of time than with single interventions.)

- Identify the specific team members (e.g., psychologist, social worker, case worker, parents) to provide services based on the prescribed interventions.

 IMPLEMENT

- Implement the interventions simultaneously.

- Fade interventions in frequency or duration systematically to transfer new skills to the classroom or home environment, without as much structure or support.

 EVALUATE

- Use progress monitoring data or repeated measures of performance to determine success or growth on the targeted attention problems.

- Track any potential medication side effects, such as changes in mood, weight or appetite, sleep patterns, or other behaviors as suggested by the physician.

- Implement booster sessions as needed.

- Review the number of interventions used and their complexity and determine their overall acceptability by those involved (e.g., ask implementers their opinion informally, survey formally).

EVIDENCE

A brief overview of research and annotated references supporting this intervention can be found on Q-global.

CONSIDERATIONS

As with individual approaches, it is important to identify the best treatment options for everyone involved. Pharmacology has generally been shown to be an effective intervention. However, the most recent findings from a comprehensive, longitudinal study suggest that while pharmacological approaches have demonstrated effectiveness at 14 and 24 months, follow-up assessments at 36 months showed pharmacological approaches to have no greater effects than behavioral or combined treatment approaches (Swanson et al., 2008a, 2008b).

As stressed in other sections of this guide, the decision to use psychopharmacological interventions is a matter for careful consideration among parents, the child, and the physician who would manage such an intervention. Small negative effects have been seen in height and weight measures at one year, but these diminish and do not appear to impact long-term growth (Faraone et al., 2008). Less intrusive interventions, such as strategy use and skill instruction, typically should be attempted before trying more complicated ones.

Parents, counselors, and teachers should not take a wait-and-see attitude or leave improvement to chance or future development. Instead, early action involves little risk, especially interventions that involve school–home communication, teaching skills, and modifying problem behavior. It is best to keep an open mind toward proactive approaches that benefit children (even those who may not warrant a diagnosis of attention problems).

In some cases, children with attention problems simply lack listening and study skills. Strategic listening and study skills can be taught. Instruments such as the School Motivation and Learning Strategies Inventory (SMALSI; Stroud & Reynolds, 2006) are specifically designed to assess listening, study skills, and related learning strategies and may be useful in determining whether the observed attention problems are the result of a lack of skills. When skill deficits are determined to be a root or related cause of attention problems, such skills can be taught effectively using common approaches taken from direct instruction methods.

 **PARENT TRAINING**

DESCRIPTION

Parenting interventions are based on a gene-environment explanation of the developmental course of attention problems in ADHD and potential negative parenting, such as coercive, intrusive, and restrictive practices (Doyle, 2004). Children who are more difficult to parent are more susceptible to negative parenting techniques and more affected by harsh parenting (Sheese et al., 2007; Swanson et al., 2008a, 2008b). The focus is on early intervention and training for the child and parents, particularly where barriers exist in the home or community to receiving services.

EXAMPLE

Juliette and Andrew are parents of two boys under the age of 8, and both boys show problems with attention. As their boys age and appear to respond less and less to their parenting techniques, they receive advice and feel the need to "clamp down" more and more when things are not working. When gentle prompting and requests appear to be ignored, the father, Andrew, increases his tone and level of punishment. The mom, Juliette, becomes increasingly agitated as she sees her two boys responding differently than other same-age children on the playground and at school with teachers and friends. Juliette is beginning to wonder if her skills are not enough and takes to heart the advice of her friends and family to be stronger and "lay down the law." As both parents become more frustrated, their parenting styles become increasingly harsh and inconsistent. The school psychologist recommends some parent training offered locally to assist Juliette and Andrew in recalibrating parenting skills specifically for children with attention problems. Parents attend the training once a week to learn skills, share experiences with other struggling parents, and receive homework to complete before each meeting. Dinner, childcare, and carpooling are provided to ease the burden of attendance.

GOAL

Help parents develop skills for encouraging attention and develop greater understanding of factors that contribute to inattention.

THE BASICS

1. Discuss goals and expected outcomes in an introduction session.

2. Teach and review parenting skills through modeling strategies and rehearsing, using videos and other prepared materials in a number of scheduled weekly sessions. Cases, shared examples, or brainstorming sessions can be used to identify parenting errors and provide effective solutions.

3. Assign homework and review in each session.

HOW TO IMPLEMENT PARENT TRAINING

 PREP

- Conduct an intake assessment with the family. This assessment includes an evaluation of the family climate to determine the needs of the family and any barriers to success, including cultural–parental expectations (Kotchick & Forehand, 2002).

- Determine if group or individual parent training will work for the implementer and the setting.

- Identify the instructor and location for trainings.

- Create or purchase materials for training (see the parent tip sheets that may be purchased to accompany this guide for prepared strategies and information).

- Determine the duration (e.g., two hours) and the number of sessions (e.g., 3, 5, or 10).

- Consider the following sample topics:
  - ▲ Defining attention problems
  - ▲ Praise and reinforcement
  - ▲ Planned ignoring
  - ▲ Anger management
  - ▲ Conflict resolution
  - ▲ Premack's principle or "grandma's rule": when you do X, then you can do Y
  - ▲ Precorrection and anticipating challenging situations
  - ▲ Contingent rewards, or tokens/points systems
  - ▲ Time out
  - ▲ Choosing your battles

- Arrange for transportation, meals, and childcare, as needed, to promote participation.

- Invite or assign parents or caregivers to training sessions.

- Provide a broad overview of the goals of the intervention, the relevance of the information to be presented, and the responsibilities of the parents in the process (e.g., follow-through, attendance).

IMPLEMENT

- Use the parent training materials that were created or purchased during the prep phase to introduce new topics.

- Explain the relevance and importance of the topics to attention problems and their consequences.

- Model or view examples of parenting errors and effective parenting skills that can serve as solutions.

- Role-play and answer questions.

- Problem-solve challenges to the skill.

- Provide corrective feedback.

- Assign simple homework.

- Encourage independent implementation by requesting the use of the technique a specific number of times before the next session. Additionally, request that the parents document the effects, problems encountered, and any questions that arise.

- Assist parents throughout the process of choosing effective and preferred parenting and child management techniques.

- After training sessions are completed, refresher sessions or periodic individual sessions may be needed to review and maintain the skills learned. In many cases, parents will receive training in three or four topics over several sessions.

 EVALUATE

- Conduct surveys at the end of each session to assess satisfaction and utility of the information.

- Directly observe changes in parenting skills during the parent training sessions and instruct or redirect accordingly.

- Have a parent or outside observer (e.g., family member, teacher) complete a progress monitoring form regarding the child's ability to pay attention.

EVIDENCE
A brief overview of research and annotated references supporting this intervention can be found on Q-global.

CONSIDERATIONS
As Anastopoulos et al. (1991) explain, a critical element for successfully implementing parent training is establishing trusting, collaborative relationships between the instructor and the parents/caregivers. To this end, instructors are advised to convey genuine understanding and support, avoid professional jargon, incorporate humor, and keep the discussion grounded in realistic examples and scenarios. Some parents may prefer to receive parent training in a multifamily group context while others may prefer an individual-family basis; this decision is based largely on parent preference, the clinical judgment of the therapist, and logistical considerations. Ideally, both parents will attend the training sessions. If this is not feasible, consider asking the parents or caregivers to alternate attendance to the training sessions or share the information via audio recording (Anastopoulos et al., 1991).

FOR AGE AND DEVELOPMENTAL LEVEL
Early intervention is often shown to be effective and is particularly relevant for parent training. Providing training to parents of young children as early as possible can have a positive effect on a child's typical behavior patterns and routines as well as on parenting styles.

For Cultural and Language Differences

Communication is critical for parent training; thus, using the primary language of the family and understanding the values of the family are essential to building an effective partnership. If beliefs about the condition or the treatment are radically different than those of the school, all key stakeholders would benefit from a discussion about expectations for success in the school setting while maintaining an attitude of tolerance and understanding for the culture of the home.

 SELF-MANAGEMENT

DESCRIPTION

Self-management strategies for attention problems are techniques that children can use to become more aware and develop better management of their own behavior. Children are taught to focus on their attention through self-observation, self-recording, self-evaluation, self-monitoring, and self-reinforcing (Harris, Friedlander, Saddler, Frizzelle, & Graham, 2005; Mace et al., 2001; Reid et al., 2005). Through self-management strategies, children continuously assess their attention behavior and self-cue appropriate behavior. They eventually learn to inhibit automatic responses (Barkley, 1997). This type of meta-cognitive activity is helpful for children across ages and settings. Children who successfully apply self-management strategies can feel a great sense of self-determination, which can have a positive impact on their opinions of themselves. There are endless variations for children or adults using one or more of the steps, and most adaptations offer similar positive results.

EXAMPLES

Ms. Wilson, an 8th-grade math teacher, instructs her students to turn in the daily assignment at the end of the class period. One student, Linda, turns her paper in with only 6 out of 20 problems completed. When the teacher asks why, Linda says she understands the work but was "thinking about something else" during independent work time. Ms. Wilson assumes Linda was daydreaming or writing a note because she was not disruptive, so Ms. Wilson assigns the remainder of the assignment to Linda as homework. The next day, Linda says that she did the work at home, but she can't find it in her backpack and can't remember where she left it. This situation creates frustration for both Linda and her teacher. A self-monitoring system could help Linda recognize when she is and is not paying attention to a task and why time gets away from her. The system could also be used to help Linda transport her homework from home to school and from her locker or backpack to the teacher's desk.

Joel, another student in Ms. Wilson's class, spends most of the independent work time sitting near the teacher's desk, where he plays with his pencil, invents games with paperclips, and looks around frequently to see what the teacher is doing. Self-monitoring with a cuing system could help Joel pay attention to his assignment and allow him to complete tasks and earn rewards. If he learns to use the system, it could help Joel to start and finish relevant tasks throughout his schooling.

GOAL

Increase the child's awareness of his or her own level of attention in order to produce an automatic response without relying on external reinforcement or prompting.

THE BASICS

1. Teach the child the skill of self-observing.
2. Teach the child the skill of self-monitoring/self-recording.
3. Instruct the child on how to self-evaluate.
4. Teach the child to reinforce him- or herself.

HOW TO IMPLEMENT SELF-MANAGEMENT

 PREP

- Determine the specific area for self-management of attention (e.g., attention to task, completion of assignments, impulsivity control, organizational skills).

- Determine the cuing method for the self-management (e.g., audio cue tape, wrist counter, teacher signal).

- Identify the paper self-recording form.

- Identify a goal.

- Determine a reinforcer.

- Gain commitment for participation from the child.

- Determine if an adult will provide simultaneous monitoring and recording for accuracy checks later. (If so, be sure to demonstrate to both the child and adult during the IMPLEMENT step.)

- Determine if whole group or individual monitoring will take place. Whole classes can record even if one child or a small group of children are the target.

 IMPLEMENT

- Explain both the rationale for using self-management techniques and the specific benefits the child might expect in a conversational and nonpunitive manner. For example, it can be important to point out that self-monitoring lets you be in charge of yourself and pay attention to things that you want to do better. It can be helpful to point out real life examples (e.g., used by athletes, strong readers, mathematicians, gamers). Benefits of this technique might include better attention, not getting into trouble as much from parents and teachers, a better reputation at school with friends, improved grades, and feeling better about yourself.

- Identify current performance and set goals. Discuss current classroom functioning using baseline data, and have the child set a goal for the target behavior (e.g., an amount of focused attention, a number of assignments completed, an organizational skill such as being prepared for class).

- Demonstrate the self-monitoring technique, and explain how to use any equipment or forms (e.g., audio cue tape, self-recording form, wrist counter).

- Explain what cuing is and how it will work. Discuss and determine how often the cue will be heard or seen (e.g., every 30 seconds for 10 minutes, or every 1 minute for 20 minutes during a certain class or instructional time).

- Demonstrate how the child will record his or her attention to task when the cue is heard. The cues or prompts can be audio recorded or generated by a watch with intermittent beeps; intervals from 15 seconds up to 2 minutes can be used, depending on the child. At the sound of each prompt, the child records if he or she is or isn't paying attention by placing a checkmark on the self-monitoring sheet.

- Ask the child to demonstrate the techniques and check for his or her understanding.

- Start the cuing and prompt if necessary to remind the child to record.

- Sum and monitor attention levels. Provide a basic level of reinforcement for participation even if goals are not met, and provide a higher level of reinforcement when goals are met.

- If an adult was monitoring the child at the same time, ask the child and adult to compare their recording forms.

  ▲ Place scores on a single graph to facilitate the comparison.

  ▲ Discuss if the scores are dramatically different—allowing for some degree of error is acceptable and expected.

  ▲ Highly praise and encourage perfectly matched scores as a goal depending on the number of intervals.

- Encourage the child to self-reinforce the behavior both for attending and for consistently and accurately recording the attending behavior. Reinforcement is phased out as naturally occurring reinforcement takes place (e.g., better grades, better skills, less discipline in classrooms).

EVIDENCE

A brief overview of research and annotated references supporting this intervention can be found on Q-global.

CONSIDERATIONS

FOR TEACHING

Self-management techniques can be effective even when a child is inaccurate in his or her recording. Accuracy, and thus attention to detail, can be encouraged by matching the child and teacher ratings. If teacher ratings aren't available or viable, the child can submit self-recorded information to another adult (for a contingent reward). The most efficient rewards using this approach are self-rewards (i.e., those given by the child to himself or herself), not rewards from the adult with whom the child has contact.

Self-management strategies can be effective in improving many aspects of daily life that require a child's attention (e.g., behavior, academic performance, and social interactions). Therefore, thoughtfully consider the goal of the intervention. If the objective is to increase attention for better academic performance, simply monitoring and recording attention to a task may not produce the same results that monitoring and recording task accuracy or completion might. However, attention to the task may be the primary goal in other situations. For example, if a child's inattention causes problems working on group assignments or creates a tense child–teacher relationship, but the child's grades aren't suffering, better attention to the task itself may be the best solution. Self-management of attention in social situations (both at home and school) can involve teaching children to paraphrase mentally, to silently count their distracting thoughts as a prompt to refocus attention, or to select only a few things to pay attention to.

FOR AGE AND DEVELOPMENTAL LEVEL

Sometimes attending to stimuli is a challenge beyond the child's abilities. The boredom factor in inattention is a lack of stimulation that everyone has experienced at one time or another in long meetings or at social activities. Individuals with strong social skills know how to read the environment for social cues and expectations and are able to effectively present the necessary cues for paying attention, even when not fully attending. As mentioned, some children with attention problems do not experience concurrent academic failure or learning problems but simply have discipline issues related to their attention problems. In some cases, speaking frankly with older children about how to present appropriate social cues, such as making eye contact, nodding, or finding ways to stay engaged so as not to disrupt someone else can do much to assist a bright child who is struggling to maintain attention when there is not enough stimulation in the environment. It is important to present children with socially acceptable methods of operating in their environment. For example, telling the geometry teacher the lecture is boring has worse consequences than a quick lesson on social skills and how to doodle discreetly.

Chapter 6

Interventions for Academic Problems

Characteristics and Conditions of Academic Problems

WHAT ARE ACADEMIC PROBLEMS?

Learning problems can encompass a variety of academic domains, including reading, writing, spelling, and mathematics. Behavior problems predict lower academic scores (Breslau et al., 2009). In fact, research consistently shows that students with emotional and behavioral disturbance demonstrate little to no improvement over time in academic areas (Siperstein, Wiley, & Forness, 2011). These students achieve significantly below grade-level expectations: 61% fall in the bottom quartile in reading; 43% fall in the bottom quartile in math; 85% score below the norm on language measures; and 68% have clinical language deficits and are unsuccessful in written expression, underperforming by more than one grade level (Coutinho, 1986; Cullinan, Epstein, & Lloyd, 1991; Epstein, Kinder, & Bursuck, 1989; Kauffman, Cullinan, & Epstein, 1987; Lochman et al., 2012; Scruggs & Mastropieri, 1986; Trout, Nordness, Pierce, & Epstein, 2003; Wagner, Kutash, Duchnowski, Epstein, & Sumi, 2005). The link between academic problems and behavior is best addressed comprehensively (McIntosh, Sadler, & Brown, 2012; Nelson, Benner, Lane, & Smith, 2004).

Learning difficulties can cause problems beyond the classroom. For example, children who have learning disorders frequently struggle with interpersonal relationships (Smith-Bonahue, Larmore, Harman, & Castillo, 2009). The pervasive nature of academic problems—their influence on numerous content areas and academic skills—often makes dealing with academic problems challenging for both teacher and student alike and requires diligence and a long-term approach to intervention strategies to achieve successful remediation.

Learning challenges can be compounded for students with emotional and behavioral disorders, whose academic failures may also be due to problems with acquiring and processing information (Lane, Carter, Pierson, & Glaeser, 2006; Mooney, Epstein, Reid, & Nelson, 2003; Wagner et al., 2005). These learning problems are significant contributors to increased risk of earning lower grades, being retained, and dropping out of school (Balfanz, Herzog, & Mac Iver, 2007; Bowers, 2010; Locke & Fuchs, 1995). Moreover, about half of students who are identified as having learning disabilities are suspended in or from school or are expelled (Cortiella & Horowitz, 2014). Therefore, academic intervention is as important as the typical social and behavioral interventions (Landrum, Tankersley, & Kauffman, 2003; Lane, 2004; Lane, Barton-Arwood, Nelson, & Wehby, 2008; Simpson, 1999; Vannest, Harrison, Temple-Harvey, Ramsey, & Parker, 2011; Vannest, Harvey, & Mason, 2009).

HOW COMMON ARE ACADEMIC PROBLEMS?

In U.S. public schools about 2.4 million students, or 5%, are classified as having learning disabilities under the *Individuals with Disabilities Education Improvement Act* (IDEIA, 2004). The number of additional students who experience academic problems because of unidentified learning disabilities and attention problems is 15% or higher (Cortiella & Horowitz, 2014). Dyslexia, which involves difficulty learning to read and spell, affects 5–17% of children (Gabrieli, 2009; Lyon, Shaywitz, & Shaywitz, 2003). Dysgraphia and writing disorders occur in similar numbers, affecting approximately 7–15% of the population (Katusic, Colligan, Weaver, & Barbaresi, 2009). Dyscalculia, difficulty with mathematical learning, is estimated to affect 3–6% of the population, according to prevalence studies conducted in the United States, Europe, and Israel (Shalev, Auerbach, Manor, & Gross-Tsur, 2000).

The BASC–3 Teacher Rating Scales (TRS) and Self-Report of Personality (SRP) use several related scales to identify potential academic problems among children and adolescents. On the TRS, academic problems are measured on the Learning Problems scale and the Study Skills scale. Items from these scales include "Has trouble keeping up in class," "Gets failing school grades," "Has reading problems," "Has good study habits," "Is well organized," and "Stays on task." The SRP assesses academic problems indirectly through the Attitude to School scale and the Attitude to Teachers scale. Items from these scales include "I don't like thinking about school," "I feel like I want to quit school," "My teacher understands me," and "I like my teacher."

Theoretical Framework for Approaching Academic Problems

Learning is defined as a change in behavior. An individual demonstrates academic learning through behaviors such as writing and speaking. Learning that is internalized (e.g., a student says, "I understand") is difficult to verify without a corresponding demonstration of the understanding through an observable behavior. Therefore, although learning is certainly a cognitive process, the behaviors associated with it make up the basis for judgment and intervention.

There are different types of learning: cognitive, affective, and psychomotor. The academic problems highlighted in this chapter are primarily related to factors included in the cognitive learning process. Cognitive learning involves knowledge and the development of intellectual skills and abilities. Its process has been conceptualized as a series of levels, progressing from simple to most complex: Knowledge, Comprehension, Application, Analysis, Synthesis, and Evaluation (Bloom, 1956). Progression from one level to the next requires mastery of the preceding one, and difficulty in any of these areas constitutes an academic problem.

The interventions presented in this chapter fit in a cognitive–behavioral model. Cognitive–behavioral approaches to academic interventions are highlighted in this chapter for two reasons. First, they have been shown to be highly effective; second, biological causes of learning problems (e.g., synaptic plasticity and structure of the cerebral cortex) are unlikely to give rise to educational intervention at the school site. There is a neurological and physiological basis of learning that involves the neural network and accounts for factors such as hormonal influences on memory and performance. However, whatever the causes, be they biological (e.g., attention deficits, head injury) or environmental (e.g., impoverished early childhood experiences, lack of language experience during critical learning periods), academic problems can be addressed by a cognitive–behavioral intervention approach.

Interventions

Academic problems can occur in isolation or with any number of other social, emotional, or behavioral problems. Fortunately, there are several academic strategies that help prevent and remediate learning problems. This discussion of interventions is not limited to content areas such as "reading interventions" or "math interventions;" rather, it represents the current literature on effective instructional practices and interventions that have evidence to support their use with the population of students who also have emotional and behavioral problems. The interventions in this chapter may be teacher directed or student directed. Student directed interventions are techniques that students can use to store, retrieve, and generalize information for academic task completion and to manage their own behavior and learning (Alberto & Troutman, 2003; Coyne, Kame'enui, & Simmons, 2001). These self-mediated strategies are not instinctive and must be explicitly taught before independent use can be expected (Good & Brophy, 2003). Evidence-based interventions for improving academic problems are listed in Table 6.1. For some of the interventions in this chapter, supplemental materials (e.g., handouts, posters, checklists, daily logs, and worksheets) that are helpful for preparing, implementing, and evaluating the interventions can be found on Q-global.

Table 6.1. Interventions for Academic Problems

Intervention	Prevention[1]	Early Intervention[2]	Intensive Intervention[3]
Advance Organizers	X	X	X
Cognitive Organizers	X	X	X
Instructional Strategies: Structure	X	X	X
Scaffolding	X	X	X
Procedural Prompting	X	X	X
Instructional Sequencing	X	X	X
Scripted Lessons	X	X	X
Instructional Strategies: Time	X	X	X
Rate and Pacing	X	X	X
Pausing	X	X	X
Allocated and Engaged Time	X	X	X
Instructional Strategies: Responding	X	X	X
Mnemonics	X	X	X
Peer Tutoring	X	X	X
Classwide Peer Tutoring	X	X	
Self-Monitoring	X	X	X
Self-Instruction	X	X	X
Reprocessing Strategies	X	X	X
Summarization	X	X	X
Paraphrasing	X	X	X
Cover, Copy, and Compare	X	X	X
Self-Questioning	X	X	X
Task-Selection Strategies		X	X

[1] Prevention refers to skills that can be taught to all children or used universally; they promote better awareness and lessen the risk of problems.

[2] Early intervention includes techniques and strategies that address early warning signs or clinical signs of the risk of future problems. Early intervention may be specifically applied to one or more problems or generically applied as a skill set to prevent the development of a chronic problem. Early interventions can be delivered to groups or individuals.

[3] Intensive intervention focuses on individuals and individual problems, which are usually chronic, intensive, and require services due to the level of interference in daily functioning.

 ADVANCE ORGANIZERS

DESCRIPTION

An advance organizer is a cognitive instructional strategy that previews unit, lesson, or topical content by explicitly connecting concepts to each other through linking questions and visual representation of organizational structures of the learning objectives. Advance organizers work because they make abstract connections between ideas more explicit. Big ideas are separated from detail; cause is represented in relation to effect. In addition, the instructional purpose is directly communicated with the learner so that students can read for focused understanding or listen for key ideas. New content and connections between new content and prior learning are scaffolded to make learning more efficient. Advance organizers retrieve prior knowledge as a foundation for new information, supply an antecedent to the main instructional activity, and provide a structure for the new information (Swanson & Deshler, 2003).

Using advance organizers requires teachers to explicitly outline the structure of the lesson and materials. This outline should reflect the relationships between concepts, describe the information to be learned, and detail how the information will be taught. Therefore, prior to the construction of the advance organizer, an analysis should be done to define the content coverage of the lesson based on previous and future lessons while considering overall expectations for the course. This stage of the process should identify the required learning outcomes for the lesson, articulate the procedures and routines for teaching those concepts, and establish the performance indicators for successful student learning.

EXAMPLES

Mr. Zhu distributes an advance organizer for a lesson on comparing themes in a reading unit about Mark Twain and then says, "Last week, we finished *The Adventures of Tom Sawyer* by Mark Twain. We learned about conflict and character development and how both were used throughout the story to represent the struggles people had with themselves and with each other. Today we will begin *The Adventures of Huckleberry Finn*, also by Mark Twain. When I introduce the main characters, be looking for the struggles the characters have with themselves and with others. See if you can find similar themes in this story." During the lesson, Mr. Zhu uses a visual display with graphics that indicates parallels between the stories, and the students complete a blank form in their notebooks that mimics what Mr. Zhu demonstrated.

Ms. Hamilton teaches an 11th-grade general education Texas history class using the required textbook that is written at a 9th-grade reading level. The reading abilities of the students in her class range from college level to 5th grade. Several of her students are English language learners and some have developmental learning problems. Ms. Hamilton provides her class with an advance organizer at the beginning of each instructional unit, such as the Battle of the Alamo. The advance organizer helps the students relate the current lesson to their previous lesson about the Battle of Goliad, showing the similar themes and concepts of both battles. She explains that the purpose of the lesson is to demonstrate the major themes of the Battle of the Alamo and states that each student will be expected to explain the sequence of events and the key players. The following lesson plan advance organizer (see Figure 6.1) and related student-completed example (see Figure 6.2) were adapted from the sample in Boudah, Lenz, Bulgren, Schumaker, and Deshler (2000); they include strictly heuristic information, presenting the key details and conceptual links.

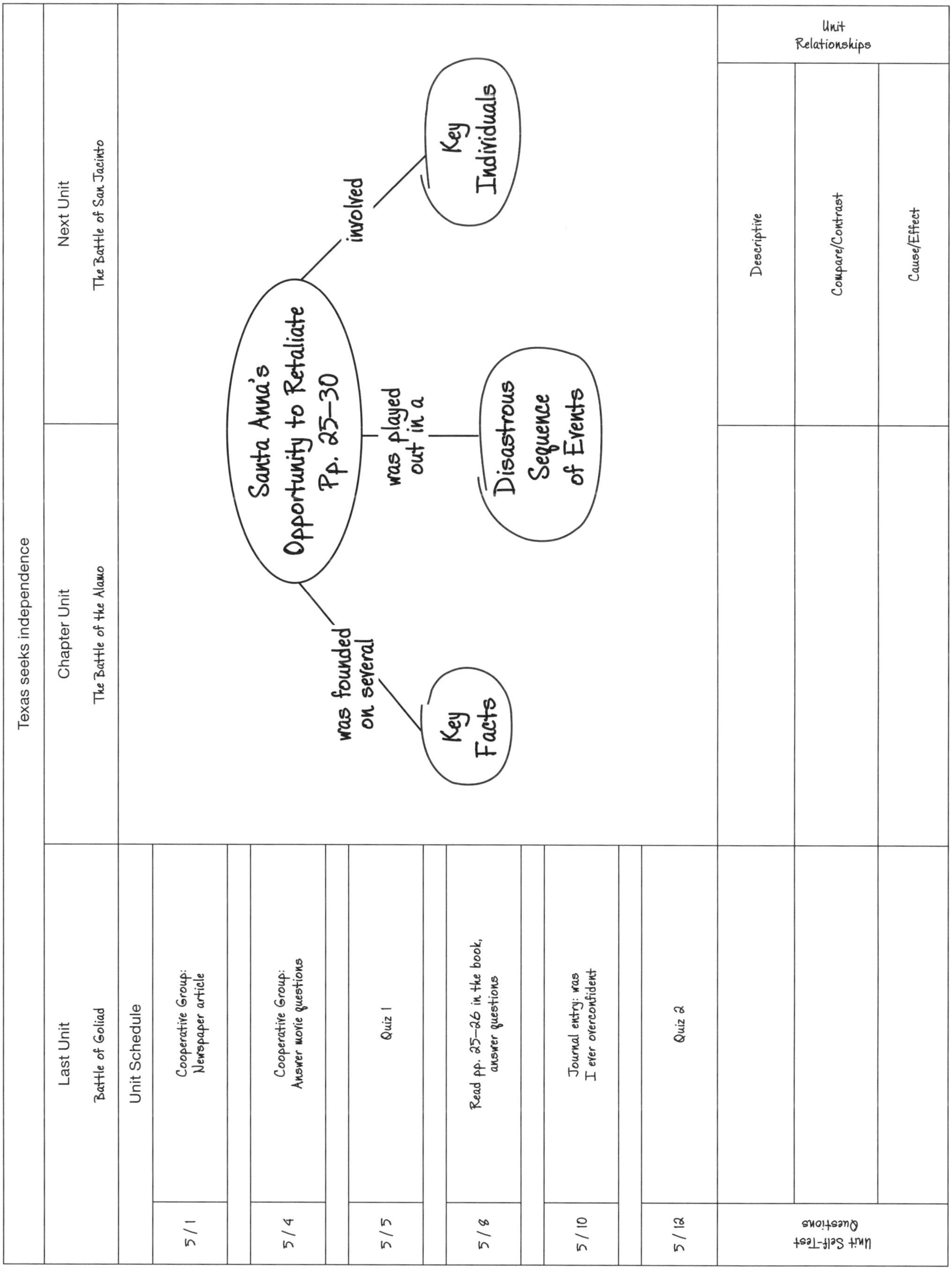

Texas seeks independence

Last Unit	Chapter Unit	Next Unit
Battle of Goliad	The Battle of the Alamo	The Battle of San Jacinto

Unit Schedule

5 / 1	Cooperative Group: Newspaper article
5 / 4	Cooperative Group: Answer movie questions
5 / 5	Quiz 1
5 / 8	Read pp. 25–26 in the book, answer questions
5 / 10	Journal entry: was I ever overconfident
5 / 12	Quiz 2
	Unit Self-Test Questions

Unit Relationships
- Descriptive
- Compare/Contrast
- Cause/Effect

Santa Anna's Opportunity to Retaliate Pp. 25–30

- involved → Key Individuals
- was played out in a → Disastrous Sequence of Events
- was founded on several → Key Facts

Figure 6.1 Example of Lesson Plan Advance Organizer

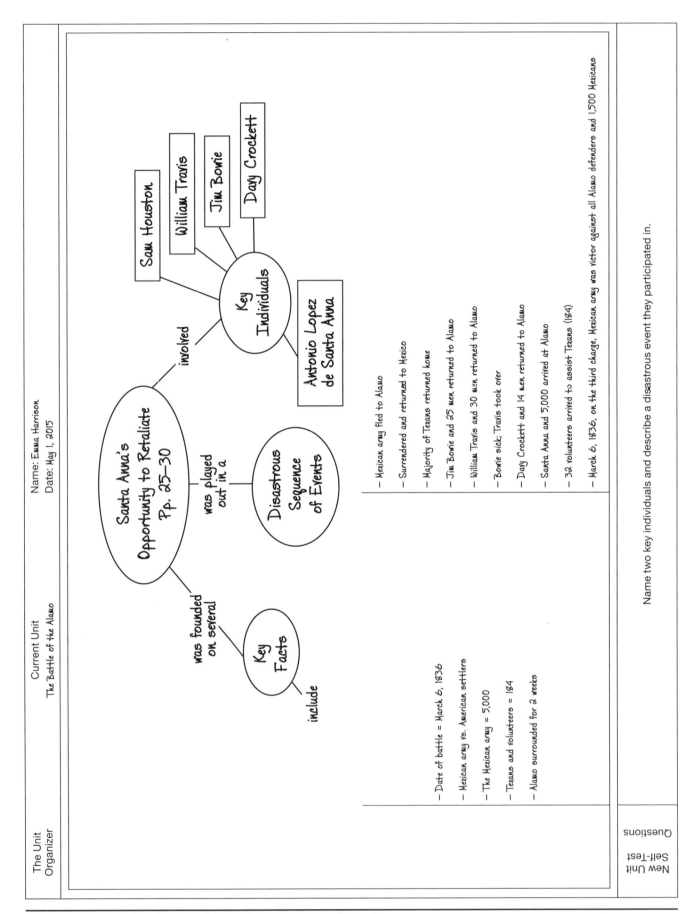

Figure 6.2 Example of Student-Completed Advance Organizer

GOAL

Facilitate retrieval of prior knowledge as a foundation for new information, supply an antecedent to the main instructional activity, and provide a structure for the new information (Swanson & Deshler, 2003).

THE BASICS

1. Review the goal and outcome of the previous lesson.

2. Review the objective of the current lesson and explain the connections using a graphic organizer.

HOW TO IMPLEMENT ADVANCE ORGANIZERS

 PREP

- Prepare the information for the advance organizer.

- Analyze the overall content of the lesson. Determine major concepts that every student must learn. Aim for a list of three or four concepts. Use concrete, specific language for objectives (e.g., describes, uses, lists), and avoid general terminology (e.g., understands, develops). Also, describe these items in terms of necessity (e.g., will describe), not conditionality (e.g., should be able to describe).

- Analyze and articulate the procedures and routines for teaching those concepts.

- Determine the performance expectations for students.

 IMPLEMENT

- Construct an advance organizer that presents the information using a graphic or visual representation that will:

  ▲ Connect and review previously learned information, emphasizing the connections between already-learned material and new information and serves a purpose similar to that of a map to help students orient themselves to the lesson and allow them to see where they are, where they were, and where they are going.

  ▲ Convey a purpose statement that explains the importance and relevance of the lesson.

  ▲ Provide a rationale statement to the student that establishes explicit expectations for successful academic performance.

  ▲ Review the relevant academic strategies for instructional routines and content.

- Teach lessons and create classroom routines that follow the outline of the organizer. Each session, as relevant, reorients the students to where they are, where they were, and where they are going, with particular emphasis on the structure and expectations of the unit or lesson.

 EVALUATE

- Consider teaching one unit or lesson with the use of an advance organizer and one without, and then compare student achievement, outcomes, and engagement.

- Monitor and make note of differences in on-task behavior or disruptive behavior with and without an advance organizer.

EVIDENCE

A brief overview of research and annotated references supporting this intervention can be found on Q-global.

CONSIDERATIONS

FOR TEACHING

Advance organizers require moderate to significant levels of preparation prior to use in instruction. However, the time spent preparing advance organizers is generally an initial investment; once the materials are created and organized, only minor investments of time are required for updating them. This preparation time pays off in additional benefits to the instruction, such as making repeated coverage of material more prescriptive for students who miss critical components and providing another method to help focus student attention, which saves time in discipline-related activities.

FOR AGE AND DEVELOPMENTAL LEVEL

Students in very early grades are unlikely to be exposed to reading materials with abstract concepts and relationships or to require this level of content knowledge. Advance organizers are most commonly used from 5th grade and up, with evidence demonstrating effective use across content areas throughout the secondary years. Recent changes in accountability and increased academic demands in grades 1–4 provide opportunity for simplified versions of advance organizers to be used for presenting relationships between content. Although no current studies exist to demonstrate the efficacy of this strategy with younger students, it is likely that the basic considerations and instructional principles would still apply.

FOR CULTURAL AND LANGUAGE DIFFERENCES

Using advance organizers creates visual memory prompts and provides nonverbal context clues that can assist English language learners in learning content. With irrelevant language stimuli removed, the visual connections to prior learning and illustrated relationships between materials are easier to grasp for students learning a new language.

 # COGNITIVE ORGANIZERS

DESCRIPTION

Cognitive organizers, also referred to as maps, diagrams, and webs, are used to represent intricate concepts and their relationships in a consistent and concrete manner (Bulgren, Lenz, Schumaker, Deshler, & Marquis, 2002). The structure of the cognitive organizer can take several different forms, including structures that are hierarchical, directional, or comparative. The information boxes are often represented by rectangles, ovals, or circles; and are typically used to represent concept names, definitions, main ideas, subtopics, or similarities and differences. The boxes are connected by lines or arrows that represent the flow or logical sequence of the various pieces of information.

Cognitive organizers come in many different forms with their structures often determined by a range of factors, including the information being presented, the goals of instruction (e.g., recall of dates, recognition of conceptual relationships), and the educational and developmental levels of the student or classroom.

In order to use cognitive organizers effectively, a student must have the prerequisite skills needed to apply or create organizational structures. These skills can be taught or scaffolded by providing outlines and graphics.

EXAMPLES

Mr. Munoz uses a hierarchical structure to determine prior student knowledge. First, Mr. Munoz draws on the board a large circle with arrows radiating from it to smaller circles. Next, he writes the main topic in the large circle and asks the students to name facts about the topic. He writes their answers in the smaller circles.

To present information such as dates or times in a sequential manner, Mrs. Sanders might provide directional cognitive organizers composed of several blank information boxes connected by arrows. To aid in comparing or contrasting two or more ideas, multiple titled information boxes may be used to provide an organizational structure for easily viewing the comparison of overall concepts, the shared or contrasting characteristics of those concepts, a summary statement of these characteristics, and any concept extensions (Bulgren et al., 2002).

GOAL

Help students learn concepts, identify associations, and understand curriculum content through graphic representations.

THE BASICS

1. Provide the basic structure of a cognitive organizer.

2. Provide information boxes.

3. Provide connecting lines or arrows.

HOW TO IMPLEMENT COGNITIVE ORGANIZERS

 PREP

- Prepare a blank and a completed (model) cognitive organizer.

- Explain to students the purpose and rationale for using cognitive organizers.

 IMPLEMENT

- Give the students a blank cognitive organizer.

- Explain to students the steps to complete the cognitive organizer (e.g., listen to the lecture or skim the material, write the name of the main concept in the primary box, write the name of the subtopics in the boxes connected to the main concept and list some characteristics or facts about them, compare and contrast subtopics).

- Model completion of the cognitive organizer (e.g., filling in blanks, creating visual representations of relationships). Write the steps on the board or project them using a visual display, model each step, and accompany the modeling verbally.

  ▲ For example, the teacher might write "Ocean Life" in the main concept box and then say, "How many kinds of ocean life are there? Let's see, plants and animals should cover it," while simultaneously writing "plants" and "animals" in the subtopic information boxes.

- Provide feedback as the students complete their own copies, saying the steps aloud.

- Have students use each completed cognitive organizer as a presentation or study guide for self-questioning or writing a prompt/outline.

- Have students verbalize the procedures for using or completing the cognitive organizer without teacher prompting.

- Instruct students to complete the same type of cognitive organizer for a similar lesson while using silent self-talk. Monitor and provide feedback as needed.

- Brainstorm different subjects or assignments in which a given cognitive organizer can be used to ensure generalization of the cognitive organizer strategy. Discuss further to identify best-practice models for those assignments or learning situations most often experienced by the students.

- Incorporate cognitive organizers in study or review sessions, for open book tests, and when completing in-class assignments.

 EVALUATE

- Consider teaching one unit or lesson with the use of a cognitive organizer and one without, and then compare student achievement, outcomes, and engagement.

- Monitor and make note of differences in on-task behavior or disruptive behavior with and without a cognitive organizer.

EVIDENCE

A brief overview of research and annotated references supporting this intervention can be found on Q-global.

CONSIDERATIONS

For Language Differences

Cognitive organizers are especially helpful for students with language differences. Material is presented in a way that reduces the use of language, thereby decreasing receptive language demands. This strategy is helpful for students whose primary language is different from the language being used in the classroom.

 # INSTRUCTIONAL STRATEGIES

DESCRIPTION

Instructional strategies may alter structure, time, and/or student responding to assist students with academic problems. These changes create optimal learning environments and provide opportunities for improved student learning. The structure of instruction may be modified by scaffolding, procedural prompts, instructional sequencing, and/or scripted lessons. The timing aspects of instruction that may be modified include the rate and pacing of instruction, pauses during instruction, and amounts of allocated and engaged time within a lesson. Responding strategies affect the frequency and types of responses and verbal exchanges between the students and teacher to provide correction or confirmation.

Instructional strategies rely on an awareness of the match (or mismatch) between a student's skill and ability levels and the requirements of the learning task. Inherent in each strategy is the planning and forethought that goes into material preparation and content delivery, with careful attention to maximizing students' learning time. The degree of structure provided within a lesson, the amount and quality of time allocated for teaching the content of the lesson, and the frequency and types of student and teacher responses required during that learning process are all components of presentation strategy. As such, each component affects how lessons are delivered.

The ineffective use of structuring, time, and responding can compound the struggles experienced by students with academic problems. Although sometimes challenging to assess, instructional presentation strategies should not be overlooked in remediating academic problems. However, these strategies should be considered a small part of the whole. For example, strong scaffolding cannot compensate for insufficient instructional time, and large quantities of engaged time cannot compensate for poor matches between instructional delivery and learner ability.

The instructional strategies have been grouped for presentation (structuring, time, and responding) to provide an overview of these components and some selected evidence for their use.

STRUCTURE

DESCRIPTION

The structure of instruction refers to the formation or development of the content and the organization of its delivery. Well-designed curriculum has an implicit structure, and good instruction presents that structure explicitly to students. Common structure methods used include the following:

1. Scaffolding

2. Procedural prompts

3. Instructional sequencing

4. Scripted lessons

Scaffolding

Scaffolding is the generic term for the instructional support provided by the teacher until the student is able to transition into independent thinking and learning (Bruner, 1985; Rosenshine & Meister, 1992; Vygotsky, 1930/1978). Teachers sometimes employ scaffolding naturally when they provide hints or clues to guide students who are struggling with an answer (e.g., pointing to a section of a page, starting to sound out a word as the student attempts to decode it). Scaffolds can be aids to developing and applying cognitive strategies (Palincsar & Brown, 1984; Swanson & Deshler, 2003). Scaffolded instruction provides an instructional bridge between existing student knowledge and new content.

Scaffolded instruction has been described as systematic sequencing (Dickson, Chard, & Simmons, 1993; Kame'enui, Carnine, Dixon, Simmons, & Coyne, 2002). One example of scaffolded instruction is providing traceable outlines of letters for students who are learning to write the alphabet. The outlines may be dark initially and then fade to dotted lines before disappearing altogether. Other examples include: the dotted half-line that appears in beginners' writing composition notebooks to provide spacing and to distinguish between uppercase and lowercase letters, the large dots that appear in touch math to assist students in counting, and worksheets that have hints or page number references for finding answers.

There are three components that typically influence the development of scaffolding applications: (1) the students' present levels of performance and their future goals, (2) the curriculum and learning objectives, and (3) providing instructional bridges (visual or verbal) between knowledge gaps based on student needs.

Scaffolding is appropriate for students of all ages, and it can circumvent language and cultural differences. The technique allows teachers to support students who struggle academically, and it can be tailored to regulate the amount of effort required to complete tasks. This strategy helps students learn independently and reduces the likelihood that they will either act out in class or ignore instruction that is above their skill level. By facilitating teacher awareness of the points at which students become bogged down in new concepts or tasks, scaffolding also provides data to the teacher for use in determining how to increase student learning.

Examples

Lauren, a 2nd grader who reads at a kindergarten level, needs to understand the food chain and water cycle in science. Visual support and scaffolding might include preteaching key vocabulary, providing diagrams with correctly spelled words to match to figures, adding more white space on the page for below-grade-level written responses (i.e., large printing), and using fewer text distracters. These methods of scaffolding result in a learning process with fewer student errors and greater focus on the science concepts rather than secondary aspects of spelling or neatness. Using these presentation strategies also may contribute to task completion by making the expectations clear and completion of the assignment more obvious.

Giancarlo is a struggling high school junior in a secondary language arts classroom. During composition writing, Giancarlo benefits from a feedback process for developing paragraphs. The process begins with Giancarlo outlining each paragraph by writing topic sentences. He then writes the numerals 1, 2, and 3 to note placement of the subsequent detail sentences of each paragraph and inserts an asterisk (*) to denote where to put each concluding sentence. The teacher first checks the initial outline and then provides suggestions for changes to the topic sentences. The teacher provides one keyword for each of the numbered sentences. Giancarlo uses the keywords to begin working through each supporting sentence. After each phase of paragraph development, the teacher provides just enough support for Giancarlo to achieve the next step. This scaffolded process limits the frustration Giancarlo normally experiences when writing by reducing effort on unrelated sentences and increasing structured thinking about the topic.

PROCEDURAL PROMPTS

Procedural prompts are visual, verbal, or auditory prompts to help students organize and remember new information (Scardamalia & Bereiter, 1985). There are two main steps to follow when applying procedural prompts. First, determine if the challenge to learning is related to memory (organization) or thinking (application). Second, ask questions that create opportunities for chunking (remembering concepts together), linking (connecting items sequentially or by relation to each other), retrieval (accessing the information more efficiently), or schema (connecting newly learned material with previously learned material).

Both memory and thinking are facilitated by prompting strategies. One of the best illustrative examples of memory function is walking through a field of tall grass or deep snow. The first time across is difficult; this is akin to learning something the first time. Subsequent crossings create a pathway that is much easier to access, and memory, like this pathway, becomes more automated. Mental connections are akin to learning a physical route. The first time driving a route, signposts are needed, a map is consulted, and landmarks are used to help in remembering the way for next time the route is travelled.

Memory's role in learning new material or concepts in education is similar. Frequent reference points are needed. Young students do not have the practical or life skills to effectively harness their memories, and they need both the strategies and signposts to learn how to recall information.

Examples of procedural prompts include the guiding questions that prompt cognitive processes and assist students in storing and retrieving information, such as:

- "How are _____ and _____ alike in the story?"
- "What other chemical process causes expansion?"
- "Do you agree with _____? Why or why not?"

These types of questions have embedded cues that prompt thinking.

INSTRUCTIONAL SEQUENCING

Instructional sequencing refers to the order in which information is presented to a student, as well as how a student structures his or her learning. Sequencing is fundamental to learning (Glynn & DiVesta, 1977; Lorch & Lorch, 1985; Van Patten, Chao, & Reigeluth, 1986). No single specific sequence is required for instruction to be successful; however, a specific example of sequencing is recommended (like the one in the next paragraph). Teachers can select other instructional methods, but students may take longer to learn, pick up errors in learning, and enter the cycle of frustration and withdrawal that sometimes accompanies unclear instruction.

Sequencing incorporates the information to be learned into the context of previously learned information. When presenting information, provide clear and explicit expectations for student performance. Information should be presented using examples and nonexamples, and should be explicitly linked or connected to previously learned information. Throughout the lesson, students should be given ample opportunities to respond to questions. They also should receive consistent reinforcement for correct responses and frequent feedback loops to correct and shape incorrect responses. Information that is learned should then be reviewed and practiced. In order to promote retention of the learned information, provide opportunities to demonstrate that information has been learned.

SCRIPTED LESSONS

Scripted lessons are a variant of the instructional sequencing concept. Teachers write scripts for lesson plans, including how the information will be presented, the desired responses by students, and the routines that will be used for learning the material. Prompts for teacher and students are included in the scripts. Although scripted lessons can take a variety of forms, they generally follow the same steps as instructional sequencing. Scripted lessons can be beneficial to teachers who want to assess the fidelity of the teaching objectives. Since the lesson plans are written, they know exactly how information was presented. If the students' performance on a particular lesson is not what was desired, the teacher can modify the lesson as needed to obtain the desired performance outcome. The nature of scripted lessons provides a structure for teachers and students, helps eliminate or reduce errors in teaching and learning, and allows for subsequent modifications that would improve the curriculum and instruction.

Example

Kim is a 3rd-grade teacher co-teaching a diverse class. She and her partner write out lessons explicitly as a script so that either teacher or a substitute can read the learning objective and begin the instruction. They create written examples illustrating new concepts ahead of time so that the illustrations are clear for students and the teachers have time to think about how to best present some of the more complex material. In addition, the teachers use symbols or write themselves notes in the margins about when to ask questions. Scripted questions help the teachers remember to ask students to participate and allow either teacher to provide the same quality of instruction and the same sequencing of content.

TIME

Time is the component of instructional strategies that refers to how much, how quickly, and how smoothly instruction is presented. These variables often directly impact student learning. For example, time is a central component and salient variable in Carroll's model of school learning (1963, 1989) and the effective instruction literature of the 1970s and 1980s. Current federal education policy seeks to improve educational outcomes through the efficient use of time (U.S. Department of Education, 1994; IDEIA, 2004).

Learning itself can be viewed as a function of time. How quickly a student acquires new knowledge and becomes fluent with that knowledge is a measure of competency. Students with learning problems are particularly susceptible to processing time issues. Difficulties arise when instructional time is not appropriately matched to student needs, particularly when the student is not engaged during the lesson.

There are three major components of time:

1. Rate and pacing

2. Pausing

3. Allocated and engaged time

RATE AND PACING

Rate and pacing refer to the speed and regularity of the presentation and of practicing new material. The speed of a lesson can determine the amount of material covered, the amount of practice in which students engage, and the interest level of the students. Quickly paced lessons tend to be more interesting, and a brisk tempo with frequent opportunities for students to respond and participate encourages a sense of excitement and urgency in learning activities. However, a pace that is too fast may lead to an instructor glossing over information without sufficiently covering content. Therefore, a good fit between the time needed for learner processing and the pace needed for effective instruction is required to optimize learning time.

PAUSING

Pausing is the delay in time between instructional prompts and expected student responses. It can help to maintain a brisk rate of instruction and provide a rhythm in which students intently listen to the instruction and process the information prior to responding. Pausing can also be used to increase exposure to material through repetition. Providing an instructional prompt, such as "The Eiffel tower was nearly dismantled because . . . (pause)," following portions of instruction in a lesson can provide students with the opportunity to consider the answer and create memory through active repetition of new knowledge.

ALLOCATED AND ENGAGED TIME

Allocated time refers to the time dedicated to instruction and learning. Engaged time is the component of allocated time that reflects the time a student spends learning tasks. Allocated and engaged times vary dramatically across teachers, students, and tasks but both are correlated with successful learning. It is suggested that teachers maximize their instructional time to reflect a minimum of 50% active instruction, 35% active monitoring, and 15% or less organizing and managing (Stallings, 1986). The level of student engagement in learning tasks can be monitored and increased individually through a variety of self-monitoring techniques or the use of reinforcers contingent on levels of on-task behavior.

The amount of both allocated and engaged time should be assessed when students are struggling with learning problems. For example, increasing instruction time by 60 minutes is ineffective if the students are not already engaged in learning during the current period of time provided for instruction. Conversely, increasing on-task learning by adding after-school or pullout instruction is ineffective if the teacher's administrative responsibilities decrease the amount of time left for instruction.

Once allocated time is maximized and engaged time is evaluated, then the instructional elements of rate, pacing, and pausing can be incorporated into the learning process to further increase a student's motivation, engagement, and success.

Example

Jack is a quick learner who rapidly completes his work and then disrupts the class. For Jack, allocated time and engaged time are not well matched because he has time left over to engage in nonproductive behavior. Katie, another student in the class, is a slow processor with language, learning, and behavior problems. The teacher's quick presentation and questioning strategies are excellent for keeping the whole class on task, but Katie needs additional time before the teacher moves from one learning objective to the next. The teacher could accommodate both the need for classroom management and Katie's processing need by asking questions that have multiple answers and having Katie answer last, providing her the additional processing time she needs while answers are given by other students. Or, the teacher could ask a question that has multiple answers and then call on Katie first so that no one will have previously given the more obvious answers.

Monitoring both instructional time and engaged time requires an awareness of how much time is spent on a variety of activities. Appropriate planning, self-recording, and self-evaluating of the use of time will allow teachers to more easily set realistic instructional goals and more readily make effective changes to curriculum or instruction. Students' engaged time can be assessed routinely by counting students who are on- and off-task. Or, for more detailed information on student engagement, record the length of time spent on- and off-task.

RESPONDING

Responding provides opportunities for students to participate by answering questions, restating instruction, or asking questions about content. The teacher provides feedback via correction or confirmation. Research has demonstrated the effectiveness of response and feedback loops in the opportunity-to-respond literature (Sutherland et al., 2003; Sutherland & Wehby, 2001; Sutherland, Wehby, & Yoder, 2002) and also in the literature about feedback (Gunter, Shores, Jack, Denny, & DePaepe, 1994; Maggs, & Morgan, 1986; McLaughlin, 1992; Schloss, Harriman, & Pfeifer, 1985).

The types and frequency of student responses and teacher feedback are fairly easy to assess and relatively pliable. With minimal training, a teacher can dramatically increase both the opportunities for student response and the immediacy and frequency of specific praise or corrective feedback provided during a lesson.

EVIDENCE

A brief overview of research and annotated references supporting this intervention can be found on Q-global.

CONSIDERATIONS

FOR TEACHING

The variety of individual backgrounds and skills training that exists in the teaching profession makes the level of difficulty in acquiring such skill wide ranging. While many teachers may come from a training program where this type of instructional vocabulary is familiar and comfortable, some programs operate from a more constructivist approach in which the expectation of structure and a mandate for explicitness may be seen as negative features of instruction. Some teachers are trained to believe that explicit expectations may minimize students' natural creativity, prevent the development of problem-solving abilities, limit students' appreciation for the subject matter, or dampen the joy of learning. However, effective instruction is not about rigid and inflexible rote memorization. Effective instruction is a skill that takes practice.

FOR AGE AND DEVELOPMENTAL LEVEL

Scaffolding is especially important for more complex academic tasks encountered in middle and high school, particularly when student reading level may interfere with comprehension and application of content area instruction (e.g., literary or historical comparisons). Models, examples, figures, and questions that guide students' thinking are all examples of the types of assisted learning that involves scaffolding.

FOR CULTURAL AND LANGUAGE DIFFERENCES

Rate and pacing are particularly critical for English language learners; implementing think time allows more opportunity for accessing information and responding to instruction. The additional time required for processing is facilitated by careful control of time use through rate, pacing, and pausing. Instructional time and time on task are essential matters for all students, regardless of culture or language, but may be more salient for students with limited background knowledge or language proficiency. The judicious use of additional time is warranted for these populations.

 **MNEMONICS**

DESCRIPTION

Mnemonics is a self-mediated method used to support learning in a variety of academic areas. Mnemonics can be used to enhance student recall of facts or other memorized information. Mnemonic devices facilitate learning by employing visual and auditory clues to aid information retrieval (Scruggs & Mastropieri, 1990).

When using mnemonics, it is important to determine which mnemonic device is appropriate for the information being learned. Then, corresponding materials must be developed. For example, in keyword picture mnemonics, the teacher determines keywords for the concepts that will be easily understood by the students. The teacher determines a way that the keyword can interact with the definition or concept being taught and then creates materials used to teach the concept (e.g., flash cards with the picture and keyword on one side of the card and the definition or explanation of the concept on the other).

There are several varieties of mnemonic methods including first letter, keyword, picture, physical, and musical. While these mnemonic devices share common pedagogical principles, their structure and instructional applications vary.

A first-letter mnemonic device can often represent the steps to an activity with a phrase made up of words corresponding to the first letter of each activity. For instance, the six steps in the process of problem solving could be represented by the phrase "Rascally dogs get extra dirty eventually" (recognize, define, generate, evaluate, design, and evaluate).

Keyword mnemonic devices use familiar words that sound similar to the term being learned to trigger past learning and assist in learning new terms. For example, carta means "letter" in Spanish so the word "cart" could be used as a keyword for remembering this definition by picturing a letter in a cart.

Mnemonic pictures reinforce learning of concepts by visualizing the concept being taught in conjunction with a more familiar concept that sounds like the concept being taught. For example, the word "carline" means "old woman," so the mnemonic picture could be of an old woman driving a car with the word "carline" written underneath the car.

Using your knuckles to represent the months of the year to remember if a month has 30 or 31 days is a physical mnemonic. Examples of musical mnemonics would be the alphabet song and the multiplication rap.

EXAMPLE

Kendra often misses problems on her math homework because she doesn't pay attention to the order of operations. To help her remember the order of operations, Kendra recites the mnemonic "Please Excuse My Dear Aunt Sally."

GOAL

Enhance student recall of facts or other memorized information by employing visual and auditory clues to aid information retrieval.

THE BASICS

1. Select and prepare the mnemonic that is best suited to the information being presented.

2. Teach the mnemonic and help in the development of new ones.

HOW TO IMPLEMENT MNEMONICS

PREP

- Determine which mnemonic device is appropriate for the information being learned.
- Develop corresponding materials to be used when presenting the mnemonic.

IMPLEMENT

- Present the mnemonic to the student and rehearse its applied use.
- Involve the student in development of additional mnemonic material.

EVALUATE

- Ask the student about preferences and interest in continuing to use mnemonics.
- Create an opportunity for independent use of a mnemonic, demonstrating a transfer of the skill.

EVIDENCE

A brief overview of research and annotated references supporting this intervention can be found on Q-global.

CONSIDERATIONS

FOR CULTURAL AND LANGUAGE DIFFERENCES

Both cultural and language differences have the possibility of making mnemonics use more difficult when learning new material. Care should be used to develop mnemonics that make sense for a primary language and cross-culturally, or the necessary steps should be taken to encourage students to create their own.

PEER TUTORING

DESCRIPTION

Peer tutoring can take many forms, but it always involves student tutors working with other students who are experiencing difficulty learning a subject or content area. Students can be paired with others who are on different academic levels, the same academic level, or of different ages. However, as discussed by Good and Brophy (2003) and Greenwood et al. (1997), and for the purposes of this discussion, peer tutoring must contain seven essential elements that are described in THE BASICS section. These elements cover both the setup for peer tutoring and the behaviors used by the peer tutors in their pairs.

Peer tutoring is the process of students assisting other students in learning through teaching (Goodlad & Hirst, 1990; Topping, 2001). Peer tutoring is also known by several other names, including peer-assisted learning, peer monitoring, peer facilitation, and peer-mediated instruction. The process is identified by some as dating back to the early Greeks (Topping, 1996). Peer tutoring is a reciprocal process and has been found to improve learning in both the tutee and the tutor in a number of studies and meta-analyses across decades (Franca & Kerr, 1990; Maher, 1982; Scruggs, Mastropieri, & Richter, 1985).

There are many types and forms of peer tutoring; however, not all arrangements are equally effective. Peer tutoring may be used to help students check for accuracy (typically by pairing same-age students) or to facilitate instruction by pairing a cross-age tutor with one or more individuals. The students work with each other on the same task but one individual remains the tutor and one (or more) remain the tutee(s). The teacher may establish age-based pairs (i.e., same- or different-aged students) as well as ability-based pairs (i.e., same or differing ability levels). No matter the arrangement, the procedures for tutoring are taught, modeled, and practiced during the first stage. Once procedures are established the peer-tutoring sessions can be implemented.

EXAMPLE

A 5th-grade social studies class that is studying U.S. national monuments has formed peer-tutoring pairs of equal skill levels. To begin, the following procedures for the tutoring session are established. The tutor first provides an example of the problem or question. The tutee then attempts a solution. If the response is correct, the tutor presents the next problem. If the tutee gives an incorrect response, the tutor requests a second attempt by saying, "Try again." After the second response attempt, the tutor either praises a correct response or provides the correct answer; provides additional supportive feedback or reteaching; or moves on to the next problem or question. Using these established procedures for the tutoring session, the teacher models the tutor role in the following exchange:

> Teacher/Tutor: "What four presidents are featured on Mount Rushmore?"

> Tutee: "Washington, Adams, Roosevelt, and Lincoln."

> Teacher/Tutor: "Good try, but you only named three of the four correctly: Washington, Roosevelt, and Lincoln. Who are the four presidents featured on Mount Rushmore?"

> Tutee: "Washington, Roosevelt, Lincoln. And, Jefferson?"

> Teacher/Tutor: "Correct. Good job. George Washington, Thomas Jefferson, Theodore Roosevelt, and Abraham Lincoln."

GOAL

Facilitate the student's learning through additional contact with instruction and feedback.

THE BASICS

1. Establish tutoring pairs.
2. Establish procedures via explanation and practice.
3. Provide tutor-to-tutee problem presentations.
4. Prompt tutee-to-tutor problem solutions.
5. Give tutor-to-tutee feedback (e.g., praise, encouragement, corrections).
6. Monitor peer tutoring time by circulating in the classroom.
7. Reinforce appropriate tutor and tutee behavior.

HOW TO IMPLEMENT PEER TUTORING

 PREP

- Define the tutoring context (e.g., when tutoring will occur, duration, general rules that apply to the tutoring sessions).

- Define the objectives of the tutoring program for the students. Objectives can be written academic or social goals, and can be individually or group based, but should include both tutor and tutee learning.

- Notify parents that peer tutoring is going to be implemented in the class. This notice should include information about the purpose of peer tutoring, the role of the students involved, the date tutoring will begin, the skills that will be practiced or taught, and the contact information for further questions.

IMPLEMENT

- Choose the subject or content area to be taught during the tutoring program.

- Select and match participants. Assign a tutor to one or more students for a specific period of time. The period of time should be long enough for the tutor and tutee to become comfortable with each other and for the tutor and tutee to work together for a defined period of time.

- Train the tutors. In the first tutoring session, the teacher provides models of the tutor role by actually doing the tutoring during this lesson. While modeling, he or she assesses the tutors' understanding of the process.

EVALUATE

- Monitor the tutoring process. During subsequent sessions, observe peer-tutoring sessions for student focus, understanding of the process, and student progress.

- Evaluate the program by determining if the initial objectives have been met.

- Provide program outcome feedback to students and other interested persons (e.g., parents, school administrators).

EVIDENCE

A brief overview of research and annotated references supporting this intervention can be found on Q-global.

CONSIDERATIONS

FOR TEACHING

Peer tutoring involves an initial investment of time in order to pair students, prepare materials, and teach procedures, but the outcomes are worth the initial investment. Students receive more instructional time and engaged time as well as additional opportunities to respond and receive corrective feedback. Also, the peer-tutoring structure allows the teacher to become the instructional leader or facilitator while monitoring a classroom of students who are teaching and learning together. This structure frees the teacher to provide more one-on-one instruction. In addition to these advantages, materials can be reused and pairs can be rotated and modified on an ongoing basis.

FOR AGE AND DEVELOPMENTAL LEVEL

Peer tutoring and cross-age tutoring both appear to work well with early grades. Naturally, the instructor should consider the developmental level of the students, the types of tasks assigned, and the training elements involved, all of which might make peer-tutoring instruction less feasible for very young children.

FOR CULTURAL AND LANGUAGE DIFFERENCES

Peer tutoring has a distinct literature on its effectiveness for English language learners. It shows evidence of effectiveness in a variety of classroom settings in both rural and urban school environments making peer tutoring a strong intervention for classroom use with these populations (Cole, 2014).

CLASSWIDE PEER TUTORING

DESCRIPTION

Classwide peer tutoring (CWPT) is a structured, prescribed variant of peer tutoring in which students in the same class help one another during the lesson (Greenwood et al., 1997). CWPT has very specific procedural requirements and a definitive body of literature. CWPT is based on the principles of maximizing student engaged time, providing frequent opportunities for practice, increasing rates of student response and feedback loops, and minimizing errors in learning and off-task behavior. CWPT also incorporates an element of progress monitoring by recording performance over time.

CWPT, like peer tutoring, focuses on improving the academic performance of students. Whereas peer tutoring can be implemented in a variety of settings however, CWPT is designed for classroom settings and can be used to facilitate large-group instruction.

Each CWPT session should last for 15 minutes and occur two to three times a week. During a session each student in the tutor–tutee pair acts as tutor for 5 minutes, and 5 minutes is reserved at the end of the session for tallying the points earned by pairs and teams (both recorded on a point chart). Individuals can earn points as either tutors or tutees by getting correct answers, giving positive feedback, following directions, and working well in pairs. Like individuals, teams earn points for correct responses, positive feedback from tutor to tutee, and accurate tutoring.

The teams compete against each other to earn the most points. Points are compiled after each session and totaled at the end of each week. Neither teams nor individual students are penalized for skill differences because both teams have an equal distribution of student skill levels. One common scoring procedure is to have the tutor provide feedback (i.e., by reading from the materials) for correct or incorrect answers and to assign 2 points for correct answers, 1 point for an answer that was initially incorrect but corrected after feedback from the tutor, and 0 points for incorrect answers left uncorrected after feedback from the tutor.

EXAMPLE

Mrs. Monroe divides her class into two rotating groups. She trains them in procedures and then constructs a visual aid to show how and when points are awarded. Two days a week the students operate as tutor and tutee by reading from prepared work that provides questions and answers related to the instruction. Correct answers receive 2 points from the tutor. If the answer is incorrect, the tutee receives a second chance during which correct answers are worth 1 point. A second incorrect answer from the tutee is awarded 0 points. The tutor and tutee switch after completing the review page. The teacher circulates and awards points for strong tutor skills.

GOAL

Improve academic and social behaviors of students by increasing engaged time with instructional materials and decreasing disruptive and/or off-task behavior.

THE BASICS

1. Divide the class into two teams and prepare a visual to record points.

2. Provide the review material for tutor and tutee to use in the sessions.

3. Prompt tutors and tutees to engage in assignments, provide feedback, and score and record points.

HOW TO IMPLEMENT CLASSWIDE PEER TUTORING

 PREP

- Create two teams by dividing the class in halves that are equal in terms of the students' skill levels, and then divide the teams into their first set of tutor–tutee pairs.
- Create and prepare the tutor–tutee folders with appropriate materials for the lesson.
- Provide directions for the presentation of practice work (e.g., how to query for spelling words, how to give correct feedback), the rules for scoring points and team play, and the guidelines for tutor–tutee interaction (e.g., rules for positive, reciprocal relationships).
- Create a visual to keep track of points.
- Train the tutors and tutees in their roles.

 IMPLEMENT

- Review the tutor–tutee rules with the students.
- Assign tutor–tutee pairs which rotate within the larger team.
- Monitor student scoring.
- Switch the tutor and tutee roles after 5 minutes.
- Record points on a class chart.

 EVALUATE

- Monitor the ability of all students to be appropriate tutors.
- Monitor the division of the teams to ensure equal opportunity to earn points.

EVIDENCE

A brief overview of research and annotated references supporting this intervention can be found on Q-global.

CONSIDERATIONS

FOR TEACHING

Classwide peer tutoring has many of the same preliminary issues as peer tutoring, such as preparation time and considerations for student abilities, curriculum levels, and pairings. It also has implementation issues, such as the need for close monitoring of student engagement and classroom behavior during tutoring. However, classwide peer tutoring also includes competition among teams. The effects of competition can sometimes include covert behaviors such as cheating or undermining of peer relationships (e.g., "I don't want Joe on my team; he brings our scores down."). The rotation of pairs ensures some degree of equality for all individuals. Matching the teams based on student scores ensures greater equality. Another solution is to concentrate on point levels rather than a win/lose system of reinforcement. The use of a raffle for any team members that beat a previous score or achieve above a certain level can be an effective deterrent for the drawbacks to competitiveness. Both strong monitoring of the peer-tutoring process and the distribution of points for appropriate behavior are important to ensure that verbal encouragement is worth as much as an accurate answer.

 **SELF-MONITORING**

DESCRIPTION

Self-monitoring, also referred to as self-recording or self-observation, requires a person to record information about his or her personal performance on a task (Alberto & Troutman, 2003) to improve self-regulation of behavior (Hallahan, Lloyd, & Stoller, 1982). Self-monitoring consists of several components, including awareness, observation, monitoring, and documentation (Mace et al., 2001). Self-monitoring places control of behavioral change in the student's sphere of influence and deemphasizes external control agents (Carter, 1993).

EXAMPLE

Ramon, an 11th grader with learning problems, is failing geometry because he doesn't complete his assignments or submit them to his teacher, Mrs. Suez. Ramon has not submitted any assignments in two weeks. He completed two out of five assignments but didn't submit them. Mrs. Suez presents this baseline data and a self-monitoring form to Ramon and asks him to write the number of problems he has completed whenever a timer rings to signal intervals throughout the class period. At the end of the lesson Ramon records the number of problems completed and submits the assignment to his teacher. Ramon is taught to self-reward by saying to himself, "I finished my work and turned it in to the teacher. I will pass geometry and graduate." His teacher presents him with a no-homework pass if he completes 90% of his work and turns in assignments for three consecutive days.

GOAL

Improve a student's skills needed for self-regulation of behavior.

THE BASICS

1. Identify the problem.
2. Identify the replacement behavior.
3. Monitor and record behavior.
4. Prompt for student self-evaluation.
5. Ensure self-rewarding or reinforcing occurs.

HOW TO IMPLEMENT SELF-MONITORING

 PREP

- Identify a behavior for change (either to increase or decrease). This may be done in conjunction with the student or identified by the teacher or other involved adult.
- Explain the behavior to the student, articulating a definition to the extent necessary (e.g., explaining what "off task" means, discussing that homework is on time if it is turned in at the beginning of class).
- Review baseline data with the student in a non-threatening, non-accusatory way.
- Emphasize the benefits of improving academic performance.

IMPLEMENT

■ Set a reasonable and achievable goal and identify the reward for achieving this goal.

■ Choose an appropriate recording form or method for tracking the selected behavior or charting the academic data. Forms and methods employed may include using a tone or stopwatch, checklist, frequency counts, tally sheets, event recording, time sampling, narrative diary, wrist counters, graphs, charts, or tangible item counters. The method for recording can be as simple as making tally marks on a piece of paper at each instance of the behavior or as complex as writing a descriptive account of the behavior. Appropriate intervals for recording can be as short as one minute for behavior that may occur more frequently (e.g., off-task behavior during class) or once per class period for a less frequent behavior (e.g., checking for homework completion at the beginning of each class).

■ Have the student practice the technique with teacher prompting and self-monitoring and self-recording.

■ Compare notes on the frequency of the behavior and provide reinforcement to the student for accurate self-recording. In some situations positive feedback alone is a sufficient reinforcer; in others, tangible rewards are needed initially.

■ Fade the use of self-monitoring supports gradually after goal mastery.

 EVALUATE

■ Assess on an ongoing basis the student's ability to self-monitor.

■ Consider the intrusiveness of any cuing.

EVIDENCE

A brief overview of research and annotated references supporting this intervention can be found on Q-global.

CONSIDERATIONS

FOR TEACHING

Self-monitoring can be used as a classwide or individual intervention. Self-monitoring is usually very well received by parents, students, and teachers (Alberto & Troutman, 2003). Peers tend to view self-monitoring as positive, mature behavior. Self-monitoring emphasizes the positive aspects of changing behavior because goals and targets usually involve increasing a desirable behavior.

The most important factor in this intervention is the self-monitoring itself and the cognitive changes that presumably occur. Stringent accuracy of monitoring is unimportant. However, if inaccuracy becomes problematic (i.e., the student does not correctly record data a majority of the time), target behaviors may need to be re-explained, self-monitoring skills and procedures may need to be retaught, or teacher matching (i.e., student self-scores and simultaneous teacher recordings matched) may need to be employed with reinforcement contingent on accuracy.

FOR AGE AND DEVELOPMENTAL LEVEL

Self-monitoring is most appropriate for students in 3rd grade or higher, although simplified variations have been effective with younger students (Goldstein, 1995). Self-monitoring is highly applicable and developmentally appropriate for use with adolescents.

 **SELF-INSTRUCTION**

DESCRIPTION

Self-instruction, a form of verbal mediation, is a learning strategy or process in which students use verbal self-prompts (i.e., self-talk) to self-direct or mediate learning behavior (Alberto & Troutman, 2003; Graham, Harris, & Reid, 1992; Harris, 1990). Self-instruction allows students to guide themselves through the steps to solve problems or complete tasks (Alberto & Troutman, 2003). Elements of self-instruction identified by Meichenbaum and Goodman (1971) include cognitive modeling, overt external guidance, overt self-guidance, faded overt self-guidance, and covert self-instruction.

The foundation for self-instruction is verbalization of necessary steps for academic task completion. For this to occur, the teacher first models task completion using verbal self-instruction. Next, the teacher provides the verbal instruction as the student completes the task. Then, the teacher provides feedback and reinforcement as the student completes the task using verbal self-instruction. Finally, verbal cues are slowly faded until the student is able to use self-instruction silently (i.e., repeat the steps silently in his or her mind only, rather than verbalize them aloud).

EXAMPLE

Keon is learning how to plot points on a graph. His teacher instructs him to say, "The first number is 3. I will start at the origin and count three squares to the right. The second number is 2. Now, I will count two squares up. I will place a dot there. I have plotted the point (3, 2)." Keon initially repeats this aloud, but over time this self-instruction is repeated silently in his mind as he plots points on graphs.

GOAL

Improve a student's academic performance through increased autonomy and self-direction, decreased learned helplessness, and bolstered independent learning.

THE BASICS

1. Verbalize the necessary steps for academic completion.

2. Model task completion using verbal self-instruction.

3. Provide verbal instruction as the student completes the task.

4. Provide feedback and reinforcement as the student completes the task using verbal self-instruction.

HOW TO IMPLEMENT SELF-INSTRUCTION

 PREP

- Identify the academic content appropriate for self-instruction.

 IMPLEMENT

- Model and verbalize the necessary steps to complete the task.
- Ask the student to complete the task.
- Verbalize the steps while the student completes the task.
- Ask the student to verbalize the steps and complete the task simultaneously.
- Ask the student to whisper the steps while completing the task.
- Ask the student to use silent self-talk while completing the task.

■ Compare the individual completion rates, grades, and/or scores for lessons completed using self-instruction strategies to those completed without them.

EVIDENCE
A brief overview of research and annotated references supporting this intervention can be found on Q-global.

CONSIDERATIONS

FOR AGE AND DEVELOPMENTAL LEVEL
Self-instruction, like self-monitoring, requires the cognitive and verbal ability to understand the steps involved in the process. Successful implementation of self-instruction requires an adult to teach the steps and the students to memorize and internalize them. Difficulty in using self-instruction typically can be resolved through thoughtful modeling, adequate practice, and honest feedback to the student who is struggling.

Self-instruction can be useful for children starting at about age 6, when attention can be focused long enough to repeat and remember steps while engaging in an action. For example, when a 4- or 5-year-old student repeats steps, it is common for his or her verbalized repetition to be quite different from what was stated initially. Similarly, if the 5-year-old student could accurately repeat the steps, he or she would likely forget them when initiating and engaging in the behavior because the cognitive demands of both repeating the steps and acting on them are too high for most 5-year-olds.

FOR CULTURAL AND LANGUAGE DIFFERENCES
Talking to oneself comes naturally to many students, but it may seem unusual to others. A literal translation for the concepts of "self-talk" or "internal dialogue" may not exist in a student's culture or primary language. Care should be taken to accurately represent self-instruction when working with students and families from different cultures, languages, and spiritual beliefs.

 ## REPROCESSING STRATEGIES

DESCRIPTION
Reprocessing strategies require a student to review material in a way that is different from that of the original presentation. Examples of reprocessing strategies include summarization; paraphrasing; cover, copy, and compare (CCC); and self-questioning. Reprocessing strategies are useful for all stages of learning ranging from acquisition through fluency and into mastery. They help a student review newly learned information to increase associations between the new information and pre-existing knowledge.

SUMMARIZATION
Summarization involves identifying important details, discarding less important details, and creating keywords or statements that simplify the most important details. Then, one key idea (sometimes a topic sentence) is constructed to represent these keywords. This process changes reading from a passive to an active cognitive task for some students.

PARAPHRASING
Paraphrasing requires reorganization of knowledge using new words. It involves focusing attention and memory on the most important concepts and their relations, and discarding or reordering the secondary details to show their relational importance. This process promotes repetition, sorting, and application of ideas by reconceptualizing them.

COVER, COPY, AND COMPARE (CCC)

CCC is the process of looking at an instructional stimulus, removing it, and responding, followed by an immediate check for accuracy. In the case of an inaccurate response, the student repeats the steps. Variations on CCC include using a verbal response instead of a written response. This process allows for near-errorless learning and immediate corrective feedback loops. It also creates a stress-free environment for learning because no outside evaluator is looking at the work until the student deems it ready.

SELF-QUESTIONING

Self-questioning is the reprocessing of information by the student asking himself or herself questions about the information he or she is reading, predicting the answers to the questions, and then finding and talking about the answers. This process assists students in locating patterns and helps them sort and discard irrelevant information.

EXAMPLE

In learning about the water cycle in their 8th-grade earth science class, students are asked to summarize a section of their textbook that covers the topic. The next assignment requires them to paraphrase what they have read, reinforcing the key elements in the process. Prior to a quiz on the water cycle, students use a graphic organizer supplied in class to review the five stages of the process and the key elements involved in each stage by covering it, copying it onto a blank organizer, and comparing the two. Next, the students use a self-questioning process while reading the section on water pollution in their textbook. By formulating questions about what they are reading and applying existing knowledge about water cycles the students begin to develop a fuller understanding of larger environmental relationships.

GOAL

Enhance learning by providing opportunities for students to process newly acquired knowledge in alternative contexts through actively restructuring, reorganizing, and re-examining material.

THE BASICS

1. Re-expose students to the academic task using reprocessing strategies.

2. Assess for comprehension and correct errors.

HOW TO IMPLEMENT REPROCESSING STRATEGIES

 PREP

- Identify the academic content to be reinforced with reprocessing strategies.

- Select the reprocessing strategy to be used.

- Prepare an example to teach the strategy.

 IMPLEMENT

- Provide academic content instruction to students.

- Instruct students in the reprocessing strategy.

- Model use of the reprocessing strategy.

- Instruct students to engage in the reprocessing strategy.

- Compare the individual completion rates, grades, and/or scores for lessons completed using reprocessing strategies to those completed without them.

EVIDENCE

A brief overview of research and annotated references supporting this intervention can be found on Q-global.

CONSIDERATIONS

FOR TEACHING

Reprocessing strategies require the preparation of practice questions, materials, or task assignments so that students can repeatedly engage with the content or material to gain mastery and fluency. Self-correcting and self-checking for errors ideally should be monitored by a classroom teacher. Answer keys should be created for repeated use and durability to save time and resources in the future. Students respond well to this type of independent work because of the fast pace, self direction, and error-free assignments turned in as a final product, which in turn eliminate frustration and prevent the need for escape.

FOR AGE AND DEVELOPMENTAL LEVEL

Young children will need additional supervision when checking their work and are unlikely to be independent. However, these children can still lead the process, evaluating and correcting as necessary. Students with cognitive challenges and attention problems may need additional scaffolding for the steps required to create and check a response, correct errors, and advance to the next assignment.

 TASK-SELECTION STRATEGIES

DESCRIPTION

Task-selection strategies focus on the tasks that students are asked to engage in. Tasks that facilitate learning have the following characteristics: (1) are relevant to the lesson at hand; (2) provide opportunities for students to become familiar with new material, practice skills, and apply knowledge; and (3) match students' abilities and goals with performance expectations (see Center, Deitz, & Kaufman, 1982; Clarke et al., 1995; Cosden, Gannon, & Haring, 1995; Rosenberg, Sindelar, & Stedt, 1985).

The tasks offered for student selection should be relevant to the curriculum or learning objectives and should not compromise the learning goals. Tasks that are relevant to life beyond the classroom are also beneficial. This relevance may be underscored by explaining the connections between the task expectations and contexts outside the classroom.

The task difficulty level should match the performance level of the student but maintain a level of instructional rigor that meets academic expectations. Tasks usually completed with a typical accuracy rate of less than 60% cause frustration, whereas those with a rate of greater than 80% cause boredom. Matching difficulty and performance within this narrow band facilitates interest, acquisition, and stamina for task completion.

The tasks should be interesting to foster student participation and attention. However, while student interest is one component that is helpful in task-selection strategies, not all students are equally willing to engage in all activities nor do they have the same level of interest in a given task. Tasks that are attractive to students, have a reasonable length, and present engaging materials are ideal.

The range of selectable tasks will vary by grade level and content area. For early grades these tasks may include art, representations, puzzles, music, dance, song, worksheets, or writing answers. As children age and curriculum progresses, tasks become more heavily dependent on verbal skills and written expression. As a result, the curriculum complexity of later grades seldom allows for representations without accompanying verbal or written descriptions.

GOAL

Increase learning by matching learner abilities and interest to curriculum requirements.

THE BASICS

1. Ensure relevance of instructional task or activity to the curriculum or lesson.

2. Assess appropriateness for student skill level and development.

3. Assess interest to the student.

HOW TO IMPLEMENT TASK-SELECTION STRATEGIES

 PREP

- Select age- and grade-appropriate tasks that are relevant to the academic content. Consider students' interests, appropriateness, skill level, and developmental level.
- Prepare materials for the tasks.
- Prepare information about the task relevance to contexts outside the classroom.

 IMPLEMENT

- Provide academic content instruction to students.
- Oversee task selection.
- Monitor selection process.
- Monitor student progress toward task completion.

 EVALUATE

- Compare the individual completion rates, grades, and/or scores for lessons completed using task-selection strategies to those completed without them.

EVIDENCE

A brief overview of research and annotated references supporting this intervention can be found on Q-global.

CONSIDERATIONS

FOR TEACHING

Teachers sometimes view allowing student choice as compromising their authority in the classroom. However, it is important to realize that allowing choice does not place students in authority. Rather, it provides equally acceptable selections that are educationally appropriate. In doing so, student needs are met through selection based on either interest or difficulty level. Task differentiation, then, can be a way to minimize resistance, prevent failure, eliminate frustration and learned helplessness, and create a culture of responsiveness.

FOR AGE AND DEVELOPMENTAL LEVEL

Task choice is most commonly used in early childhood settings where free-time periods provide students an opportunity to engage in preferred activities or to demonstrate skills in ways they find most comfortable. Teachers of older grade levels may have less exposure to methods that encourage flexibility in how students demonstrate content knowledge mastery or engage in the curriculum because they typically are trained first in subject or content area and second in pedagogy or teaching methods. Although less common in secondary settings, choice and varied difficulty provide the same opportunities for older students and should be encouraged.

Tasks that range in difficulty level or language acquisition requirements facilitate learning by providing students with learning difficulties opportunities to complete reasonable assignments, access content, and demonstrate mastery. Label assignments based on the content or activity involved (rather than as easy or hard) to ensure students are comfortable selecting the task which best matches their current performance level.

General Intervention Considerations for Academic Problems

There are a variety of types and causes of academic problems; however, they all have enough in common to indicate several general considerations for intervention and remediation. When addressing academic problems, it is important to reflect on learning as a function of ability as well as a student's age, developmental progression, and the expectations established for the student. Teacher-, student-, and peer-mediated strategies are affected by each of these issues.

Conceptualization of learning as a function of an individual's ability to acquire new material over time lends itself to the principle of repetition. It is understood intuitively that individuals learn some material at first glance and other material only after extended and repeated exposures, and some material is never learned. This principle of time to acquire new information can sometimes create conditions in which educators overdrill (i.e., employ constant repetition of concepts and/or information). In some situations continual and repeated teaching is ineffective and alternative approaches should be considered. For example, an adolescent who continues to be taught basic math facts after more than 10 years of instruction should have the opportunity to use a calculator or learn other compensatory strategies.

Innate ability, environmental conditions, learning history, injury or illness, and internal states (e.g., motivation) all contribute to an individual's propensity for learning new material. Based on these factors, learning problems have various degrees of resolution. For example, memory and learning problems resulting from a brain injury or other medical conditions have specific curves of recovery with general expected durations for when and to what degree healing occurs. Learning problems that are a result of environmental deprivation may become permanent conditions, especially in cases of language acquisition. Learning problems that are manifestations of poor instruction or lack of opportunity for education may resolve differently depending on the duration of the absence of good instruction. Students with two consecutive years of bad classroom teaching or learning experiences are significantly more likely to drop out of school, and they have higher probabilities of nonrecovery (Hughes, 2007). Retention is the single most powerful predictor for dropping out (Rumberger, 1995), and retaining students by two grades increases their risk of dropping out of high school by 90% (Roderick, 1995).

Age is also a factor to consider. Early intervention for learning problems, much like interventions for behavior problems, is critical to successful remediation. Consider a young child experiencing problems learning to read. Treating the reading problem right away may prevent learning problems in other content areas. For example, a 4th-grade child experiencing reading problems may struggle with reading as well as history, science, geography, and any other subject matter that uses reading as a means of learning. Thus, as children age and develop, learning problems become more pronounced. Just as there are negative consequences for a wait-and-see attitude toward behavioral problems, there can be negative consequences with this approach for learning problems. Therefore, false positives in learning problem identification and treatment should be more acceptable to school professionals than false negatives. In any case, treatment should involve strategies for more effective instruction, strategies to empower students to help themselves learn, and strategies to create environments using peers as mediators to assist cooperatively in the teaching and learning processes.

The remediation of skill deficits versus performance deficits should also be considered, as each involves different interventions. In the case of skill deficits, no amount of motivation or punishment can teach a student to exhibit a skill that he or she does not possess. Motivation to earn or avoid something may increase a student's intention or attention to learn the skill, but paying him or her to speak Latin will only work if he or she already knows enough Latin to speak. A skill-deficit learning problem requires effective instruction, strategy training, and creation of a positive learning environment from acquisition through mastery of the new skill. A performance deficit, on the other hand, calls for instructional techniques or strategies and behavior management that create conditions for optimal performance and reinforce appropriate skill use. It is common to find performance-deficit techniques used inappropriately to remediate skill deficits and skill-deficit techniques used inappropriately to address performance deficits.

Individual versus small-group instruction is another consideration in academic problem remediation. Participation in pullouts; extended school time; or alternative classrooms, campuses, or districts each have a place in the remediation of learning problems. The most effective and responsive instructional model may be a one-to-one ratio of teacher to student. However, in most public school settings this ratio is not a realistic expectation for all children because classrooms generally have more than 20 students and a reasonable rate of learning is expected. Some states regulate class size by grade level or topic (e.g., kindergarten classes tend to be smaller; an advanced placement class may be smaller than the average class size). Students who struggle with learning disabilities tend to require more individualized time and instruction. An efficient method for teaching new skills may be to structure the learning environment in small groups within a large group. Large groups can sometimes facilitate modeling or demonstration requirements, and small groups or individual sessions can be used for practice and queries.

English language learners experience learning problems not unlike their native English-speaking peers. The challenges of learning in a language other than the primary involve complexities of both language and cultural differences as they apply to academic performance. For example, hand raising, volunteering, working alone or in groups, sharing answers, debating peers or teachers, defending responses, or elaborating on thinking may be cultural artifacts that do not translate universally. It is important to consider the general, not explicitly articulated expectations held by U.S. schools and teachers. Consider how your school context may create an environment that inhibits the identification and remediation of learning problems. Some examples of this include the role of parental involvement, the value of homework, the right or ability to challenge a teacher or school about decision making, or an instructional style that may seek participation and democratic equality between classes or genders.

Expectation for change is a final consideration. In general, individuals rise to expectations. However, unrealistic or inappropriate goals can deflate student efforts and leave a student feeling a loss of control and experiencing a lack of opportunities to succeed. Such feelings and experiences create learned helplessness. Thorough assessment of family history, school records, and standardized assessments of academic performance can assist in gauging appropriate goals. When appropriate, students can also be included in the goal-setting process to create an internal locus of control and prepare them to be lifelong learners who can incorporate learning into their daily lives outside the classroom.

Considerations for Assessment of Learning Problems

Many students without disabilities experience difficulties or frustrations in the classroom with learning and/or test taking. A variety of constructs associated with academic motivation and learning strategies can be assessed using the School Motivation and Learning Strategies Inventory (SMALSI; Stroud & Reynolds, 2006). Constructs assessed include study strategies, time management, organizational techniques, attention and concentration, writing and research skills, test-taking strategies, and test anxiety, each of which has an established history in educational psychology and general education literature.

The SMALSI is useful in identifying specific problem areas for students whose academic problems may be remediated prior to a referral for formal assessment or evaluation for special education. Poor learning strategies, study skills, and test-taking skills are often overlooked due to a lack of appropriate measures that allow accurate conceptualization and assessment of these problem areas.

The SMALSI is for group or individual administration. Group administration allows teachers to screen entire classrooms so they can detect individual students with specific motivation and learning strategy problems as well as trends in the classroom that could be targeted for specific, classwide remedial activities.

Chapter 7

Interventions for Anxiety

Characteristics and Conditions of Anxiety

WHAT IS ANXIETY?

Anxiety disorders are characterized by excessive worry, nervousness, specific or general fears or phobias, and self-deprecation (Reynolds & Kamphaus, 2015). Children who have anxiety disorders may feel overwhelmed easily; feel a sense of dread; and suffer from obsessive, intrusive, and bothersome thoughts. Anxiety disorders are often accompanied by somatic complaints, and anxiety may itself be a symptom of depression (Reynolds & Kamphaus, 2015). A detailed examination of a child's symptoms is needed in order to determine whether the symptoms are caused by an anxiety disorder, somatic symptom or related disorder, depressive disorder, or a combination thereof.

Anxiety disorders include panic disorder, social anxiety disorder (social phobia), specific phobias, agoraphobia, generalized anxiety disorder (GAD), and separation anxiety disorder (APA, 2013). Symptoms for each of these disorders are different, but the common presentation for all anxiety disorders involves excessive and/or irrational level of fear and worry.

Anxiety is believed to have both a biological and environmental component. Two areas of the brain, the amygdala and the hippocampus, play a significant role in anxiety disorders (McNaughton & Corr, 2004). Parents who are anxious may model anxious behavior for children or expect children to also be anxious (Aschenbrand & Kendall, 2012), so anxiety is also learned. Anxiety disorders are the result of a complex set of interactions between experiences and genetics. Research shows that anxiety is highly treatable (Hunsley, Elliott, & Therrien, 2014).

HOW COMMON IS ANXIETY?

Anxiety problems affect a number of children across the U.S. Some studies have reported anxiety disorders occurring in approximately 8% of children ages 13–18 (National Institute of Mental Health, n.d.), with a lifetime prevalence rate for this age group of 25.1% (Merikangas et al., 2010). Other studies have suggested that 15–20% of children through age 18 have had anxiety disorders (Beesdo, Knappe, & Pine, 2009). Prevalence rates for specific anxiety disorders are estimated to be somewhat lower (e.g., separation anxiety at about 4%, panic disorders less than 1% [APA, 2013]).

The BASC–3 measures anxiety through the Anxiety scale and the Withdrawal scale. The Teacher Rating Scales (TRS), the Parent Rating Scales (PRS), and the Self-Report of Personality all include items that measure general fears, nervousness, and worry, which contribute to the Anxiety scale. Items from the scale include "Is easily stressed," "Is nervous," and "Worries about things that cannot be changed." The TRS and PRS also measure the Withdrawal scale, with items related to general shyness, preference for being alone, and engagement in situations involving others. These items include "Avoids other children/adolescents," "Quickly joins group activities," and "Prefers to play alone." It is important to keep in mind that the child may show symptoms of anxiety that require intervention but may not warrant a formal diagnosis. Children scoring in the At-Risk or Clinically Significant range on the BASC–3 Anxiety or Withdrawal scales will likely benefit from some type of intervention strategy.

Theoretical Framework for Approaching Anxiety

The anxiety interventions in this chapter reflect behavioral, cognitive–behavioral, psychoeducational, and neurobiological frameworks. A behavioral approach is based on the idea that anxiety is a classically conditioned response to specific stimuli and is maintained by negative reinforcement (Compton et al., 2004). For example, if a child who feels anxious in social situations experiences relief when he or she withdraws from a group and seeks solitude, the removal of the anxious sensation may reinforce the child's tendency to withdraw again in subsequent social situations. Cognitive–behavioral theory, on the other hand, conceptualizes the behaviors associated with anxiety as being influenced by a combination of cognitive, behavioral, affective, and social factors (Kendall, Kortlander, Chansky, & Brady, 1992). For instance, a child's anxiety about speaking in class may be related to his or her dislike of particular classmates. In such a case, addressing affective and social factors are key components of effective intervention. Psychoeducation aims to demystify the disorder and to enhance the likelihood of successful treatment through greater understanding. In a similar way, neurobiology studies the biological foundations at the neuronal level for explanations of behavior.

The treatment effects for a prevention or an intervention rest on a number of factors. The level of anxiety, hereditary factors, and parental characteristics (e.g., depression, hostility, paranoia) all may impact the success of an intervention for a child (Berman, Weems, Silverman, & Kurtines, 2000). Changes in a child's environment (e.g., peer teasing, adult reprimands) can also negatively affect an intervention's success. Finally, the level of skill and fidelity in implementation may mediate outcome effects.

Interventions

Interventions for childhood anxiety—in particular, fears and phobias—are among the oldest evidence-based psychological treatments. A variety of interventions have been shown to reduce, or show promise for reducing, feelings of anxiety. Specific phobias (e.g., fear of dogs, school, water) are typically treated with behavioral interventions, whereas cognitive–behavioral interventions are often used for general anxiety disorders.

Most of the research studying the effects of interventions on reducing anxiety in children occurs in clinical or therapeutic settings rather than school-based environments. The research included in this chapter provides evidence for interventions that are expected to generalize to anxiety-related problems typically encountered by those persons working in a school setting. Evidence-based interventions for improving problems with anxiety are listed in Table 7.1. For some of the interventions in this chapter, supplemental materials (e.g., handouts, posters, checklists, daily logs, and worksheets) that are helpful for preparing, implementing, and evaluating the interventions can be found on Q-global.

Table 7.1 Interventions for Anxiety

Intervention	Prevention[1]	Early Intervention[2]	Intensive Intervention[3]
Cognitive–Behavioral Therapy Integrated Approach	X	X	X
Cognitive Restructuring		X	X
Contingency Management	X	X	X
Exposure-Based Techniques (Imaginal and In Vivo Desensitization, Emotive Imagery)		X	X
Family Therapy		X	X
Modeling (Live and Video)		X	X
Psychoeducational Approach		X	X
Relaxation Training	X	X	X
Self-Monitoring and/or Self-Assessment		X	X

[1] Prevention refers to skills that can be taught to all children or used universally; they promote better awareness and lessen the risk of problems.

[2] Early intervention includes techniques and strategies that address early warning signs or clinical signs of the risk of future problems. Early intervention may be specifically applied to one or more problems or generically applied as a skill set to prevent the development of a chronic problem. Early interventions can be delivered to groups or individuals.

[3] Intensive intervention focuses on individuals and individual problems, which are usually chronic, intensive, and require services due to the level of interference in daily functioning.

COGNITIVE–BEHAVIORAL THERAPY INTEGRATED APPROACH

DESCRIPTION

The cognitive–behavioral therapy (CBT) integrated approach for anxiety includes training in both cognitive and behavioral techniques within a prescribed number of therapy sessions. CBT is used to produce changes in thought patterns to affect changes in behaviors. CBT typically includes 5–16 sessions. The first half of the sessions focus on cognitive techniques, and the second half of the sessions focus on practicing exposure-based techniques (e.g., systematic desensitization).

Like most CBT interventions, the basic elements of those used to treat anxiety problems consist of identifying the problem (e.g., recognizing anxious feelings), creating a treatment plan, and evaluating progress throughout the sessions. Anxiety CBT sessions typically include as part of the treatment plan combinations of cognitive strategies, behavioral or exposure-based strategies (supplemented with relaxation activities), and relapse prevention strategies (Flannery-Schroeder & Kendall, 2000).

EXAMPLES

Shay, a 14-year-old female of average height and weight, refused to go into the high school cafeteria or out to eat in public with her family. When asked about the behavior, Shay related that she felt fat and said, "The other kids watch me eat and think I'm a pig. When they're watching me, I can't swallow and I start sweating. Then I feel sick." The school psychologist implemented CBT with the dual goal of helping Shay use problem-solving techniques to challenge her own negative self-talk (a cognitive technique) and gradually practice eating in the school cafeteria (a behavioral technique).

Lola, a 5-year-old girl who lost her father in a military campaign, often cried and had tantrums before school. Her mother frequently kept her home. After evaluating Lola, the school psychologist worked with both Lola and her mom over five sessions to talk about a routine of going to school and how Lola may feel when getting ready to leave. They discussed Lola's description of feeling "tickly" and together they practiced taking five deep breaths to see if that made the feeling go away. Lola's mom was then taught to help Lola practice taking five deep breaths before they get dressed and to record it with a colorful sticker on a wall chart. They learned to do five more deep breaths in the car before Lola got out. Her mom would give her a warm hug in the car for the breathing and reassure her that she would pick her up right after the bell rings at the end of the day.

GOAL

Integrate education, self-awareness, relaxation techniques, cognitive changes, and self-monitoring to reduce anxiety in children and adolescents.

THE BASICS

1. Identify the anxious behavior and hypothesize why it is occurring.
2. Reconceptualize the anxious behavior.
3. Determine a replacement behavior.
4. Practice the new behavior.
5. Evaluate the transfer of the new behavior to the child's actual setting.

HOW TO IMPLEMENT COGNITIVE–BEHAVIORAL THERAPY INTEGRATED APPROACH

 PREP

- Identify the cause of the anxiety and determine the best strategies to incorporate (e.g., cognitive restructuring and systematic desensitization).

- Determine if the sessions will occur in an individual or group format.

- Choose the strategies that best fit with the child's age and needs.

- Determine the total number of planned sessions and create a session schedule listing topics and goals.

 IMPLEMENT

- Start with a session to provide anxiety education (e.g., anxiety is influenced by brain chemistry and may have a genetic component; adults may model anxious behavior; anxiety is treatable).

- Conduct a session to teach the first strategy (e.g., relaxation training or visualization).

- Conduct one session apiece to teach each subsequent strategy (e.g., cognitive restructuring, addressing cognitive distortions, in-vivo exposure, self-rewarding).

- Conduct a session that focuses on integrating the strategies previously learned in a way that is a pattern of behavior or a seamless group of skills that can be used in specific situations or in all situations (e.g., breathing may work for social situations, cognitive restructuring may be better in classroom situations).

- Teach the child self-monitoring and self-evaluation strategies.

 EVALUATE

- Identify with the child where and when skills were used successfully. Review self-monitoring data if available. Note skills that are not used across situations (e.g., a skill used in social situations, but not in an academic setting).

- Identify possible opportunities for transfer by reviewing self-monitoring data with the child. Discuss strategies successfully used in only one setting (e.g., school) and if they could reduce anxiety when used in other settings (e.g., home, recreation).

- Discuss any existing barriers to generalization across settings.

- Identify solutions to overcome existing barriers.

EVIDENCE
A brief overview of research and annotated references supporting this intervention can be found on Q-global.

CONSIDERATIONS

FOR TEACHING
Many aspects of CBT can be taught for use by laypersons and incorporated as small skills training in classroom or classwide applications. For example, teachers may learn in a faculty development workshop to demonstrate taking deep breaths prior to distributing an exam. Teachers may walk students through visualization of performing well, remembering what they studied, and earning a good grade on the exam.

FOR AGE AND DEVELOPMENTAL LEVEL

Very young children will likely have difficulty participating in many of the cognitive aspects of CBT. Interventions that have moderate cognitive demands (e.g., cognitive restructuring) should be used primarily with children or adolescents who have the emotional development and executive functioning to perform the tasks they are asked to do (e.g., verbalize fears and phobias, and conceptualize them as a cognitive trait).

 # COGNITIVE RESTRUCTURING

DESCRIPTION

Cognitive restructuring teaches children to identify their own negative irrational thoughts and supplant them with healthier, more realistic thoughts. Children are taught to identify and classify the irrational thoughts they have during anxiety-provoking events and to challenge and modify their irrational thoughts by making realistic appraisals of the events (Hops & Lewinsohn, 1995). Cognitive restructuring techniques include rational analysis (i.e., examining evidence for and against thoughts), decatastrophising (i.e., reconsidering how bad the worst-case scenario actually is), cognitive self-control (i.e., planning, evaluating, and self-regulating problem-solving activities and attention to a task), decentering (i.e., increasing awareness through perspective shifting of focus from self to others), reattribution training (i.e., helping children determine attributes of failure that are not internal, global, or stable in nature), reframing/relabeling (i.e., identifying and disputing maladaptive thoughts), cognitive rehearsal (i.e., rehearsing a particular situation that may occur in the future), behavioral experiments, and verbal self-instruction. These strategies can be used to reinforce positive thinking and promote more positive and productive behaviors.

Successful cognitive restructuring results in improved self-evaluation and self-reward skills. Self-evaluation and self-reward are key ingredients for social phobia and anxiety treatment (Albano, Detweiler, & Logsdon-Conradsen, 1999). The ability to self-evaluate and self-reward increases self-confidence in anxiety-provoking situations.

EXAMPLES

Carlos is a 17-year-old boy who suffers from anxiety. Carlos has a fear of using public bathrooms. The therapist uses cognitive restructuring to help him recognize the aspects of the bathroom that worry him and discuss what actual effects these aspects may have on him. For example, Carlos is taught that anxious thoughts about getting germs can be reduced by using a paper towel when touching the bathroom faucet or door handle to decrease exposure to germs. The therapist challenges Carlos to reconsider using public bathrooms while using the newly learned behavior (i.e., protecting his hands with paper towels). Carlos is taught to use self-talk to remind himself about the effects of the newly learned behaviors (e.g., "Using a paper towel when touching things in the bathroom helps to keep germs off of me"). In this way, Carlos begins to reinterpret the experience of using a public bathroom, seeing it in a more positive light.

Janet is an 8-year-old girl who really worries that she may say something wrong in class and be embarrassed by the teacher. The teacher and counselor meet with Janet and help her recognize that simply thinking she may be embarrassed does not make it so. They ask Janet to identify times she has spoken up and to recognize what really happened. They complete a role-play exercise, asking questions with the teacher responding a few times. The teacher leaves a sticky-note on Janet's desk that says, "I want to hear your voice, I am on your side." This serves to remind Janet to participate in class and helps to reduce Janet's anxiety.

GOAL

Modify the cognitions associated with anxiety, thereby reducing the anxiety.

THE BASICS

1. Identify erroneous beliefs or anxious thinking.

2. Challenge the reality of these beliefs or thoughts.

3. Modify thoughts to be more rational or probable.

HOW TO IMPLEMENT COGNITIVE RESTRUCTURING

 PREP

- Identify the child's anxiety symptoms.

- Select cognitive restructuring techniques that may be particularly effective for a given situation (e.g., cognitive rehearsal may be helpful in recurrent anxiety-provoking situations such as being asked to read aloud to a class).

 IMPLEMENT

- Teach the child how to recognize thoughts that are negative. Young children may find cartoons helpful for this purpose. For example, draw a thought bubble over the head of a character and ask the child to write in what the character is thinking. Older children might keep a diary or journal of their thoughts.

- Explain how negative thoughts are connected to anxious feelings or exaggerated and unproductive thinking (as described above, the use of a cartoon or journal might be helpful).

- Explore specific actions the child can take to think more adaptively.

  ▲ Thought stopping: Ask the child to imagine a stop sign when negative thinking occurs. This cue can be used to replace a negative thought with a positive one.

  ▲ Self-tracking: Choose one negative thought (e.g., "other kids are laughing at me") and ask the child to record how often it occurs. Agree on a new thought to replace the negative one (e.g., "I'm okay just how I am.").

- Plan for relapse-prevention training after anxiety interventions are successfully implemented. Consider holding a refresher session to reduce the likelihood of a relapse of the problematic behaviors or emotions. The relapse-prevention training typically occurs during a single session in which the therapist assists the child in identifying future stressors that may trigger anxiety.

- Encourage the child to practice consistently.

 EVALUATE

- Have the child record or journal anxiety symptoms daily.

- Discuss the child's anxiety symptoms with parents or other involved adults as appropriate.

- Monitor the strategy use frequency if changes are not at the desired level.

EVIDENCE

A brief overview of research and annotated references supporting this intervention can be found on Q-global.

CONSIDERATIONS

FOR AGE AND DEVELOPMENTAL LEVEL

Interventions that have moderate cognitive demands (e.g., cognitive restructuring) should be used primarily with children or adolescents who have the emotional development and executive functioning skills to perform the necessary tasks (e.g., verbalize fears and phobias and conceptualize them as a cognitive trait). Such interventions will likely be inappropriate with young or nonverbal children. For younger children, tools or methods such as songs, rhymes, or video representations may be helpful in identifying negative cognitions and understanding the connections among thoughts, feelings, and behaviors.

 # CONTINGENCY MANAGEMENT

DESCRIPTION

Contingency management relies on the use of natural consequences and reinforcers for reducing anxieties associated with specific behaviors or events (Flood & Wilder, 2004). Contingency management for anxiety includes shaping, positive reinforcement, and extinction (King, Muris, & Ollendick, 2005).

Contingency management requires rewards and consequences tailored to the needs and preferences of each child. To be effective, reinforcers must be desirable to the child, and consequences must be focused on changing maladaptive behavior (e.g., truancy, avoidance, lying to escape) rather than punishing the anxiety. Tangible reinforcers are gradually replaced by social reinforcers (e.g., attention, praise) and ultimately by internal management and reinforcement (e.g., feeling good about the situation and accomplishments). Fading out reinforcers increases the likelihood that desired behavior will continue beyond the period of direct intervention and that the child will learn how to handle future anxiety.

EXAMPLES

Jennifer, a high school student, experiences severe test anxiety. She has an identified disability and is permitted to take tests in the library, which is quiet, relaxing, and welcoming. Her test anxiety is real as are the escape contingencies. Contingency management requires Jennifer to complete tests in the classroom, thereby earning a reward of library time to be used at her discretion. Additional reinforcers (e.g., creating a more relaxing environment, receiving an external reward upon completion of the test, forgoing the completion of certain parts of the test) may be needed to help Jennifer remain in the classroom when taking tests.

Linus, a preschooler with previously identified anxiety problems, crawls under his desk when it is time to participate in a group activity. Linus engages in negative behaviors (e.g., biting) in an effort to remain under the desk when his teacher attempts to redirect him. Reinforcement for joining the group and participating could be used to change Linus's behavior.

GOAL

Alter the child's anxious or fear-based behavior by eliminating the contingencies that support them and by creating more powerful contingencies for replacement behavior.

THE BASICS

1. Identify contingencies currently maintaining the problem behavior resulting from the anxiety.

2. Ignore problem behavior and eliminate any prior contingencies maintaining undesirable behavior.

3. Institute frequent and powerful reinforcers for engaging in the desirable behavior.

HOW TO IMPLEMENT CONTINGENCY MANAGEMENT

 PREP

- Identify the specific anxiety-related behaviors to be addressed.
- Ask the child to choose from an existing list of preferred reinforcers.
- Create a reinforcement schedule.
- Determine appropriate consequences for maladaptive behaviors (e.g., what will happen if the child responds to anxiety by throwing a tantrum, destroying property, or refusing to engage in a desired activity).

 IMPLEMENT

- Review the reinforcement schedule with the child.
- Review the consequences for maladaptive behaviors with the child.
- Use shaping techniques (i.e., reinforce successive approximations to engage in the desired behavior) during the initial stages of treatment.
- Replace tangible reinforcers with social reinforcers. This transition should be planned and gradual, at a pace designed to meet the needs of the child while maintaining the effect of the reinforcement for appropriate behavior.

 EVALUATE

- Monitor and record the frequency of inappropriate and appropriate behaviors.
- Monitor the strategy use frequency if changes are not at the desired level.
- Reassess the reinforcer strength and reinforcement schedule if the strategy is implemented faithfully with poor results. Consider aspects such as: Is the reinforcement schedule a 1:1 ratio? Is shaping needed? Is the reinforcement maintaining interest?

EVIDENCE
A brief overview of research and annotated references supporting this intervention can be found on Q-global.

CONSIDERATIONS
Competing reinforcement outside the control of the therapist can affect the effectiveness of this intervention. For example, reinforcers such as reward tokens or extra computer time may be weaker than other available reinforcers (e.g., attention from peers, the feeling of relief from crying or making up an excuse to avoid taking a test). Finally, consider the effects of satiation. If the child has extensive access to the reinforcer its reinforcement properties may weaken.

FOR AGE AND DEVELOPMENTAL LEVEL
When asking children to generate a list of desired reinforcers it is important to remind them to list things that are both realistic and age-appropriate. In order to avoid problems, consider asking a parent to provide some examples of attainable reinforcers and then give the child the option to choose from such a list. When generating a list of reinforcers, consult with teachers or other adults because they can sometimes provide clues about preferences and high-interest activities. Young children may be more comfortable with small numbers of choices, such as a fruit snack, rocking in a chair, or choosing a song for circle time. Older children may prefer access to music, social time with peers, or one-on-one time with a teacher.

FOR CULTURAL AND LANGUAGE DIFFERENCES

Be aware that apparent anxiety may actually be post-traumatic stress in individuals who immigrated under stressful conditions. A new culture, a new language, and the accompanying expectations may create performance anxiety that is difficult to escape at school, where both academic and social expectations are tied to a specific culture. Carefully consider all factors that may contribute to anxious behavior.

FOR SAFETY

Anxiety or phobic reactions to certain events may be rooted in violence, abuse, or neglect. Carefully consider the antecedents to anxiety. For example, fear of showering in a locker room could require great sensitivity in treatment (more than just rewards for performance) if the showering fear is associated with abuse. Likewise, the gender of some teachers, appearance, tone of voice, or other similarities to an abuser may be hidden triggers of anxiety.

EXPOSURE-BASED TECHNIQUES (IMAGINAL AND IN VIVO DESENSITIZATION, EMOTIVE IMAGERY)

DESCRIPTION

Exposure-based techniques are variants of systematic desensitization (Wolpe, 1958), including emotive imagery (Lazarus & Abramovitz, 1962), imaginal desensitization, and in vivo desensitization. Such techniques are counter-conditioning strategies that require a child to confront a series of anxiety-producing stimuli in a gradual, systematic progression (building slowly from the least to the most anxiety producing) while simultaneously engaging in behaviors that are incompatible with anxiety (Akande et al., 1999; Compton et al., 2004; Wolpe, 1958). The stimuli may be either imaginal or real. The use of relaxation techniques, such as progressive muscle relaxation or breathing exercises, applied concurrently with gradual exposure to aversive stimuli, enables the eventual elimination of escape and avoidance behaviors (Compton et al., 2004).

A key component of this strategy is establishing a child's "anxiety hierarchy." This can be accomplished in a number of ways. A simple technique is to record each anxiety-producing event or stimulus on a note card and ask the child to rank the cards from least to most anxiety provoking (Akande & Akande, 1994; Morris, 1980). The resulting anxiety hierarchy can serve as a guide for dealing with anxiety problems, starting with the event or stimulus that is least anxiety provoking and working up toward events or stimuli that are most anxiety provoking.

Emotive imagery, a variant of imaginal exposure, uses themes with positive emotional resonance for the child, such as superheroes or favorite TV characters, to counter-condition the child's anxiety. While the child is focused on a positive image of the hero in the story, the therapist introduces an anxiety hierarchy item into the plot, and the positive emotions associated with the hero interfere with the child's usual anxious response to the stimulus.

EXAMPLES

Kwan experiences intense anxiety every day when required to attend 1st grade. Kwan cries and refuses to get out of bed when his mother wakes him each morning. It is determined that no specific negative event led to his anxious feelings (i.e., there is no functional cause). The therapist uses exposure-based techniques to work with Kwan and his mother to develop Kwan's tolerance for going to school. The therapist first shows Kwan pictures of the school until Kwan is able to look at the pictures without crying. Then, the therapist has Kwan and his mother drive up to the school but not get out of the car until Kwan can handle driving up to the school without feeling anxious. Next, he progresses to walking up to the school without going in, then to going inside the building, and finally to entering his classroom. Kwan uses a variety of relaxation techniques throughout the progression to calm himself along the way. Kwan concentrates on counting to 30 when driving up to the school to distract himself from his anxious feelings, and he focuses on maintaining a steady rate of breathing when walking to the school doors.

Zuri walks to school every day and is afraid of dogs. A new neighbor keeps a dog in the front yard. Zuri has been skipping school because she is unable to walk past the new neighbor's yard. The therapist explains to Zuri that he is going to teach her some relaxation techniques. Zuri is reassured that nothing anxiety-provoking will happen during these sessions and that she will learn to overcome her fear of dogs. The therapist also reassures Zuri that she may leave the room whenever she needs to, but that he hopes she will practice her breathing while thinking about her favorite place. The first exposure is to a cartoon image of a dog. The therapist guides her to pick a favorite place and imagine it in her mind's eye while she counts her breathing. Zuri is taught to inhale for five seconds and exhale for five seconds. She responds, "That is not a real dog." She is guided to count her breathing and recall her favorite place. Next, the therapist exposes her to a photo of a very small, fluffy dog at a dog show. They proceed through several photos until Zuri identifies one as scary: a Doberman. The exposure continues across sessions through static images, video clips of dogs playing, then video clips of dogs barking. Finally, Zuri observes a real dog and approaches it. Each time the therapist debriefs, emphasizing to Zuri that nothing bad happened.

GOAL
Counter-condition the child's anxiety response and gradually decrease symptoms of situational anxiety.

THE BASICS
1. Teach relaxation training methods.
2. Develop skills that enable the recognition of anxiety hierarchies.
3. Implement desensitization strategies.

HOW TO IMPLEMENT EXPOSURE-BASED TECHNIQUES

PREP

- Conduct an initial meeting with the child (and as appropriate) to determine/identify the anxiety hierarchy. List items in the hierarchy according to the degree of fear or anxiety produced by each, beginning with the stimulus that produces the least amount of anxiety or fear and then increasing gradually. It may be helpful to include the parent(s) in this step as well.

- Acquire the materials that will be used during exposure. These could include actual objects or videos that will be used for exposure, or identifying and arranging for situations in which the exposure will take place.

IMPLEMENT

- Establish a warm, supportive, therapeutic environment that is based on the individual needs or situation of the child.

- Teach the child to recognize physical sensations that signal anxiety (e.g., muscle tension, hands shaking, stomach uneasiness).

- Teach the child relaxation techniques (e.g., progressive muscle relaxation, breathing exercises).

- Lead the child through the anxiety hierarchy established during the PREP stage. Start by having the child spend 3–5 minutes focusing on relaxing the body, then use imaginal desensitization techniques. For example, guide a young child through a series of carefully scripted emotive imagery exercises that incorporate the child's favorite superheroes while gradually introducing items from the child's anxiety hierarchy into the plot of the story.

- Instruct the child to close his or her eyes and concentrate on clearly imagining the scene that is described from the anxiety hierarchy, focusing on the senses of sight, hearing, smell, and touch.

- Have the child describe the scene in detail from the perspective of all senses.

- Use a carefully constructed script to tell a story that incorporates the child's name, heightens the child's positive feelings, and (if using emotive imagery) connects the child to his or her hero.

- Ask the child if the scene is too frightening; if it is, stop the script and help the child refocus on the positive aspects of the scene.

- Gradually work toward in vivo exposure.

EVALUATE

- Observe or ask for self-report of successful desensitization.

EVIDENCE

A brief overview of research and annotated references supporting this intervention can be found on Q-global.

CONSIDERATIONS

When implementing exposure-based techniques, it is important to keep in mind that some anxieties may require particular sensitivity (e.g., fear and anxiety experienced by a person who has been bullied, threatened, or abused) because that anxiety may accompany post-traumatic stress disorder.

FOR AGE AND DEVELOPMENTAL LEVEL

Exposure-based techniques may be inappropriate for very young children if they lack the social and verbal skills necessary to request ending a stressful therapy session. In addition, imaginal desensitization exercises may be too abstract for a very young child to understand.

DESCRIPTION

Involving family members in anxiety intervention strategies can increase effectiveness. Research has examined the effects of several strategies for increasing parental involvement or modifying the type of involvement that currently exists, including modifying attachment levels and caregiving practices, decreasing maternal control, and providing communication training (Ginsburg, Silverman, & Kurtines, 1995; Howes, Galinsky, & Kontos, 1998; Kochanska & Aksan, 1995).

While the implementation of various family involvement approaches varies, most will require several educational sessions to teach the common causes, consequences, and strategies to combat anxiety. Examples of common training topics include anxiety management, discipline management, and communication. Each of these strategies involves distinct procedural steps for implementation, so these steps are not listed in this chapter.

EXAMPLE

Emily experiences anxiety from several sources, including fears of the dark, speaking out in school, and talking to other children. One parent is very supportive bordering on enabling. The other parent believes Emily needs to be forced to sleep in the dark, speak in class, and make friends. Emily's parents receive training in the basis of anxiety, the common consequences of it, and two techniques for managing anxiety to use at home. The techniques are indicated to support Emily when she feels anxious. Both parents monitor Emily's use of the techniques. The parents are also taught how to work with Emily in a more positive way to help her overcome anxiety. They learn not to blame her for wanting attention and not to overindulge all of her fears.

GOAL
Reduce the child's anxiety through education and support.

THE BASICS

1. Identify the child's specific anxiety problems and find related instructional materials.

2. Involve family members in training.

3. Provide opportunities for family members to practice skills.

HOW TO IMPLEMENT FAMILY THERAPY

 PREP

- Identify family candidates and organize small group or private training sessions.

- Develop or acquire materials, such as curriculum or lessons on key topics.

 IMPLEMENT

- Teach anxiety management strategies, such as recognizing positive and negative thoughts.

- Use modeling and role-play to teach strategies.

- Teach how to recognize and reinforce courageous behavior.

- Teach techniques for parents to minimize anxiety in children.

- When appropriate, teach methods for parents to manage their own anxiety and thus prevent modeling.

- Teach strategies to effectively communicate anxiety in an appropriate way.

- Teach self-evaluation skills and self-reward skills to reinforce appropriate behavior.

 EVALUATE

- Monitor session attendance and participation.

- Observe behaviors while practicing targeted skills.

- Assess knowledge of learned strategies and behaviors.

- Use role-play or daily logs to assess understanding of content.

EVIDENCE
A brief overview of research and annotated references supporting this intervention can be found on Q-global.

CONSIDERATIONS

For Cultural and Language Differences
Families deserve respect as autonomous units that may have different values and structures than either those of the school professional or the school normative culture. The important consideration is sharing of education and expectations, and providing training to the extent it is desired. The focus should be on supporting the family members while they support the child, rather than attributing blame or trying to change a family or child. Culture and language can certainly be challenges to working together, but they can also be strengths. It is important to find common ground and seek a platform of understanding so that information is accurately and helpfully translated.

MODELING (LIVE AND VIDEO)

DESCRIPTION

Showing children examples of successful outcomes in anxiety-provoking situations can effectively reduce anxiety-related beliefs and behaviors. Both live and video modeling are based on the concept of vicarious conditioning (Bandura, 1977; Berger, 1962). One variation of this approach is to use participant modeling, in which the child becomes an active participant in the exercise. The child observes a therapist or other trusted individual successfully confront an anxiety-provoking stimulus then mimics the model's behavior to confront the anxiety-provoking stimulus successfully.

EXAMPLES

Ray is afraid of birds and will not go into the nurse's office at school because he has to pass a cage with a parrot in it. The nurse uses her phone to record video of a boy that is the same size as Ray walking past the bird and into her office. Ray watches the video several times and they discuss how nothing bad happened to the boy. The video helped Ray to recognize that he could also walk by the bird without anything bad happening. Ray then observes another child interacting with a real bird, and the therapist and Ray discuss how nothing bad happened to the other child.

Riley, who has Down syndrome, has high anxiety when going to the dentist's office. The therapist shows her a video of other children going to the dentist. Scenes are comprised of children walking in, sitting in the chair, being greeted by the dental hygienist, watching TV or listening to headphones while having their teeth worked on, and then exiting with a new toothbrush. Riley watches the video to learn that you can wear headphones or watch TV to help distract yourself from any anxious feelings.

GOAL

Reduce the child's anxiety by demonstrating the event and consequences in a non-anxiety provoking manner, and help the child acquire a new skill to manage the anxiety.

THE BASICS

1. Identify the anxiety-provoking scenario.

2. Present the scenario live or using a video in a way that demonstrates a desirable and successful outcome.

3. Have the anxious child narrate or debrief the events that happened during modeling and practice what was learned.

HOW TO IMPLEMENT MODELING

 PREP

- Identify the anxiety-related problem.
- Determine if live or video models will be used.
- Create or acquire a video and any props needed for modeling or recording video.

 IMPLEMENT

- Assess the child's current responses to the anxiety-related situation.
- Identify, describe, and discuss the anxiety problem with the child.
- Discuss the concept of watching a model and how it can assist in reducing anxiety.

- Reassure the child that nothing bad will happen during the demonstration.
- Show the child an anxiety-provoking situation or event using live or recorded models.
- Discuss with the child the events in the demonstration.
- Identify the antecedents to the event, the event itself, and the consequences of the event.
- Ask the child to identify the responses and behaviors used by the models that would feel comfortable.
- Ask the child to describe how he or she would engage in such responses and behaviors.
- Practice the desired responses and behaviors with the child.
- Ask the child (and/or involved adults as appropriate) to track the child's responses to the anxiety-provoking situation.

 EVALUATE

- Monitor changes in the child's responses to the anxiety-provoking situation.
- Review practice sessions.
- Provide additional modeling as necessary and appropriate.
- Provide feedback as needed.

EVIDENCE
A brief overview of research and annotated references supporting this intervention can be found on Q-global.

CONSIDERATIONS
The primary concept in modeling—critical to the effectiveness of the intervention—is a successful experience with the anxiety-provoking event. If at any time the modeling or video becomes stressful for the child the session should cease. Resistance should build through gradual exposure. Videos or models should be sensitive to culture, language, and age appropriateness. Subjects who are similar to the child are more relatable to the child (e.g., an adult male is unlikely to be a good model for a 6-year-old girl).

 # PSYCHOEDUCATIONAL APPROACH

DESCRIPTION
The psychoeducational component of cognitive intervention for anxiety focuses on teaching children and sometimes their families about the causes and symptoms of anxiety. It also involves teaching how and why certain events or behaviors may lead to an emotional response (Kearney, 2005; March & Ollendick, 2004). By learning about the thoughts and behaviors that bring about anxiety, children can begin to recognize their interrelations. This recognition lays the groundwork for behavioral and emotional change.

EXAMPLES
Darius has generalized anxiety and rubs his thumb and finger together until they are chapped and raw. Darius is taught that this is a signal from his brain to stay calm and to focus on something rather than worry. Darius also learns to focus on his breathing rather than rub his fingers as a way to make the worrying go away.

Jeannie, a bright high-school student, pulls out the hair behind her ear whenever she feels anxious. Jeannie is taught about the limbic system and the brain chemistry involved in anxiety. She does a small Internet-based research project and learns a mindfulness technique where she stills her body and pays attention to the sounds in the environment around her.

GOAL

Teach children the nature of anxiety, its symptoms, and the goal(s) of therapy in order to demystify, decrease, and help them recognize anxiety.

THE BASICS

1. Review the common causes of anxiety with the child.

2. Generate a list of anxiety-provoking stimuli.

3. Discuss the affective responses that are caused by the anxiety-provoking stimuli.

HOW TO IMPLEMENT THE PSYCHOEDUCATIONAL APPROACH

 PREP

- Obtain basic knowledge about and prepare information explaining brain chemistry and/or the condition of anxiety.

- Gather visual aids for instructional purposes.

 IMPLEMENT

- Teach awareness. Anxiety is sometimes generalized and nonspecific, but typically it is tied to an initial negative experience that triggers a fight or flight response. Individual predispositions vary.

- Teach the child about physiological and biological responses to anxiety. Physiological responses to events are real, not imagined, and can become generalized. Demonstrate or view relevant images (e.g., neurons, the limbic system, or brain scans showing anxiety as a chemical process).

- Teach the concept of generalization. For example, a child read a frightening story may transfer that feeling to other similar or possibly unrelated events.

- Develop strategies to reduce anxiety and fear based on the information learned. Anxiety can be reduced simply by realizing that the physiological response is natural and not something that is unusual about the child.

- Identify the triggers or stimuli for eliciting the anxiety and any consequences that result.

 EVALUATE

- Use the information gained by the child during psychoeducational sessions as a basis for creating effective behavioral strategies tailored to the child's specific needs.

- Monitor the treatment as it proceeds to determine if additional psychoeducation is necessary. As the need becomes evident, reinstruct the child about relevant information that he or she does not retain.

EVIDENCE

A brief overview of research and annotated references supporting this intervention can be found on Q-global.

CONSIDERATIONS

FOR AGE AND DEVELOPMENTAL LEVEL

For maximum effectiveness, children should have adequate verbal skills and be able to comprehend the concepts presented at a high level. Written materials to supplement verbal instructions, and visual materials to increase understanding of the abstract concepts of brain chemistry, are helpful in promoting comprehension and retention.

RELAXATION TRAINING

DESCRIPTION

Physical discomfort caused by muscle tension can exacerbate common anxiety symptoms, causing a child to become even more anxious. Relaxation training teaches children to employ relaxation techniques (e.g., monitor and intentionally reduce muscle tension created by stressful situations and events, control irregular breathing by slowly breathing in through the nose and out through the mouth) to reduce muscle tension (Kearney, 2005; Ollendick & Cerny, 1981).

Relaxation techniques include counting and breathing, recall, mental imagery, and progressive muscle relaxation (Kahn, Kehle, Jenson, & Clarke, 1990). Counting and breathing are simple for children of all ages and require the child to concentrate on counting or breathing when he or she feels anxiety symptoms. The recall technique requires a child to think about a previous successful or pleasant event. Reexperiencing pleasant feelings and emotions associated with the event can help reduce negative feelings and emotions. Mental imagery and progressive muscle relaxation require a child to focus on a specific event or part of the body and to envision the steps needed to succeed at the event or to relax the affected part of the body. All these techniques involve identifying the emotional triggers and their corresponding physical symptoms, engaging in an activity designed to reduce the negative emotions associated with the anxiety symptoms, and recognizing when the negative emotions and feelings start to improve.

EXAMPLE

Luanna, a 4th grader, experiences extreme anxiety when placed in new surroundings. Luanna learns from a community volunteer how to practice relaxation training. She is taught three techniques. First, she learns to close her eyes and imagine scenes from her favorite movie. She pictures the princess singing at a fountain and riding her horse through the forest. Second, she learns to count so her breaths take twice as long to exhale as to inhale; she counts and breathes in for three seconds then counts and breathes out for six seconds. Third, she learns to relax her body starting at the top of her head. She first concentrates on her scalp and then relaxes her facial muscles until she feels like her jaw will drop open. Then she moves down her neck and lowers her shoulders, and so on, until she gets to her toes. When Luanna is asked which technique is her favorite she states it is the third technique (i.e., body relaxation).

GOAL

Reduce the child's anxiety through physiological responses to slowed breathing and positive imagery.

THE BASICS

1. Identify the context in which anxiety occurs.

2. Provide options for relaxation training based on strengths and interest.

3. Teach procedures through modeling, practice, and feedback.

HOW TO IMPLEMENT RELAXATION TRAINING

 PREP

- Identify a specific symptom of the child's anxiety, along with the effect it has on the child (e.g., increased sweating results in embarrassment).
- Introduce the concept of relaxation training prior to initiating the intervention.
- List feasible relaxation techniques and inquire about the child's preferences when appropriate.
- Select among the various types of relaxation techniques.

IMPLEMENT

- Teach the child how to perform the preferred relaxation technique. Model the steps for the child as necessary.

- Ask the child to imagine a situation that typically causes the undesired symptoms.

- Practice the technique with the child until he or she is able to perform the steps by himself or herself.

EVALUATE

- Monitor the child's progress by checking in with the child periodically to determine if the relaxation techniques are being practiced correctly and at the appropriate times.

- Assess ongoing anxiety symptoms.

- Provide refresher training as necessary.

EVIDENCE

A brief overview of research and annotated references supporting this intervention can be found on Q-global.

CONSIDERATIONS

FOR AGE AND DEVELOPMENTAL LEVEL

Young children may not have the requisite cognitive skills to successfully perform all relaxation techniques. Specifically, mental imagery and recall may be too abstract for a young child to comprehend and implement.

SELF-MONITORING AND/OR SELF-ASSESSMENT

DESCRIPTION

In self-monitoring and/or self-assessment, the child learns to self-monitor aversive physiological reactions, irrational thoughts, and avoidance behavior (Ginsburg & Walkup, 2004). Diaries, charts, or logbooks can be used to self-monitor. Children are taught to recognize the antecedents (or triggers) and consequences of anxiety. Self-talk is incorporated as part of self-monitoring. A component of this is accurate self-awareness and meta-cognition.

The elements essential to self-monitoring training include monitoring, recording, and evaluating behaviors and emotions; learning to recognize when and how to implement new behaviors to reduce the effects of anxiety; and learning when to reinforce changes in behavior. Self-monitoring typically involves recording physiological reactions using paper and pencil, audio, and/or video. Recording sheets can be as simple as a chart or table for the child to fill in or a piece of graph paper from a tablet. Some children prefer journaling but may need structure to guide them to record specific behaviors or feelings rather than just private musings. Type and frequency of recording vary depending on the type and degree of symptomatology.

EXAMPLES

Gwen, a junior in high school, sits by herself during social times or open activities. With the help of a professional Gwen begins recording how she spends her free time. She records free time as either "alone" or "with a friend" and checks how she feels using a 3-point scale (i.e., upset, nervous, or normal). Gwen is then given a target to try and tell herself that she is fine and has many friends willing to spend time with her when she wants them. After select social situations, Gwen is highly self-critical and endures self-admonishment for what she said or how she acted as she replays the interactions of the social event in her mind. The professional works with Gwen for a more accurate self-appraisal.

Bobby, a kindergartner, avoids the boy's bathroom and is taught to record his level of apprehension by circling a red, yellow, or green light on a stop sign graphic prior to the class bathroom breaks. Bobby frequently circles red, and with his teacher, decides to try and move the feeling from red to yellow before entering the bathroom by visualizing the routine of waiting in line in the hall, taking a turn in the bathroom, washing his hands, and walking to the library.

GOAL
Reduce the child's anxiety through a methodological approach to greater self-awareness.

THE BASICS

1. Identify the child's trigger(s) for anxiety.

2. Identify reaction(s) to anxiety and record presence, absence, or level of distress.

3. Provide corrective feedback for inaccurate recordings.

HOW TO IMPLEMENT SELF-MONITORING AND/OR SELF-ASSESSMENT

 PREP

- Generate a form the child can use to monitor and track emotions and behavior. Forms used for tracking could be a calendar, notebook, or journal.

- Develop a procedure for the child to follow when using the form. Recordings could be made hourly or daily. Shorter intervals (e.g., every 15 minutes) might be helpful when there are a number of different transitions made during a day (e.g., classroom changes during school).

- Determine how frequently to check in or meet with the child and establish a time to review the tracking form.

 IMPLEMENT

- Choose one or two problem emotions or behaviors to monitor and evaluate.

- Train the child to use the tracking form to monitor the selected emotions or behaviors.

- Review the child's completed tracking form.

- Discuss with the child how distorted thoughts may affect his or her everyday behavior.

- Monitor feelings, problems, and replacement behaviors.

 EVALUATE

- Check in with the child to mark progress and provide feedback. This check-in can be done at the beginning and end of the school day, for example, or more frequently as needed (particularly in the early stages of intervention).

- Reward positive efforts regardless of success, including consistent use of the tracking form and any steps made to resolve problem emotions and behaviors.

EVIDENCE

A brief overview of research and annotated references supporting this intervention can be found on Q-global.

CONSIDERATIONS

FOR AGE AND DEVELOPMENTAL LEVEL

Age and developmental level of the child will have an impact on the types of ratings and sophistication of the self-evaluation. Icons, graphics, and symbols should be used with children under the age of 12. As children become more self-aware, assessments may be more abstract. Use concrete descriptions of feelings and behaviors whenever possible. Use clear representations in any self-recording that may occur with self-monitoring. Repetition will be necessary for most children.

Chapter 8

Interventions for Depression

Characteristics and Conditions of Depression

WHAT IS DEPRESSION?

Depression is a condition in which a person experiences significant distress and impaired life functioning. With a major depressive episode, mood may be depressed most or all of the day every day for two weeks. Depression generally manifests with a persistent sad or irritable mood and with a decrease in pleasure derived from activities that were previously enjoyable (APA, 2013).

Depression can occur after a stressful event and can cause temporary or permanent changes in the brain. Genetics also plays a role in susceptibility to depression due to life events, stressors, and development (APA, 2013).

The *DSM–5* states that children and adolescents with depression may be irritable or moody, exhibit changes in eating patterns, have difficulty sleeping or concentrating, have feelings of worthlessness and inappropriate guilt, experience loss of energy or extreme fatigue, and have recurrent thoughts or fears of death or suicide (APA, 2013).

A child may show depressive symptoms that may not warrant a formal diagnosis but still require intervention. Historically, professionals did not know that children could have depression. Treatment was not provided, and children and adolescents with depression were assumed merely to have difficult personalities. Fortunately, this is no longer the case. Depression is recognized as an illness that occurs in children and adolescents and as a chemical change in the brain precipitated by any number or combination of neurological and biological factors.

HOW COMMON IS DEPRESSION?

Depression is a common condition in childhood and adolescence, with estimates of 8–10% prevalence among school-aged children, and it is the leading cause for suicide in adolescents. As many as 20% of adolescents report experiencing depression by age 18 (Bansal, Goyal, & Srivastava, 2009). Depression is increasingly diagnosed in younger children, with 1–2% of preschool children receiving diagnoses (Egger & Angold, 2006).

The BASC–3 Depression scale measures feelings of unhappiness, sadness, and stress that may result in an inability to carry out everyday activities or may bring on thoughts of suicide. Depression scale items on the Teacher Rating Scales, Parent Rating Scales, and Self-Report of Personality assess many symptoms related to *DSM–5* criteria for a major depressive episode. Items include "Is sad," "Is irritable," or "I feel depressed" (depressed mood), "Says, 'I want to die' or 'I wish I were dead'" (suicidal ideation), and "Says, 'Nobody likes me'" or "I don't seem to do anything right" (feelings of worthlessness). Children scoring in the At-Risk or Clinically Significant range on the BASC–3 Depression scale may well require intervention.

Theoretical Framework for Approaching Depression

Depression is a brain illness. It is a condition resulting from a combination of distorted cognitions; a lack of positive reinforcement for rational cognitions and behaviors; and an abundance of negative reinforcement for dysfunctional emotions, thinking, and behaviors (Jacobson et al., 1996; Kanter, Callaghan, Landes, Busch, & Brown, 2004; Lewinsohn, Hoberman, Teri, & Hautzinger, 1985).

This chapter focuses primarily on the cognitive and behavioral aspects of depression and effective cognitive–behavioral interventions. Pharmacology treatments (medicine) are not discussed; while these are effective, they usually produce the highest gains when used in combination with cognitive–behavioral approaches.

Cognitive theory finds the source of depression in negative or depression-producing thoughts or schemas. Negative events experienced by a person are linked to internal attributes, resulting in negative thinking that is used to interpret new events, which can ultimately lead to depression (Beck, 1976). For example, Krystal, an 11-year-old girl, rarely has had success in school and has little interest in hobbies or interacting with other children. Her inability to get good grades and make friends has led to a sense of worthlessness. Even when Krystal received an invitation to a party from a classmate, she refused to go, saying "I won't fit in," and "Nobody really wants me there anyway."

Behavioral theory, on the other hand, considers depression to be a result of stressful events that lead to a disruption of adaptive behavior or stem from a lack of positive reinforcement and an excess of negative consequences (Weersing & Brent, 2006). For example, Isaac, a 9-year-old boy who was always considered normal, experienced a series of negative events over the course of a year (e.g., moved into a new school district and was unable to make new friends, parents pursued a divorce) that led to symptoms of depression. Isaac started to perform poorly in school and was reprimanded frequently by his parents and teachers for poor academic performance and failing to socialize with others. Isaac's performance continued to worsen, as did his depressive symptoms. Isaac had experienced several significant, stressful events that resulted in negative consequences.

Interventions

A variety of interventions are effective in reducing depressive symptomatology. In this chapter, school- and community-based cognitive–behavioral interventions are presented. Cognitive interventions assume distorted cognitions about oneself and circumstances are at the center of the depressive symptomatology. Behavioral interventions assume depression results from stressful events causing disruption in adaptive behaviors (Beck, Rush, Shaw, & Emery, 1979; Lewinsohn, Clarke, Rohde, Hops, & Seeley, 1996; Meichenbaum, 1977). Cognitive–behavioral approaches may include one (or more) of the strategies listed in Table 8.1. For some of the interventions in this chapter, supplemental materials (e.g., handouts, posters, checklists, daily logs, and worksheets) that are helpful for preparing, implementing, and evaluating the interventions can be found on Q-global.

Table 8.1 Interventions for Depression

Intervention	Prevention[1]	Early Intervention[2]	Intensive Intervention[3]
Cognitive–Behavioral Therapy (which typically includes one or more of the strategies below)		X	X
Psychoeducation		X	X
Problem-Solving Skills Training		X	X
Cognitive Restructuring		X	X
Pleasant-Activity Planning	X	X	X
Relaxation Training	X	X	X
Self-Management Training	X	X	X
Family Involvement		X	X
Interpersonal Psychotherapy			X

[1] Prevention refers to skills that can be taught to all children or used universally; they promote better awareness and lessen the risk of problems.

[2] Early intervention includes techniques and strategies that address early warning signs or clinical signs of the risk of future problems. Early intervention may be specifically applied to one or more problems or generically applied as a skill set to prevent the development of a chronic problem. Early interventions can be delivered to groups or individuals.

[3] Intensive intervention focuses on individuals and individual problems, which are usually chronic, intensive, and require services due to the level of interference in daily functioning.

COGNITIVE–BEHAVIORAL THERAPY

Cognitive behavioral therapy (CBT) as an intervention for depression integrates cognitive, behavioral, affective, and social strategies to change thought patterns. Changes to these thought patterns result in a change in behavior (Corey, 1991; Kendall et al., 1992). The emphasis during treatment is placed on changing unhealthy thoughts and emotions over the course of a relatively brief period of time, generally 5–16 sessions, depending on the specific needs of the child (Lewinsohn & Clarke, 1999; Roberts, Lazicki-Puddy, Puddy, & Johnson, 2003). The total number of sessions is typically determined within the first few sessions and the determination is made explicit to both the child and the parent(s). If the goals for behavioral change are not reached by the end of the prescribed treatment period, booster sessions are sometimes added to increase the effectiveness of the treatment (Lewinsohn & Clarke, 1999).

Most CBT interventions consist of the same basic elements. A general planning stage defines what is covered over the prescribed number of sessions. Between sessions, individuals often receive homework assignments that are reviewed during the next session. Throughout treatment, participants track their progress and the treatment plan is modified as needed.

While most often used on an individual basis, CBT also can be implemented in group formats. The advantage of group implementation is the perception that it is a form of general education rather than therapy as with one-on-one sessions (Lewinsohn & Clarke, 1999). For example, in group CBT a number of children might meet to listen to a 30-minute session on a commonly shared topic, such as self-image (depression-related) or family relationships, and the leader would provide instruction on the elements of problem solving based on a general scenario. The instructional presentation and group dynamics simulate a typical classroom session in a school setting. Individual CBT might include a one-on-one session that leads the child through the same elements. This format looks the class-like feel of a group session but offers the advantage of individualization, allowing for greater focus on specific issues that are troubling the child. Components of CBT could be implemented as universal preventative approaches. For example, relaxation training, problem solving, and awareness of what depression "is" may all serve as resiliency-building strategies.

Several CBT strategies are discussed below, including psychoeducation, problem-solving skills training, cognitive restructuring, pleasant-activity planning, relaxation training, and self-management training. Family involvement is discussed as a strategy although it is often used in conjunction with many other childhood CBT strategies.

PSYCHOEDUCATION

DESCRIPTION
The psychoeducational component of CBT focuses on informing children and their parents about depression's causes and symptoms and presenting them as factors that can be changed (Kaslow & Racusin, 1994). This approach can demystify mental health issues and permit comparison to something a family already understands, such as a chronic illness. Additionally, children gain some understanding that is necessary to manage their depression. By learning about the thoughts and behaviors that cause and maintain depressive symptomatology and about the possible cognitive–behavioral intervention techniques used to address depression, children can begin to recognize the relationship between these two factors and lay the groundwork for change in their behavior and emotions.

EXAMPLE
Will is in an individualized treatment program for depression. To clarify the connection between behavior and outcome for him, the therapist illustrates using another child's behavior as an example. Will views a movie scene in which a child experiences depressive symptoms such as anger and feelings of low self-worth. The scene shows how these emotions affect relationships with family and friends and conveys the possible effects on school performance (e.g., acting out in class and then feeling bad about being sent from the classroom). The therapist uses the scene to illustrate how the child learns that his emotions and behavior are unhealthy and that they may be related to learning difficulties. The scene provides a vehicle for initially understanding the connection between emotional stress and behavioral reaction, as well as the negative effects of these two components. As a result, Will begins to develop greater emotional understanding. From that basic insight, Will can attempt to make behavioral changes.

GOAL

Decrease or resolve depression and depressive episodes by de-mystifying the condition; removing barriers to treatment; and removing any blame, unfair expectations, or judgment placed on the child.

THE BASICS

1. Teach the nature of depression to children and families.

2. Teach the symptomatology.

3. Introduce treatment options.

HOW TO IMPLEMENT PSYCHOEDUCATION

 PREP

- Create or acquire information about depression to share with the child and parents.

- Prepare to dispel myths and dispute bias with that information and knowledge.

  ▲ Visuals of the brain or brain chemistry, and examples of other illnesses that are not the "fault" of the child may be particularly helpful.

- Organize a time and space that is private and non-threatening.

- Consider whether the parents and child will attend sessions jointly or separately.

 IMPLEMENT

- Review the common causes of depression with the child and family.

- Brainstorm with the child about the possible causes for his or her depressed feelings. Involve the family if the child does not articulate possible causes.

- Discuss how the possible causes might be related to the child's depressive symptoms.

- Explain the treatment options to the child and family. Discuss specific therapeutic activities and how they may be effective in this situation.

- Create a treatment plan together with the child and family, including the goals of treatment and criteria for success. This plan may describe the use of specific activities; define the duration of each treatment component; describe expectations of the therapist, family, and child; and determine what behavioral change is expected.

 EVALUATE

- Consider the use of a post-training survey for the family asking about satisfaction with the information.

- Assess understanding throughout the process by asking open-ended (rather than yes/no) questions and requesting that the child and family rephrase the causes/effects, options, and goals discussed to ensure understanding.

PROBLEM-SOLVING SKILLS TRAINING

DESCRIPTION

Problem solving enables a child to identify negative thinking that occurs in a specific situation, recognize how those thoughts can lead to depression, and replace those thoughts and subsequent feelings with healthier ones. These may be erroneous thoughts or true thinking about events. Generally, the therapist teaches the child to view situations more objectively in order to solve them as problems (Nicolson & Ayers, 2004).

EXAMPLES

Asia is suffering from depressive feelings about her relationships with family and friends. The therapist working with Asia teaches her to reframe her negative thoughts. During clinical sessions, Asia might express feelings or thoughts such as, "My family doesn't love me," or "I have no friends." The therapist treats these thoughts as problems to be solved by either disputing them or thinking differently. Through reframing, Asia learns to state these feelings or thoughts more realistically (e.g., "My family shows love by. . ."; "I can make friends by asking one person to go to a movie"), therefore making them more manageable. By reframing the negative feelings and emotions more positively and as actionable behaviors, Asia gains more control over the specific situation and can use the reframing technique to further promote emotional and behavioral improvement.

Terry loses a friend in a car accident and suffers from repetitive thinking about the loss. The therapist meets with him to identify methods of reducing the negative thinking in order to diminish the suffering caused by sadness, guilt, or fear.

GOAL

Help a child to view situational depression (caused by a lack of positive reinforcement) as a dilemma to be resolved rather than as a hopeless situation or an incurable disease (Nicolson & Ayers, 2004).

THE BASICS

1. Define the problem (e.g., thinking patterns, loss of appetite, decreased interest, agitation) as actionable.

2. Generate potential actions or solutions.

3. Evaluate these options.

4. Select the option that is the best fit and try it out.

5. Evaluate and revise as desired.

HOW TO IMPLEMENT PROBLEM-SOLVING SKILLS TRAINING

 PREP

- Identify acceptable times and locations to meet privately with the child or the child and parent(s) as appropriate.

- Prepare to gather information from outside sources about the types of challenges and problems the child is facing if the child is not forthcoming or has limited self-awareness.

 IMPLEMENT

- Discuss with the child the likely causes of his or her depression and the resulting symptoms.

- Reframe these in the context of problems to be solved rather than an illness to be treated.

- Brainstorm with the child to generate solutions to the problem.

  ▲ For example, a child may begin to experience feelings of loneliness after quitting the swim team. Solutions to this problem might include rejoining the team or joining a similar or more interesting social group.

  ▲ Divorce, death, and other incidents involving bereavement and loss of control require solutions that focus on the child's feelings, thoughts, or behaviors rather than the event itself. The event itself cannot be changed, but the feelings, thoughts, and behaviors that result from the event may be actionable.

- Together, evaluate the pros and cons of each solution and choose the best option to try.

- Be aware of and sensitive to the desires, strengths, and needs of the child during solution generation and selection. Start with simple solutions to avoid overwhelming the child.

- Work out a gradual approach with the child as you would for a homework assignment, outlining the steps needed and setting a target date for completion.

 EVALUATE

- Monitor the child's progress. Consider revising the plan as necessary. Provide plenty of encouragement both for attempts and for successes.

COGNITIVE RESTRUCTURING

DESCRIPTION

Cognitive restructuring involves identifying, challenging, and changing depressive thoughts (Hops & Lewinsohn, 1995). Cognitive restructuring teaches children to identify their own negative irrational thoughts and to supplant them with healthier, more rational ones. Children are taught to identify negative thoughts and are shown how these thoughts can lead to negative beliefs, emotions, and behaviors. For younger children, tools or methods such as songs, rhymes, or video representations may be helpful in identifying negative cognitions and understanding the connections among thoughts, feelings, and behaviors. After awareness is obtained, children are taught strategies that can be used to reinforce positive thinking and promote more positive and productive behaviors.

EXAMPLE

Lee is suffering from depression and has irrational thoughts about his self-worth. Whenever he makes a mistake while completing a task he thinks, "This proves that I am useless." Using cognitive restructuring the therapist helps Lee recognize these negative thoughts and understand their effects. The therapist then challenges Lee to view his mistakes as lessons learned. Lee is taught to use self-talk and to think, "It is okay to make mistakes; it's how we learn." In this way, he begins to reinterpret his response to the negative event of making a mistake, seeing it as a more positive event and changing his response into a healthier one.

GOAL

Modify distorted thinking that contributes to depressive cognitions and replace it with rational thinking.

THE BASICS

1. Identify the child's irrational depressive thoughts.

2. Challenge these thoughts by identifying ones that are more rational.

3. Schedule sessions for guided rehearsal and independent practice.

HOW TO IMPLEMENT COGNITIVE RESTRUCTURING

 PREP

- Identify the child's negative cognitions and determine if they are irrational and subject to challenge or replacement.

  ▲ For example, a child is sad about a recently deceased parent. This sadness is not subject to challenge. However, if the child thinks the loss is "my fault," such thinking is subject to challenge.

 IMPLEMENT

- Teach the child how to recognize negative thoughts.

  ▲ Young children may find cartoons to be helpful illustrations. Draw a thought bubble over the head of a character and ask the child to write in (or describe) the thoughts.

  ▲ Older children might keep diaries or journals of their thoughts.

- Explain how negative thoughts connect with unpleasant feelings or exaggerated and unproductive thinking. Use a cartoon or journal if these methods are helpful with a particular child.

- Explore specific actions the child can take to think more adaptively.

  ▲ For example, ask the child to imagine a stop sign when negative thinking occurs. This strategy can help the child to stop a negative thought so that it can be replaced with a positive one.

- Practice self-tracking. Choose one negative thought (e.g., "Other kids are laughing at me") and ask the child to record how often it occurs. Then, agree on a new thought to replace the negative one (e.g., "I'm okay just how I am."). Encourage the child to practice the replacement consistently.

 EVALUATE

- Monitor progress at future sessions through self-recordings or discussions, or by checking with parents or other adults who work with the child.

- Evaluate any changes to symptomatology, such as sleeping, eating, and participation levels. Do not focus exclusively on feelings or thinking patterns.

PLEASANT-ACTIVITY PLANNING

DESCRIPTION

Pleasant-activity planning encourages children to plan activities and social interactions that they consider pleasurable. When struggling with depression, children may lose interest in the activities that once made them feel happy, and they may lack the motivation to join them again. Pleasant-activity planning for depression includes goal setting, developing a plan to engage in an activity, behavioral contracting, and self-reward (Hops & Lewinsohn, 1995). Participating in fun activities can promote a more positive outlook and a greater sense of self-worth. Participating in fun activities provides reinforcement that eventually is replaced by natural environmental and social reinforcers, resulting in positive feelings that serve to encourage continued participation in the activity.

EXAMPLE

Jeanette is suffering from depression and she stops participating in French club after school. When asked why, she responds by saying, "I just don't feel like going." Using pleasant-activity planning, a therapist works with Jeanette to try to select a different after-school activity. While they talk, Jeanette discusses her interest in the drama club, which is having its first meeting the following week. Together they decide that she will attend the drama club meeting and make a list of questions she has about the club. As an added incentive for following through on her plan to attend, Jeanette's parents will take her to dinner afterward, and they will talk about the meeting over dinner.

GOAL

Help the child plan pleasant activities to decrease depressive symptoms and make the scheduling process a fun experience.

THE BASICS

1. Plan preferred or "fun" activities.

2. Develop a behavior contract that specifies the reward for participating in the activity.

HOW TO IMPLEMENT PLEASANT-ACTIVITY PLANNING

 PREP

- Interview the child and parents (or seek information otherwise) about preferred activities to prepare suggestions appropriate for the age and interests of the child.

 IMPLEMENT

- Teach the child about the benefits of planning for fun activities. Describe how planning and participating in an activity can improve depressive symptoms.

- Tailor suggestions to the child's needs and interests.

- Create a list of five or so feasible activities that the child finds enjoyable. Ask the child to rank order them by preference.

- Create the plan in a way that embeds "looking forward" and anticipation. This may include the child creating a detailed plan for participating.

  ▲ If so, help the child discover all the considerations and steps for participating in the activities (e.g., costs, transportation). Try to let the child lead the organization and planning of the activities as much as possible.

  ▲ If the child is unwilling to engage, simply organize the schedule and help facilitate the child's participation.

- Choose a reward for participating in each activity. Rewards could be given during the event (e.g., purchasing popcorn while at a movie) or after the event (e.g., getting more computer time for a day or week).

 EVALUATE

- Track the number of activities or events the child participates in.

- Inform the child about his or her increased participation levels and discuss how the child's emotions and behavior may have changed during that time.

RELAXATION TRAINING

DESCRIPTION

Relaxation training teaches children to relax by monitoring muscle tension created by stressful situations and events (Ollendick & Cerny, 1981). Tension-related physical discomfort can exacerbate common depressive symptoms and cause a child to feel even worse about him- or herself and the situation. As with the pleasant-activity planning intervention, improvements made to an aspect of a child's life (in this case, physical well-being) can influence his or her thoughts and emotions and lead to a reduction in depressive symptomatology.

There are a number of relaxation techniques available, including counting, breathing exercises, recall, mental imagery, and progressive muscle relaxation (Kahn et al., 1990). Children of all ages easily learn counting and breathing techniques as they simply require the child to concentrate on counting or breathing when feeling symptoms of depression. The recall technique requires a child to think about a previous successful or pleasant event; pleasant feelings and emotions associated with the past event will help reduce negative feelings and emotions in the present. Mental imagery requires a child to focus on a specific event and envision the steps needed to succeed at the event. Similarly, progressive muscle relaxation techniques require the child to mentally focus on a specific part of the body and concentrate on relaxing it.

The essential elements of all these techniques include identifying emotional triggers and their corresponding physical symptoms, engaging in an activity designed to reduce the negative emotions associated with the depressive symptoms, and recognizing when emotions and feelings start to improve.

EXAMPLE

Carmen has experienced many traumatic events and she is showing signs of depression. One of the symptoms of her depression is a fear of attending preschool twice a week. She becomes agitated, restless, defiant, weepy, and resistant. To relieve some of her emotional distress Carmen's foster mother describes a favorite part of school for Carmen (e.g., snack time, the playground, story time). As she talks, she selects an image and describes it in detail and then asks Carmen to do the same. This dialogue is part of their morning routine and it continues in the car on the way to preschool. Once in the parking lot, they take four deep breaths together before Carmen exits the car. Even 4-year-old Carmen can rehearse deep breathing and imagery, and she can verbalize the practice to her foster mom, indicating independent use.

GOAL

Help the child learn to use physiological changes in his or her body to relieve depressive symptoms.

THE BASICS

1. Identify emotional triggers and their corresponding physical symptoms.

2. Teach the child the selected relaxation techniques.

HOW TO IMPLEMENT RELAXATION TRAINING

 PREP

- Identify a specific symptom of the child's depression, along with the effect it has on the child (e.g., crying, headaches).

 IMPLEMENT

- Teach the child to use a relaxation technique.

- Ask the child to imagine a situation that causes the undesired symptoms.

- Practice the technique with the child until he or she is able to perform the steps independently. Discuss how the technique can help the child feel calmer in the imagined situation. Model the steps for the child as needed.

 EVALUATE

- Check in with the child periodically to assess whether the relaxation technique is being used correctly and at the appropriate times.

- Provide refresher training as necessary.

SELF-MANAGEMENT TRAINING

DESCRIPTION

Self-management techniques that can be used with feelings or thinking are sometimes called "affect regulation." They require a child to use information obtained while monitoring his or her behavior to modify and control negative feelings and emotions (Braswell & Kendall, 2001; Friedberg et al., 2003; Nicolson & Ayers, 2004).

Self-management typically involves physical recording of some kind (e.g., paper and pencil, audio, or video tools). Recording sheets can be as simple as a chart or table the child can fill out. Some children prefer journaling but may require structure to guide them in recording specific behaviors or feelings rather than just private musings. The frequency and type of recording vary depending on the severity and variety of depressive symptoms.

EXAMPLE

Isabel reported feeling sad for no reason every day for 6 months before entering therapy, and the sadness was something she wanted to change. The therapist taught Isabel to record her mood on a daily basis using a small notebook. Isabel and her therapist decided that Isabel should keep the notebook with her throughout the day. Isabel recorded her mood when she woke up and any sad thoughts, noting the precipitating event. During therapy sessions, Isabel and the therapist reviewed the notebook together and used it as a tool to develop interventions and to discuss the impact of the interventions. Isabel identified and recorded walking her dog and going to movies as favorite activities. Isabel's goal was to manage her sadness through increasing participation in favorite activities and finding two new positive activities.

GOAL

Decrease the child's depression through awareness, targeted monitoring, and self-reinforcement.

THE BASICS

1. Set goals with the child for self-monitoring and recording.

2. Teach the child to monitor and record changes in feelings or thoughts and to identify precipitating events.

3. Evaluate the records to determine opportunities for intervention.

4. Reinforce positive activities and encourage the child to do the same while continuing to look for new opportunities to manage negative emotions.

HOW TO IMPLEMENT SELF-MANAGEMENT TRAINING

 PREP

- Evaluate if the child is a good candidate for self-management.

- Identify methods for recording that fit the child.

- Consider generating a form the child can use for recording, along with a procedure for him or her to follow. Forms used for recording could be a calendar, notebook, or journal.

- Identify the duration of self-monitoring intervals. The child can record observations hourly or daily. Shorter intervals (e.g., every 15 minutes) might be helpful when there are a number of transitions in a daily schedule (e.g., classroom changes during school).

- Determine how often you will check in or meet with the child, and set a time to review the child's records.

IMPLEMENT

- Teach the child self-management procedures. Coach the child in the identification of personal goals and, if necessary, provide goals for the child; keep these as specific to the child as possible.

- Review the child's records. Discuss with the child how distorted thoughts might be affecting his or her current behavior.

- Choose one or two problem emotions or behaviors to modify, and suggest a solution that the child can implement independently.

 EVALUATE

- Monitor progress and provide feedback often (e.g., at the beginning and end of the school day). Consider providing frequent feedback in early stages of intervention.

- Encourage self-rewarding and praise positive efforts (e.g., consistent record keeping, steps taken to resolve problem emotions and behaviors). Provide rewards whether the steps are successful or not.

FAMILY INVOLVEMENT

DESCRIPTION

Involving family members can be a helpful strategy with any CBT intervention. Family members may provide support and mentoring to help a child cope with depressive symptoms. It is often helpful to educate family members about depressive symptoms and for them to learn about common causes and consequences. Family members may learn new ways of interacting with the child through training in communication skills, negotiation skills, conflict resolution, and problem solving (Beardslee et al., 1997; Hops & Lewinsohn, 1995; Lewinsohn & Clarke, 1999; Stark & Kendall, 1996). In general, meet with family members whose involvement will likely be most impactful. Observing the child's interaction with these family members may also help in determining the extent to which family will be involved in a given intervention.

EXAMPLE

Jada is upset because she and her boyfriend broke up. Although this seems minor and irritating to the family members, for Jada, the boyfriend represented a positive and stable component of her life and a buffer against other problems at school with friends. The therapist schedules a home visit with some members of the family to create allies for Jada and promote sensitivity to the feelings that Jada is having. If the family is contributing to the depression, this information may be helpful in developing treatment plans.

GOAL

Help family members deal with the child's depressive symptoms or participate in therapy aimed at resolving extended family issues.

THE BASICS

1. Determine if the child could benefit from family involvement in an intervention. Gather information relevant to this decision from discussions with the child and parents and an assessment of the child's home situation and level of support.

2. Involve family members strategically on an as-needed basis.

3. Consider involving the family in bolstering the child's practice of the learned cognitive-behavioral techniques.

4. Evaluate effectiveness through discussions with the child (and parents as appropriate).

HOW TO IMPLEMENT FAMILY INVOLVEMENT

 PREP

- Evaluate if members of the family or the entire family should be involved in treatment and to what extent.
- Determine which members to invite to a session and what information will be conveyed.
- Set an initial plan for the duration and intensity of involvement.

 IMPLEMENT

- As appropriate, train family members to provide support and mentoring to the child in coping with his or her depressive symptoms.
- As appropriate, educate family members on depression-related symptoms, common causes, and consequences.
- As appropriate, train family members on new strategies for interacting with the child.

 EVALUATE

- Evaluate the effectiveness and impact on the child's depressive symptoms through discussion with the child (and parents as appropriate).

EVIDENCE

A brief overview of research and annotated references supporting this intervention can be found on Q-global.

CONSIDERATIONS

FOR TEACHING

Many CBT interventions blend well with classroom-based approaches because of their inherent teaching nature. Classroom environments are appropriate settings to discuss identification of problems, causes, triggers, replacements, and solutions. Problem-solving and self-management skills generalize to a variety of behavioral and academic concerns. Posters that illustrate the steps of particular techniques (e.g., breathing in self-relaxation) are useful. Classwide instruction can be conducted by a counselor or school psychologist. Teachers can provide time for children with depression or depressive symptoms to record symptoms and thoughts.

Even during regular class periods, children can self-record in an inconspicuous manner (e.g., make a check mark on a page in a notebook) or can write sentences about their feelings in a journal. The self-monitoring and self-recording should involve checking in with an adult who reviews the records, tracks progress, and provides feedback. This check-in can occur in the morning or afternoon of each school day or more frequently if needed. A teacher may perform such check-ins, if appropriate.

FOR CULTURAL AND LANGUAGE DIFFERENCES

Depending on the origins and trajectory of the depression, parental involvement may be limited. Communicate expectations for parental involvement clearly and in person to the parent(s), with awareness of and respect for the family's perceptions of depression and treatment. Some parents may not be interested in learning about depression and may view it as a weakness in the child. Others may reinforce the depression with protection, attention, and caretaking that enables the depressive behavior. Culture, language, and personal experience with depressive symptomatology and treatment will all have an impact on parent involvement and interest in training or treatment.

FOR AGE AND DEVELOPMENTAL LEVEL

Age and developmental level should be primary considerations when selecting a CBT intervention. Many CBT interventions require a child to articulate and document feelings, emotions, and behaviors. As such, the effectiveness may be limited for children with poor verbal, language, or writing skills. It is unlikely that young children or children with developmental delays can truly examine their thought patterns or the origin of those thoughts until they have reached Piaget's stage of formal operations, typically at adolescence (Lewinsohn & Clarke, 1999).

Psychoeducational interventions should consider both the information provided to a child and his or her ability to understand and act on it. For example, young children may not understand the purpose of relaxation training at first; they must receive adequate, age-appropriate information to understand the nature and use of the technique.

Problem-solving skills training, cognitive restructuring, and self-management training may also be difficult to implement for young children (i.e., ages 7 and younger) or for children who have minimal verbal skills. In contrast, pleasant-activity planning can be easily understood and effective for children of most ages.

The type of monitoring and recording used for self-management depends on the child's age and ability level, level of independence, and desire to use self-help strategies. Very young children are more likely to be successful if taught a simple recording strategy, such as making a check mark in the sad or happy face column on a recording sheet, while older children may prefer to write about their feelings in narrative form.

FOR SAFETY

Depression is a very serious condition that can lead to physical harm. Take all suicidal threats and any signs or reports of self-injury seriously, and keep parents and other caregivers informed. When appropriate, provide 24-hour support information (e.g., suicide prevention telephone numbers, emergency room telephone numbers and addresses). Request permission to inform family physicians. Make clear to the child that suicide attempts and self-injury are not options and that such actions do not result in increased peer or adult attention or in revenge. For more information on suicide prevention, see one of the many online resources from the U.S. Department of Health and Human Services or the National Institute of Mental Health.

 # INTERPERSONAL PSYCHOTHERAPY

DESCRIPTION

Interpersonal psychotherapy for adolescents (IPT or IPT-A) with depression is based on the premise that depression occurs because of limitations in an individual's ability to adapt to changes in interpersonal relationships. Depression is conceptualized as beginning with cognitions and feelings associated with interpersonal relationships across several situations, including grief, role transitions, role disputes, and interpersonal deficits (Klerman, Weissman, Rounsaville, & Chevron, 1984; Mufson & Sills, 2006; Rosselló & Bernal, 1999). Although it originated from psychodynamic theories, IPT is generally considered a cognitive–behavioral approach because its primary effects include increases in communication ability, self-efficacy, autonomy, and adaptability. IPT also seeks to address cognitive aspects of depression. The child and therapist identify the issues and select specific treatment goals, interventions, and strategies collaboratively. IPT is typically a short-duration treatment used to understand the child's personality, relationships with others, and relationship to the environment (Mufson, Dorta, Moreau, & Weissman, 2004; Weissman, Markowitz, & Klerman, 2000). Successful outcomes of IPT involve establishment of autonomy and an individual's sense of self, development of appropriate and responsible romantic relationships, acceptable management of peer pressure, and, when applicable, successful coping with initial experiences of death and loss (Mufson & Sills, 2006). These outcomes are achieved by applying the essential elements of IPT, including education, development of interpersonal skills, and prevention of relapse (Mufson & Sills, 2006; Rosselló & Bernal, 1999).

EXAMPLE

Brittany, a 15-year-old female, was very close to her grandmother who had lived with the family since Brittany's birth. Since her grandmother's death, Brittany has had difficulty adjusting to life without her grandmother's presence. The use of IPT in grief recovery may help Brittany understand and manage her grief while adjusting to the change. Specifically, IPT may help Brittany understand the transition she is experiencing and identify the changes that the loss of her grandmother may cause in her life. For example, she may need to discuss whom she can confide in and how to help with tasks that her grandmother often did for the family (e.g., laundry, meal preparation). Brittany may also feel out of control, particularly because this is her first experience with death. She may wonder when and how the grief will end. The education and interpersonal skill building components of IPT should help with each of these identified issues.

GOAL

Decrease the child's depressive symptoms by improving his or her interpersonal functioning.

THE BASICS

1. Teach the child about interpersonal skills.
2. Coach the child in the use and improvement of new skills.

HOW TO IMPLEMENT INTERPERSONAL PSYCHOTHERAPY

 PREP

- Identify acceptable times and locations to meet privately with the child or the child and parent(s) as appropriate.

 IMPLEMENT

- Conduct an interview or interpersonal inventory with the child.
- Discuss his or her feelings or behaviors related to the depression.
- Identify any interpersonal skills that need improvement.
- Assess the child's communication and decision-making skills by discussing a painful or difficult event.
- Create a treatment contract with the child that includes a clear statement of the problem, the expectations of both the child and the therapist, and the specific course of treatment (including parameters of the treatment and articulation of desired behaviors). Clarify any necessary points.
- Teach behavior change techniques, including identifying activities that trigger more pleasurable mood responses as a way to learn or practice interpersonal skills.

 EVALUATE

- Assess the effectiveness in the reduction of depressive symptoms.
- Identify and review the behavioral and emotional signs of relapse. Ask the child to practice identifying these signs between sessions.
- Phase out treatment gradually, over the course of about three sessions.

EVIDENCE

A brief overview of research and annotated references supporting this intervention can be found on Q-global.

CONSIDERATIONS

FOR AGE AND DEVELOPMENTAL LEVEL

Generally IPT strategies are used with adolescents due to the relatively high cognitive demands of this approach. Younger children may have difficulty articulating feelings or attributing them to an event. Symptoms of depression can occur during times of developmental change, such as the transition to adolescence. Malaise and other depressive symptoms may be the result of uncertainty about the future of adolescence or adulthood.

FOR CULTURAL, RELIGIOUS, AND LANGUAGE DIFFERENCES

Different coping skills and belief sets may correspond to certain religious or cultural values. Respect these belief sets while teaching skills to create more adaptive behaviors. For example, a child who is experiencing depression due to the death of a parent may be hearing from other adults that the parent is in a better place, and that there should be no sadness. If the child's feelings differ from these beliefs, cognitive distortions may result. This disconnect between what the child feels and what adults say he or she should feel may contribute to the depression, and both issues may need to be addressed.

Chapter 9

Interventions for Somatization

Characteristics and Conditions of Somatization

WHAT IS SOMATIZATION?

Somatization symptom disorder and related disorders are characterized by somatic symptoms that are very distressing and accompanied with excessive and disproportionate thoughts, feelings, and behaviors concerning those symptoms (APA, 2013). An important update for the *DSM–5* is that there is no longer a requirement for a specific number of somatic complaints for somatic symptom disorder (APA, 2013). It is only required that somatic symptoms be persistently present and significantly distressing or disruptive to daily functioning for at least six months. Furthermore, somatic symptom related disorders do not require that the somatic symptoms be medically unexplained. In other words, symptoms may or may not be explained by another medical condition.

The *DSM–5* criteria focus identification of this disorder on the degree to which thoughts, feelings, and behaviors related to somatic symptoms are disproportionate or excessive. Somatic symptom and related disorders are debilitating and chronic (Allen, Woolfolk, Escobar, Gara, & Hamer, 2006). Health care is costly for these disorders and is estimated as being 10% of total health care costs (Allen et al; 2006; Magallon et al., 2008). Patients should be strongly encouraged to receive a comprehensive assessment for an accurate diagnosis. Holistic care is recommended for treatment.

The *DSM–5* states that specific somatic symptom and related disorder diagnoses include somatic symptom disorder, illness anxiety disorder, conversion disorder (functional neurological symptoms disorder), factitious disorder, other specified somatic symptom and related disorder, and unspecified somatic symptom and related disorder. While most somatic symptom and related disorders do not reflect a conscious effort to invent symptoms, factitious disorder is distinct from malingering and other somatic symptom and related disorders because it is associated with fabricating or intentionally causing physical symptoms even in the absence of external incentives (APA, 2013).

HOW COMMON IS SOMATIZATION?

The overall prevalence of somatic symptom and related disorders has been estimated to be anywhere from 0.2–2% among women and less than 0.2% in men (APA, 2013). Some studies have examined the prevalence rates of somatization in children. Somatic symptoms are reported as common among adolescents and are often related to depression (Rhee, Miles, Halpern, Holditch-Davis, 2005) or anxiety. One third of pediatric patients with headaches may actually be expressing depressive symptoms (Bohman et al., 2010). In one study, of the 10–15% of children complaining of recurrent abdominal pain or other somatic symptoms, only one in ten had a verified underlying medical condition (Apley, 1975). Another study found that somatic symptom disorder was diagnosed in 27 of 276 children with headaches (Emich-Widera, Kazek, Szwed-Białożyt, Kopyta, & Kostorz, 2012).

Professionals often consider somatic complaints to be an attempt by the child or adolescent to communicate emotional or social difficulties (Taylor & Garralda, 2003). Somatization has been found to co-occur with anxiety and mood disorders (Reynolds & Kamphaus, 2015). Although somatization may or may not be related to physiological problems, it can produce adverse consequences and impact daily functioning. For example, there is evidence that children who often express somatic complaints run a higher risk of academic problems (Hughes, Lourea-Waddell, & Kendall, 2008).

The BASC–3 Somatization scale is designed to identify the tendency to be overly sensitive and complain about relatively minor physical problems or ailments and to over-report the occurrence of various physical complaints. Children's verbal complaints are the primary behaviors identified as problematic; such complaints typically are not associated with an actual physical origin. Items on the BASC–3 Somatization scale include "Complains of pain," "Complains of physical problems," "Has headaches," and "Gets sick."

Some conditions may mirror somatization but have different underlying causes. Bullying, abuse, neglect, or exposure to drugs may result in somatic complaints among children, but the key to resolving these complaints in such cases lies not in treating the child for somatization, but rather in changing some aspect of the child's interpersonal relationships or environment. For example, Tanya, a 7th grader, regularly complains of headaches, leg cramps, and other physical symptoms. Her teachers perceive her complaints as attempts to avoid the locker room. When the teachers begin watching more closely, they discover that Tanya is being harassed in the locker room. As soon as the root of the problem (harassment) is eliminated, Tanya no longer complains about her physical symptoms.

For this reason, it is important to assess fully the child's environment to determine whether there are other medical or nonmedical causes of somatic complaints. The child's case history also should be examined to determine if the complaints have been long-standing or are recent. For example, children who have been abused are more likely to express somatic complaints. If a recent acute onset of these complaints is noted, an interview exploring this possibility is reasonable. Somatic complaints can also accompany the onset of a more generalized anxiety disorder, and the BASC–3 or a stand-alone anxiety inventory may assist in clarifying a diagnosis. School personnel should consider that a sudden increase in physical complaints from multiple children may indicate there is a specific individual (e.g., a new student, a new staff member) contributing to these complaints. The use of additional staff or support on the playground or in the lunchroom where a large student population is supervised less closely may also be helpful.

Theoretical Framework for Approaching Somatization

The theoretical framework for understanding somatization in youth is a wellness model—a multidisciplinary rehabilitative approach. The term "multidisciplinary" is included to stress the necessity for parents and school personnel to work closely in a collaborative effort with medical providers (Haugaard & Hazan, 2004). The rehabilitative framework involves both behavioral and cognitive–behavioral approaches and frames physical symptoms and wellness behavior as a challenge for the child (i.e., a challenge to be managed internally by the child with outside support) as opposed to an illness that must be controlled via external measures (Campo & Fritz, 2001).

Interventions

Experimental studies of interventions for childhood and adolescent somatization remains an emerging area. No single program or manualized system has a sufficient number of studies to recommend its use. However, each program tends to fall into one of two generalized categories of treatments, either behavioral or cognitive–behavioral therapy. Evidence-based interventions for improving somatic symptom and related disorders are listed in Table 9.1. For some of the interventions in this chapter, supplemental materials (e.g., handouts, posters, checklists, daily logs, and worksheets) that are helpful for preparing, implementing, and evaluating the interventions can be found on Q-global.

Table 9.1 Interventions for Somatization

Intervention Name	Prevention[1]	Early Intervention[2]	Intensive Intervention[3]
Behavioral Intervention			X
Cognitive–Behavioral Therapy			X

[1] Prevention refers to skills that can be taught to all children or used universally; they promote better awareness and lessen the risk of problems.

[2] Early intervention includes techniques and strategies that address early warning signs or clinical signs of the risk of future problems. Early intervention may be specifically applied to one or more problems or generically applied as a skill set to prevent the development of a chronic problem. Early interventions can be delivered to groups or individuals.

[3] Intensive intervention focuses on individuals and individual problems, which are usually chronic, intensive, and require services due to the level of interference in daily functioning.

BEHAVIORAL INTERVENTIONS

DESCRIPTION

When applied to somatization, the use of positive and negative reinforcement or response-cost treatments involves the systematic presentation or removal of stimuli to increase coping skills and healthy behaviors (Campo & Fritz, 2001). It is imperative that both the child and adult jointly identify reinforcers that will be used during the intervention. Negative reinforcement is the removal of an aversive stimulus that has been jointly identified by the child and adult contingent on the child engaging in an appropriate healthy behavior or coping behavior. In the literature, punishment for somatic symptoms is frequently reported as a form of timeout (removal) from preferred activities. When used appropriately, this method of punishment leads the child to see removal from enjoyable activities as a natural, automatic consequence of any sick episode. If timeouts do not result in a decrease in somatic complaints it is possible the child desires to escape from the given activity, in which case the timeout is actually functioning as a reinforcer rather than as a punishment.

EXAMPLES

Holly, age 8, complains daily of a stomachache, which often causes her to be absent from school. When she attends school, she complains to the school nurse and requests to be allowed to return home. When Holly returns home, she remains in bed. Typically, her mother entertains her with books and games, or they watch television. Holly's mother has repeatedly taken her to several doctors, none of whom have found any physiological reason for her stomachaches. Holly's mother, doctor, psychiatrist, and psychologist identify three factors that are serving to reinforce Holly's behavior: (1) being home, (2) attention from her mother, and (3) attention from doctors. They identify reading time with Mom as an appropriate reinforcer for Holly's staying at school without complaints of a stomachache. Holly's adherence to a no-complaints policy is to be communicated using a school–home note filled out by the school nurse. Healthy behavior at school results in Holly being able to exchange the school–home note for immediate reading time with Mom. In contrast, if Holly complains of a stomachache and goes home from school, she will be subjected to a no-reading, no-TV, no-play-date condition for 24 hours or until the next time she receives a school–home note from the nurse for healthy behavior.

Tom, age 6, frequently reports minor daily injuries, such as scrapes, bumps, and bruises from the playground, calling them "broken" arms and legs. He elects to sit out the remainder of recess, requests bandages or wraps from the school nurse, and sometimes wants to call home to report his injuries.

Denise, a junior high student, greets her teacher each morning with a complaint about how heavy her backpack is and how much her shoulders hurt, requesting time to lie down before starting to work. Denise also lets the teacher know that she might not be able to use a pencil, displaying her arm hanging limply at her side. Sometimes, Denise complains about the bumpy bus ride that "jars her spine," resulting in a need to stand for a while in the classroom. At other times, she expresses a belief that the air conditioner filter is dusty and reports having difficulty breathing.

In both Tom's and Denise's cases, somatization behaviors are enabling them to receive additional one-on-one adult attention. On some occasions they receive perceived special treatment and possibly escape a non-preferred activity. Both children are old enough to engage in conversations about their behavior, including how it differs from their peers' behavior in similar situations and how it may be interfering with their relationships with other children. They are also old enough to self-monitor and to learn cognitive coping strategies that can help them handle their perceived pain. For example, to encourage Tom to remain active at recess (e.g., prosocial, healthy behavior) the playground monitor arranges for him to play with a different group of children who like to look for rocks and plants and who avoid the soccer field. If Tom gets through recess without complaining of injuries, he is rewarded with one-on-one time with his teacher after school to show her the rocks he collected. In Denise's case, she acknowledges that although her back and arms do hurt, she might be able to wait until lunch time to discuss them with her teacher, and she begins to use a self-monitoring chart to keep a list of her physical complaints. Denise's teacher consistently reinforces Denise with praise and encouragement when she successfully limits her complaints to the number agreed upon (two per day). When Denise and Tom begin engaging in more prosocial behaviors they naturally receive more social reinforcement, which in turn reduces their urges to engage in attention-seeking behavior; consequently, their complaints decrease.

GOAL

Reduce somatization behaviors that are interfering with daily functional activities and increase prosocial behavior, allowing the child to return to pre-illness functioning (e.g., attending school, demonstrating responsible behavior).

THE BASICS

1. Identify specific somatization behavior(s) to change.

2. Determine appropriate reinforcers or punishments.

3. Confirm complete cooperation from all team members (e.g., parents, teachers) on a continual basis to ensure reinforcers and punishments will be effective.

HOW TO IMPLEMENT BEHAVIORAL INTERVENTIONS

 PREP

- Consult with the child's physician (and psychiatrist, if applicable) to ensure that no medical conditions exist that could explain the child's complaints. Maintain consistent communication to track possible medical conditions that may arise throughout the intervention.

- Work with the multidisciplinary team to establish agreement between all key stakeholders (e.g., physician, parents, teachers, school administrators, counselor, school psychologist) about the use of contingent reinforcers and punishments (e.g., timeout from preferred activities is the intervention of choice).

- Complete a functional behavioral assessment to clearly identify, define and document the specific somatization behavior(s) to be changed. In addition, identify any activities or personal interactions that are reinforcing the somatization behavior (e.g., being able to watch movies while home sick, getting one-on-one attention from a parent).

- Work with the child and parent(s) to identify appropriate reinforcers and punishments for use in the intervention.

- In collaboration with other members of the multidisciplinary team (e.g., physician, psychologist, counselor, teacher, parent), design an intervention plan to address the underlying cause of the somatization behavior, and communicate the plan to all stakeholders. The intervention should include these components:

  ▲ use of a functional behavioral assessment to identify reinforcements for engagement in alternative (i.e., healthy) behavior and punishments (e.g., timeout from preferred activities) for engaging in illness-related behavior,

  ▲ psychoeducation for the family (e.g., parent and child),

  ▲ parent training on how specific techniques and intervention methods should be administered,

  ▲ creation of a list of the child's specific somatization behaviors and healthy coping strategies to share with all stakeholders, and

  ▲ coordination with the multidisciplinary team to maintain consistent communication and monitor the child's progress throughout the entire intervention.

IMPLEMENT

- Work with the multidisciplinary team to implement all intervention components.

- In psychoeducational sessions, clearly explain somatization to the child and family, clarify the goals of behavioral treatment, and discuss the planned intervention methods.

- Provide training in the effective use of reinforcers and punishments with the child.

- Along with other team members, encourage the child to return to pre-illness functioning (e.g., attend school, complete homework and chores).

- Assist the teacher(s) and parents in implementing the program of contingent reinforcement and punishment with the child.

- Maintain communication with the family and other stakeholders (e.g., physician, teachers) throughout treatment.

- Coordinate a plan for fading (gradual withdrawal of) positive reinforcement and timeout from preferred activities as the child attains specified goals for reducing somatization behavior and increasing healthy behavior.

 EVALUATE

- Monitor or survey home practices to ensure compliance with the behavioral intervention.

EVIDENCE

A brief overview of research and annotated references supporting this intervention can be found on Q-global.

CONSIDERATIONS

In order for behavioral interventions for somatization to be successful, practitioners must recognize that effective reinforcers and punishments must be individualized. Some individuals may be strongly reinforced by chocolate ice cream while others could easily forego it. Likewise, attention may function as a reinforcer for some children but not for others. Indeed, some adolescents may view teacher attention as a punishment rather than a reinforcer, just as some children may find increased social time to be aversive—something to be avoided at all costs. It is important to examine the function of the somatization, or inadvertent reinforcement of the maladaptive behavior may occur. Discussing the likes and dislikes of the child and conducting a reinforcement survey may be useful in identifying appropriate reinforcers. In addition, a functional behavioral assessment may be useful for providing information on environmental influences that affect specific contingencies.

"Reinforcement" and "punishment" are very loaded terms in the lay population. Some parents and therapists may have a misconception that reinforcement is a form of bribery or mind control, or that it discounts feelings. Likewise, the word "punishment" can elicit frightening images of corporal punishment (e.g., spanking) or other harsh disciplinary measures. Therefore, accurate definitions of reinforcement and punishment, as they relate to the goals of the intervention, should be presented: Reinforcement is something that results in an increase in the target behavior, while punishment results in a decrease in the behavior. Parents should also understand that reinforcement may be accomplished either through providing something pleasant (positive reinforcement) or through removing something unpleasant (negative reinforcement). Clarifying these terms helps with team communication when implementing interventions or measuring the integrity of an intervention.

Ongoing communication between school, family, and medical staff is critical to detect and effectively treat the child's somatic symptoms. Nothing could be more damaging to the trust relationship between the child and the adults involved than if the child's accounts of somatic symptoms were ignored, minimized, or discounted as existing merely in the child's head. In addition, young children may use physical descriptions (e.g., "a tummy ache") to talk about completely unrelated feelings or issues (e.g., fear) or to respond to a traumatic event. A young child may not be able to articulate an episode of sexual abuse but may describe "not feeling well" or "feeling funny." Open communication is important to maintain trust and to accommodate the development of appropriate interventions as symptoms occur.

Hormonal cycles in adolescents may mirror somatic complaints (e.g., stomachache, headache) although no specific physical cause can be identified. In addition, normal physical changes may account for some behavior and should not be completely discounted.

FOR AGE AND DEVELOPMENTAL LEVEL

Consider the age and developmental level of the child when planning interventions. Consider to what degree the observed behavior is expected or deemed within normal limits based on the child's age and developmental level. Be aware of other disabling conditions (e.g., cognitive delay) that could interfere with the child's ability to articulate physical complaints accurately enough to ensure a correct medical diagnosis

FOR CULTURAL DIFFERENCES

Consider the culture of the child's family when planning interventions. Consider to what degree the observed behavior is expected or deemed within normal limits based on the child's culture.

 # COGNITIVE–BEHAVIORAL THERAPY

DESCRIPTION

Cognitive–behavioral therapy (CBT) as an intervention for somatization is an approach that incorporates multiple methods of intervention based on the individual needs of the child. A number of CBT programs are manualized (i.e., described in a manual with steps and sequence to ensure they are standardly applied) for anxiety and are likely to show results for somatization problems. A number of commercially-available manualized programs are available (James, James, Cowdrey, Soler, & Choke, 2015). CBT approaches place an overall emphasis on coping and encourage children to continue functional activities with minimal complaints of illness (Schulman, 1988). Helpful strategies may include breathing exercises, defocusing from physical symptoms, problem solving, or family therapy (Kushwaha, Chadda & Mehta, 2013). Strategies should be selected based on individual assessment data as well as the age and development of the child.

THERAPEUTIC COMPONENTS

PROBLEM RE-CONCEPTUALIZATION

Problem re-conceptualization involves assisting the child in conceptualizing the problem as less threatening and working to shift attention from illness to treatment. The parents and child will need to successfully reframe the problem as something to *cope with* rather than to *cure*. Emphasis is placed on the child's role in treatment as an active agent coping with a difficult but manageable problem. Improvement is conceptualized as the child's personal success. It is important that the child understands that the duration of symptoms cannot be fully anticipated. Therefore, returning to typical life functioning (without a cure) is important for day to day success.

Once the focus on the problem shifts from identifying the cause or cure to selecting a coping strategy, assist the parents in evaluating and articulating the impact of the illness on the child and family. Help them to determine how somatization is impacting the child's functioning and what is necessary for the child to return to normal functioning. Provide examples of others with severe illnesses who continue normal activities. While emphasizing the need for improvement and normalization, assure the child and parents that the child's physical complaints are not being ignored.

Acknowledge the child's suffering, address any parental concerns, and reassure the family about the treatment plan and potential for symptom reduction. Ensure that the parents, child, and physician all agree to the coping and behavioral techniques that will be implemented. Provide information to the parents and the child in an honest and direct manner in order to build a trusting relationship. Reassure the parents and the child that the symptoms can be reduced.

PSYCHOEDUCATION

Psychoeducation involves helping parents understand somatic symptoms and stressing that the child's physical symptoms are not based on any known illness. Reassure the parents and child that coordination with the primary physician occurs continually during the intervention. Educate the child and parents about the connection between distress and symptoms. Help the child and parents to determine sources of stress and anxiety and to identify alternative coping strategies. Educate family members about how their habitual reactions to the child's sick role may reinforce the maladaptive behavior. Help them develop a plan to remove such reinforcements. Emphasize the importance of education and school attendance and stress that the child is required to follow school district attendance policies. Educate the child about the benefits and importance of participating in routine activities.

THERAPEUTIC STRATEGIES

There are a variety of therapeutic strategies to select from when implementing CBT as a somatic symptom intervention. Coping skills training, including self-monitoring and self-instruction, involves teaching the child to monitor the somatic symptoms and teaching the child to identify certain situations as antecedents (i.e., triggers for somatic complaints). Training in problem-solving techniques is helpful so that after triggers are identified the child can collaboratively approach the trigger as a problem and identify an alternate method to solve the problem. For example, a child identifies being asked to write on the board in front of the class because she feels nervous as a trigger for stomachaches and is able to escape the situation through the somatic complaint. The therapist can teach the child to choose a signal she can use to let the teacher know she feels nervous and does not want to write on the board. Assess for reinforcement of the somatization behaviors and determine how alternate behaviors can be reinforced instead. Reinforcement for somatization behavior should be removed and competing, healthy behavior should be reinforced. Relaxation training, breathing, and distraction techniques, as described in Chapter 7 of this guide, are also helpful techniques for reducing somatic symptoms.

Additional parent training may be warranted to help parents support basic behavioral approaches used in therapy. Training in how to manage contingencies, how to prompt and reinforce coping behaviors, how to use negative reinforcement to encourage healthy behavior, and the importance of withdrawing attention from sickness-related behavior, as described in Chapter 7 of this guide, may be useful to support treatment.

Generalization training involves spreading the newly learned and practiced coping strategies to other somatic problems or other settings. Consider scenarios where successful strategies are used with other problem behaviors or in other problem settings. Provide support for successful generalization but fade as quickly as possible. Address relapses quickly by reinstating relevant components.

GOAL

Decrease the child's exaggeration of physical symptomatology and increase his or her functional behavior (Gutsch, 1988).

THE BASICS

1. Gather information about the somatic symptoms.

2. Conceptualize the problem by reframing it as something to cope with rather than to cure.

3. Evaluate and articulate the impact of the illness on the child and family.

4. Provide psychoeducation to the child and parents about somatic symptom and related disorders and the nature of the child's somatic symptoms (i.e., not originating from any known illness and related to distress).

5. Plan with the child (and family as appropriate) and implement therapeutic strategies.

6. Work to generalize strategies and coping skills to other contexts.

HOW TO IMPLEMENT COGNITIVE–BEHAVIORAL THERAPY

 PREP

- Assess and gather information about the somatic symptoms. In collaboration with the multidisciplinary team, coordinate and consult with the child's primary care physician and/or psychiatrist and the child's parents or caregivers to ensure that the child's symptoms have been thoroughly investigated for a possible medical diagnosis.

- Conduct a functional behavioral assessment to clearly define and document the specific somatization behavior(s) to be changed. In addition, identify any factors that are currently reinforcing the somatization behaviors.

- Interview the child and parents, gathering a broad base of information about the child's background. During the interviews, explore the following issues:

  ▲ child and family attitudes about the child's illness,

  ▲ possible anxieties and stressors in the child's life or prior experiences,

  ▲ previous counseling and/or treatments and their effectiveness,

  ▲ family complaints about the child's behavior,

  ▲ the extent to which the child has stopped participating in normal activities,

  ▲ possible underlying emotional causes for the child's behavior, and/or

  ▲ possible cultural factors that may explain somatization behaviors.

 IMPLEMENT

- Help the child develop and implement a plan for reducing or effectively coping with stressors.

- Establish a set daily or weekly time for the child to explain his or her plan to the parents.

- Encourage the child to return to his or her usual activities and responsibilities.

- Implement strategies to support the child's return to previous activities and to encourage the child to increase social activities and exercise.

- Enlist all members of the multidisciplinary team in actively discouraging the child's illness-related behaviors and providing positive reinforcement for healthy behaviors.

- Decrease possible gains from illness-related behavior by insisting on school attendance.

- Ensure that the parents do not allow attention and pleasant activities at home during sickness-related episodes.

- Choose, in collaboration with the multidisciplinary team, the therapeutic strategies to be implemented.

- Implement the selected therapeutic strategies.

 EVALUATE

- Monitor somatic complaints through observations in school and/or at home, nurse records, absenteeism, journals, or logs. Somatic complaints can be recorded by frequency counting or narrative descriptions.

- Modify the treatment plan as needed.

- Reevaluate with the multidisciplinary team any continued or new somatic complaints on an ongoing basis.

EVIDENCE

A brief overview of research and annotated references supporting this intervention can be found on Q-global.

CONSIDERATIONS

For Teaching

School personnel should remain in contact with the child's primary care physician and proceed with school-based interventions only with the approval of both the physician and the child's parent(s). Physical illness, neglect, and abuse must be ruled out before intervention for somatization proceeds; therefore, collaboration and communication with the child's primary care physician and family are essential (Campo & Fritz, 2001). Intervention by a pediatrician made early and explained clearly and with certainty to the child and parent(s) may expedite and ease parental acceptance of the diagnosis and child recovery (Zeharia et al., 1999).

For Families

The child's family/home environment should be considered to determine how it interacts with the maladaptive behavior and to identify ways in which these factors may affect response to the intervention. Gender and cultural differences may also account for familial belief systems about how illness (mental or physical) is viewed and handled. For example, some individuals and families may view occasionally calling in sick as an adaptive behavior (e.g., by considering the sick day a "mental health day" and dedicating the time off to activities that reduce stress and enhance coping), whereas in other families the same behavior may be maladaptive (e.g., avoiding specific problems at work or at school).

Practitioners should recognize that parental acceptance of the concept of somatization may vary. Similarly, parental beliefs about which types of treatments are acceptable may vary. A preference for self-reliance versus community responsibility differs by family, culture, and gender of the dominant parent.

For Age and Developmental Level

Attention should be given to developmental characteristics of youth, particularly since diagnosis of youth and adults with somatic symptom disorders is not differentiated (Eminson, 2007). Age and development are key factors that may affect creation and implementation of the self-evaluation or self-monitoring components of interventions. For instance, language development and cognitive development are important considerations. If the verbal or cognitive abilities of the individual are not well suited to comprehending and using self-awareness and self-regulatory strategies, these components will be less successful. In situations where age or developmental readiness is a factor, more direct environmental approaches such as reinforcement and timeout from preferred activities have a greater likelihood of success.

For Cultural Differences

The child's culture should be evaluated to determine how it relates to the maladaptive behavior and to identify ways in which it may cause response to the intervention to differ. When prosocial repertoires are limited, avoidant behavior may be a function of limited skills or a culturally appropriate response to conflict. As discussed, cultural differences may also account for familial belief systems about how illness (mental or physical) is viewed and handled, and preference for self-reliance versus community responsibility differs by culture of the dominant parent. Consideration should also be given to cultural expectations about physical appearance and self-presentation (APA, 2013), which may lead to behaviors that appear somatic.

Chapter 10

Interventions for Adaptability Problems

Characteristics and Conditions of Adaptability Problems

WHAT IS ADAPTABILITY?

Adaptability is described as the ability to adapt readily to environmental changes (Reynolds & Kamphaus, 2015). Deficits in adaptability are demonstrated in a variety of behaviors. For some children with adaptability problems, a change in a routine may result in defiance or resistance. For others, a change in a routine may result in crying, throwing tantrums, abandoning the original task, or other problem behaviors. Children with deficits in adaptability skills often appear rigid or inflexible, and they depend on predictability, order, and consistency.

Deficits in adaptability are characteristic of children with autism spectrum disorder (ASD), attention-deficit/hyperactivity disorder (ADHD; Reynolds & Fletcher-Janzen, 2007), and/or obsessive compulsive and related disorders (Reynolds & Livingston, 2010). In addition, decreases in adaptability in children who have previously adapted to change might be associated with high levels of anxiety, as is often observed in children with social phobia and/or anxiety-based school refusal. If assessment indicates that the decrease in adaptability is a manifestation of anxiety experienced in the school setting, the therapist should also reference the interventions in Chapter 7 of this guide.

HOW COMMON ARE ADAPTABILITY PROBLEMS?

Problems with adaptability are experienced across a variety of conditions, including ASD, ADHD, and obsessive compulsive and related disorders. The prevalence rate for children with ASD is estimated to be at about 1.5% (Kim et al., 2011). For ADHD, the prevalence rate for children is about 10% (Visser et al., 2014). Obsessive compulsive disorder prevalence rates are markedly lower, around 0.5% for children (Rapoport et al., 2000).

The BASC–3 Adaptability scale measures positive behaviors and skills related to the child's ability to adjust to changes in routine and environment, to shift from one task to another, and to share toys or possessions with other children. Adaptability scale items on the Teacher Rating Scales and Parent Rating Scales include "Recovers quickly after a setback," "Adjusts well to changes in routine," and "Adjusts well to new teachers (or caregivers)."

Theoretical Framework for Approaching Adaptability Problems

The theoretical orientations described in this chapter are a mix of behavioral and cognitive–behavioral approaches. The behavioral aspect addresses the distinct, observable problems associated with adaptability deficits, and the cognitive–behavioral aspect addresses the potential causes and origins of these issues. Behavioral approaches presume that problems are learned and expressed as physical or verbal behaviors. Cognitive–behavioral approaches rely on the combination of metacognitive processes with antecedent and consequent changes to modify the mental and physical aspects that sustain the problem behavior.

Children who have deficits in adaptability are often mistakenly described as "strong-willed," "stubborn," or "challenging." Due to these misconceptions, there can be a tendency to use punishment or harsh verbal redirections, ultimatums, or even shaming with children who are resistant compared to their compliant peers. Punishment should not be used for treating adaptability deficits. Antecedent interventions and reinforcement for alternative, healthy behaviors and/or lower rates of the maladaptive behavior are the most effective and least intrusive interventions. Also, note that parents, teachers, peers, and other well-meaning individuals may have unintentionally reinforced the child's fear, anxiety, and troubling behaviors associated with a lack of adaptability if they have responded to the maladaptive behavior by giving the child attention or an opportunity to escape the situation. Teachers, parents, and other caregivers may need additional training and assistance to cease reinforcing the maladaptive behavior and to provide effective intervention in classroom or home settings.

Interventions

This chapter presents six interventions for increasing or enhancing adaptability to help children develop the skills to adapt to planned and unplanned changes without exhibiting aberrant or inappropriate behavior. When selecting interventions to treat adaptability deficits, the therapist should first consider the child's specific characteristics and the function served by the child's negative behavioral response to changes in routines or activities. This information may be gathered systematically by conducting a functional behavioral assessment (FBA). While FBA is not necessarily an intervention, research indicates that conducting an FBA is necessary with some children who experience adaptability problems— particularly children with ASD and other developmental disorders—in order to select effective interventions (Flannery, O'Neill, & Horner, 1995; Sterling-Turner & Jordan, 2007). Evidence also suggests that interventions selected based on FBA are three times as likely to be successful as those selected without conducting an FBA (Newcomer & Lewis, 2004). For this reason, FBA is included as an intervention in this chapter.

The intervention strategies for enhancing adaptability discussed in this chapter fall into two broad categories: behavioral and cognitive–behavioral. Behavioral interventions focus on changing some aspect of the antecedent events (i.e., trigger situations) that tend to bring about the maladaptive behavior. Cognitive–behavorial interventions seek to improve the child's ability to self-regulate through cognitive and behavioral training. The behavioral interventions discussed in this chapter include: (1) precorrection, in which the therapist gives the child advance warning of any activity or schedule change and teaches expected transition behaviors ahead of time, and (2) procedural prompts—visual, verbal, or auditory signals that cue appropriate behavior during transitions (Schmit, Alper, Raschke, & Ryndak, 2000). The use of behavioral momentum (e.g., issuing several "easy" requests to build momentum in favor of compliance before issuing a "difficult" request) is also included in the discussion of procedural prompts as well as on its own. The two cognitive–behavioral interventions presented in this chapter include cognitive behavior management (CBM) and self-management training. CBM seeks to increase adaptability through the use of exercises that focus on thinking about behavior paired with reinforcement procedures. The use of self-management training allows the child to learn skills to manage their own behavior in the absence of receiving treatment. Lastly, although FBA is not an intervention, per se, gathering information about the antecendents, behaviors, and consequences is vital to designing an effective behavioral or cognitive-behavioral intervention to reduce problem behaviors and to facilitate positive behaviors (Witt, Daly, & Noell, 2000). Evidence-based interventions for improving adaptability in children are listed in Table 10.1. For some of the interventions in this chapter, supplemental materials (e.g., handouts, posters, checklists, daily logs, and worksheets) that are helpful for preparing, implementing, and evaluating the interventions can be found on Q-global.

Table 10.1 Interventions for Adaptability Problems

Intervention	Prevention[1]	Early Intervention[2]	Intensive Intervention[3]
Behavioral Momentum	X	X	X
Cognitive Behavior Management	X	X	X
Functional Behavioral Assessment		X	X
Precorrection	X	X	X
Procedural Prompts		X	X
Self-Management Training		X	X

[1] Prevention refers to skills that can be taught to all children or used universally; they promote better awareness and lessen the risk of problems.

[2] Early intervention includes techniques and strategies that address early warning signs or clinical signs of the risk of future problems. Early intervention may be specifically applied to one or more problems or generically applied as a skill set to prevent the development of a chronic problem. Early interventions can be delivered to groups or individuals.

[3] Intensive intervention focuses on individuals and individual problems, which are usually chronic, intensive, and require services due to the level of interference in daily functioning.

BEHAVIORAL MOMENTUM

DESCRIPTION

Behavioral momentum is based on the idea that issuing several behavioral requests with a high probability of compliance creates positive momentum that, in turn, increases the likelihood of a child fulfilling a request that would ordinarily have a low probability of compliance (Nevin, 1996). The greater the rate of reinforcement, the greater the behavioral momentum (Mace et al., 1988). Verbal reinforcement is incorporated as frequently as is feasible with comments such as "Right," "Thanks," or "You bet."

EXAMPLE

Maria, a high school senior with borderline intellectual functioning, frequently says "no" to teacher requests and is known for her stubbornness toward faculty members; however, she readily engages with teachers socially. One of her teachers, Mrs. Wayne, instructs Maria to move from working on the history mural to the computer, but Maria continues to paint. In the past, if Mrs. Wayne confronted Maria about not following directions, Maria's noncompliant behavior would quickly escalate to shouting or running out of the classroom. Mrs. Wayne finds she is more successful with Maria's transitions when she approaches her with a series of easy questions or high-compliance requests in rapid succession. For example, Mrs. Wayne stands next to Maria, smiles, and says, "Tell me your name." Maria smiles back and says, "Maria." Mrs. Wayne then asks, "Maria, what color is this paint?" Maria answers that it is green. Mrs. Wayne says, "Maria, please keep painting," and Maria does. Mrs. Wayne then asks, "Maria, do you like painting the Statue of Liberty?" and Maria says, "Yes." Finally, Mrs. Wayne says, "Maria, let's move to the computer," and Maria complies with the transition request.

GOAL

Increase the child's compliance with transitions by asking a series of easy questions or requests for high-probability behaviors before requesting compliance with a difficult request.

THE BASICS

1. Identify and deliver a selection of easy questions or high-compliance requests.

2. Reinforce compliance with each request.

3. Deliver several easy requests continuously and immediately before a difficult request.

HOW TO IMPLEMENT BEHAVIORAL MOMENTUM

 PREP

- Identify high probability requests, such as simple questions or verbal requests that will very likely result in compliance. For example, "Pat your head," "Jump up and down," "Stick out your tongue," "Turn around," and "Do you like chocolate?"

 IMPLEMENT

- Use the high-probability requests identified during prep when a potentially problematic transition is about to occur, and have the child respond in quick succession to several of the easy questions or requests.

- Provide verbal reinforcement immediately after compliance with each request.

- Give the request related to the desired transition behavior (e.g., "Let's line up to go to lunch now") after the child has complied with all of the easy requests. Verbally reinforce compliance.

EVALUATE

- Consider if it is necessary to modify the number of task requests in the sequence depending on the age and cognitive development of the child.
- Check for understanding and participation in the rapid request sequences.

EVIDENCE

A brief overview of research and annotated references supporting this intervention can be found on Q-global.

CONSIDERATIONS

FOR AGE AND DEVELOPMENTAL LEVEL

For behavioral momentum interventions to succeed, children need to first possess the cognitive and receptive and expressive language abilities necessary to comprehend and respond to questions or requests. They must also be capable of understanding the final request and exhibiting the requested behavior.

COGNITIVE BEHAVIOR MANAGEMENT

DESCRIPTION

The purpose of cognitive behavior management (CBM) is for the child to become aware of how he or she feels, thinks, and behaves and how his or her behavior affects performance as well as interactions with others (Versi, 1995). CBM encompasses a number of teaching strategies, including cognitive restructuring to teach self-control and increase awareness of cognitive processes, and systematic desensitization to increase awareness of the effect of behavior on academic and behavior outcomes.

EXAMPLE

Jemal is a bright high school senior who appreciates structure and is fairly rigid in his daily routine. Any changes to plans or events that impact his daily routine upset him, resulting in agitation that can lead to aggression. Rather than try to send Jemal to the principal or punish him (more change that causes agitation), the school counselor talks to Jemal about the consequences of his lack of adaptability: fewer friends, teachers who shy away from trying to help him, and problems with his job and girlfriend. The counselor identifies several positive things that could happen if Jemal learns to become more adaptable. Together they agree to try some ways to become more adaptable. First, Jemal lists triggers of his agitation (e.g., too many people standing in front of his locker, social studies teacher schedules a particular activity for class and then changes it, compulsory attendance for a pep assembly). The counselor and Jemal agree to focus on the school-related issues first and tackle other problems later.

Jemal and the counselor meet again to discuss Jemal's thoughts when these events occur. Jemal thinks his classmates are rude when they crowd his locker, and that they may step on his toes or get fingerprints on his locker. Jemal believes the social studies teacher is disorganized. He also thinks that his daily activities are more important than interruptions such as pep rallies. Jemal worries that these interruptions will cause him to miss out on important information that he will need to write essays for college applications.

Jemal and the counselor identify the irrational or catastrophic thinking in these scenarios and talk through the realities (e.g., his toes might get stepped on but it won't kill him). Replacement thinking is identified as "it is cool to have others by my locker," and "my teacher cares about me and what I need and is looking out for me." Jemal begins to practice the new thinking and reports his progress and feelings back to his counselor. Jemal and the counselor track the number of setbacks Jemal has. They discuss Jemal's belief that the new strategies are working.

GOAL

Increase the child's adaptive or compensatory strategies to deal with change, mitigate any negative effects of change on the child, and decrease any maladaptive or aberrant behaviors that the child employs to cope or to achieve a particular desire.

THE BASICS

1. Help the child recognize antecedents (i.e., settings or events that tend to trigger the problem behavior).

2. Help the child identify maladaptive behaviors and/or catastrophic self-talk and any appropriate replacement behaviors.

3. Create opportunities to practice recognizing problem events and associated feelings.

4. Create opportunities to practice thinking through options and making good choices about replacement thinking and behavior.

5. Evaluate and reward good performance.

HOW TO IMPLEMENT COGNITIVE BEHAVIOR MANAGEMENT

 PREP

- Identify the triggers for problem behaviors associated with the child's adaptability deficits by talking with teachers, parents, or the child, and/or conducting a functional behavioral assessment (FBA).

- Work with the child to identify the antecedents, behaviors, and consequences involved, as well as the associated thoughts and feelings.

- Create a list of alternative "thinking scripts" (e.g., more positive, appropriate thoughts) and behaviors that are adaptive replacements for the problem thinking and behavior.

 IMPLEMENT

- Role-play or model the problem scenarios to allow the child opportunities to practice the alternative thinking and behavior.

- Have the child try using alternative thinking and behavior independently, and have him or her report back on the results. If necessary, repeat modeling and role-play of the new skills.

- Use a predetermined reinforcement schedule to reward the child for successfully implementing the strategies.

 EVALUATE

- Use the child's self-report of progress to reinforce use of the strategies or to make adaptations as necessary.

- Identify individuals in the child's environment who can observe the CBM use in action and report progress or continuation of existing problems.

- Ask the child to teach the strategy to another child in a mentoring activity. The ability to successfully teach the procedures and explain them to someone else is one sign of mastery.

EVIDENCE

A brief overview of research and annotated references supporting this intervention can be found on Q-global.

CONSIDERATIONS

FOR TEACHING

CBM can be implemented in small group settings; however, carefully consider gender, age, and sensitivity of topics prior to leading group discussions or group therapy for issues that are potentially embarrassing or that involve personally identifiable attributes. For example, children may not be embarrassed by some adaptability issues related to food consumption (e.g., a child's refusal to try any food in the school cafeteria). On the other hand, an issue related to personal hygiene routines may be more likely to cause embarrassment.

FOR AGE AND DEVELOPMENTAL LEVEL

To successfully learn and use CBM techniques, children need to first possess the cognitive and verbal abilities necessary to articulate problem behaviors, feelings, and thoughts. If the child cannot initially articulate feelings or demonstrate understanding of his or her own cognition, at a minimum, he or she should have the ability to respond when a skilled professional names or describes different feelings to choose from.

Self-awareness is also imperative for success of CBM techniques. For that reason, CBM may be inappropriate for very young children or those with developmental delays. In such cases, a strictly behavioral approach will probably be sufficient. Most adolescents in late elementary school or older grades possess the cognitive skills and self-awareness needed to benefit from CBM techniques.

 # FUNCTIONAL BEHAVIORAL ASSESSMENT BASED INTERVENTION

DESCRIPTION

A functional behavioral assessment (FBA) is a method for identifying the purpose or communicative function of a behavior. It should not be confused with a functional analysis (FA), which refers to the use of experimental manipulation of environmental events to assess the functions these events have on behavior (Horner, 1994). An FBA does not manipulate or attempt to control the environment. The use of an FBA is not a single test or observation, but rather a multi-method strategy consisting of observations, interviews, and a review of records regarding the child's behavior and environmental conditions associated with presence or absence of problem behaviors (Gresham, Watson, & Skinner, 2001). An FBA for a child with adaptability problems allows therapists to determine the reason for the particular maladaptive behaviors—in other words, what the child hopes to achieve through the behavior (e.g., to gain attention; to gain access to objects, events, or people; to escape certain events, situations, or people). Knowing the behavior's function helps the therapist address effectively the two primary goals of an adaptability intervention: (1) eliminating problem behaviors by modifying the antecedents and/or consequences of the behavior, and (2) teaching appropriate replacement behaviors. Through an FBA, therapists assess the effect of antecedents and consequences on the observed behavior. Antecedents to behaviors associated with adaptability deficits (e.g., aberrant, rigid, and/or inflexible behavior) may be identified as unscheduled changes in routine or environment, and the function of the subsequent aberrant behavior may be stimulation, such as self-soothing or escape from the change. The results of an FBA can be used to select interventions aimed at increasing acceptable behaviors that are functionally equivalent (i.e., accomplish the same purpose) to the problem behaviors.

EXAMPLES

The results of an FBA determined that Boris exhibits aberrant behavior for self-soothing purposes. He may be given access to a rocking chair when he is agitated, thus replacing the maladaptive behavior with an acceptable alternative behavior that accomplishes the same purpose.

Whenever Tabori arrives in class and sees a substitute teacher, he cries and complains of a stomachache, and consequently, is allowed to go lie down in the nurse's office. The school psychologist completes an FBA and determines that the function of Tabori's behavior is to escape from unexpected situations or changes in routine. Interventions are planned that familiarize Tabori with substitute teachers in advance and prevent him from escaping to the nurse's office. To provide Tabori with a sense of familiarity and continuity during the regular teacher's absence, a preferred peer, Susan, is allowed to sit next to Tabori as long as he does not cry and he remains in the classroom.

An FBA could reveal that another child with behavior like Tabori's may use the same behavior to achieve a different purpose—for instance, to escape not from the substitute teacher, but rather from peers who often engage in teasing when the regular classroom teacher is not present. Intervention in this case may include teaching and reassuring the child that substitute teachers do not allow teasing either. The child could also be granted a new place to sit that is a safe distance away from the children who are teasing, thus allowing a more limited form of escape without reducing the child's time in the classroom. Self-management techniques, precorrection, or procedural prompts (e.g., verbalizing rather than crying or complaining when upset, using a "seating pass" to move away from teasing children rather than escaping to the nurse's office) could be used to increase appropriate behavior and decrease problem behavior.

GOAL

Increase the child's adaptive behavior by identifying and changing or eliminating environmental conditions which support problems in adaptability.

THE BASICS

1. Conduct an FBA (including interviews and direct observation).

2. Operationalize the target behavior.

3. Observe and record the antecedents.

4. Observe and record the consequences.

5. Develop hypotheses for why the behavior occurs.

6. Evaluate or test the hypotheses.

7. Select a functionally equivalent replacement or intervention.

HOW TO IMPLEMENT AN FBA-BASED INTERVENTION

 PREP

- Gather collateral information (e.g., interview with parents and teachers, review of records) and observe the child in the environment in which the adaptability problems are occurring.

 IMPLEMENT

- Identify and operationally define the target behavior. Interview parent(s) and teacher(s) to gather information about the problematic elements of transitions. Determine the specific situations (e.g., expected and/or unexpected changes in routine) in which the child tends to exhibit problem behaviors reflecting a deficit in adaptability. Focus on the child's adaptability problems.

- Determine if the problem is related to a change in the sequence in which events occur, the time at which a particular event occurs, changes in the content of the situation (e.g., different people, location, or materials than usual), or the introduction of something new (e.g., doing a new activity, meeting a new teacher).

- Use carefully phrased questions to determine the key variables that predict problem behavior.
  - ▲ Sequence: Is the problem behavior associated with a change in the order of events/activities?
  - ▲ Time: Is the problem behavior associated with a change in the time at which expected events/activities occur?
  - ▲ Content: Is the problem behavior associated with a change in materials, location, procedure for an activity, or the people present?
  - ▲ Novelty: Is the problem behavior associated with the addition of new items, activities, or people?
- Identify observers to collect data before and after the targeted behavior. Observers may include the therapist or other adults involved with the child's day-to-day activities.
- Observe (or have other adults observe) the child during problematic transitions or changes. For example, if the parent indicated that the child has problems with schedule changes, observe the child during transitions on days when schedule changes occur.
- Generate a testable hypothesis about the function of the behavior and test it when possible.
- Observe the child again to test the hypothesis, targeting the identified problem situations (e.g., transitions on days with schedule changes, days with substitute teachers). If needed, revise the hypotheses based on these observations.
- Using the results of the FBA, choose an appropriate intervention to help the child develop the skills to accomplish the same function through socially acceptable behaviors.

 EVALUATE

- Assess the use of the intervention or the functional equivalence of any replacement behavior to determine if the adaptive problems identified in the FBA have decreased.
- Use parent, student, and teacher reports to provide information about the level of adaptive functioning. Use direct observations—and frequency, duration, latency, or rating scales—to monitor effects and/or progress.

EVIDENCE
A brief overview of research and annotated references supporting this intervention can be found on Q-global.

CONSIDERATIONS
FBA is a technically sound approach to intervention planning; however, an assessment is only as reliable as the data that are collected. In some situations, the function of a child's behavior may be nearly self-evident and minimal effort may be required to collect high-quality data that are both valid and reliable. For example, in the case of a child who throws tantrums whenever a stranger enters the classroom, parent and teacher interviews are likely to yield an accurate hypothesis about the function of the child's tantrum behavior. In this case, data collection to confirm the hypothesis simply involves observing the child on several different occasions when a stranger enters the classroom and documenting the child's response. However, some other behaviors related to adaptability deficits may belong to behavior classes that are more difficult to operationally define and whose antecedents are more difficult to determine. In these situations, collecting good data and finding clear patterns in the child's behavior will be much more challenging. In instances where the behavior is topographically complicated or not readily observed (e.g., occurs with high intensity but low frequency or occurs at times or in locations not accessible to school personnel), a team of professionals should remain involved until sufficient data are gathered to produce a solid hypothesis about the behavior's function.

Therapists who already have extensive professional experience working with a certain child may be tempted to draw conclusions about the function of a particular behavior without formal data collection procedures. This practice is inadvisable. It is crucial to view preliminary ideas about the behavior's possible function as a hypothesis only and to enter the observation/hypothesis-testing step with an open mind. Data tend to become a self-fulfilling prophecy when the observer feels strongly invested in an a priori hypothesis. This is not to suggest that professional knowledge of and history with the child should not influence what kind of data are collected and what data collection methods are used (e.g., identifying the conditions or behaviors of interest and choosing the time periods for observation). However, there is a marked difference between drawing on one's experience to conduct informed data collection and undertaking data collection to support a biased or predetermined attribution of cause.

FOR TEACHING

Some teachers and/or administrators may be hesitant to participate in formal data collection due to the time-consuming nature of the process. This may be particularly true if the problem behavior interferes with classroom or campus life or if parents are demanding immediate, effective intervention. In some cases, a "best match" approach, in which the intervention is based on professional judgment and informal assessment of the conditions surrounding the problem behavior, is warranted. Teachers may need support in classroom settings; including training, help supervising students, or assistance in data collection responsibilities.

 **PRECORRECTION**

DESCRIPTION

Precorrection involves providing prompts for desired behaviors in certain circumstances that are determined to be antecedents to problem behavior (De Pry & Sugai, 2002). Precorrection may also familiarize children with behavior that is acceptable during expected or unexpected changes in routine or schedule by explaining, teaching, and/or practicing the desired behavior prior to the event or task (VanDerHeyden, Witt, & Gatti, 2001). Precorrection can take the form of verbal directions, visual schedules (i.e., schedules that use a picture or photo to represent each task), or both. Combining symbols with written schedules is helpful in establishing expectations for all stages of transitions (Olive, 2004). The terms previewing, systematic preparation, and priming all refer to similar precorrection techniques in which the child is prepared for an upcoming event through modeling (either filmed or in vivo), practice, and/or verbal instruction (Schreibman, Whalen, & Stahmer, 2000). Often, precorrection activities are conceptualized as "readiness signals" for changes that will occur in the near future.

EXAMPLES

Harrison, a 6th grader with ASD, becomes highly agitated on days when the school schedule is changed for pep rallies or other assemblies. Using precorrection, on the day before an expected schedule change, Harrison's teacher explains to him that the schedule the next day will be different, tells him how to follow the new schedule, and shows him a visual schedule that lists the new class times. She sends Harrison home that day with a note asking his mother to remind him about the schedule change in the morning. The next day, when Harrison arrives at school, his teacher greets him with a familiar visual cue representing a pep rally or assembly day, as well as a class schedule for the day that Harrison can carry with him. Harrison's teacher's precorrection through the use of a visual schedule and verbal direction the day before helps to familiarize Harrison with the schedule changes, and as a result, lowers his level of agitation the next day.

Roberto, an adolescent with obsessive-compulsive disorder, often becomes angry and starts fights when his gym teacher changes the arrangement of the physical fitness weight equipment. To help Roberto deal effectively with the change, the teacher gives Roberto a map of the new arrangement the day before moving the equipment. Arrows and numbers on the map show the correct order in which to use the machines and the number of repetitions to do at each station. The advance knowledge of the change and having a map to refer to alleviates Roberto's anxiety and allows him to function as part of the class the next day without starting any fights.

GOAL

Decrease adaptability problems by increasing predictability of routines and increasing a priori explanations for alterations. Increase predictability by using prompts and explaining expectations for behavior when there are expected or unexpected changes in schedules, tasks, and activities.

THE BASICS

1. Identify transitions or events that might lead to problems by reviewing the results of the child's FBA.

2. Verbalize and/or model expected behavior through precorrection procedures (e.g., visual schedules and social stories).

HOW TO IMPLEMENT PRECORRECTION

 PREP

- Identify problematic changes, transitions, or problem behavior related to adaptability (e.g., by reviewing the results of the child's FBA).

- Determine if the child responds to verbal or visual precorrection.

- Identify potential prospects for unscheduled changes or scheduled but infrequent changes to daily routines that could be sources of threat for the child (e.g., an assembly at school, being pulled out for a doctor appointment, someone sitting in the child's chair or favorite place in a room).

- Provide scripted scenarios or instruction on modeled behavior to children who need them and are not able to implement precorrection "on the fly."

 IMPLEMENT

- Implement precorrection before unscheduled changes or scheduled but infrequent changes to the child's daily routines occur.

- Name, describe, and discuss the problem situation with the child to engage in verbal precorrection. Describe the problematic transition or schedule change and the expected behavior to the child. Model the behavior and then practice it with the child, reinforcing correct responses and effort. If it is obvious that the child does not understand the transition or schedule change or has not mastered the appropriate behavior, repeat the steps until the child demonstrates mastery.

- Point to, show, or refer to the photo, drawing, or symbol that represents the problem situation or establish a visual schedule for the child to engage in visual precorrection. Use the visual aid to alert and prepare both for expected transitions and for unexpected schedule changes. A special change symbol may be used to call the child's attention to parts of the schedule that differ from the norm.

 EVALUATE

- Assess the use of precorrection to determine if implementation increased the child's predictability when there were expected or unexpected changes in schedules, tasks, and activities.

- If the child continues to engage in problematic behavior or has difficulty adapting to changes in schedule, review and/or make modifications to determine if the child responds better to verbal or visual precorrection.

- Use parent, student, and teacher reports to provide information about the level of adaptive functioning. Use direct observations—and frequency, duration, latency, or rating scales—to monitor effects and or progress.

EVIDENCE
A brief overview of research and annotated references supporting this intervention can be found on Q-global.

CONSIDERATIONS

FOR TEACHING

Precorrection is an effective and efficient technique for school professionals. Those who are skilled at using precorrection strategies can incorporate them into regular interactions with students, anticipate the potential for problems in certain situations, and teach behavioral expectations before the problematic scenarios present themselves. Extensive use of precorrection may cause some children to become dependent on outside prompting in order to engage in appropriate behavior. Care should be taken to precorrect only when needed to prevent children from learning to rely on this external source of information processing. To help children with adaptability deficits develop their ability to independently engage in appropriate transition behavior, precorrection can gradually be transferred from an adult's voice to children's own voices as they learn to signal themselves, cognitively process scenarios, and effectively prepare for transitions.

Larger but less-frequent transitions (e.g., moving from one grade to the next or from one campus to another, or seasonal changes in routine) are good candidates for precorrection. Children can be prepared for these types of transitions using video or pictures of new staff and environments. Ideally, children should spend time in the new classroom or on the new campus to practice the transition, decrease uncertainty, and become familiar with the skills and expectations that accompany the new place. Precorrection is especially helpful when it focuses on the positive aspects of what is coming next.

 PROCEDURAL PROMPTS

DESCRIPTION

Procedural prompts (often referred to as visual or auditory cuing or signaling) help to increase adaptability by (1) providing information that cues the child to transition from one activity or event to another, or (2) informing the child about changes in schedules and/or events (Dalrymple, 1995). Procedural prompts are similar to precorrection activities but are used as a stimulus to prompt the child to transition at the time of the new event or activity, while precorrection is used as an antecedent for appropriate behavior and is implemented before the transition or change in activity.

There are three main categories of procedural prompts: visual, verbal, and auditory. Visual prompts can be pictures, gestures, or written directions. Verbal prompts are language cues, such as words, songs, or spoken directions. Auditory prompts include music, beeps, chimes, bells, whistles, buzzers, or the ringing of a timer or alarm clock. For children who respond better to kinesthetic prompting, objects may be used as an alternative to visual or auditory cues (e.g., the teacher may hand the child a basketball to signal that it is time to go to gym class). Other examples of commonly used prompts are dimming the lights, visual timers (e.g., timers that represent the amount of time left in an activity with a colored wedge that grows smaller as the end time approaches), stop lights, transition songs like "Clean Up," or call-and-response clapping routines such as the teacher clapping twice and the students clapping once in response. These signals all serve to communicate that a particular type of behavior or transition will occur.

EXAMPLE

Jerrod has difficulty disengaging from one activity and beginning the next. His teacher uses an auditory prompt (a doorbell chime) to signal Jerrod that it is time to put away his reading books and begin math. Jerrod's teacher also uses a toy chirping bird (a combination of a visual and an auditory prompt) to signal Jerrod and other students that it is time to listen. In this example, using prompts helped to give both Jerrod and the other children information about the upcoming change and its nature, allowing them additional time to adapt and transition to the new task.

GOAL

Increase adaptation to changes in routine or schedule by providing the child with a prompt for the activity or event transition.

THE BASICS

1. Identify an appropriate form of prompting.

2. Teach the child to associate the prompt with the target behavior through pairing.

3. Use the prompt as an antecedent to solicit the desired behavior.

HOW TO IMPLEMENT PROCEDURAL PROMPTS

 PREP

- Identify problematic changes, transitions or problem behavior related to adaptability (e.g., by reviewing the results of the child's FBA).

- Determine the minimum level of prompting that is effective for the child, as well as the most effective type(s) of prompts (e.g., visual, verbal, auditory, or kinesthetic).

- Provide scripted instructions on how to properly implement procedural prompts to professionals working with the child, if needed.

 IMPLEMENT

- Teach the child to associate each prompt with its meaning. As necessary, model the appropriate response to the prompt or guide the child to demonstrate the expected action.

- Practice procedures with the child as necessary to ensure mastery.

- Assess the use of procedural prompts by checking to see if implementation increased the child's adaptability and decreased problematic behaviors associated with transitioning to another task.

- Provide reinforcement for every effort while new behaviors are being taught. As the child becomes more comfortable with and skilled at performing the new behavior, reinforcement can fade to an interval or ratio schedule (e.g., praise offered every five minutes or after every five good efforts).

- Use behavioral momentum to ease a difficult transition (refer to the section on behavioral momentum in this chapter).

 EVALUATE

- If the child continues to have difficulties adapting to task or schedule changes, review and/or make modifications to determine if the child responds better to verbal, auditory, visual, kinesthetic, or a combination of procedural prompt types.

- Use parent, child, and teacher reports to provide information about the level of adaptive functioning. Use direct observations—and frequency, duration, latency, or rating scales—to monitor effects and or progress.

EVIDENCE

A brief overview of research and annotated references supporting this intervention can be found on Q-global.

CONSIDERATIONS

Avoid prompting techniques that could be stigmatizing by asking relevant adults or observing classrooms or work environments. One method for avoiding stigmatizing or calling attention to one child is to implement a classwide prompt. When this approach is used, the prompts often improve performance for various children, even if they are truly required for just one. Classwide prompting may take the form of a single cue that all children see or hear at the same time (e.g., songs, chimes, lights), or individual cues (e.g., providing a separate, portable picture schedule for each child).

FOR TEACHING

The use of various prompting procedures to assist children with ASD is supported as effective (Peterson, McLaughlin, Weber, & Anderson, 2008). Studies support procedural prompts as an effective and efficient way to enhance adaptability and ease task transition (Taber, Seltzer, Heflin, Alberto, 1999) and completion. Despite this evidence of successful use of prompts, selective attention and need for a high level of assistance may create difficulties for school professionals using this technique.

Prompts may increase the child's reliance on others to prompt his or her every move (Taber et al., 1999). This strategy relies heavily on continuous teacher participation to ensure skill acquisition but fails to promote maintenance and generalization. It is of importance when using prompts to successfully fade prompts, so that the original prompt or cue becomes a functioning stimulus that is reinforced without dependence on prompts. The use of time delay and reinforcement procedures have been found to facilitate the generalization of prompts. Once the child consistently models the appropriate response after receiving the prompt or cue, the time between the prompt and the child's appropriate response and the presentation of a reward can be gradually increased until the child learns to move to another task with greater ease.

Research has found that children with ASD have difficulty responding to multiple simultaneously presented cues or "stimulus overselectivity" (Schreibman, 1975). Lovaas, Schreibman, Koegel, and Rehm (1971) employed a discrimination task involving complex simultaneous visual, auditory, and tactile cues and found that children with ASD characteristically responded to only one of the components, while children without ASD responded normally to all three cues. Furthermore, early research has found that the use of auditory prompting may not be effective cue for children with ASD due to auditory speech suppression and problems related to processing auditory information (Blackstock, 1978; Hermelin & O'Connor, 1975).

FOR AGE AND DEVELOPMENTAL LEVEL

Select signals that are age appropriate. Singing about "clean-up time" is appropriate for 4-year-olds, but high school students should have age-appropriate transition signals that are typical in a high school setting (e.g., a bell). It also is important to consider any potential for stigma or an inability to transfer to post-school settings. Complex sequences of bells or chimes are not typical of a household or work environment; however, some use of alarms and timers is certainly a common adaptive behavior for most adults. Picture schedules, often used as visual cues, might easily transfer to a personal calendar as the child becomes an adult.

 # SELF-MANAGEMENT TRAINING

DESCRIPTION

Self-management training to increase adaptability aims to help children independently monitor and self-reinforce behaviors associated with adaptability, such as following schedules and sharing (Stahmer & Schreibman, 1992). Children are taught to monitor their own behavior when transitioning to new locations or activities, responding to expected or unexpected changes in routine, and sharing toys. The decreased need for staff assistance suggests that self-management techniques are ideal for persons with developmental disabilities in integrated academic and community settings (Koegel, Koegel, Hurley, & Frea, 1992).

EXAMPLE

Lydia frequently refused to stop working on tasks before she was finished with them, even if the class period was over. This led to many verbal conflicts with her teachers and caused her to be late routinely to the next class. The desired transition behavior for Lydia was defined as "Putting my work in my 'To Finish Later' box quickly when the class period is over." It was represented by a stop sign on her self-monitoring checklist. At the end of each activity, Lydia wrote a Y next to the stop sign if she had stopped working quickly, and an N if she had not. Her teachers initially prompted her to complete the checklist after each activity, but lessened the prompts as Lydia learned to remember to complete it on her own. At the end of each day, Lydia gave the checklist to the school psychologist, who added up the total number of Y's and N's. Initially,

---

the psychologist provided reinforcement in the form of a sticker or a token on any day when Lydia achieved more Y's than N's. Each week, the performance required for reinforcement became more challenging until Lydia needed to limit her N's to a certain number to receive a reward. In addition, the responsibility for tallying up the day's Y's and N's and choosing a reinforcer (if she had earned one) gradually transitioned to Lydia.

GOAL

Enhance adaptability and increase the child's ability to independently adapt or transition to new routines or activities.

THE BASICS

1. Identify the behavior to target.

2. Identify the occasions and function of the target behavior to monitor and record problematic behavior.

3. Create a self-monitoring form (e.g., checklist, table with pictures) for the child to track his or her own behavior.

4. Teach the child how to use the self-monitoring form and expected behavior during transitions.

5. Use reinforcers to reward the child for engaging in desired behavior.

HOW TO IMPLEMENT SELF-MANAGEMENT TRAINING

 PREP

- Identify the targeted problematic behavior for self-management.

- Determine the type of reinforcement to be used.

- Identify any cuing systems that will be employed (e.g., a bell or timer, automated or manual).

- Create a self-monitoring form. For example, prepare a self-management form, such as a simple table or checklist, with an appropriate level of sophistication (e.g., reading level, layout, use of pictures) for the child.

 IMPLEMENT

- Define with the child the target behavior to be reduced (i.e., what it is and is not, where it occurs, what it looks like). If needed, define a replacement behavior or "fair-pair." Define and discuss this (i.e., what it is and is not, where and when it should occur).

- Teach the child the expected behavior during transitions by verbally explaining the behavior, modeling it, and practicing it with the child.

- Introduce the self-monitoring form to the child and model how to complete it. Discuss how often the form should be used (e.g., for the first 10 minutes of each class, at the end of each activity, once every 5 minutes).

- Cue or prompt the child when it is time to complete the form. Gradually discontinue prompting as the child adjusts to the task.

- Reinforce successful performance and monitoring of the target behavior. Increase the requirements for reinforcement over time. Teach the child to independently select reinforcers and gradually transition the responsibility for reinforcing the target behavior to the child.

EVALUATE

- Assess the child's use of the self-monitoring form by checking with parent, child, and teacher reports to see if implementation increased the child's adaptability and helped decrease problematic behaviors associated with transitioning to another task.

- If the child continues to have difficulties adapting to task or schedule changes, review and/or make modifications to the type of self-monitoring form and/or reinforcers given for the target behavior.

EVIDENCE

A brief overview of research and annotated references supporting this intervention can be found on Q-global.

CONSIDERATIONS

FOR TEACHING

Self-management is readily adopted by classroom teachers and philosophically fits with most professionals' view of teaching children to learn self-responsibility. Intervals for monitoring and recording need to be appropriate both for the behavior in question and for the nature of the classroom. A child is probably unable to monitor him- or herself in 45-second intervals and may require cuing from a teacher or other source (e.g., a watch or other auditory or visual prompt). Keep in mind that frequent cuing can be distracting to the child and to the other children. Tailor cues and self-monitoring methods to fit the environment. For example, if all children keep a calendar or planner on their desks, consider using it as a cuing device. Paper comes in a variety of shapes, sizes, and colors and can be used as an inexpensive form for children who are frequency counting. Print shops can also reproduce custom forms with a sticky back and/or can print forms with a tear-off gummy binding; both can be convenient ways to attach forms to a child's desk.

FOR AGE AND DEVELOPMENTAL LEVEL

Self-management is generally considered most appropriate for children ages 4 and above (note that ages 4–6 will probably need adult coaching to determine if they are engaged in the targeted behavior). Teachers can help coach by talking about why a child did or did not successfully monitor the behavior. For young children, a simple yes/no or green/red face may work well. For older children, a simple rating scale can be used for monitoring behavior, like completing an assignment or handling a transition, or for evaluating the amount and quality of effort given to a task. For a child who struggles with adaptability, introducing a new routine or procedure requires time, discussion, modeling, and close connection to reinforcement.

Chapter 11

Interventions for Functional Communication Problems

Characteristics and Conditions of Functional Communication Problems

WHAT IS A FUNCTIONAL COMMUNICATION PROBLEM?

Communication takes many forms across a person's life span. It can be spoken or written, and it can be direct or symbolic. It can also encompass a variety of nonverbal characteristics such as posture, facial expression, eye contact, and non-language based sounds. Functional communication problems occur when needs, wants, desires, feelings, and/ or preferences of those communicating are unmet or unfulfilled (Kaiser, 2000). Ultimately, this results in a communication breakdown that prevents a message from being properly understood. Put another way, functional communication refers to skills and behaviors that enable a successful interaction between a person delivering a message and those persons who are receiving it (Charlop & Trasowech, 1991; Kaiser, 2000). (Related communication problems not addressed in this chapter for intervention include fluency, voice, and language problems. These problems may either be part of a stage in normal human development, or they may be specific speech and communication problems that need intervention.)

HOW COMMON ARE FUNCTIONAL COMMUNICATION PROBLEMS?

Communication disorders are a significant problem for a large number of children. A study by Pinborough-Zimmerman et al. (2007) found that over 6% of 8-year-olds had a communication disorder, with boys having an incidence rate double that found in girls, resulting in a major educational and public health concern.

Communication disorders are often comorbid with other disabilities, resulting in communication deficits that interfere with independence and functioning. For example, the prevalence rates of functional communication disorders for children receiving services for emotional or behavioral disorders (EBD) range from 42–88%, with many children being undiagnosed and untreated (Benner, 2005; Benner, Nelson, & Epstein, 2002). Functional communication problems are also frequently evident in children with autism spectrum disorder (ASD) and attention-deficit hyperactivity disorder (ADHD).

The BASC–3 Functional Communication scale assesses the child's ability to express ideas and communicate in ways that others can easily understand. The Teacher Rating Scales and Parent Rating Scales address various levels of functional communication skills. Rudimentary and advanced expressive-communication skills are measured by items such as "Provides full name when asked" and "Communicates clearly;" receptive-communication skills are measured by items such as "Responds appropriately when asked a question;" and written skills are measured by items such as "Accurately takes down messages."

Theoretical Framework for Approaching Functional Communication Problems

Most interventions for remediating functional communication problems emphasize social interaction theory that includes both behavioral and functional components. Each intervention is influenced by the individual needs of the child. For example, whereas some children have little or no spontaneous speech, others need assistance only in conversational speech and social interactions.

Typically, functional communication research examines the effects of interventions for children who are diagnosed with autism spectrum disorder or intellectual disability. A common characteristic of children with these problems is limited or severely limited speech-language ability that causes social or communication problems. The interventions presented in this chapter are generally designed for children with these types of speech-language issues. However, with respect to the BASC–3 Teacher Rating Scales and Parent Rating Scales, the Functional Communication scale provides a more general view of one's ability to effectively communicate with others. As such, a child who receives a score in the At-Risk or Clinically Significant range may have adequate speech but have difficulty conveying basic information to others. Interventions discussed in this chapter cover a range of functional and social communication skills but are less appropriate for children with adequate speech skills. For these children, the video modeling intervention strategy will be most applicable.

Interventions

The interventions presented in this chapter are predominately used with individual children with the most significant language needs. Two of the interventions (i.e., functional communication training and video modeling) may also be useful to prevent developing problems from worsening. Interventions included in this chapter should be carried out by all key stakeholders (e.g., parents, teachers, siblings) in all of the child's relevant environments (e.g., home, school, daycare), and not just in conjunction with clinical practitioners. The success of skill acquisition dramatically improves when all adults can be "teachers" and are trained to use the communication methods being taught to the child. Evidence-based interventions for improving functional communication in children are listed in Table 11.1. For some of the interventions in this chapter, supplemental materials (e.g., handouts, posters, checklists, daily logs, and worksheets) that are helpful for preparing, implementing, and evaluating the interventions can be found on Q-global.

Table 11.1. Interventions for Improving Functional Communication

Intervention	Prevention[1]	Early Intervention[2]	Intensive Intervention[3]
Functional Communication Training		X	X
Milieu Language Teaching			X
Picture Exchange Communication System (PECS)			X
Pivotal Response Training			X
Video Modeling		X	x

[1] Prevention refers to skills that can be taught to all children or used universally; they promote better awareness and lessen the risk of problems.

[2] Early intervention includes techniques and strategies that address early warning signs or clinical signs of the risk of future problems. Early intervention may be specifically applied to one or more problems or generically applied as a skill set to prevent the development of a chronic problem. Early interventions can be delivered to groups or individuals.

[3] Intensive intervention focuses on individuals and individual problems, which are usually chronic, intensive, and require services due to the level of interference in daily functioning.

 FUNCTIONAL COMMUNICATION TRAINING

DESCRIPTION

Functional communication training (FCT) is the process of teaching a child to communicate effectively (i.e., without the use of aberrant behavior) to satisfy his or her needs and wants. It can be applied in social situations or in any routine that requires good communication. FCT is used to determine the function of aberrant behavior and then to teach a replacement communication behavior with a functionally equivalent response (Mancil, 2006; Mancil & Boman, 2010). The replacement communication behaviors are communication skills that may be verbal or nonverbal. For example, some children can learn to verbalize questions or preferences while others might learn to use gestures (e.g., pointing, signing). Other communication options include assistive technology and picture card systems (discussed later in this chapter).

The procedural steps included in the How to Implement Functional Communication Training section incorporate the basic elements of FCT that are needed for successful application of this method (Brady & Halle, 1997; Lalli, Casey, & Kates, 1995).

EXAMPLES

Gary, an 11-year-old with autism spectrum disorder, shrieks loudly and points at the computer when he wants to play a game. Using FCT, he can be taught to say, "Game, please," or to give a picture of the computer to his teacher, in order to be given contingent access to the game. By using the replacement communication behavior, Gary learns that the aberrant behavior will no longer be effective and that appropriate communication will be successful.

Kay, an 8-year-old, frequently has trouble during lunchtime. She often throws food and cries, and it is hard for the other children or lunchroom attendants to know how to help her. Her counselor, after talking with her parents and lunchroom staff, suspects that Kay's outbursts are expressions of frustration about her food choices. Instead of asking, she throws her chocolate milk because she wants plain milk. He tests this hypothesis by giving Kay plain milk instead of chocolate milk and observing her response. The counselor chooses a communication behavior to replace the aberrant behavior of throwing and crying. Although the cafeteria staff does not use American Sign Language and Kay is still learning to sign, the staff is taught to recognize the letter "C" for chocolate milk and "P" for plain milk. Kay's teacher also provides her with training to wait for attention and to hold her place in line until she receives the milk she wants. Both Kay and the cafeteria staff practice before the lunch rush. The lunchroom staff can encourage Kay by providing her milk choice immediately and also by praising her for using her signs.

GOAL

Increase the child's functional communication (e.g., verbal responses, gestures, sign language) and decrease aberrant behavior.

THE BASICS

1. Complete a functional behavioral assessment (FBA).

2. Teach the child functionally equivalent replacement communication behavior(s).

HOW TO IMPLEMENT FUNCTIONAL COMMUNICATION TRAINING

 PREP

- Identify the aberrant behavior.

- Interview the parents, teachers, and other caregivers about the aberrant behavior that is being used for communication.

- Identify the setting and situations in which the aberrant behavior occurs.

- Observe the child's aberrant behavior in all relevant environments.

- Identify who will complete the FBA; this should correspond with the setting where the behavior occurs most frequently.

- Complete an FBA of the aberrant behavior. Possible causes might include wanting something tangible (e.g., a toy), intangible (e.g., attention), or sensory (e.g., rocking in the teacher's chair, using special school supplies), or it might include escaping something unpleasant (e.g., a chore, a social situation, a sensory experience).

- Form a hypothesis regarding the function of the behavior. Use the interview and observation data to support any hypotheses.

- Manipulate or change the consequences of the behavior to validate the hypotheses.

- Identify a replacement communication behavior. Optimal replacement communication behaviors should:
  - ▲ be within the child's ability level,
  - ▲ be applicable to other situations and in other environments,
  - ▲ clearly result in the same outcome as the undesirable behavior,
  - ▲ be as equal as possible to the degree of effort expended for the undesirable behavior, and
  - ▲ be as efficient as the undesirable behavior.

- Teach the child the replacement communication behavior. The replacement communication behavior is taught by modeling, providing verbal mands (i.e., requests), and, when appropriate, including hand-over-hand prompting (i.e., putting the child's hand where it belongs, with the instructor's hand on top guiding it).

- Prompt the child to use the replacement communication behavior and consistently ignore the aberrant behavior (in order to extinguish it).

- Reinforce the replacement communication behavior. It is important that the communication partner respond immediately. Acknowledge the use of the replacement communication behavior with praise or other reinforcers, such as smiles or preferred/requested objects.

- Collect data on the frequency of the use of the replacement communication behavior and on the frequency or duration of the aberrant behavior that was targeted.

- Use of the replacement communication behavior should increase, and use of the aberrant behavior should decrease. If this does not occur, evaluate whether the replacement communication behavior is as efficient as the aberrant behavior. Does it provide as immediate a response and result in the same outcome as the aberrant behavior? If not, go back and identify how to make the replacement communication behavior equally effective for the child. If this is not the issue, do the same process for efficiency: Is the replacement communication behavior just as easy as the aberrant behavior?

EVIDENCE

A brief overview of research and annotated references supporting this intervention can be found on Q-global.

CONSIDERATIONS

FOR TEACHING

The success of FCT will depend on finding the best possible replacement communication behavior. Using a child's preferences increases the likelihood of success for FCT. It is also important that the replacement communication behaviors are recognizable to individuals besides those who trained the response. For example, Voice Output Communication Aids (VOCAs) can be used as the replacement communication behavior, as can picture cards or some gesticulation, as long as these responses are reasonably universal, and thus functional in the community beyond the classroom.

As hypotheses are formed, it is important to note that there are some behavioral influences that should not be (or cannot be) manipulated during FCT (Durand & Merges, 2001). For instance, if the child cries for attention only when he or she is ill, the illness condition cannot be manipulated to determine if it truly is influencing the child's behavior. In this case, the aberrant behavior should be redirected. For example, self-injury cannot be ignored, but the potential sensory reinforcement could be redirected to another sensory activity (e.g., dragging fingers through rice, wearing wrist bands, stretching yoga bands) while the replacement communication behavior is being taught and learned.

Two important parts of implementing FCT are to make the aberrant behavior as nonfunctional as possible (Durand & Merges, 2001) and to create scenarios for using the replacement communication behavior. For example, a child who yells out in class may receive attention; ideally a group of classmates could support the use of verbal or other communication and ignore the yelling. It is also possible that attention and/or escape may not be the function of the behavior; instead, it may be sensory or it may be used to receive access to something tangible. It is critical to identify the function of the behavior in any case.

 MILIEU LANGUAGE TEACHING

DESCRIPTION
Milieu language teaching is a "naturalistic, conversation-based teaching procedure in which the child's interest in the environment is used as a basis for eliciting elaborated child communicative responses" (Kaiser, 1993, p. 77). Milieu language teaching is the combination of behavioral principles, incidental teaching, the time-delay procedure, and the mand-model procedure (Alpert & Kaiser, 1992). The time-delay procedure involves the adult waiting a period of time for a response prior to prompting or attempting another teaching strategy (U.S. Department of Education, Institute of Education Sciences, What Works Clearinghouse, 2012). The mand-model procedure involves requesting (i.e., asking a question or giving the child a directive to respond) and/or modeling an appropriate response (U.S. Department of Education et al., 2012). Milieu language teaching allows the therapist to optimize generalization of communicative initiations and responses throughout the day by observing naturally occurring teachable moments in child activity.

This application of the word "milieu" means the physical or social setting where something commonly takes place; therefore, milieu language teaching can include such everyday situations as parents at a park asking a child to name objects and then asking for the child to describe the objects using attributes (color or size) or a function of the object. These natural interactions encourage the use of spontaneous speech. Through the use of spontaneous speech, children have more social interactions and can solicit information, objects, and attention (Charlop & Trasowech, 1991).

EXAMPLES
A parent might ask a child, "What is this?" while pointing to a slide in the park, and the child would respond, "Slide." The parent would then ask, "What color is the slide?" to further engage the child, and the child would respond, "Red." This exchange could be followed with, "What do we do on a slide?" The child might say, "Go down."

In a classroom setting, a teacher could ask one child, "What is Allia doing?" while pointing to another child in the room. The child might answer, "Drawing." The teacher might then affirm the response and ask, "What is she drawing a picture of?" The dialog would continue with prompting, pausing, and natural events.

GOAL
Increase appropriate spontaneous speech in natural settings.

THE BASICS

1. Assess the child's current language needs.

2. Identify the environment where the language would most naturally occur and create teaching arrangements.

3. Use the time-delay procedure.

4. Incorporate incidental teaching.

5. Model spontaneous speech whenever possible.

6. Use the mand-model procedure.

*Elements 3 through 6 are not required when implementing a minimally intrusive process.

HOW TO IMPLEMENT MILIEU LANGUAGE TEACHING

 PREP

- Identify the communication needs (e.g., Asking for items? Expressing desires? Social communication?).

- Identify and select the most natural environment for this type of communication to occur based on the child's typical daily routines

 IMPLEMENT

TIME-DELAY PROCEDURE

- Present the target item or activity (e.g., cookie, mom walking into the bedroom in the morning) and model the expected response for the child.

- Increase the amount of time between the presentation of the target item and a prompt gradually.

  ▲ For example, Jimmy wants an apple from the refrigerator. When the door is open, he points at the apple. His mother says, "Do you want one green apple?" His mom waits for him to respond with "one green apple" and then gives it to him. Each day, Jimmy's mother increases the time between Jimmy seeing or pointing to the apple and the time that she prompts him to ask for the apple. The response can later be generalized to other environments. Jimmy's mother can integrate a new skill by prompting Jimmy with the question, "Do you want two green apples?" Jimmy's mother intermittently asks Jimmy if he wants one green apple or two green apples, thus associating a new skill (in this case, assigning a quantity of one or two) with an old skill (naming a green apple).

- Observe the child in a natural setting to find teachable moments and to encourage the child to communicate by using prompts that increase in intensity (as needed).

- Implement the lowest of the four prompt levels necessary to enhance the communicative response of the child. The four levels identified by Hart & Risley (1974) include: (1) a 30-second delay; (2) a prompt to request an object; (3) a prompt that is a more elaborate request; and (4) a response that is modeled and the child is encouraged to mimic.

  ▲ Level 1: Note items or activities that the child seems to like. When the child indicates a desire for an item or activity or to engage with peers, first wait 30 seconds for the child to initiate communication without prompting.

  ▲ Level 2: After 30 seconds, provide a verbal prompt to request the object (e.g., "Eat?" or "What do you want?").

  ▲ Level 3: The next prompt is a more elaborate question, such as, "Do you want to eat now?" or "Would you like a green apple to eat?"

  ▲ Level 4: The final prompt is a phrase to be repeated, such as, "I want apple," or, "I want to eat green apple." This most intensive prompt requires modeling the correct response, and the child imitating the adult or peer behavior.

MODELING AND MAND MODELING

- Use modeling and mand modeling techniques with the child. Modeling and mand modeling techniques are similar.

  ▲ Modeling involves observing the child showing interest in an item and modeling the correct communicative response for the item (e.g., "That's a toy car.").

  ▲ Mand modeling, however, involves observing the child's natural interest in an item or activity and requesting a communicative response from him or her (e.g., "Tell me what you want."). Give the child the item or allow him or her to engage in the activity immediately if he or she provides the correct response. Model the correct response for the child (e.g., "Say *toy car*") if the child provides an incorrect response.

 EVALUATE

- Evaluate the child's increased spontaneous use of language. Evaluation methods can be as simple as frequency counting (e.g., the frequency and rate of words produced, length of utterances, or spontaneous use of new words or target words and phrases).

- Consider employing a "topographical" description where the behavior can be described qualitatively (e.g., what the communication looks and sounds like, including body gestures, facial expressions, or other descriptions that could be relevant in identifying improvement or fluency).

EVIDENCE

A brief overview of research and annotated references supporting this intervention can be found on Q-global.

CONSIDERATIONS

FOR TEACHING

Teaching children with speech and language delays involves a curricular focus on adaptive or functional skills that depend on the age of the child. Academic goals and behavioral goals will co-vary and overlap; as verbal skills improve, maladaptive behavior should decrease. Generalization and transfer of skills to other educational and home settings are important considerations that are also based, at least in part, on age and developmental level. Community issues, transportation needs, workplace transitions, and social needs will all vary according to the environmental demands associated with both school and home.

PICTURE EXCHANGE COMMUNICATION SYSTEM (PECS)

DESCRIPTION

The Picture Exchange Communication System (PECS; Bondy & Frost, 1994) teaches communication skills to primarily nonverbal children with developmental delays (Bondy & Frost, 1994). PECS is an alternative communication system that involves exchanging a picture or symbol for a desired event or item (Carr & Felce, 2007; Charlop-Christy, Carpenter, Le, LeBlanc, & Kellet, 2002). Its conceptual simplicity and positive results make it an appealing intervention choice when working with nonverbal children. It can be considered augmentative communication, which takes the form of both aided and unaided language. Speech or sign language are "unaided" and picture systems or icon symbol systems are "aided" (Bondy, 2012; Mirenda, 2003). PECS is distinct from a communication or gesture dictionary, which is a picture or symbol book of all possible words or signals that may potentially be needed for an individual. Instead, PECS uses select words that are likely to be needed. PECS is designed to increase spontaneous and functional communication and to foster meaningful interactions between the child, his or her environment, and a communication partner (Bondy & Frost, 1994; Charlop-Christy et al., 2002; Howlin, Gordon, Pasco, Wade, & Charman, 2007; Magiati & Howlin, 2003).

EXAMPLE

Shandalynn, a 6-year-old with autism, wants to watch her favorite movie, *Bambi*. She takes her mom's hand, sits in front of the television, and begins to cry when she realizes the movie is not the one she wanted to watch. Using PECS, Shandalynn can get her communication book and select a picture of movie and animal (from which her mom might infer *Bambi*) or a photo of the exact movie, or she may create a more complete sentence strip with pictures representing, "this movie is wrong and I want Bambi," using symbols to represent movie and wrong or no, and then movie and her selection.

GOAL

Increase the child's spontaneous functional augmented communication to foster meaningful interactions.

THE BASICS

1. Determine which frequently requested items or activities the child needs to communicate about.

2. Create picture symbols.

3. Identify and train communication partners.

4. Exchange access to wants and needs for communicative use of symbols.

5. Provide positive reinforcement.

HOW TO IMPLEMENT PICTURE EXCHANGE COMMUNICATION SYSTEM

 PREP

- Conduct a needs assessment so that the pictures for the picture library are age appropriate, related to the needs of the child, and match frequently requested items or activities. A large component of a picture exchange communication system is the development of the picture library. Picture symbols can be made from digital photographs or reproduced from commercially distributed computer programs.

- Ask someone who knows the child to create lists of desired food, entertainment, and activities; or place an assortment of things (e.g., food, toys, games, movies) within the child's reach and watch to see which items the child selects first. Compile a list of communication settings (e.g., classroom, home, cafeteria, playground, bus, grocery store, park). Be creative and consider the widest range of relevant environments.

- Create the communication board or book. Depending on the child's physical ability or developmental level, choose either a laminated piece of cardboard on which the child can place his or her picture cards, or create flip pages or a portable flip-type book. Place the reusable adhesive strips on the board or in the book, making it a place to keep all the cards a child may want to use.

- Create sentence strips with picture representations of phrases like "I want," "I see," "I have," or "I hear." Eventually, these can be added together to enhance communication and help further develop word and object recognition in a variety of settings.

- Identify communication partners for the child (e.g., parents, other family members, teachers, paraprofessionals, principals). Choosing a variety of communication partners from a number of environments will help the child begin to apply new skills to different situations. Individuals who will be communication partners must be trained.

 ## IMPLEMENT

The implementation stage is broken into six phases that are based primarily on Bondy & Frost (1994, 2001) and Bondy (2012).

PHASE ONE: Teach the child how to communicate a basic need by exchanging a picture for a desired object.

- Place the desired object within the child's view.

- Watch as the child reaches for the object, physically block access to the object, and place a picture of the object in the child's hand.

- Guide the child to give the picture to the communication partner.

- Have the communication partner accept the picture, state the name of the picture, and immediately give the object to the child.

- Fade physical prompts gradually.

- Continue this phase until the child reaches for the picture and places it in the communication partner's hand without prompting.

PHASE TWO: Expand the child's spontaneity when requesting desired objects.

- Move the communication partner and the picture of the desired object away from the child, and have the communication partner avoid making eye contact with the child.

- Touch the communication partner (modeling) or prompt the child to touch the communication partner to draw attention and initiate eye contact if the child does not initiate eye contact with the communication partner.

- Have the communication partner make immediate eye contact and open his or her hand to receive the picture from the child when the child touches the communication partner. Fade this gesture during the intervention.

- Immediately give the reinforcing object to the child when the child places the picture in the communication partner's hand. Ensure no verbal interactions occur until the picture is placed in the communication partner's hand. At this point, the communication partner may confirm verbally the item or activity the child is requesting.

PHASE THREE: Teach the child to discriminate between different pictures or symbols.

■ Place one preferred and one nonpreferred object (to be used as a distracter) within the child's reach, and present two corresponding pictures to the child.

■ Have the communication partner give the object to the child, provide reinforcement, and allow the child to play with the object for a few seconds if the child places the picture of the preferred object in the communication partner's hand.

■ Have the communication partner give the child the nonpreferred object if the child gives the picture of the nonpreferred object to the communication partner.

▲ Complete an error correction sequence by modeling the selection of the appropriate picture to receive the preferred object when the child indicates that the wrong object was selected.

▲ Prompt the child to select the correct picture and praise him or her when the correct selection is made; however, the object is not given to the child.

▲ Remove the picture of the nonpreferred object and repeat the process, this time allowing the child to receive the object.

▲ Replace both pictures and repeat the process.

■ Have the communication partner replace handing the child the object with the words "take it" after this skill is mastered.

■ Block the preferred object from the child's reach and repeat the error correction sequence if the child chooses the picture of the nonpreferred object but reaches for the preferred object.

■ Add more items to the communication book or board and repeat the process when the child masters the skill of selecting the picture of the preferred object.

PHASE FOUR: Teach the child to differentiate between requesting and commenting phrases.

■ Add a sentence strip to the communication board or book with icons representing the words "I want."

■ Model placing the picture of the preferred object on the communication board or book and receiving the desired object.

■ Remove the picture, and when the child places the picture next to icons representing the words "I want," give the child the desired object and say, "I want a (name the desired object)."

PHASE FIVE: Continue to delineate between phrase types as the child is taught to answer the question "What do you want?"

■ Say, "What do you want?" while placing the "I want" sentence strip on the communication book or board.

■ Give the child the desired object after the child places the picture on the communication book or board.

■ Delay placing the sentence strip on the board gradually until enough time has passed for the child to place the sentence strip on the board without prompting.

PHASE SIX: Teach the child how to comment.

■ Introduce a new sentence strip that includes icons representing comment phrases such as "I hear" or "I see."

■ Arrange interesting items for the child to hear or see.

■ Ask the child, "What do you see?" while pointing to the symbol representation of "I see."

■ Wait for the child to place a symbol on the board.

■ Provide a social response, such as "I see a (name pictured object), too!"

- Add more commenting phrases, such as "I hear" in response to "What do you hear?" or "I have," in response to "What do you have?"

- Gradually fade the use of the question.

- Wait for the child to request or comment by independently approaching multiple communication partners in multiple environments without prompting (see also Carr & Felce, 2007).

 EVALUATE

- Consider collecting communication data in a variety of ways. At the most basic level, frequency counts of word use can be tallied. In addition, the use of prompts can also be tallied (e.g., counting the number of times a prompt is used, coding and counting the use of general versus specific prompts). Beyond these counts, the number of communication partners that are being used can be monitored, as well as the type (e.g., home, school, cafeteria, bus, grocery store) and number of settings in which the behaviors are being counted.

EVIDENCE

A brief overview of research and annotated references supporting this intervention can be found on Q-global.

CONSIDERATIONS

FOR TEACHING

PECS requires a 1:1 ratio of child to communication partner. School psychologists, counselors, and/or speech-language pathologists are encouraged to train and assist teachers in using PECS procedures, practicing generalization, and creating materials. Some research suggests that modifications to the classroom and teacher training are needed (Howlin et al., 2007). Teacher assistance teams can provide this type of support.

PECS, like all communication systems or strategies, is most effective when used across settings, such as home or nonschool environments. Language differences would imply that families would need to be involved in either dual-language applications for sentence strips or in developing pictures that reflect activities that are important to the family and the family's culture.

 PIVOTAL RESPONSE TRAINING

DESCRIPTION

Pivotal response training (PRT) is an intervention that targets specific central response areas in natural environments that, if modified, will generalize to other behaviors and result in widespread behavioral change (Koegel & Koegel, 1995; Koegel, Koegel, Harrower, & Carter, 1999; Koegel, et al., 1989). Examples of central response areas that are often targeted include: initiation, motivation, responsiveness to multiple cues, and self-direction (Koegel & Koegel, 1995). Motivation is assessed by observable characteristics, such as responding to the environment or rate of responding. If children are taught pivotal skills (e.g., initiation, motivational behaviors), these skill sets will generalize to a variety of other behaviors across multiple settings.

EXAMPLES

Elmer is taught to ask WH- questions, such as "What is that?" or "Where is X?" These questions are socially appropriate in a variety of settings, provide social interactions, and initiate communication with others.

Leon is taught to carry a pen and a small notebook in his pocket. When he is bored (self-assessment, self-management), he knows that he can practice written communication (i.e., signing his name) rather than rocking or wandering about the room.

GOAL

Enhance the child's ability to engage in spontaneous interactions more frequently by engaging in new communication behaviors.

THE BASICS

1. Identify pivotal responses that will affect multiple conditions and behaviors.

2. Teach these behaviors and reinforce clear communication.

3. Introduce the use of descriptive responses using multiple examples.

HOW TO IMPLEMENT PIVOTAL RESPONSE TRAINING

 PREP

- Identify the communication partner (e.g., parents, teachers, caregivers, other professionals, peers and/or siblings of typical development).

- Identify environments for optimal use of PRT (i.e., those environments where multiple variables exist and more specific language is required).

 IMPLEMENT

- Teach the communication partner to provide stimuli that encourage the child to engage in more communication behaviors.

  ▲ For example, Joey enjoys riding a bicycle. Joey's mother makes sure the bicycle is available when they are playing outside.

- Have the communication partner provide prompts to encourage a communicative response from the child. The communication partner can turn the child's attention to a task by stating the child's name, touching the child, or making eye contact. The communication partner asks questions only when needed to provide clear and simple instructions for the opportunity to respond.

  ▲ For example, Joey grabs the bike from his brother when he wants to ride. His brother holds Joey's hands, makes eye contact, and says, "Do you want to ride the bike?"

- Make sure the communication partner allows time for the child to respond, models the targeted behavior, and reinforces each attempt by the child to respond.

- Ensure that the communication partner provides reinforcers that are logically and naturally related to the targeted communicative response for all attempts at communication. Ultimately, tasks that have been mastered by the child are combined with new tasks.

 EVALUATE

- Track improvements in language usage by targets. Consider identifying areas of communication such as social expression and self-care or getting desired items.

- Keep track of word use and/or sentence use.

- Develop goals to improve the number of words used and to expand choices and variety as the child maximizes vocabulary in an area.

EVIDENCE

A brief overview of research and annotated references supporting this intervention can be found on Q-global.

 **VIDEO MODELING**

DESCRIPTION

Video modeling is the use of video technology to help children see the accurate performance of a target behavior (Apple, Billingsley, & Schwartz, 2005; Bellini & Akullian, 2007; Charlop-Christy, Le, & Freeman, 2000). Video modeling is founded on the observational learning principles of Bandura (1977), who said that observational learning "refers to cognitive and behavioral change that results from observation of others engaged in similar actions" (p. 39). For the purpose of this guide, the targeted or observed behaviors are functional communication skills.

Video modeling has two basic elements: observation and imitation of functional communication skills. These two elements are incorporated into the three stages for implementation: (1) video planning and production, (2) video observation, and (3) generalization.

EXAMPLES

Ivan, a 14-year-old with ASD, constantly attempts to talk to his peers about a black hole in outer space that can be utilized to create energy for Earth. His peers typically are not interested and walk away. However, Ivan does not notice and continues to engage in this topic of discussion. Video modeling can help Ivan identify external cues that signal how well a message is being received by others.

Beth, a 5-year-old with ASD, sits in front of the toy shelf and makes different sounds for each of her favorite toys when she wants to play with them. Beth's mother understands what each sound means, but other caregivers might not. Data gathered from her mother and from other assessment instruments suggest that communicative behaviors that model requesting items would be good content for Beth's video.

Andre, a 10-year-old with ASD, requests items by using two- or three-word phrases, but he pushes other children when he wants to play with them. Communication skills related to initiating play with other children might be selected as the video content for Andre.

GOAL

Increase the child's exposure to accurate performance of targeted behaviors to improve his or her ability to sustain functional and social communication with peers and other communication partners.

THE BASICS

1. Create (or find) a video that models the desired behavior(s).

2. Conduct sessions in which the child watches the video.

3. Train teachers or others in various settings to prompt for and reinforce desired behaviors.

HOW TO IMPLEMENT VIDEO MODELING

 PREP

- Determine the most appropriate video models (e.g., the child, a preferred peer, familiar adults and peers), and select the individual video models if someone other than the child will be included.

- Determine the content of the video. It should include specific communicative needs of the child discovered during prior assessments (e.g., making a request, initiating a conversation). Consider use of a formal or informal preference assessment, observation, and interviews with others (e.g., parents, teachers) to select child-preferred activities or objects.

IMPLEMENT

- Write and record the script for each video segment. The scripts should be brief, typically between 1–4 minutes long.

- Find a natural setting (e.g., classroom, hallway, home, cafeteria) for the video. Multiple natural settings can be used and may be helpful. Determine how many segments or scenarios to include.

- Record the models performing the targeted communication behavior. Edit the videos if needed.

- Watch the video with the child. Explain and model appropriate video-watching behavior (e.g., ask the child to sit and watch quietly). Sit beside the child and prompt him or her to maintain attention (e.g., say, "Good watching.").

- Play the video for the child on another occasion.

  ▲ Remind the child to sit and watch quietly. (If needed, model the correct way to pay attention to a video, and the child can practice this behavior prior to viewing.)

  ▲ Provide encouraging prompts during the video, such as "See what a good time you (they) are having."

  ▲ Watch the video a second time, and then have the child role-play the communication skills learned in the video to reinforce the newly acquired behaviors.

- Repeat the video-watching session if the child does not master the content after two separate viewings.

- Role-play the video content with the child in other common settings to reinforce the application of the newly learned behavior.

- Train peers and/or significant adults (e.g., parents, teachers, siblings, caregivers) to prompt the child to use the skill modeled in the video in different environments (e.g., classroom, playground, home).

- Teach peers and significant adults to fade prompts.

- Encourage the child to use the skill in common settings.

- If appropriate, involve the child in the evaluation by including a self-management phase in which the child self-monitors and self-reinforces the use of the communication skill.

- If needed, create a contract with the child to perform the skill with reinforcement (activity or tangible) and keep track of the child's performance.

- Create a self-management data collection instrument with the child.

- Model and practice the use of the self-management instrument with the child.

- Ask the child to self-monitor use of the communication skill and to provide reinforcement with a visual schedule, such as a progress chart.

EVALUATE

- Track the child's performance of targeted communication behaviors demonstrated in the video modeling.

- Return to the IMPLEMENT steps as necessary if the frequency of targeted communication behaviors does not increase.

EVIDENCE

A brief overview of research and annotated references supporting this intervention can be found on Q-global.

CONSIDERATIONS

FOR TEACHING

Teaching specific linguistic rules prior to the use of video modeling or embedded within the video model increases the effectiveness of the intervention (Apple et al., 2005; Hepting & Goldstein, 1996). Make videos as realistic as possible by using peers as models or the child as a lead actor, as well as by filming in natural settings such as classrooms. For some children, using adults to model behavior may not be as effective.

FOR SAFETY

Talk with the child's family about protecting his or her privacy; everyone should understand that the video content is confidential material. Children and their families must be reassured that use of any video imagery or photos will be strictly controlled to prevent misuse (e.g., getting posted on social networking websites). Use permission forms checked by school administration regarding video use.

Chapter 12

Intervention for Social Skills Problems

Characteristics and Conditions of Social Skills Problems

WHAT ARE SOCIAL SKILLS?

Social skills are learned, situation-specific behaviors (both verbal and nonverbal) that are demonstrated in particular social contexts (Spitzberg & Dillard, 2002; Van Hasselt, Hersen, Whitehill, & Bellack, 1979). Interpersonal skills, typically classified as a type of social skills, are needed to interact effectively with people; as such, they form the foundation for social relationships. Deficits in social skills interfere with social, emotional, and academic functioning (Bellini, Peters, Benner, & Hopf, 2007; Welsh, Parke, Widaman, & O'Neil, 2001; Whitted, 2011). They are frequently observed in children with learning disabilities and children with emotional and behavioral disorders, especially autism spectrum disorder, attention-deficit/hyperactivity disorder (ADHD), conduct disorder, and social anxiety (Bellini et al., 2007; Forness & Knitzer, 1992; Foster & Bussman, 2008; Kavale & Forness, 1996; Sullivan & Mastropieri, 1994; Walker, Colvin, & Ramsey, 1995).

Social skills are necessary for developing and maintaining social relationships. A child with strong social and interpersonal skills is considered to have achieved social competence. Social competence includes the absence of significant maladaptive behaviors and the presence of positive relationships with others, accurate and age-appropriate social cognition, and effective social behaviors needed for children to be accepted by peers (Bierman, Miller, & Stabb, 1987).

Social skills deficits can be classified into three categories: (1) skill or acquisition deficits, (2) performance deficits, and (3) self-control deficits (Gresham, 1981, 1998; Gresham, Elliott, & Kettler, 2010; Gresham, Sugai, & Horner, 2001). Children with skill or acquisition deficits lack the knowledge necessary to perform a social skill. Children with performance deficits know how to perform a social skill but do not perform it or perform it in an awkward fashion. Children with self-control deficits may not exhibit appropriate social skills due to the presence of competing problem behaviors. For example, verbal aggression might compete with the social skill of expressing understanding for the feelings of others. Similarly, a child who knows how to respond positively may not do so because of issues associated with another developmental issue (e.g., ADHD) for which impulsive responding may overpower the individual's knowledge of how to respond appropriately. In such instances, interventions for the underlying disorder, as well as methods that are specific to treating social skills knowledge or performance deficits, should be utilized.

HOW COMMON ARE SOCIAL SKILLS DEFICITS?

Social skills deficits have been shown to be relatively uncommon in the general population, with the prevelence of performance deficits being markedly higher (average of 3.5% of children) than skill acquisition deficits (average of less than 1% of children; Gresham et al., 2010). Social skills deficits are commonly observed in and hallmark characteristics of a number of behavioral and emotional problems, such as autism spectrum disorder, ADHD, and conduct disorder (APA, 2013).

The BASC–3 measures social skills through two related positive scales, the Social Skills scale (from the Teacher Rating Scales and Parent Rating Scales) and the Interpersonal Relations scale (from the Self-Report of Personality). Social skills develop resiliency, increase desirable behaviors, and mediate behaviors associated with externalizing and internalizing problems, such as aggression, conduct problems, anxiety, somatization, depression, hyperactivity, and inattention. Items from the Social Skills scale include "Compliments others," "Encourages others to do their best," and "Says, 'please' and 'thank you.'" Items from the Interpersonal Relations scale include "I get along well with others" and "I have a hard time making friends."

Theoretical Framework for Approaching Social Skills Problems

Childhood behavioral problems involving relationships often are linked to the absence of particular social skills. This lack of social skills indicates a deficiency in the child's social competency. While social skills and social competency may seem synonymous, the two are not. Social competency encompasses social skills and other important factors, such as positive relationships with others, accurate and age-appropriate social cognition, absence of maladaptive behaviors, and effective social behaviors (Vaughn & Hogan, 1990). Social competency, therefore, is the necessary construct for successful treatment and remediation of problem behaviors of a social and interpersonal nature.

Social competency is made up of discrete skills that must be taught separately but integrated seamlessly into the individual's life and actions. Typically, when a child lacks social competency, his or her behavioral deficiency is remediated through a training program based on a series of related skills. For example, it is insufficient to teach a child to be nice, behave, or play fair, because the skills that make up being nice and playing fair (e.g., taking turns and sharing) have to be taught individually before being incorporated into the child's repertoire of generalized social skills.

Social skills, as a part of social competency, consist of the interpersonal behaviors that allow individuals to work cooperatively with others, form groups and bonds, communicate, and develop relationships. These behaviors may be demonstrated when an individual exhibits interpersonal skills such as empathy and sympathy, which motivate or predispose a person to relate to others and to want to work cooperatively with them.

Social skills are learned, although innate abilities or predispositions for certain behaviors may enhance the rate and degree of mastery in acquiring these skill sets. The intervention strategy for increasing or enhancing social skills presented in this chapter is considered a cognitive–behavioral approach because it addresses both the mental factors involved (e.g., self-awareness) and the tendency for certain behaviors to be reinforced by the environment.

Intervention

The intervention presented in this chapter has broad applications for building or strengthening social and interpersonal skills. It can be used for prevention, early intervention, or intensive intervention, in multiple settings, and in conjunction with other needed interventions. Supplemental materials (e.g., handouts, posters, checklists, daily logs, and worksheets) that are helpful for preparing, implementing, and evaluating the intervention can be found on Q-global.

Ratings from multiple informants are useful in focusing interventions on the most appropriate settings. It is possible for a child to exhibit better social skills in one setting than another; for example, a child may exhibit more skilled behaviors with parents somewhere in the community than without parents at school. Thus, intervention implementation may focus on only the home or school setting for some children, while some children may need training in both settings. For a child who primarily displays skill deficits in interacting with peers, implementation may focus on the development of interpersonal social skills.

When selecting interventions for any behavioral or emotional disorder, therapists should take into account whether social or interpersonal skills have been identified as strengths or weaknesses. If they are strengths, therapists can use those strengths to address co-morbid deficits by allowing the child to draw on stronger social skills to mediate other identified behavioral deficits (e.g., aggression). In contrast, for a child with scores that fall within the At-Risk or Clinically Significant range on the Social Skills or Interpersonal Relations scales, the therapist should consider the child's specific externalizing or internalizing behavior problems and use this information to help select the skills to be taught within social skills training (Reynolds & Kamphaus, 2015).

For example, if Campbell was identified by the BASC–3 rating scales as being At-Risk for problems with aggression, but he scored high on the Social Skills scale, the therapist should consider Campbell's social skills strength when selecting from evidence-based interventions identified in the Aggression chapter of this guide (Chapter 2). Knowing Campbell's strength, the therapist might select peer-mediated conflict resolution as the intervention, teaching Campbell to use his social skills to take on the role of peer mediator. Conversely, if Campbell had score in the Clinically Significant range on both the Social Skills and Aggression scales, and the therapist noted that Campbell tended to respond to others' anger by using physical aggression, the therapist might choose to focus Campbell's social skills training on responding to others' anger.

SOCIAL SKILLS TRAINING

DESCRIPTION

Social skills training is a cognitive–behavioral approach to teaching prosocial concepts needed for children to function successfully in multiple social environments. Social skills training includes teaching interpersonal skills and subskills that enable children to function cooperatively and effectively with other individuals.

The term "social skills" generally refers to skills that enable effective functioning when interacting with others. Gresham (1986) notes that social skills also include dimensions of peer acceptance, behavioral skills, and social validity (i.e., the social importance of the targeted skills). Social skills training and similar intervention programs generally present a child with a series of lessons that each target a specific social skill so that the newly learned skills can be applied by the child when opportunities arise.

Social skills training lessons or curricula can be created by individuals or teams, or they can be purchased from a wide variety of educational publishers. Training programs often require a child to generate multiple strategies for engaging in appropriate social behavior. These strategies may include broad skills (e.g., expressing empathy, being aware of the consequences of one's own and others' behavior, and identifying appropriate paths to reach desired goals) and discrete skills (e.g., making friends, expressing disagreement, waiting for one's turn, and listening). The procedural steps presented in this chapter for implementing social skills training are adapted from several sources, including Foster and Bussman (2008); Quinn, Kavale, Mathur, Rutherford, and Forness (1999); Rutherford, Quinn, and Mathur (1996); and Spitzberg and Dillard (2002).

EXAMPLE

Barry, a 6-year-old boy with social skills deficits, takes toys out of his peers' hands when he wants to play. Barry's teacher helps him to learn the developmentally appropriate interpersonal skill of sharing, which involves asking politely, taking turns, and remaining calm when playing with others.

GOAL

Help the child develop skills that enable him or her to engage in appropriate interactions with others by remediating the behavioral challenges associated with his or her social skills deficits.

THE BASICS

1. Identify the target social skills to develop.

2. Teach the skills and talk about why each is useful or important.

3. Model the skills through active demonstration.

4. Help the child practice the skills in a controlled environment while receiving feedback.

5. Assist the child in generalizing the skills by practicing them in new environments.

HOW TO IMPLEMENT SOCIAL SKILLS TRAINING

 PREP

- Determine whether the training is an intervention or if it is preventative.

  ▲ If it is an intervention, assess the child's social skills and determine the specific skill(s) the child needs to master. Instruction should be tailored to a child's specific needs, not based on a set list or a fixed curriculum. For example, if the child throws tantrums to get desired objects, the therapist should specifically teach the skill of asking for objects.

  ▲ If it is preventative, the organizational or leadership team should identify target social skills for instruction and either all children or small groups of at-risk children should learn similar sets of critical social skills to prevent problems.

- Determine the format of instruction. The target social skills can be taught to a group or to individuals, and the skills can be taught in either a clinical or natural environment.

  ▲ A natural environment is the ideal training scenario for generalization; however, training sessions are not always possible in school settings due to environmental constraints (e.g., lack of personnel, lack of adequate training, competing demands of classroom settings).

  ▲ Groups can have children with similar social skills deficits (homogeneous grouping) or children with different deficits (heterogeneous grouping). When working with a homogeneous group, particularly one with children who exhibit antisocial behavior, be sure to provide enough supervision and structure to prevent modeling of inappropriate behaviors (i.e., behaviors that contradict the skills being taught). For example, if some children in a social skills training group frequently mimic wrestling moves or use inappropriate language, others in the group may adopt these behaviors. The selection of members for group-based social skills training should be made based on information about the specific behavioral challenges and social skills deficits of the individual children.

- Schedule consistent times for social skills training keeping in mind that high training intensity (both frequency of meetings and overall program duration) is desirable (Taylor et al., 1999).

  ▲ If the skill is taught to an individual child in his or her natural environment, select a time based on the child's current schedule (e.g., getting along with others might be taught during recess).

  ▲ If the skill is taught in a pull-out group session, select a specific time during the day that does not interfere with academic instruction. Determine the behavioral expectations for the group and post them in a highly visible area.

 IMPLEMENT

- Explain the purpose of the training and define the concept of social skills for the children.

- Teach the children the steps to master the selected skills, focusing on one skill per lesson.

  ▲ Begin with a visual representation (written or pictorial, depending on the children's abilities) of the steps required for performing the skill, and then ask the children to write down the steps on note cards or paper to help them remember the steps.

  ▲ Instruct the children to verbalize the steps of a social skill using choral responding (i.e., reciting them aloud and in unison) if desired, and verbally reinforce children as they recite the steps.

- Demonstrate appropriate use of the skill by modeling it with another adult or with other children.

- Ask the children to provide examples of appropriate times to use this skill and situations in the recent past when this skill could have been useful.

- Ask the children to reenact some of the situations described and encourage them to incorporate the newly learned social skill. Assign other children to be monitors of the process so that they feel included even though they are not role-playing the situation.

  - ▲ Provide feedback and reinforcement during the role-play to both the actors and the children who are monitoring the use of the steps.

  - ▲ Elicit feedback after the role-play from all children, including the actors, on how effectively the skill was used.

- Provide relevant adults (e.g., teachers, parents, tutors, classroom volunteers) with a copy of the steps of the skill. Ask the adults to model the skill, encourage the child to apply the new skill, and reinforce all efforts.

- At the beginning of the next session, review the steps for the skill taught in the previous session.

- Provide reinforcement to the children for situational use of the skill to increase the likelihood of skill maintenance and generalization, which are vital to all skills training programs.

EVALUATE

- Ask children who can write to record all social situations in which they use the skill in a journal. Children who cannot write can report daily to parents or to a teacher who can record their experiences.

- Monitor and continually assess the children's use of the skill (either through direct observation or by reviewing their journals) to identify any skills that need to be re-taught or reinforced.

- Hold periodic refresher courses on the skills taught in order to maintain skill acquisition.

EVIDENCE

A brief overview of research and annotated references supporting this intervention can be found on Q-global.

CONSIDERATIONS

Social skills training programs have been found to be more effective for children at risk of developing internalizing or externalizing disorders than for children already diagnosed with such disorders (Beelmann, Pfingsten, & Lösel, 1994; Quinn et al., 1999). In addition, social skills training has been found to be more effective for children with internalizing disorders than for children with externalizing disorders (Erwin, 1994). Therefore, early identification of potential deficits increases the likelihood of successful intervention.

FOR TEACHING

Social skills training is implemented easily within the classroom because it can be presented as a lesson. In fact, many social skills curricula are structured and formatted to be taught campus-wide as a lesson within a relevant content area, such as social studies or health.

Prior to teaching social skills, practitioners should consider which specific social skills should be taught and, if desired, which social skills program should be used. A social skills program with established social validity (Bullis, Walker, & Sprague, 2001; Foster & Bussman, 2008; Gresham, Sugai, & Horner, 2001) should be chosen based on the needs of the individual children (Quinn et al., 1999). Interventions should be systematically matched to the type of skill deficit (i.e., acquisition, performance, or self-control) the children exhibit (Gresham, Sugai, & Horner, 2001; Quinn et al., 1999). There are a number of commercially available social skills programs; a quick Internet search can provide many options.

For maximum effectiveness, social skills training should be implemented in an intense and frequent manner (Bierman, 2004; Bullis et al., 2001; Gresham, Sugai, & Horner, 2001), with more than 30 hours of instruction over a 10- to 12-week period. This schedule may be difficult to achieve in school environments that focus on academics only. Social skills training can also be incorporated as one component of a multiple-stage or -tier approach to preventing or remediating behavior disorders (Quinn et al., 1999). Strong consideration should be given to the possible negative impact of conducting social skills training with a homogenous group if working with a group of children with behavior disorders (Bierman, 2004; Dishion, McCord, & Poulin, 1999).

Finally, if social skills training is adopted as a school-wide program, administrators should plan for certain potentially problematic aspects of implementation. Specifically, administrators should plan strategies for preventing and dealing with missed sessions, engaging students actively in the curriculum, managing disruptions and attention problems, and enhancing generalization and maintenance by involving all relevant adults. Further, administrators should (1) consider the educational goals of the school and of those practitioners implementing the social skills interventions; (2) identify methods for monitoring the fidelity of implementation; (3) develop appropriate training for the implementers of the social skills program; and (4) assess the needs for community, administrative, and technical support.

Failure to consider methods for maintaining and generalizing the newly learned skills is common, and such failure often compromises the effectiveness of social skills training interventions (Bierman, 2004; Gresham, Sugai, & Horner, 2001). In situations where the skills are taught in pull-out programs, rather than in the children's natural environments, practitioners can increase maintenance and generalization by practicing and reinforcing skills in more natural settings. Further, all relevant adults should have knowledge of the procedural steps for the skill being taught and should be encouraged to model, reinforce, and practice the skill with the children (Taylor et al., 1999).

FOR AGE AND DEVELOPMENTAL LEVEL

Social skills training can be implemented across a wide variety of ages and developmental levels. However, the curriculum, lesson structure, and materials used must be appropriate for each child's age and developmental level. For instance, showing pictures representing the steps of a given social skill rather than providing written descriptions is more helpful for a child who is not yet reading.

FOR CULTURAL AND LANGUAGE DIFFERENCES

Careful consideration must be given to the acceptance of specific social skills within different cultures. For instance, the procedural steps for socially engaging in conversation might be different across families. When uncertain, asking is the best practice, because social norms such as gender expectations and making eye contact may vary by culture. By the same token, children can and should be taught to differentiate appropriate social skills for various environments. For instance, Jake's father uses phrases such as, "Only dummies use calculators" and "Laundry is women's work." Although neither statement is generally considered socially acceptable, and both could result in unusual looks from other adults, the social norms of a family can be rigid, shaped as they are by region and economics. Teaching Jake to navigate his different social environments could help him maintain appropriate social skills when presented with conflicting social norms.

Parent involvement in social skills training is the optimal solution, but it may not always be practical. It may be helpful to involve parents in understanding the social norms of the school culture and to identify familial vernacular. In cases of second-language families, providing the social skills steps in their native language is the first step to overcoming any additional barriers.

References

Abikoff, H., Courtney, M. E., Szeibel, P. J., & Koplewicz, H. S. (1996). The effects of auditory stimulation on the arithmetic performance of children with ADHD and nondisabled children. *Journal of Learning Disabilities, 29*(3), 238–246.

Abikoff, H., & Hechtman, L. (1994). Multimodal treatment of ADHD: One year treatment outcome data. *Proceedings of the Sixth Annual CHADD Conference*, 50–56.

Abramowitz, A. J., & O'Leary, S. G. (1991). Behavioral interventions for the classroom: Implications for students with ADHD. *School Psychology Review, 20,* 220–234.

Akande, A., & Akande, B. E. (1994). On becoming a person: Activities to help children with their anger. *Early Child Development and Care, 102,* 31–62.

Akande, A., Osagie, J. E., Mwaiteleke, P. B., Botha, K. F. H., Ababio, E. P., Selepe, T. J., & Chipeta, K. (1999). Managing children's fears and anxieties in classroom settings. *Early Child Development and Care, 158,* 51–69.

Albano, A. M., Detweiler, M. F., & Logsdon-Conradsen, S. (1999). Cognitive–behavioral interventions with socially phobic children. In S. W. Russ & T. H. Ollendick (Eds.), *Handbook of psychotherapies with children and families* (pp. 255–280). New York, NY: Kluwer Academic/Plenum.

Alberg, J., Petry, C. A., Eller, S., Warger, C. L., Cook, B., & Cross, D. (1994). *The social skills planning guide.* Longmont, CO: Sopris West.

Alberto, P. A., & Troutman, A. C. (2003). *Applied behavior analysis for teachers* (6th ed.). Upper Saddle River, NJ: Prentice Hall.

Allen, L. A., Woolfolk, R. L., Escobar, J. I., Gara, M. A., & Hamer, R. M. (2006). Cognitive-behavioral therapy for somatization disorder: A randomized controlled trial. *Archive of Internal Medicine, 166,* 1512–1518.

Alpert, C. L., & Kaiser, A. P. (1992). Training parents as milieu language teachers. *Journal of Early Intervention, 16*(1), 31–52.

American Psychiatric Association. (2013). *Diagnostic and statistical manual of mental disorders* (5th ed.). Washington, DC: Author.

Anastopoulos, A. D., DuPaul, G. J., & Barkley, R. A. (1991). Stimulant medication and parent training therapies for attention deficit-hyperactivity disorder. *Journal of Learning Disabilities, 24*(4), 210–218.

Apley, J. (1975). *The child with abdominal pains.* London: Blackwell.

Apple, A. L., Billingsley, F., & Schwartz, I. S. (2005). Effects of video modeling alone and with self-management on compliment-giving behaviors of children with high-functioning ASD. *Journal of Positive Behavior Interventions, 7*(1), 33–46.

Arbuthnot, J., & Gordon, D. A. (1986). Behavioral and cognitive effects of a moral reasoning development intervention for high-risk behavior-disordered adolescents. *Journal of Consulting and Clinical Psychology, 54*(2), 208–216.

Arnold, D. H., Kupersmidt, J. B., Voegler-Lee, M. E., & Marshall, N. A. (2012). The association between preschool children's social functioning and their emergent academic skills. *Early Childhood Research Quarterly, 27*(3), 376–386.

Aschenbrand, S. G., & Kendall, P. C. (2012). The effect of perceived child anxiety status on parental latency to intervene with anxious and nonanxious youth. *Journal of Consulting and Clinical Psychology, 80*(2), 232–238.

Association for Play Therapy. (n.d.). *Play therapy makes a difference.* Retrieved from https://a4pt.site-ym.com/?PTMakesADifference

Atkins, M. S., Pelham, W. E., & Licht, M. H. (1985). A comparison of objective classroom measures and teacher ratings of attention deficit disorder. *Journal of Abnormal Child Psychology, 13*(1), 155–167.

Axline, V. M. (1947). *Play therapy: The inner dynamics of childhood.* Oxford, England: Houghton Mifflin.

Baddeley, A. D., & Hitch, G. J. (1974). Working memory. In G. A. Bower (Ed.), *Recent advances in learning and motivation*, (Vol. 8, pp. 47–89). New York, NY: Academic Press.

Balfanz, R., Herzog, L., & Mac Iver, D. J. (2007). Preventing student disengagement and keeping students on the graduation path in urban middle-grades schools: Early identification and effective interventions. *Educational Psychologist, 42*(4), 223-235.

Bandura, A. (1969). *Principles of behavior modification.* New York, NY: Holt, Rinehart, & Winston.

Bandura, A. (1977). *Social learning theory.* Englewood Cliffs, NJ: Prentice Hall.

Bandura, A. (1986). *Social foundations of thought and action: A social cognitive theory.* Englewood Cliffs, NJ: Prentice Hall.

Bansal, V., Goyal, S., & Srivastava, K. (2009). Study of prevalence of depression in adolescent students of a public school. *Industrial Psychiatry Journal, 18*(1), 43–46.

Barkley, R. A. (1997). Behavioral inhibition, sustained attention, and executive functions: Constructing a unifying theory of ADHD. *Psychological Bulletin, 121*(1), 65–94.

Barkley, R. A. (2006). *Attention-deficit hyperactivity disorder: A handbook for diagnosis and treatment* (3rd ed.). New York, NY: Guilford Press.

Barrish, H. H., Saunders, M., & Wolf, M. M. (1969). Good behavior game: Effects of individual contingencies for group consequences on disruptive behavior in a classroom. *Journal of Applied Behavior Analysis, 2*(2), 119–124.

Beardslee, W. R., Versage, E. M., Wright, E. J., Salt, P., Rothberg, P. C., Drezner, K., & Gladstone, T. R. G. (1997). Examination of preventive interventions for families with depression: Evidence of change. *Development and Psychopathology, 9,* 109–130.

Beck, A. T. (1976). *Cognitive therapy and the emotional disorders.* New York, NY: International Universities Press.

Beck, A. T., Rush, A. J., Shaw, B. F., & Emery G. (1979). *Cognitive therapy of depression.* New York, NY: Guilford Press.

Beelmann, A., Pfingsten, U., & Lösel, F. (1994). Effects of training social competence in children: A meta-analysis of recent evaluation studies. *Journal of Clinical Child Psychology, 23*(3), 260–271.

Beesdo, K., Knappe, S., & Pine, D. S. (2009). Anxiety and anxiety disorders in children and adolescents: Developmental issues and implications for DSM–V. *Psychiatric Clinics of North America, 32*(3), 483–524. doi:10.1016/j.psc.2009.06.002

Bellini, S., & Akullian, J. (2007). A meta-analysis of video modeling and video self-modeling interventions for children and adolescents with autism spectrum disorders. *Exceptional Children, 73*(3), 264–287.

Bellini, S., Peters, J. K., Benner, L., & Hopf, A. (2007). A meta-analysis of school-based social skills interventions for children with autism spectrum disorders. *Remedial and Special Education, 28*(3), 153–162.

Benner, G. (2005). Language skills of elementary-aged children with emotional and behavioral disorders. *Great Plains Research, 15,* 251–265.

Benner, G. J., Nelson, J. R., & Epstein, M. H. (2002). Language skills of children with EBD: A literature review. *Journal of Emotional and Behavioral Disorders, 10*(1), 43–56.

Berger, S. M. (1962). Conditioning through vicarious instigation. *Psychological Review, 69*(5), 450–466.

Berk, L. (1992). Children's private speech: An overview of theory and the status of research. In R. M. Diaz & L. E. Berk (Eds.), *Private speech: From social interaction to self-regulation* (pp. 17–53). Hillsdale, NJ: Erlbaum.

Berman, S. L., Weems, C. F., Silverman, W. K., & Kurtines, W. M. (2000). Predictors of outcome in exposure-based cognitive and behavioral treatments for phobic and anxiety disorders in children. *Behavior Therapy, 31,* 713–731.

Bierman, K. L. (2004). *Peer rejection: Developmental processes and intervention strategies.* New York, NY: Guilford Press.

Bierman, K. L., Miller, C. L., & Stabb, S. D. (1987). Improving the social behavior and peer acceptance of rejected boys: Effects of social skill training with instructions and prohibitions. *Journal of Consulting and Clinical Psychology, 55*(2), 194–200.

Blackman, G. J., & Silberman, A. (1980). *Modification of child and adolescent behavior* (3rd ed.). Belmont, CA: Wadsworth.

Blackstock, E. G. (1978). Cerebral asymmetry and the development of early infantile autism. *Journal of Autism and Childhood Schizophrenia, 8*(3), 339–353. doi:10.1007/BF01539636

Block, M. F., & Blazej, B. (2005). *Resolving conflict with a peer mediation program: A manual for grades 4–8.* Retrieved from: http://umaine.edu/peace/files/2011/01/PEER_MEDIATION_FINAL_11.pdf

Bloom, B. S. (Ed.). (1956). *Taxonomy of educational objectives. Handbook I: Cognitive domain.* White Plains, NY: Longman.

Bohman, H., Jonsson, U., von Knorring, A.-L., von Knorring, L., Määren, A., & Olsson, G. (2010). Somatic symptoms as a marker for severity in adolescent depression. *Acta Paediatrica, 99,* 1724–1730.

Bondy, A. (2012). The unusual suspects: Myths and misconceptions associated with PECS. *The Psychological Record, 62,* 789–816.

Bondy, A., & Frost, L. (1994). The picture exchange communication system. *Focus on Autistic Behavior, 9*(3), 1–19.

Bondy, A., & Frost, L. (2001). The picture exchange communication system. *Behavior Modification, 25*(5), 725–744.

Bor, W., & Sanders, M. R. (2004). Correlates of self-reported coercive parenting of preschool-aged children at high risk for the development of conduct problems. *Australian and New Zealand Journal of Psychiatry, 38*(9), 738–745.

Borduin, C. M., Mann, B. J., Cone, L. T., Henggeler, S. W., Fucci, B. R., Blaske, D. M., & Williams, R. A. (1995). Multisystemic treatment of serious juvenile offenders: Long-term prevention of criminality and violence. *Journal of Consulting and Clinical Psychology, 63*(4), 569–578.

Borduin, C. M., & Schaeffer, C. M. (1998). Violent offending in adolescence: Epidemiology, correlates, outcomes, and treatment. In T. P. Gullotta, G. R. Adams, & R. Montemayor (Eds.), *Delinquent violent youth: Theory and interventions* (pp. 144–174). Newbury Park, CA: Sage.

Boudah, D. J., Lenz, B. K., Bulgren, J. A., Schumaker, J. B., & Deshler, D. D. (2000). Don't water down! Enhance content learning through the unit organizer routine. *Teaching Exceptional Children, 32*(3), 48–56.

Bowers, A. J. (2010). Grades and graduation: A longitudinal risk perspective to identify school dropouts. *Journal of Educational Research, 103*(3), 191-207.

Bowman-Perrott, L., Burke, M., Zaini, S., Zhang, N., & Vannest, K. (in press). Promoting positive behavior using the Good Behavior Game: A meta-analysis of single-case research. *Journal of Positive Behavior Interventions.*

Brady, N. C., & Halle, J. W. (1997). Functional analysis of communicative behaviors. *Focus on Autism and Other Developmental Disabilities, 12*(2), 95–104.

Braswell, L., & Kendall, P. C. (2001). Cognitive-behavioral therapy with youth. In K. S. Dobson (Ed.), *Handbook of cognitive-behavioral therapies* (2nd ed., pp. 167–213). New York, NY: Guilford Press.

Bratton, S. C., Ceballos, P. L., Sheely-Moore, A. I., Meany-Walen, K., Pronchenko, Y., & Jones, L. D. (2013). Head Start early mental health intervention: Effects of child-centered play therapy on disruptive behaviors. *International Journal of Play Therapy, 22*(1), 28–42.

Bratton, S. C., Ray, D., Rhine, T., & Jones, L. (2005). The efficacy of play therapy with children: A meta-analytic review of treatment outcomes. *Professional Psychology: Research and Practice, 36*(4), 376–390. doi:10.1037/0735-7028.36.4.376

Breslau, J., Miller, E., Breslau, N., Bohnert, K., Lucia, V., & Schweitzer, J. (2009). The impact of early behavior disturbances on academic achievement in high school. *Pediatrics, 123*(6), 1472–1476. doi:10.1542/peds.2008-1406

Brestan, E. V., & Eyberg, S. M. (1998). Effective psychosocial treatments of conduct-disordered children and adolescents: 29 years, 82 studies and 5,272 kids. *Journal of Clinical Child Psychology, 27*(2), 180–189.

Brigman, G., & Campbell, C. (2003). Helping students improve academic achievement and school success behavior. *Professional School Counseling, 7*(2), 91–98.

Brown, R. T., & Sammons, M. T. (2002). Pediatric psychopharmacology: A review of new developments and recent research. *Professional Psychology: Research and Practice, 33*(2), 135–147.

Bruner, J. (1985). Vygotsky: A historical and conceptual perspective. In J. V. Wertsch (Ed.), *Culture, communication and cognition: Vygotskian perspectives.* Cambridge, England: Cambridge University Press.

Bulgren, J. A., Lenz, B. K., Schumaker, J. B., Deshler, D. D., & Marquis, J. G. (2002). The use and effectiveness of a comparison routine in diverse secondary content classrooms. *Journal of Educational Psychology, 94*(2), 356–371.

Bullis, M., Walker, H. M., & Sprague, J. R. (2001). A promise unfulfilled: Social skills training with at-risk and antisocial children and youth. *Exceptionality, 9*(1/2), 67–90.

Burke, M. D., & Vannest, K. J. (2008). Behavioral-progress monitoring using the electronic daily behavioral report card (e-DBRC) system. *Preventing School Failure, 52*(3), 51–60.

Bushell, D. (1973). *Classroom behavior: A little book for teachers.* Englewood Cliffs, NJ: Prentice Hall.

Campo, J. V., & Fritz, G. (2001). A management model for pediatric somatization. *Psychosomatics, 42*, 467–576.

Cao, M., Shu, N., Cao, Q., Wang, Y., & He, Y. (2014). Imaging functional and structural brain connectomics in attention-deficit/hyperactivity disorder. *Molecular Neurobiology, 50*(3), 1111–1123. doi:10.1007/s12035-014-8685-x

Carbone, E. (2001). Arranging the classroom with an eye (and ear) to students with ADHD. *Teaching Exceptional Children, 34*(2), 72–81.

Carr, D., & Felce, J. (2007). The effects of PECS teaching to phase III on the communicative interactions between children with autism and their teachers. *Journal of Autism and Developmental Disorders, 37*(4), 724–737.

Carroll, J. B. (1963). A model of school learning. *Teachers College Record, 64*, 723–733.

Carroll, J. B. (1989). The Carroll model: A 25-year retrospective and prospective view. *Educational Researcher, 18*(1), 26–31.

Carter, J. F. (1993). Self-management: Education's ultimate goal. *Teaching Exceptional Children, 25*(3), 28–32.

Center, D. B., Deitz, S. M., & Kaufman, M. E. (1982). Student ability, task difficulty, and inappropriate classroom behavior: A study of children with behavior disorders. *Behavior Modification, 6*(3), 355–374.

Centers for Disease Control and Prevention. (2014). Key findings: Trends in the parent-report of health care provider-diagnosis and medication treatment for ADHD: United States, 2003–2011. Retrieved from http://www.cdc.gov/ncbddd/adhd/features/key-findings-adhd72013.html

Chafouleas, S. M., Riley-Tillman, T. C., & McDougal, J. L. (2002). Good, bad, or in-between: How does the daily behavior report card rate? *Psychology in the Schools, 39*(2), 157–169.

Chang, Y.-K. Hung, C.-L., Huang, C.-J., Hatfield, B. D., & Hung, T.-M. (2014). Effects of an aquatic exercise program on inhibitory control in children with ADHD: A preliminary study. *Archives of Clinical Neuropsychology, 29,* 217–223. doi:10.1093/arclin/acu003

Charlop, M. H., & Trasowech, J. E. (1991). Increasing autistic children's daily spontaneous speech. *Journal of Applied Behavior Analysis, 24*(4), 747–761.

Charlop-Christy, M. H., Carpenter, M., Le, L., LeBlanc, L. A., & Kellet, K. (2002). Using the Picture Exchange Communication System (PECS) with children with autism: Assessment of PECS acquisition, speech, social-communicative behavior, and problem behavior. *Journal of Applied Behavior Analysis, 35*(3), 213–231.

Charlop-Christy, M. H., Le, L., & Freeman, K. A. (2000). A comparison of video modeling with in vivo modeling for teaching children with autism. *Journal of Autism and Developmental Disorders, 30*(6), 537–552.

Christie, D. J., Hiss, M., & Lozanoff, B. (1984). Modification of inattentive classroom behavior: Hyperactive children's use of self-recording with teacher guidance. *Behavior Modification, 8*(3), 391–406.

Chronaki, G., Garner, M., Hadwin, J. A., Thompson, M. J. J., Chin, C. Y., & Songua-Barke, E. J. S. (2015). Emotion-recognition abilities and behavior problem dimensions in preschoolers: Evidence for a specific role for childhood hyperactivity. *Child Neuropsychology, 21*(1), 25–40. doi:10.1080/09297049.2013.863273

Chronis, A. M., Chacko, A., Fabiano, G. A., Wymbs, B. T., & Pelham, W. E., Jr. (2004). Enhancements to the behavioral parent training paradigm for families of children with ADHD: Review and future directions. *Clinical Child and Family Psychology Review, 7,* 1–27.

Chronis, A. M., Fabiano, G. A., Gnagy, E. M., Wymbs, B. T., Burrows-MacLean, L., & Pelham, W. E., Jr. (2001). Comprehensive, sustained behavioral and pharmacological treatment for attention-deficit/hyperactivity disorder: A case study. *Cognitive and Behavioral Practice, 8,* 346–359.

Chronis, A. M., Jones, H. A., & Raggi, V. L. (2006). Evidence-based psychosocial treatments for children with attention-deficit/hyperactivity disorder. *Clinical Psychology Review, 26,* 486–502.

Clarke, S., Dunlap, G., Foster-Johnson, L., Childs, K. E., Wilson, D., White, R., & Vera, A. (1995). Improving the conduct of students with behavioral disorders by incorporating student interests into curricular activities. *Behavioral Disorders, 20*(4), 221–237.

Cole, M. W. (2014). Speaking to read: Meta-analysis of peer-mediated learning for English language learners. *Journal of Literacy Research, 46*(3), 358–382. doi:10.1177/1086296X14552179

Colter, S. B., & Guerra, J. J. (1976). *Assertion training: A humanistic-behavioral guide to self-dignity.* Champaign, IL: Research Press.

Comings, D. E., Gade-Andavolu, R., Gonzalez, N., Wu, S., Muhleman, D., Blake, H., . . . MacMurray, J. P. (2000). Multivariate analysis of associations of 42 genes in ADHD, ODD and conduct disorder. *Clinical Genetics, 58*(1), 31–40.

Compton, S. N., March, J. S., Brent, D., Albano, A. M., Weersing, V. R., & Curry, J. (2004). Cognitive-behavioral psychotherapy for anxiety and depressive disorders in children and adolescents: An evidence-based medicine review. *Journal of the American Academy of Child and Adolescent Psychiatry, 43*(8), 930–959.

Cook, E. H., Stein, M. A., Krasowski, M. D., Cox, N. J., Olkon, D. M., Kieffer, J. E., & Leventhal, B. L. (1995). Association of attention-deficit disorder and the dopamine transporter gene. *American Journal of Human Genetics, 56,*993–998.

Corey, G. (1991). *Theory and practice of counseling and psychotherapy* (4th ed.). Pacific Grove, CA: Brooks/Cole.

Cortiella, C., & Horowitz, S. H. (2014). The state of learning disabilities: Facts, trends and emerging issues (3rd. ed.). Retrieved from http://www.ncld.org/wp-content/uploads/2014/11/2014-State-of-LD.pdf

Cosden, M., Gannon, C., & Haring, T. G. (1995). Teacher-control versus student-control over choice of task and reinforcement for students with severe behavior problems. *Journal of Behavioral Education, 5*(1), 11–27.

Council for Exceptional Children. (1992). *Children with ADD: A shared responsibility.* Reston, VA: Author.

Coutinho, M. J. (1986). Reading achievement of students identified as behaviorally disordered at the secondary level. *Behavioral Disorders, 11,* 200–207.

Coyne, M. D., Kame'enui, E. J., & Simmons, D. C. (2001). Prevention and intervention in beginning reading: Two complex systems. *Learning Disabilities Research and Practice, 16*(2), 62–73.

Crenshaw, T. M., Kavale, K. A., Forness, S. R., & Reeve, R. E. (1999). Attention deficit hyperactivity disorder and the efficacy of stimulant medication: A meta-analysis. In T. J. Scruggs and M. Mastropieri (Eds.), *Advances in Learning and Behavioral Disabilities* (Vol. 13, pp. 135–165). Greenwich, CT: JAI.

Crocker, A. G., Mercier, C., Lachapelle, Y., Brunet, A., Morin, D., & Roy, M. E. (2006). Prevalence and types of aggressive behaviour among adults with intellectual disabilities. *Journal of Intellectual Disabilities Research, 50*(9), 652–661.

Cullinan, D., Epstein, M. H., & Lloyd, J. W. (1991). Evaluation of conceptual models of behavior disorders. *Behavioral Disorders, 16,* 148–157.

Dalrymple, J. (1995). It's not as easy as you think! Dilemmas and advocacy. In J. Dalrymple & J. Hough (Eds.), *Having a voice: An exploration of children's rights and advocacy.* Birmingham, England: Venture Press.

Daly, B. P., Creed, T., Xanthopoulos, M., & Brown, R. T. (2007). Psychosocial treatments for children with attention deficit/ hyperactivity disorder. *Neuropsychology Review, 17,* 73–89.

de Haan, A. D., Prinzie, P., & Deković, M. (2010). How and why children change in aggression and delinquency from childhood to adolescence: Moderation of overreactive parenting by child personality. *Journal of Child Psychology and Psychiatry, 51*(6), 725–733. doi:10.1111/j.1469-7610.2009.02192.x

De Pry, R. L., & Sugai, G. (2002). The effect of active supervision and pre-correction on minor behavioral incidents in a sixth grade general education classroom. *Journal of Behavioral Education, 11*(4), 255–267.

Dean, C., Myors, K., & Evans, E. (2003). Community-wide implementation of a parenting program: The South East Sydney Positive Parenting Project. *Australian e-Journal for the Advancement of Mental Health, 2*(3). Retrieved June 4, 2006, from http://www.auseinet. com/journal/vol2iss3/dean.pdf

DeNisco, S., Tiago, C., & Kravitz, C. (2005). Evaluation and treatment of pediatric ADHD. *Nurse Practitioner, 30,* 14–23.

Dickson, S. V., Chard, D. J., & Simmons, D. C. (1993). An integrated reading/writing curriculum: A focus on scaffolding. *LD Forum, 18*(4), 12–16.

Dishion, T. J., & Andrews, D. W. (1995). Preventing escalation in problem behaviors with high-risk young adolescents: Immediate and 1-year outcomes. *Journal of Consulting and Clinical Psychology, 63*(4), 538–548.

Dishion, T. J., McCord, J., & Poulin, F. (1999). When interventions harm: Peer groups and problem behavior. *American Psychologist, 54*(9), 755–764.

Doyle, R. (2004). The history of adult attention-deficit/hyperactivity disorder. *Psychiatric Clinics of North America, 27,* 203–214. doi:10.1016/j.psc.2004.01.001

Drechsler, R., Rizzo, P., & Steinhausen, H.-C. (2010). The impact of instruction and response cost on the modulation of response-style in children with ADHD. *Behavioral and Brain Functions : BBF, 6,* 31. doi:10.1186/1744-9081-6-31

Dunlap, G., dePerczel, M., Clarke, S., Wilson, D., Wright, S., White, R., & Gomez, A. (1994). Choice making to promote adaptive behavior for students with emotional and behavioral challenges. *Journal of Applied Behavior Analysis, 27*(3), 505–518.

DuPaul, G. J., & Eckert, T. L. (1997). The effects of school-based interventions for attention deficit hyperactivity disorder: A meta-analysis. *School Psychology Review, 26,* 5–27.

DuPaul, G. J., & Eckert, T. L. (1998). Academic interventions for students with attention-deficit/hyperactivity disorder: A review of the literature. *Reading and Writing Quarterly, 14*(1), 59–82.

DuPaul, G. J., & Ervin, R. A. (1996). Functional assessment of behaviors related to attention deficit/hyperactivity disorder: Linking assessment to intervention design. *Behavior Therapy, 27,* 601–622.

DuPaul, G. J., & Weyandt, L. L. (2006). School-based interventions for children and adolescents with attention-deficit/hyperactivity disorder: Enhancing academic and behavioral outcomes. *Education and Treatment of Children, 29*(2), 341–358.

DuPaul, G. J., & White, G. P. (2006). ADHD: Behavioral, educational, and medication interventions. *Education Digest, 71*(7), 57–60.

Durand, V. M., & Merges, E. (2001). Functional communication training: A contemporary behavior analytic intervention for problem behaviors. *Focus on Autism and Other Developmental Disabilities, 16*(2), 110–119.

Dweck, C. S. (2000). *Self-theories: Their role in motivation, personality, and development.* Philadelphia, PA: Psychology Press.

Dyer, K., Dunlap, G., & Winterling, V. (1990). Effects of choice making on the serious problem behaviors of students with severe handicaps. *Journal of Applied Behavior Analysis, 23,* 515–524.

Egger, H. L., & Angold, A. (2006). Common emotional and behavioral disorders in preschool children: Presentation, nosology, and epidemiology. *Journal of Child Psychology and Psychiatry, 47*(3/4), 313–337.

Ellis, A. (1962). *Reason and emotion in psychotherapy.* New York, NY: Lyle Stuart.

Ellis, A. (1986). An emotional control card for inappropriate and appropriate emotions in using rational-emotive imagery. *Journal of Counseling and Development, 65*(4), 205–206.

Embry, D. D., & Straatemeier, G. (2001). *The PAX acts game manual: How to apply the good behavior game.* Tucson, AZ: PAXIS Institute.

Emich-Widera, E., Kazek, B., Szwed-Białożyt, B., Kopyta, I., & Kostorz, A. (2012). Headaches as somatoform disorders in children and adolescents. *Mental Illness, 4*(9), 35–37.

Eminson, D. M. (2007). Medically unexplained symptoms in children and adolescents. *Clinical Psychology Review, 27*(7), 855–871.

Epstein, M. H., Kinder, D., & Bursuck, B. (1989). The academic status of adolescents with behavioral disorders. *Behavioral Disorders, 14*(3), 157–165.

Ervin, R. A., DuPaul, G. J., Kern, L., & Friman, P. C. (1998). Classroom-based functional and adjunctive assessments: Proactive approaches to intervention selection for adolescents with attention deficit/hyperactivity disorder. *Journal of Applied Behavior Analysis, 31*(1), 65–78.

Erwin, P. G. (1994). Social problem solving, social behavior, and children's peer popularity. *Journal of Psychology, 128*(3), 299–307.

Espelage, D. L., Polanin, J. R., & Low, S. K. (2014). Teacher and staff perceptions of school environment as predictors of student aggression, victimization, and willingness to intervene in bullying situations. *School Psychology Quarterly, 29*(3), 287–305. doi:10.1037/spq0000072

Evans, S. W., Pelham, W., & Grudberg, M. V. (1995). The efficacy of notetaking to improve behavior and comprehension of adolescents with attention deficit hyperactivity disorder. *Exceptionality, 5*(1), 1–17.

Evans, S. W., Timmins, B., Sibley, M., White, C., Serpell, Z. N., & Schultz, B. (2006). Developing coordinated, multimodal, school-based treatment for young adolescents with ADHD. *Education and Treatment of Children, 29*(2), 359–378.

Fair, D. A., Posner, J., Nagel, B. J., Bathula, D., Dias, T. G. C., Mills, L. K., . . . Nigg, J. T. (2010). Atypical default network connectivity in youth with attention-deficit/hyperactivity disorder. *Biological Psychiatry, 68*(12), 1084–1091. doi:10.1016/j.biopsych.2010.07.003

Faraone, S. V., Biederman, J., Morley, C. P., & Spencer, T. J. (2008). Effect of stimulants on height and weight: A review of the literature. *Journal of the American Academy of Child & Adolescent Psychiatry, 47*(9), 994–1009. doi:10.1097/CHI.ObO13e31817eOea7

Fischer, S. M., Iwata, B. A., & Mazalesk, J. L. (1997). Noncontingent delivery of arbitrary reinforcers as treatment for self-injurious behavior. *Journal of Applied Behavior Analysis, 30*(2), 239–249.

Flannery, K. B., O'Neill, R. E., & Horner, R. H. (1995). Including predictability in functional assessment and individual program development. *Education and Treatment of Children, 18*(4), 499–509.

Flannery-Schroeder, E. C., & Kendall, P. C. (2000). Group and individual cognitive-behavioral treatments for youth with anxiety disorders: A randomized clinical trial. *Cognitive Therapy and Research, 24*(3), 251–278.

Flora, S. R., & Polenick, C. A. (2013). Effects of sugar consumption on human behavior and performance. *The Psychological Record, 63*(3), 513–524. doi:10.11133/j.tpr.2013.63.3.008

Flood, W. A., & Wilder, D. A. (2004). The use of differential reinforcement and fading to increase time away from a caregiver in a child with separation anxiety disorder. *Education and Treatment of Children, 27*(1), 1–8.

Forehand, R., & Kotchick, B. A. (2002). Behavioral parent training: Current challenges and potential solutions. *Journal of Child and Family Studies, 11*(4), 377–384.

Forness, S. R., & Knitzer, J. (1992). A new proposed definition and terminology to replace "serious emotional disturbance" in Individuals with Disabilities Education Act. *School Psychology Review, 21*(1), 12–20.

Foster, S. L., & Bussman, J. R. (2008). Evidence-based approaches to social skills training with children and adolescents. In R. G. Steele, T. D. Elkin, & M. C. Roberts (Eds.), *Handbook of evidence-based therapies for children and adolescents: Bridging science and practice* (pp. 409–427). New York, NY: Springer.

Franca, V. M., & Kerr, M. M. (1990). Peer tutoring among behaviorally disordered students: Academic and social benefits to tutor and tutee. *Education and Treatment of Children, 13*(2), 109–128.

Frey, K. S., Hirschstein, M. K., & Guzzo, B. (2000). Second step: Preventing aggression by promoting social competence. *Journal of Emotional and Behavioral Disorders, 8*(2), 102–112.

Frick, P. J. (2000). A comprehensive and individualized treatment approach for children and adolescents with conduct disorders. *Cognitive and Behavioral Practice, 7*(1), 30–37.

Frick, P. J. (2006). Developmental pathways to conduct disorder. *Child and Adolescent Psychiatric Clinics of North America, 15*(2), 311–331.

Friedberg, R. D., McClure, J. M., Wilding, L., Goldman, M. L., Long, M. P., Anderson, L., & DePolo, M. R. (2003). A cognitive-behavioral skills training group for children experiencing anxious and depressive symptoms: A clinical report with accompanying descriptive data. *Journal of Contemporary Psychotherapy, 33*(3), 157–175.

Friman, P. C., Barnard, J. D., Altman, K., & Wolf, M. W. (1986). Parent and teacher use of DRO and DRI to reduce aggressive behavior. *Analysis and Intervention in Developmental Disabilities, 6*(4), 319–330.

Gabrieli, J. D. E. (2009). Dyslexia: A new synergy between education and cognitive neuroscience. *Science, 325,* 280–283. doi:10.1126/science.1171999

Gest, S. D., Madill, R. A., Zadzora, K. M., Miller, A. M., & Rodkin, P. C. (2014). Teacher management of elementary classroom social dynamics: Associations with changes in student adjustment. *Journal of Emotional and Behavioral Disorders, 22*(2), 107–118. doi:10.1177/1063426613512677

Gimpel, G. A., & Holland, M. L. (2003). *Emotional and behavioral problems of young children: Effective interventions in the preschool and kindergarten years.* New York, NY: Guilford Press.

Ginsburg, G. S., Silverman, W. K., & Kurtines, W. K. (1995). Family involvement in treating children with phobic and anxiety disorders: A look ahead. *Clinical Psychology Review, 15*(5), 457–473.

Ginsburg, G. S., & Walkup, J. T. (2004). Specific phobia. In T. H. Ollendick & J. S. March (Eds.), *Phobic and anxiety disorders in children and adolescents: A clinician's guide to effective psychosocial and pharmacological interventions* (pp. 175–197). New York, NY: Oxford Press.

Gjervan, B., Torgersen, T., Rasmussen, K., & Nordahl, H. M. (2014). ADHD symptoms are differentially related to specific aspects of quality of life. *Journal of Attention Disorders, 18*(7), 598–606. doi:10.1177/1087054712445183

Glynn, S. M., & DiVesta, F. J. (1977). Outline and hierarchical organization as aids for study and retrieval. *Journal of Educational Psychology, 69*(2), 89–95.

Goldstein, A. P. (1988). *The PREPARE curriculum: Teaching prosocial competencies.* Champaign, IL: Research Press.

Goldstein, S. (1995). *Understanding and managing children's classroom behavior.* New York, NY: John Wiley & Sons.

Good, T. L., & Brophy, J. E. (2003). *Looking in classrooms* (9th ed.). Boston, MA: Allyn & Bacon.

Goodlad, S., & Hirst, B. (Eds.). (1990). *Explorations in peer tutoring.* Oxford: Blackwell Education.

Gordijn, B. (2015). Moral improvement through ethics education. In H. A. M. J. ten Have (Ed.), *Advancing global bioethics: Vol. 4. Bioethics education in a global perspective: Challenges in global bioethics* (pp. 177–193), New York, NY: Springer.

Graham, S., Harris, K. R., & Reid, R. (1992). Developing self-regulated learners. *Focus on Exceptional Children, 24*(6), 1–16.

Greenwood, C. R., Delquadri, J. C., & Carta, J. J. (1997). *Together we can! Class wide peer tutoring to improve basic academic skills.* Longmont, CO: Sopris West.

Greenwood, C. R., Maheady, L., & Carta, J. J. (1991). Peer tutoring programs in the regular education classroom. In G. Stoner, M. R. Shinn, & H. M. Walker (Eds.), *Interventions for achievement and behavior problems* (pp. 179–200). Washington, DC: National Association of School Psychologists.

Greenwood, C. R., Maheady, L., & Delquadri, J. (2002). Class-wide peer tutoring. In G. Stoner, M. R. Shinn, & H. M. Walker (Eds.), *Interventions for achievement and behavior problems: Preventive and remedial approaches* (2nd ed., pp. 611–649). Washington, DC: National Association of School Psychologists.

Gresham, F. M. (1981). Social skills training with handicapped children: A review. *Review of Educational Research, 51*(1), 139–176.

Gresham, F. M. (1986). Conceptual and definitional issues in the assessment of children's social skills: Implications for classification and training. *Journal of Clinical Child Psychology, 15*, 3–15.

Gresham, F. M. (1998). Social skills training: Should we raze, remodel, or rebuild? *Behavioral Disorders, 24*(1), 19–25.

Gresham, F. M., Elliott, S. N., & Kettler, R. J. (2010). Base rates of social skills acquisition/performance deficits, strengths, and problem behaviors: An analysis of the Social Skills Improvement System—Rating Scales. *Psychological Assessment, 22*(4), 809–815.

Gresham, F. M., Sugai, G., & Horner, R. H. (2001). Interpreting outcomes of social skills training for students with high-incidence disabilities. *Exceptional Children, 67*(3), 331–344.

Gresham, F. M., Watson, T. S., & Skinner, C. H. (2001). Functional behavioral assessment: Principles, procedures, and future directions. *School Psychology Review, 30,* 156–172.

Gunter, P. L., Shores, R. E., Jack, S. L., Denny, R. K., & DePaepe, P. A. (1994). A case study of the effects of altering instructional interactions on the disruptive behavior of a child identified with severe behavior disorders. *Education and Treatment of Children, 17*(4), 435–444.

Gutsch, K. U. (1988). *Psychotherapeutic approaches to specific DSM-III-R categories: A resource book for treatment planning.* Springfield, IL: Charles C. Thomas Publisher.

Habboushe, D. F., Daniel-Crotty, S., Karustis, J. L., Leff, S. S., Costigan, T. E., Goldstein, S. G., & Power, T. J. (2001). A family-school homework intervention program for children with attention-deficit/hyperactivity disorder. *Cognitive and Behavioral Practice, 8*(2), 123–136.

Hallahan, D. P., Lloyd, J. W., & Stoller, L. (1982). *Improving attention with self-monitoring: A manual for teachers.* Charlottesville, VA: University of Virginia, Learning Disabilities Research Institute.

Halperin, J. M., & Healey, D. M. (2011). The influences of environmental enrichment, cognitive enhancement, and physical exercise on brain development: Can we alter the developmental trajectory of ADHD? *Neuroscience and Biobehavioral Reviews, 35*(3), 621–634. doi:10.1016/j.neubiorev.2010.07.006

Hancock, P. A., & Warm, J. S. (2003). A dynamic model of stress and sustained attention. *Human Performance in Extreme Environments, 7*(1), 15–28.

Harlacher, J. E., Roberts, N. E., & Merrell, K. W. (2006). Classwide interventions for students with ADHD: A summary of teacher options beneficial for the whole class. *Teaching Exceptional Children, 39*(2), 6–12.

Harris, K. R. (1990). Developing self-regulated learners: The role of private speech and self-instructions. *Educational Psychologist, 25*(1), 35–49.

Harris, K. R., Friedlander, B. D., Saddler, B., Frizzelle, R., & Graham, S. (2005). Self- monitoring of attention versus self-monitoring of academic performance: Effects among students with ADHD in the general education classroom. *Journal of Special Education, 39*(3), 145–156.

Harris, K. R., Wong, B. Y. L., & Keogh, B. K. (Eds.). (1985). Cognitive-behavior modification with children: A critical review of the state of the art [Special issue]. *Journal of Abnormal Child Psychology, 13*(3).

Harris, V. W., & Sherman, J. A. (1973). Use and analysis of the "good behavior game" to reduce disruptive classroom behavior. *Journal of Applied Behavior Analysis, 6*(3), 405–417.

Hart, B., & Risley, T. R. (1974). Using preschool materials to modify the language of disadvantaged children. *Journal of Applied Behavior Analysis, 7*(2), 243–256.

Hartley, M. M. M. (1998). *The relationships among disruptive behaviors, attention, and academic achievement in a clinic referral sample* (Unpublished doctoral dissertation). University of Georgia, Athens, GA.

Haugaard, J. J., & Hazan, C. (2004). Recognizing and treating uncommon behavioral and emotional disorders in children and adolescents who have been severely maltreated: Somatization and other somatoform disorders. *Child Maltreatment, 9*(2), 169–176.

Hogel, M. T., & Ferguson, R. J. (2000). Differential reinforcement of other behavior to reduce aggressive behavior following traumatic brain injury. *Behavior Modification, 24*(1), 94–101.

Hemphill, S. A., Toumbourou, J. W., Herrenkohl, T. I., McMorris, B. J., & Catalano, R. F. (2006). The effect of school suspensions and arrests on subsequent adolescent antisocial behavior in Australia and the United States. *Journal of Adolescent Health, 39*(5), 736–744.

Henggeler, S. W., Cunningham, P. B., Pickrel, S. G., Schoenwald, S. K., & Brondino, M. J. (1996). Multisystemic therapy: An effective violence prevention approach for serious juvenile offenders. *Journal of Adolescence, 19,* 47–61.

Henggeler, S. W., Halliday-Boykins, C. A., Cunningham, P. B., Randall, J., Shapiro, S. B., & Chapman, J. E. (2006). Juvenile drug court: Enhancing outcomes by integrating evidence-based treatments. *Journal of Consulting and Clinical Psychology, 74*(1), 42–54.

Henggeler, S. W., Melton, G. B., & Smith, L. A. (1992). Family preservation using multisystemic therapy: An effective alternative to incarcerating serious juvenile offenders. *Journal of Consulting and Clinical Psychology, 60*(6), 953–961.

Henggeler, S. W., Schoenwald, S. K., Borduin, C. M., Rowland, M. D., & Cunningham, P. B. (1998). *Multisystemic treatment of antisocial behavior in children and adolescents.* New York, NY: Guilford Press.

Hepting, N. H., & Goldstein, H. (1996). Requesting by preschoolers with developmental disabilities: Videotaped self-modeling and learning of new linguistic structures. *Topics in Early Childhood Special Education, 16*(3), 407–427.

Hermelin, B., & O'Connor, N. (1975). The recall of digits by normal, deaf and autistic children. *British Journal of Psychology, 66*(2), 203–209. doi:10.1111/j.2044-8295.1975.tb01456.x

Hinshaw, S. P., & Arnold, L. E. (2014). Attenetion-deficit hyperactivity disorder, multimodal treatment, and longitudinal outcome: Evidence, paradox, and challenge. *WIREs Cognitive Science, 6,* 39–52. doi:10.1002/wcs.1324

Hinshaw, S. P., & Erhardt, D. (1991). Attention deficit-hyperactivity disorder. In P. C. Kendall (Ed.), *Child and adolescent therapy: Cognitive-behavioral procedures* (pp. 98–128). New York, NY: Guilford Press.

Hoffmann, H. (1845). *Lustige geschichten und drollige bilder mit 15 schön kolorierten tafeln für kinder von 3⬜6 jahren* [Funny stories and jocose pictures with 15 beautifully coloured panels for children aged 3 to 6]. Frankfurt, Germany: Literarische Anstalt Rütten & Loening.

Hops, H., & Lewinsohn, P. M. (1995). A course for the treatment of depression among adolescents. In K. D. Craig & K. S. Dobson (Eds.), *Anxiety and depression in adults and children* (pp. 230–245). Thousand Oaks, CA: Sage.

Horner, R. H. (1994). Functional assessment: Contributions and future directions. *Journal of Applied Behavior Analysis, 27*(2), 401–404. doi:10.1901/jaba.1994.27-401

Howes, C., Galinsky, E., & Kontos, S. (1998). Child care caregiver sensitivity and attachment. *Social Development, 7*(1), 25–36.

Howlin, P., Gordon, R. K., Pasco, G., Wade, A., & Charman, T. (2007). The effectiveness of Picture Exchange Communication System (PECS) training for teachers of children with autism: A pragmatic, group randomised controlled trial. *Journal of Child Psychology and Psychiatry, 48*(5), 473–481.

Hughes, J. N. (2007, November). *Emotions are academic: Promoting children's academic and life success through social and emotional learning.* Distinguished Lecture Series. Office of the Provost and Executive Vice President for Academics, Texas A & M University, College Station, Texas.

Hughes, A. A., Lourea-Waddell, B., & Kendall, P. C. (2008). Somatic complaints in children with anxiety disorders and their unique prediction of poorer academic performance. *Child Psychiatry and Human Development, 39*, 211–220. doi:10.1007/s10578-007-0082-5

Hunsley, J., Elliott, K., & Therrien, Z. (2014). The efficacy and effectiveness of psychological treatments for mood, anxiety, and related disorders. *Canadian Psychology, 55*(3), 161–176.

Individuals With Disabilities Education Improvement Act of 2004, 20 U.S.C. § 1400 *et seq.* (2004).

Jacobson, N. S., Dobson, K. S., Truax, P. A., Addis, M. E., Koerner, K., Gollan, J.K., . . . Prince, S. E. (1996). A component analysis of cognitive-behavioral treatment for depression. *Journal of Consulting and Clinical Psychology, 64*(2), 295–304. doi:10.1037/0022-006X.64.2.295

James, A. C., James, G., Cowdrey, F. A., Soler, A., & Choke, A. (2015). Cognitive behavioural therapy for anxiety disorders in children and adolescents. *Cochrane Database of Systematic Reviews* 2015, Issue 2, Art. No.: CD004690. doi:10.1002/14651858.CD004690.pub4

Johnson, D. W., & Johnson, R. (2005). *Teaching students to be peacemakers* (4th ed.). Minneapolis, MN: Burgess Publishing Company.

Johnson, M., Bullis, M., Mann, S., Benz, M., & Hollenbeck, K. (1999). *The CONNECTIONS curriculum.* Eugene, OR: Institute on Violence and Destructive Behavior, College of Education, University of Oregon.

Johnson, M. R., Turner, P. F., & Konarski, E. A. (1978). The good behavior game. A systematic replication in two unruly transitional classrooms. *Education and Treatment of Children, 1*(3), 25–33.

Kahn, J. S., Kehle, T. J., Jenson, W. R., & Clark, E. (1990). Comparison of cognitive-behavioral, relaxation, and self-modeling interventions for depression among middle-school students. *School Psychology Review, 19*(2), 196–211.

Kaiser, A. P. (1993). Parent implemented language intervention: An environmental system perspective. In A. P. Kaiser & D. B. Gray (Eds.), *Enhancing children's communication: Research foundations for interventions* (pp. 63–84). Baltimore, MD: Brookes.

Kaiser, A. P. (2000). Teaching functional communication skills. In M. E. Snell & F. Brown (Eds.), *Instruction of students with severe disabilities* (5th ed., pp. 453–492). Upper Saddle River, NJ: Prentice Hall.

Kame'enui, E. J., Carnine, D. W., Dixon, R. C., Simmons, D. C., & Coyne, M. D. (2002). *Effective teaching strategies that accommodate diverse learners* (2nd ed.). Columbus, OH: Merrill.

Kanne, S. M., & Mazurek, M. O. (2011). Aggression in children and adolescents with ASD: Prevalence and risk factors. *Journal of Autism and Developmental Disorders, 41,* 926–937.

Kanter, J. W., Callaghan, G. M., Landes, S. J., Busch, A. M., & Brown, K. R. (2004). Behavior analytic conceptualization and treatment of depression: Traditional models and recent advances. *The Behavior Analyst Today, 5*(3), 255–274.

Kaplan, J., & Carter, J. (1995). *Beyond behavior modification: A cognitive–behavioral approach to behavior management in the school* (3rd ed.). Austin, TX: Pro-Ed.

Kaslow, N. J., & Racusin, G. R. (1994). Family therapy for depression in young people. In W. M. Reynolds & H. F. Johnston (Eds.), *Handbook of depression in children and adolescents* (pp. 345–364). New York, NY: Plenum Press.

Katusic, S. K., Colligan, R. C., Weaver, A. L., & Barbaresi, W. J. (2009). The forgotten learning disability: Epidemiology of written language disorder in a population-based birth cohort (1976–1982), Rochester, Minnesota. *Pediatrics, 123*(5), 1306–1313. doi:10.1542/peds.2008-2098

Kauffman, J. M., Cullinan, D., & Epstein, M. H. (1987). Characteristics of students placed in special programs for the seriously emotionally disturbed. *Behavioral Disorders, 12*(3), 175–184.

Kavale, K. A., & Forness, S. R. (1996). Social skill deficits and learning disabilities: A meta-analysis. *Journal of Learning Disabilities, 29*(3), 226–237.

Kazdin, A. E. (2005). *Parent management training: Treatment for oppositional, aggressive, and antisocial behavior in children and adolescents.* New York, NY: Oxford University Press.

Kazdin, A. E., Siegel, T. C., & Bass, D. (1992). Cognitive problem-solving skills training and parent management training in the treatment of antisocial behavior in children. *Journal of Consulting and Clinical Psychology, 60*(5), 733–747.

Kearney, C. A. (2005). *Social anxiety and social phobia in youth: Characteristics, assessment, and psychological treatment.* New York, NY: Springer.

Kendall, P. C., Kortlander, E., Chansky, T. E., & Brady, E. U. (1992). Comorbidity of anxiety and depression in youth: Treatment implications. *Journal of Consulting and Clinical Psychology, 60*(6), 869–880.

Kern, L., Bambara, L., & Fogt, J. (2002). Class-wide curricular modification to improve the behavior of students with emotional or behavioral disorders. *Behavior Disorders, 27*(4), 317–326.

Kern, L., Childs, K. E., Dunlap, G., Clarke, S., & Falk, G. D. (1994). Using assessment-based curricular intervention to improve the classroom behavior of a student with emotional and behavioral challenges. *Journal of Applied Behavior Analysis, 27*(1), 7–19.

Kern, L., & Clemens, N. H. (2007). Antecedent strategies to promote appropriate classroom behavior. *Psychology in the Schools, 44*(1), 65–75.

Kerns, K. A., Eso, K., & Thomson, J. (1999). Investigation of a direct intervention for improving attention in young children with ADHD. *Developmental Neuropsychology, 16*(2), 273–295.

Kim, Y. S., Leventhal, B. L., Koh, Y.-J., Fombonne, E., Laska, E., Lim, E.-C., . . . Grinker, R. R. (2011). Prevalence of autism spectrum disorders in a total population sample. *The American Journal of Psychiatry, 168*(9), 904–912. doi:10.1176/appi.ajp.2011.10101532

King, N. J., Muris, P., & Ollendick, T. H. (2005). Childhood fears and phobias: Assessment and treatment. *Child and Adolescent Mental Health, 10*(2), 50–56.

Klerman, G. L., Weissman, M. M., Rounsaville, B. J., & Chevron, E. S. (1984). *Interpersonal psychotherapy of depression.* New York, NY: Basic Books.

Kochanska, G., & Aksan, N. (1995). Mother-child mutually positive affect, the quality of child compliance to requests and prohibitions, and maternal control as correlates of early internalization. *Child Development, 66*(1), 236–254.

Koegel, L. K., Koegel, R. L., Harrower, J. K., & Carter, C. M. (1999). Pivotal response intervention I: Overview of approach. *The Journal of the Association for Persons with Severe Handicaps, 24*(3), 174–185.

Koegel, L. K., Koegel, R. L., Hurley, C., & Frea, W. D. (1992). Improving social skills and disruptive behavior in children with autism through self-management. *Journal of Applied Behavior Analysis, 25*(2), 341–353. doi:10.1901/jaba.1992.25-341

Koegel, R. L., Dyer, K., & Bell, L. K. (1987). The influence of child preferred activities on autistic children's social behavior. *Journal of Applied Behavior Analysis, 20*, 243–252.

Koegel, R. L., & Koegel, L. K. (Eds.). (1995). *Teaching children with autism: Strategies for initiating positive interactions and improving learning opportunities.* Baltimore, MD: Brookes.

Koegel, R. L., Schreffirnan, L., Good, A., Cerniglia, L., Murphy, C., & Koegel, L. K. (1989). *How to teach pivotal behaviors to children with autism: A training manual.* Retrieved from http://www.users.qwest.net/~tbharris/prt.htm

Kohlberg, L. (1969). Stage and sequence: The cognitive-developmental approach to socialization. In D. A. Goslin (Ed.), *Handbook of socialization theory and research* (pp. 347–480). Chicago, IL: Rand McNally.

Kotchick, B. A., & Forehand, R. (2002). Putting parenting in perspective: A discussion of the contextual factors that shape parenting practices. *Journal of Child and Family Studies, 11*(3), 255–269.

Kushwaha, V., Chadda, R. K., & Mehta, M. (2013). Psychotherapeutic intervention in somatization disorder: Results of a controlled study from India. *Psychology, Health, & Medicine, 18*(4), 445–450. doi:10.1080/13548506.2013.765020

LaBerge, D. (2002). Attentional control: brief and prolonged. *Psychological Review, 66,* 220–233.

Lalli, J. S., Casey, S., & Kates, K. (1995). Reducing escape behavior and increasing task completion with functional communication training, extinction, and response chaining. *Journal of Applied Behavior Analysis, 28*(3), 261–268.

Landreth, G. L. (2012). *Play therapy: The art of the relationship* (3rd ed). New York, NY: Routledge.

Landrum, T. J., Tankersley, M., & Kauffman, J. M. (2003). What is special about special education for students with emotional or behavioral disorders? *Journal of Special Education, 37,* 148–156.

Lane, K. L. (2004). Academic instruction and tutoring interventions for students with emotional/behavioral disorders: 1990 to present. In R. B. Rutherford, M. M. Quinn, & Mathur, S. R. (Eds.), *Handbook of research of emotional and behavioral disorders* (pp. 462–486). New York, NY: Guilford Press.

Lane, K. L., Barton-Arwood, S. M., Nelson, J. R., & Wehby, J. (2008). Academic performance of students with emotional and behavioral disorders served in a self-contained setting. *Journal of Behavioral Education, 17*(1), 43–62.

Lane, K. L., Carter, E. W., Pierson, M. R., & Glaeser, B. C. (2006). Academic, social, and behavioral characteristics of high school students with emotional disturbances or learning disabilities. *Journal of Emotional and Behavioral Disorders, 14*(2), 108–117.

Lazarus, A. A., & Abramovitz, A. (1962). The use of "emotive imagery" in the treatment of children's phobias. *Journal of Mental Science, 108,* 191–195.

Lazarus, P. J., & Pfohl, W. (2010). *Bullying prevention and intervention: Information for educators.* Retrieved from: http://www.nasponline.org/resources/bullying/bullying_info_educators.pdf

Lemberger, M. E., Brigman, G., Webb, L., & Moore, M. M. (2011/2012). Student success skills: An evidence-based cognitive and social change theory for student achievement. *Journal of Education, 192,* 89–100.

Lerman, D. C., Kelley, M. E., Vorndran, C. M., Kuhn, S. A., & Larue, R. H. (2002). Reinforcement magnitude and responding during treatment with differential reinforcement. *Journal of Applied Behavior Analysis, 35*(1), 29–48.

Lewinsohn, P. M., & Clarke, G. N. (1999). Psychosocial treatments for adolescent depression. *Clinical Psychology Review, 19*(3), 329–342.

Lewinsohn, P. M., Clarke, G. N., Rohde, P., Hops, H., & Seeley, J. R. (1996). A course in coping: A cognitive–behavioral approach to the treatment of adolescent depression. In E. D. Hibbs & P. S. Jensen (Eds.), *Psychosocial treatments for child and adolescent disorders: Empirically based strategies for clinical practice* (pp. 109–136). Washington, DC: American Psychological Association.

Lewinsohn, P. M., Hoberman, H. M., Teri, L., & Hautzinger, M. (1985). An integrated theory of depression. In S. Reiss & R. R. Bootzin (Eds.), *Theoretical issues in behavior therapy* (pp. 331–359). New York, NY: Academic Press.

Lindblom, C. E. (1959). The science of "muddling through." *Public Administration Review, 19,* 79–88.

Lipsey, M. W., & Wilson, D. B. (1998). Effective intervention for serious juvenile offenders: A synthesis of research. In R. Loeber & D. P. Farrington (Eds.), *Serious and violent juvenile offenders: Risk factors and successful interventions* (pp. 313–345). London, England: Sage.

Lochman, J. E., Boxmeyer, C. L., Powell, N. P., Qu, L., Wells, K., & Windle, M. (2012). Coping power dissemination study: Intervention and special education effects on academic outcomes. *Behavioral Disorders, 37*(3), 192–205.

Lochman, J. E., & Wells, K. C. (2004). The Coping Power Program for preadolescent aggressive boys and their parents: Outcome effects at the 1-year follow-up. *Journal of Consulting and Clinical Psychology, 72*(4), 571–578.

Locke, W. R., & Fuchs, L. S. (1995). Effects of peer-mediated reading instruction on the on-task behavior and social interaction of children with behavior disorders. *Journal of Emotional and Behavioral Disorders, 3*(2), 92–99.

Loge, D. V., Staton, R. D., & Beatty, W. W. (1990). Performance of children with ADHD on tests sensitive to frontal lobe dysfunction. *Journal of the American Academy of Child and Adolescent Psychiatry, 29*(4), 540–545.

Lorch, R. F., Jr., & Lorch, E. P. (1985). Topic structure representation and text recall. *Journal of Educational Psychology, 77*(2), 137–148.

Lovaas, O. I., Schreibman, L., Koegel, R., & Rehm, R. (1971). Selective responding by autistic children to multiple sensory input. *Journal of Abnormal Psychology, 77*(3), 211–222.

Loya, F. (2011). *The developmental trajectory of ADHD in females: Predictors and associations of symptom change from childhood to young adulthood* (Doctoral dissertation, University of California, Berkeley). Retrieved from: http://escholarship.org/uc/item/7wc3q211#page-3

Lyon, G. R., Shaywitz, S. E., & Shaywitz, B. A. (2003). Part I: Defining dyslexia, comorbidity, teachers' knowledge of language and reading: A definition of dyslexia. *Annals of Dyslexia, 53,* 1–14.

Mace, F. C., Belfiore, P. J., & Hutchinson, J. M. (2001). Operant theory and research on self-regulation. In B. J. Zimmerman & D. H. Schunk (Eds.), *Self-regulated learning and academic achievement: Theoretical perspectives* (2nd ed., pp. 39–66). Mahwah, NJ: Erlbaum.

Mace, F. C., Hock, M. L., Lalli, J. S., West, B. J., Belfiore, P., Pinter, E., & Brown, D. K. (1988). Behavioral momentum in the treatment of noncompliance. *Journal of Applied Behavioral Analysis, 21,* 123–141.

Magallón, R., Gili, M., Moreno, S., Bauzá, N., García-Campayo, J., Roca, M., . . . Andrés, E. (2008). Cognitive behavior therapy for patients with abridged somatization disorder in primary care: A randomized controlled study. Retrieved from: http://www.biomedcentral.com/1471-244X/8/47

Maggs, A., & Morgan, G. (1986). Effects of feedback on the academic engaged time of behaviour disordered learners. *Educational Psychology, 6*(4), 335–351.

Magiati, I., & Howlin, P. (2003). A pilot evaluation study of the Picture Exchange Communication System (PECS) for children with autistic spectrum disorders. *Autism, 7*(3), 297–320.

Maher, C. A. (1982). Behavioral effects of using conduct problem adolescents as cross-age tutors. *Psychology in the Schools, 19*(3), 360–364.

Mancil, G. R. (2006). Functional communication training: A review of the literature related to children with autism. *Education and Training in Developmental Disabilities, 41*(3), 213–224.

Mancil, G. R., & Boman, M. (2010). Functional communication training in the classroom: A guide for success. *Preventing School Failure, 54*(4), 238–246.

March, J. S., & Ollendick, T. H. (2004). Integrated psychosocial and pharmacological treatment. In T. H. Ollendick & J. S. March (Eds.), *Phobic and anxiety disorders in children and adolescents: A clinician's guide to effective psychosocial and pharmacological interventions* (pp. 141–174). New York, NY: Oxford Press.

Marcus, R. F. (2007). *Aggression and violence in adolescence.* New York, NY: Cambridge University Press.

Margolin, G., Burman, B., & John, R. S. (1989). Home observations of married couples reenacting naturalistic conflicts. *Behavioral Assessment, 11,* 101–118.

Martinez, C. R., & Forgatch, M. S. (2001). Preventing problems with boys' noncompliance: Effects of a parent training intervention for divorcing mothers. *Journal of Consulting and Clinical Psychology, 69*(3), 416–428.

Mash, E. J., & Barkley, R. A. (2003). *Child psychopathology* (2nd ed.). New York, NY: Guilford Press.

McGinnis, E. (2012). *Skillstreaming the elementary school child: A guide for teaching prosocial skills* (3rd ed.). Champaign, IL: Research Press.

McGinnis, E., Sprafkin, R. P., Gershaw, N. J., & Klein, P. (2012). *Skillstreaming the adolescent: A guide for teaching prosocial skills.* Champaign, IL: Research Press.

McIntosh, K., Sadler, C., & Brown, J. A. (2012). Kindergarten reading skill level and change as risk factors for chronic problem behavior. *Journal of Positive Behavior Interventions, 14,* 17–28.

McLaughlin, T. F. (1992). Effects of written feedback in reading on behaviorally disordered students. *Journal of Educational Research, 85*(5), 312–316.

McNaughton, N., & Corr, P. J. (2004). A two-dimensional neuropsychology of defense: Fear/anxiety and defensive distance. *Neuroscience and Biobehavioral Reviews, 28,* 285–305.

Meichenbaum, D. (1977). *Cognitive–behavior modification: An integrative approach.* New York, NY: Plenum Press.

Meichenbaum, D. (1985). *Stress inoculation training.* New York, NY: Pergamon.

Meichenbaum, D. H., & Goodman, J. (1971). Training impulsive children to talk to themselves: A means of developing self-control. *Journal of Abnormal Psychology, 77*(2), 115–126.

Merikangas, K. R., He, J., Burstein, M., Swanson, S. A., Avenevoli, S., Cui, L., . . . Swendsen, J. (2010). Lifetime prevalence of mental disorders in U.S. adolescents: Results from the National Comorbidity Study-Adolescent Supplement (NCS-A). *Journal of the American Academy of Child and Adolescent Psychiatry, 49*(10), 980–989.

Milani, A., Nikmanesh, Z., & Farnam, A. (2013). Effectiveness of mindfulness-based cognitive therapy (MBCT) in reducing aggression of individuals at the juvenile correction and rehabilitation center. *International Journal of High Risk Behaviors and Addiction, 2*(3), 126–131. doi:10.5812/ijhrba.14818

Mirenda, P. (2003). Toward functional augmentative and alternative communication for students with autism: Manual signs, graphic symbols, and voice output communication aids. *Language, Speech, and Hearing Services in Schools, 34,* 203–216.

Montague, M., & Warger, C. (1997). Helping students with attention deficit hyperactivity disorder succeed in the classroom. *Focus on Exceptional Children, 30*(4), 1–16.

Mooney, P., Epstein, M. H., Reid, R., & Nelson, J. R. (2003). Status and trends of academic intervention research for students with emotional disturbance. *Remedial and Special Education, 24,* 273–287.

Morris, D. (1980). *Infant attachment and problem solving in the toddler: Relations to mother's family history* (Unpublished doctoral dissertation). University of Minnesota. Minneapolis, MN.

Moustakas, C. (1959). *Psychotherapy with children: The living relationship.* Oxford, England: Harper.

Mpofu, E., & Crystal, R. (2001). Conduct disorder in children: Challenges and prospective cognitive–behavioural treatments. *Counselling Psychology Quarterly, 14*(1), 21–32.

MTA Cooperative Group. (1999). A 14-month randomized clinical trial of treatment strategies for attention-deficit/hyperactivity disorder (ADHD). *Archives of General Psychiatry, 56,* 1073–1086.

MTA Cooperative Group. (2004). National Institute of Mental Health multimodal treatment study of ADHD follow-up: 24-month outcomes of treatment strategies for attention-deficit/hyperactivity disorder. *Pediatrics, 113*(4), 754–761.

Mufson, L., Dorta, K. P., Moreau, D., & Weissman, M. M. (2004). *Interpersonal psychotherapy for depressed adolescents* (2nd ed.). New York, NY: Guilford Press.

Mufson, L., & Sills, R. (2006). Interpersonal psychotherapy for depressed adolescents (IPT-A): An overview. *Nordic Journal of Psychiatry, 60*(6), 431–437.

Naoi, N. (2011). Functional skill replacement training. In J. L. Matson & P. Sturmey (Eds.), *International handbook of autism and pervasive developmental disorders* (pp. 355–366). New York, NY: Springer Science + Business Media, LLC. doi:10.1007/978-1-4419-8065-6_22

National Institute of Mental Health. (n.d.) What is anxiety disorder? Retrieved from: http://ftp.nimh.nih.gov/health/topics/anxiety-disorders/index.shtml

National Institute of Mental Health. (2006). *Attention deficit hyperactivity disorder.* Bethesda, MD: Author. (NIH Publication Number: NIH 5124)

Nelson, J. R., Benner, G. J., Lane, K., & Smith, B. W. (2004). Academic achievement of K–12 students with emotional and behavioral disorders. *Exceptional Children, 71,* 59–73.

Nevin, J. A. (1996). The momentum of compliance. *Journal of Applied Behavior Analysis, 29*(4), 535–547.

Newcomer, L. L., & Lewis, T. J. (2004). Functional behavioral assessment: An investigation of assessment reliability and effectiveness of function-based interventions. *Journal of Emotional and Behavioral Disorders, 12*(3), 168–181.

Nicolson, D., & Ayers, H. (2004). *Adolescent problems: A practical guide for parents, teachers, and counsellors* (2nd ed.). London, England: David Fulton Publishers.

Office of Applied Studies, Substance Abuse and Mental Health Services Administration. (August 19, 2010). *The NSDUH report: Violent behaviors and family income among adolescents.* Retrieved from: http://www.oas.samhsa.gov/2k10/189/ViolentBehaviorsHTML.pdf

Offord, D. R., Boyle, M. H., Fleming, J. E., Blum, H. M., & Grant, N. I. R. (1989). Ontario child health study: Summary of selected results. *Canadian Journal of Psychiatry, 34,* 483–491.

Olive, M. L. (2004). Assessment and intervention for young children with nonphysiological feeding concerns. *Young Exceptional Children, 7,* 10–19.

Ollendick, T. H., & Cerny, J. A. (1981). *Clinical behavior therapy with children.* New York, NY: Plenum Press.

O'Rourke, K., & Worzbyt, J. C. (1996). *Support groups for children.* New York, NY: Routledge.

Palincsar, A. S., & Brown, A. L. (1984). Reciprocal teaching of comprehension-fostering and comprehension-monitoring activities. *Cognition and Instruction, 1*(2), 117–175.

Palmer, E. J. (2005). The relationship between moral reasoning and aggression, and the implications for practice. *Psychology, Crime & Law, 11*(4), 353–361.

Parker, A. E., Kupersmidt, J. B., Mathis, E. T., Scull, T. M., & Sims, C. (2014). The impact of mindfulness education on elementary school students: Evaluation of the Master Mind program. *Advances in School Mental Health Promotion, 7*(3), 184–204. doi:10.1080/1754730X.2014.916497

Patterson, G. R., Chamberlain, P., & Reid, J. B. (1982). A comparative evaluation of a parent-training program. *Behavior Therapy, 13*(5), 638–650.

Patterson, G. R., & Narrett, C. M. (1990). The development of a reliable and valid treatment program for aggressive young children. *International Journal of Mental Health, 19*(3), 19–26.

Patterson, G. R., Reid, J. B., & Dishion, T. J. (1992). *Antisocial boys.* Eugene, OR: Castalia.

Pelham, W. E., Jr., & Gnagy, E. M. (1999). Psychosocial and combined treatments for ADHD. *Mental Retardation and Developmental Disabilities Research Reviews, 5*(3), 225–236.

Peters, J. R., Smart, L. M., Eisenlohr-Moul, T. A., Geiger, P. J., Smith, G. T., & Baer, R. A. (2015). Anger rumination as a mediator of the relationship between mindfulness and aggression: The utility of a multidimensional mindfulness model. *Journal of Clinical Psychology.* Advance online publication. doi:10.1002/jclp.22189

Peterson, L., McLaughlin, T. F., Weber, K. P., & Anderson, H. (2008). The effects of model, lead, and test technique with visual prompts paired with a fading procedure to teach "where" to a 13-year-old echolalic boy with autism. *Journal of Developmental and Physical Disabilities, 20*, 31–39.

Pfiffner, L. J., & Haack, L. M. (2014). Behavior management for school-aged children with ADHD. *Child and Adolescent Psychiatric Clinics of North America, 23*(4), 731–746.

Pfiffner, L. J., & O'Leary, S. G. (1987). The efficacy of all-positive management as a function of the prior use of negative consequences. *Journal of Applied Behavior Analysis, 20*, 265–271.

Piaget, J. (1932). *The moral judgment of the child.* New York, NY: Harcourt Brace Jovanovich.

Pilania, V. M., Mehta, M., & Sagar, R. (2015). Anger management. In M. Mehta & R. Sagar (Eds.), *A practical approach to cognitive behavior therapy for adolescents* (pp. 109–130). New Delhi, India: Springer.

Pinborough-Zimmerman, J., Satterfield, R., Miller, J., Bilder, D., Hossain, S., & McMahon, W. (2007). Communication disorders: Prevalence and comorbid intellectual disability, autism, and emotional/behavioral disorders. American *Journal of Speech-Language Pathology, 16*, 359–367.

Polsgrove, L., & Smith, S. (2004). Informed practice in teaching students self-control. In R. Rutherford, Jr., M. Quinn, & S. Mathur (Eds.), *Handbook of research in emotional and behavioral disorders* (pp. 399–425). New York, NY: Guilford Press.

Powell, S., & Nelson, B. (1997). Effects of choosing academic assignments on a student with attention deficit hyperactivity disorder. *Journal of Applied Behavior Analysis, 30*(1), 181–183.

Quinn, M. M., Kavale, K. A., Mathur, S. R., Rutherford, S. R., Jr., & Forness, S. R. (1999). A meta-analysis of social skill interventions for students with emotional or behavioral disorders. *Journal of Emotional and Behavioral Disorders, 7*(1), 54–64.

Raggi, V. L., & Chronis, A. M. (2006). Interventions to address the academic impairment of children and adolescents with ADHD. *Clinical Child and Family Psychology Review, 9*(2), 85–111.

Rapoport, J. L., Inoff-Germain, G., Weissman, M. M., Greenwald, S., Narrow, W. E., Jensen, P. S., . . . Canino, G. (2000). Childhood obsessive-compulsive disorder in the NIMH MECA study: Parent versus child identification of cases. *Journal of Anxiety Disorders, 14*(6), 535–548.

Reid, R., Trout, A. L., Schartz, M. (2005). Self-regulation interventions for children with attention deficit/hyperactivity disorder. *Exceptional Children, 71*(4), 361–377.

Reynolds, C. R., & Fletcher-Janzen, E. (Eds.). (2007). *Encyclopedia of special education: A reference for the education of children, adolescents, and adults with disabilities and other exceptional individuals* (3rd ed., Vol. 1). New York, NY: John Wiley & Sons.

Reynolds, C. R., & Kamphaus, R. W. (2015). *Behavior assessment system for children* (3rd ed.). Bloomington, MN: NCS Pearson.

Reynolds, C. R., & Livingston, R. A. (2010). *Children's measure of obsessive compulsive symptoms.* Los Angeles, CA: Western Psychological Services.

Reynolds, C. R., Vannest, K. J., & Harrison, J. R. (2012). *The energetic brain: Understanding and managing ADHD.* San Fransisco, CA: John Wiley & Sons.

Rhee, H., Miles, M. S., Halpern, C. T., & Holditch-Davis, D. (2005). Prevalence of recurrent physical symptoms in U.S. adolescents. *Pediatric Nursing, 31*(4), 314–319, 350.

Riccio, C. A., Reynolds, C. R., & Lowe, P. A. (2001). *Clinical applications of continuous performance tests: Measuring attention and impulsive responding in children and adults.* New York, NY: Wiley.

Rietveld, M. J. H., Hudziak, J. J., Bartels, M., van Beijsterveld, C. E. M., & Boomsma, D. I. (2004). Heritablility of attention problems in children: Longitudinal results from a study of twins, age 3 to 12. *Journal of Child Psychology Psychiatry, 45*(3), 577–588.

Riley-Tillman, T. C., Chafouleas, S. M., & Briesch, A. M. (2007). A school practitioner's guide to using daily behavior report cards to monitor student behavior. *Psychology in the Schools, 44*(1), 77–89.

Robbins, M. S., Liddle, H. A., Turner, C. W., Dakof, G. A., Alexander, J. F., & Kogan, S. M. (2006). Adolescent and parent therapeutic alliances as predictors of dropout in multidimensional family therapy. *Journal of Family Psychology, 20*(1), 108–116.

Roberts, M. C., Lazicki-Puddy, T. A., Puddy, R. W., & Johnson, R. J. (2003). The outcomes of psychotherapy with adolescents: A practitioner-friendly research review. *Journal of Clinical Psychology, 59*(11), 1177–1191.

Roderick, M. (1995). Grade retention and school dropout: Policy debate and research questions. *Phi Delta Kappa Research Bulletin, 15,* 1–6.

Rosenberg, M. S., Sindelar, P. T., & Stedt, J. (1985). The effects of supplemental on-task contingencies on the acquisition of simple and difficult academic tasks. *Journal of Special Education, 19*(2), 189–203.

Rosenshine, B., & Meister, C. (1992). The use of scaffolds for teaching higher-level cognitive strategies. *Educational Leadership, 49*(7), 26–33.

Rosselló, J., & Bernal, G. (1999). The efficacy of cognitive–behavioral and interpersonal treatments for depression in Puerto Rican adolescents. *Journal of Consulting and Clinical Psychology, 67*(5), 734–745.

Rumberger, R. W. (1995). Dropping out of middle school: A multilevel analysis of students and schools. *American Educational Research Journal, 32*(3), 583–625.

Rutherford, R., Chipman, J., DiGangi, S., & Anderson, C. (1992). *Teaching social skills: A practical instructional approach.* Reston, VA: Exceptional Innovations.

Rutherford, R. B., Jr., Quinn, M. M., & Mathur, S. R. (1996). *Effective strategies for teaching appropriate behaviors to children with emotional/behavioral disorders.* Reston, VA: Council for Children with Behavior Disorders.

Sagiv, S. K., Epstein, J. N., Bellinger, D. C., & Korrick, S. A. (2013). Pre- and postnatal risk factors for ADHD in a nonclinical pediatric population. *Journal of Attention Disorders, 17*(1), 47–57. doi:10.1177/1087054711427563

Salend, S. J., Elhoweris, H., & van Garderen, D. (2003). Educational interventions for students with ADD. *Intervention in School and Clinic, 38*(5), 280–288.

Scardamalia, M., & Bereiter, C. (1985). Fostering the development of self-regulation in children's knowledge processing. In S. F. Chipman, J. W. Segal, & R. Glaser (Eds.), *Thinking and learning skills: Vol. 2 Research and open questions* (pp. 563–578). Hillsdale, NJ: Erlbaum.

Schloss, P. J., Harriman, N. E., & Pfefier, K. (1985). Application of a sequential prompt reduction technique to the independent composition performance of behaviorally disordered youth. *Behavioral Disorders, 11*(1), 17–23.

Schmit, J., Alper, S., Raschke, D., & Ryndak, D. (2000). Effects of using a photographic cueing package during routine school transitions with a child who has autism. *Mental Retardation, 38*(2), 131–137.

Schreibman, L. (1975). Effects of within-stimulus and extra-stimulus prompting on discrimination learning in autistic children. *Journal of Applied Behavior Analysis, 8,* 91–112.

Schreibman, L., Whalen, C., & Stahmer, A. C. (2000). The use of video priming to reduce disruptive transition behavior in children with autism. *Journal of Positive Behavior Interventions, 2*(1), 3–11.

Schulman, J. L. (1988). Case study: Use of a coping approach in the management of children with conversion reactions. *Journal of the American Academy of Child and Adolescent Psychiatry, 27*(6), 785–788.

Scott, T. J. (1970). The use of music to reduce hyperactivity in children. American *Journal of Orthopsychiatry, 40*(4), 677–680.

Scruggs, T. E., & Mastropieri, M. A. (1986). Academic characteristics of behaviorally disordered and learning disabled students. *Behavioral Disorders, 11*(3), 184–190.

Scruggs, T. E., & Mastropieri, M. A. (1990). The case for mnemonic instruction: From laboratory research to classroom applications. *Journal of Special Education, 24*(1), 7–32.

Scruggs, T. E., Mastropieri, M. A., & Richter, L. (1985). Peer tutoring with behaviorally disordered students: Social and academic benefits. *Behavioral Disorders, 10*(4), 283–294.

Searight, H. R., Robertson, K., Smith, T., Perkins, S., & Searight, B. K. (2012). Complementary and alternative therapies for pediatric attention deficit hyperactivity disorder: A descriptive review. *International Scholarly Research Network: Psychiatry, 2012,* 804127. doi:10.5402/2012/804127

Semrud-Clikeman, M., Nielsen, K. H., Clinton, A., Sylvester, L., Parle, N., & Connor, R. T. (1999). An intervention approach for children with teacher- and parent-identified attentional difficulties. *Journal of Learning Disabilities, 32*(6), 581–590.

Shalev, R. S., Auerbach, J., Manor, O., & Gross-Tsur, V. (2000). Developmental dyscalculia: Prevalence and prognosis. *European Child & Adolescent Psychiatry, 9*(Suppl 2), S58–S64. doi:10.1007/s007870070009

Sheese, B. E., Voelker, P. M., Rothbart, M. K., & Posner, M. I. (2007). Parenting quality interacts with genetic variation in dopamine receptor D4 to influence temperament in early childhood. Development and Psychopathology, 19, 1039–1046.

Sheridan, S. M. (1995). *The tough kid social skills book.* Longmont, CO: Sopris West.

Simpson, R. L. (1999). Children and youth with emotional and behavioral disorders: A concerned look at the present and a hopeful eye for the future. *Behavioral Disorders, 24*(4), 284–292.

Singh, N. N., Lancioni, G. E., Karazsia, B. T., Winton, A. S. W., Myers, R. E., Singh, A. N. A., ... Singh, J. (2013). Mindfulness-based treatment of aggression in individuals with mild intellectual disabilities: A waiting list control study. Mindfulness, 4(2), 158–167. doi:10.1007/s12671-012-0180-8

Siperstein, G. N., Wiley, A. L., & Forness, S. R. (2011). School context and the academic and behavioral progress of students with emotional disturbance. Behavioral Disorders, 36(3), 172–184.

Skinner, B. F. (1931). The concept of the reflex in the description of behavior. Journal of General Psychology, 5, 427–458.

Skinner, B. F. (1953). Science and human behavior. New York, NY: Macmillan.

Skinner, C. H., Johnson, C. W., Larkin, M. J., Lessley, D. J., & Glowacki, M. L. (1995). The influence of rate of presentation during taped-words interventions on reading performance. Journal of Emotional and Behavioral Disorders, 3(4), 214–223.

Smith-Bonahue, T., Larmore, A., Harman, J., & Castillo, M. (2009). Perceptions of parents and teachers of the social and behavior characteristics of children with reading problems. Learning Disabilities: A Contemporary Journal, 7(2), 19–34.

Sohlberg, M. M., McLaughlin, K. A., Pavese, A., Heidrich, A., & Posner, M. I. (2000). Evaluation of attention process training and brain injury education in persons with acquired brain injury. Journal of Clinical and Experimental Neuropsychology, 22(5), 656–676.

Solden, S. (1995). Women with attention deficit disorder: Embracing disorganization at home and in the workplace. Nevada City, CA: Underwood Books.

Spitzberg, B. H., & Dillard, J. P. (2002). Social skills and communication. In M. Allen, R. W. Preiss, B. M. Gayle, & N. Burrell (Eds.), Interpersonal communication research: Advances through meta-analysis (pp. 89–107). Mahwah, NJ: Erlbaum.

Stahmer, A. C., & Schreibman, L. (1992). Teaching children with autism appropriate play in unsupervised environments using a self-management treatment package. Journal of Applied Behavior Analysis, 25(2), 447–459. doi:10.1901/jaba.1992.25-447

Stallings, J. A. (1986). Effective use of time in secondary reading programs. In J. V. Hoffman (Ed.), Effective teaching of reading: Research and practice (pp. 85–106). Newark, DE: International Reading Association.

Stark, K. D., & Kendall, P. C. (1996). Treating depressed children: Therapist manual for "taking action." Ardmore, PA: Workbook Publishing.

Sterling-Turner, H. E., & Jordan, S. S. (2007). Interventions addressing transition difficulties for individuals with autism. Psychology in the Schools, 44(7), 681–690.

Stormont-Spurgin, M. (1997). I lost my homework: Strategies for improving organization in students with ADHD. Intervention in School and Clinic, 32(5), 270–274.

Stroud, K., & Reynolds, C. R. (2006). School motivation and learning strategies inventory (SMALSI). Los Angeles, CA: Western Psychological Services.

Sullivan, G. S., & Mastropieri, M. A. (1994). Social competence of individuals with learning disabilities. In T. E. Scruggs & M. A. Mastropieri (Eds.), Advances in learning and behavioral disabilities (Vol. 8, pp. 171–213). Greenwich, CT: JAI Press.

Sutherland, K. S., Alder, N., & Gunter, P. L. (2003). The effect of varying rates of opportunities to respond to academic requests on the classroom behavior of students with EBD. Journal of Emotional and Behavioral Disorders, 11(4), 239–248.

Sutherland, K. S., & Wehby, J. H. (2001). Exploring the relationship between increased opportunities to respond to academic requests and the academic and behavioral outcomes of students with EBD: A review. Remedial and Special Education, 22(2), 113–121.

Sutherland, K. S., Wehby, J. H., & Yoder, P. J. (2002). Examination of the relationship between teacher praise and opportunities for students with EBD to respond to academic requests. *Journal of Emotional and Behavioral Disorders, 10*(1), 5–13.

Swanson, H. L., & Deshler, D. (2003). Instructing adolescents with learning disabilities: Converting a meta-analysis to practice. *Journal of Learning Disabilities, 36*(2), 124–135.

Swanson, J., Arnold, L. E., Kraemer, H., Hechtman, L., Molina, B., Hinshaw, S., & . . . Wigal, T. (2008a). Evidence, interpretation, and qualification from multiple reports of long-term outcomes in the multimodal treatment study of children with ADHD (MTA): Part I: Executive summary. *Journal of Attention Disorders, 12*(1), 4–14. doi:10.1177/1087054708319345

Swanson, J., Arnold, L. E., Kraemer, H., Hechtman, L., Molina, B., Hinshaw, S., & . . . Wigal, T. (2008b). Evidence, interpretation, and qualification from multiple reports of long-term outcomes in the multimodal treatment study of children with ADHD (MTA): Part II: Supporting details. *Journal of Attention Disorders, 12*(1), 15–43. doi:10.1177/1087054708319525

Taber, T. A., Seltzer, A., Heflin, J., & Alberto, P. A. (1999). Use of self-operated auditory prompts to decrease off-task behavior for a student with autism and moderate mental retardation. *Focus on Autism and Other Developmental Disabilities, 14*(3), 159–166.

Tamm, L., & Carlson, C. L. (2007). Task demands interact with the single and combined effects of medication and contingencies on children with ADHD. *Journal of Attention Disorders, 10*(4), 372–380.

Tarolla, S. M., Wagner, E. F., Rabinowitz, J., & Tubman, J. G. (2002). Understanding and treating juvenile offenders: A review of current knowledge and future directions. *Aggression and Violent Behavior, 7*(2), 125–143.

Taylor, S., & Garralda, E. (2003). The management of somatoform disorder in childhood. *Current Opinion in Psychiatry, 16*(2), 227–231.

Taylor, T. K., Eddy, J. M., & Biglan, A. (1999). Interpersonal skills training to reduce aggressive and delinquent behavior: Limited evidence and the need for an evidence-based system of care. *Clinical Child and Family Psychology Review, 2*(3), 169–182.

Thomas, C. R. (2006). Evidence-based practice for conduct disorder symptoms. *Journal of the American Academy of Child and Adolescent Psychiatry, 45*(1), 109–114.

Todd, R. D., & Botteron, K. N. (2001). Is attention deficit/hyperactivity disorder an energy deficiency syndrome? *Biological Psychiatry, 50*(3), 151–158.

Topping, K. J. (1996). The effectiveness of peer tutoring in further and higher education: A typology and review of the literature. *Higher Education, 32*(3), 321–345.

Topping, K. (2001). *Peer assisted learning: A practical guide for teachers.* Cambridge, MA: Brookline Books.

Trout, A. L., Nordness, P. D., Pierce, C. D., & Epstein, M. H. (2003). Research on the academic status of children with emotional and behavioral disorders: A review of literature from 1961 to 2000. *Journal of Emotional and Behavioral Disorders, 11*(4), 198–210.

U.S. Department of Education. (1994). *16th annual report to congress on the implementation of P.L.* (pp. 94–142). Washington, DC: U.S. Government Printing Office.

U.S. Department of Education, Institute of Education Sciences, What Works Clearinghouse. (2012, April). *Early childhood interventions for children with disabilities intervention report: Milieu teaching.* Retrieved from http://ies.ed.gov/ncee/wwc/interventionreport.aspx?sid=567

U.S. Food and Drug Administration. (2011). *How do you know if you child has ADHD?* Retrieved from: http://www.fda.gov/ForConsumers/ConsumerUpdates/ucm269188.htm#top

van der Put, C. E., Stams, G. J. J. M., Hoeve, M., Deković, M., Spanjaard, H. J. M., van der Laan, P. H., & Barnoski, R. P. (2012). Changes in the relative importance of dynamic risk factors for recidivism during adolescence. *International Journal of Offender Therapy and Comparative Criminology, 56*(2), 296–316. doi:10.1177/0306624X11398462

Van Hasselt, V. B., Hersen, M., Whitehill, M. B., & Bellack, A. S. (1979). Social skill assessment and training for children: An evaluative review. *Behaviour Research and Therapy, 17*(5), 413–437.

Van Patten, J., Chao, C. I., & Reigeluth, C. M. (1986). A review of strategies for sequencing and synthesizing instruction. *Review of Educational Research, 56*(4), 437–471.

VanDerHeyden, A. M., Witt, J. C., & Gatti, S. (2001). Research into practice: Descriptive assessment method to reduce overall disruptive behavior in a preschool classroom. *School Psychology Review, 30*(4), 548–567.

Vannest, K. J., Davis, J. L., Davis, C. R., Mason, B. A., & Burke, M. D. (2010). Effective intervention for behavior with a daily behavior report card: A meta-analysis. *School Psychology Review, 39*(4), 654–672.

Vannest, K. J., Harrison, J. R., Temple-Harvey, K., Ramsey, L., & Parker, R. I. (2011). Improvement rate differences of academic interventions for students with emotional and behavioral disorders. *Remedial and Special Education, 32*(6), 521–534. doi:10.1177/0741932510362509

Vannest, K. J., Harvey, K., & Mason, B. (2009). Meeting annual yearly progress through better teaching for students with emotional and behavioral disorders. *Preventing School Failure, 53*(2), 73–84.

Vannest, K. J., Reynolds, C. R., & Kamphaus, R. W. (2008). *Intervention guide: Part of the BASC–2 family*. Minneapolis, MN: NCS Pearson.

Vaughn, S., & Hogan, A. (1990). Social competence and learning disabilities: A prospective study. In H. L. Swanson & B. Keogh (Eds.), *Learning disabilities: Theoretical and research issues* (pp. 175–191). Hillsdale, NJ: Erlbaum.

Versi, M. (1995). Differential effects of cognitive behavior modification on seriously emotionally disturbed adolescents exhibiting internalizing or externalizing problems. *Journal of Child and Family Studies, 4*(3), 279–292. doi:10.1007/BF02233963

Villares, E., Lemberger, M., Brigman, G., & Webb, L. (2011). Student success skills: An evidence-based school counseling program grounded in humanistic theory. *Journal Of Humanistic Counseling, 50*, 42–55.

Visser, S. N., Danielson, M. L., Bitsko, R. H., Holbrook, J. R., Kogan, M. D., Ghandour, R. M., . . . Blumberg, S. J. (2014). Trends in the parent-report of health care provider-diagnosed and medicated attention-deficit/hyperactivity disorder: United States, 2003–2011. *Journal of The American Academy of Child & Adolescent Psychiatry, 53*(1), 34–46. doi:10.1016/j.jaac.2013.09.001

Vygotsky, L. S. (1978). *Mind in society: The development of higher mental processes* (M. Cole, V. John-Steiner, S. Scribner, & E. Souberman, Eds. & Trans.). Cambridge, MA: Harvard University Press. (Original work published 1930, 1933, & 1935)

Vygotsky, L. S. (1987). Thinking and speech. In R. W. Rieber & A. S. Carton (Eds.), *The collected works of L. S. Vygotsky* (Vol. 1, pp. 37–285). New York, NY: Plenum Press. (Original work published 1934)

Wagner, M., Kutash, K., Duchnowski, A. J., Epstein, M. H., & Sumi, C. (2005). The children and youth we serve: A national picture of the characteristics of students with emotional disturbances receiving special education. *Journal of Emotional and Behavioral Disorders, 13*(2), 79–96.

Walen, S. R., DiGiuseppe, R., & Wessler, R. (1980). *A practitioner's guide to rational-emotive therapy* (1st ed.). New York, NY: Oxford University Press.

Walker, H. M., Colvin, G., & Ramsey, E. (1995). *Antisocial behavior in school: Strategies and best practices.* Pacific Grove, CA: Brooks/Cole.

Walker, H. M., McConnell, S., Holmes, D., Todis, B., Walker, J., & Golden, N. (1983). *The Walker social skills curriculum: The ACCEPTS program.* Austin, TX: Pro-Ed.

Webster-Stratton, C., & Hammond, M. (1997). Treating children with early-onset conduct problems: A comparison of child and parent training interventions. *Journal of Consulting and Clinical Psychology, 65*(1), 93–109.

Weersing, V. R., & Brent, D. A. (2006). Cognitive behavioral therapy for depression in youth. *Child and Adolescent Psychiatric Clinics of North America, 15*(4), 939–957.

Weiner, B. (1985). An attributional theory of achievement motivation and emotion. *Psychological Review, 92*(4), 548–573.

Weiss, M., & Murray, C. (2003). Assessment and management of attention-deficit hyperactivity disorder in adults. *Canadian Medical Association Journal, 168*(6), 715–722.

Weissman, M. M., Markowitz, J. C., & Klerman, G. L. (2000). *Comprehensive guide to interpersonal psychotherapy.* New York, NY: Basic Books.

Welsh, M., Parke, R. D., Widaman, K., & O'Neil, R. (2001). Linkages between children's social and academic competence: A longitudinal analysis. *Journal of School Psychology, 39*(6), 463–481.

Wessler, R. A., & Wessler, R. L. (1980). *The principles and practice of rational-emotive therapy* (1st ed.). San Francisco: Proquest Info & Learning.

Whitted, K. S. (2011). Understanding how social and emotional skill deficits contribute to school failure. *Preventing School Failure, 55*(1), 10–16.

Whitted, K. S., & Dupper, D. R. (2005). Best practices for preventing or reducing bullying in schools. *Children & Schools, 27*(3), 167–175.

Wilkinson, J., & Canter, S. (1982). *Social skills training manual: Assessment, program design, and management of training.* New York, NY: Wiley.

Wilson, D. B., Gottfredson, D. C., & Najaka, S. S. (2001). School-based prevention of problem behaviors: A meta-analysis. *Journal of Quantitative Criminology, 17*(3), 247–272.

Witt, J. C., Daly, E. M., & Noell, G. (2000). *Functional assessments: A step-by-step guide to solving academic and behavior problems.* Dallas, TX: Sopris West.

Wolpe, J. (1958). *Psychotherapy by reciprocal inhibition.* Stanford, CA: Stanford University Press.

Wolpe, J., & Lazarus, A. (1966). Behavior therapy techniques: *A guide to the treatment of neuroses.* New York, NY: Pergamon Press.

Wolery, M., Bailey, D. B., & Sugai, G. M. (1988). *Effective teaching: Principles and procedures of applied behavior analysis with exceptional students.* Boston, MA: Allyn & Bacon.

Woolgar, M., & Scott, S. (2005). Evidence-based management of conduct disorders. *Current Opinion in Psychiatry, 18*(4), 392–396.

Wymbs, F. A., Cunningham, C. E., Chen, Y., Rimas, H. M., Deal, K., Waschbusch, D. A., & Pelham, W. E., Jr. (2015). Examining parents' preferences for group and individual parent training for children with ADHD symptoms. *Journal of Clinical Child and Adolescent Psychology.* Advance online publication. doi:10.1080/15374416.2015.1004678

Xu, C., Reid, R., & Steckelberg, A. (2002). Technology applications for children with ADHD: Assessing the empirical support. *Education and Treatment of Children, 25*(2), 224–248.

Yeager, D. S., & Dweck, C. S. (2012). Mindsets that promote resilience: When students believe that personal characteristics can be developed. *Educational Psychologist, 47*(4), 302–314.

Yeager, D. S., Trzesniewski, K. H., & Dweck, C. S. (2013). An implicit theories of personality intervention reduces adolescent aggression in response to victimization and exclusion. *Child Development, 84*(3), 970–988. doi:10.1111/cdev.12003

Young, H. S. (1977). Counseling strategies with working class adolescents. In J. L. Wolfe & E. Brand (Eds.), *Twenty years of rational therapy: Proceedings of the first national conference on rational psychotherapy.* New York, NY: Institute for Rational Living.

Zeharia, A., Mukamel, M., Carel, C., Weitz, R., Danziger, Y., & Mimouni, M. (1999). Conversion reaction: Management by the paediatrician. *European Journal of Pediatrics, 158*(2), 160–164.

Zentall, S. S. (1983). Learning environments: A review of physical and temporal factors. *Exceptional Education Quarterly, 4*(2), 90–115.

Zentall, S. S. (1989). Attentional cuing in spelling tasks for hyperactive and comparison regular classroom children. *The Journal of Special Education, 23*(1), 83–93.

Zentall, S. S. (1993). Research on the educational implications of attention deficit hyperactivity disorder. *Exceptional Children, 60*(2), 143–153.

Zentall, S. S., & Dwyer, A. M. (1989). Color effects on the impulsivity and activity of hyperactive children. *Journal of School Psychology, 27,* 165–173.

Zentall, S. S., & Leib, S. L. (1985). Structured tasks: Effects on activity and performance of hyperactive and comparison children. *Journal of Educational Research, 79*(2), 91–95.

Zentall, S. S., & Meyer, M. J. (1987). Self-regulation of stimulation for ADD-H children during reading and vigilance task performance. *Journal of Abnormal Child Psychology, 15*(4), 519–536.

Zentall, S. S., & Shaw, J. H. (1980). Effects of classroom noise on performance and activity of second-grade hyperactive and control children. *Journal of Educational Psychology, 72*(6), 830–840.